73
166

Scenes 1 + 2

Questions at back

Portia lives at Belmont

who is the merchant of venice = antonio

a Comedy Tragedy

WILLIAM SHAKESPEARE
(The Droeshout Portrait. From Title-page of the First Folio, 1623)

FIVE PLAYS OF

SHAKESPEARE

JULIUS CAESAR · MACBETH
MERCHANT OF VENICE · AS YOU LIKE IT
HAMLET

EDITED BY

H. C. SCHWEIKERT

CENTRAL HIGH SCHOOL
ST. LOUIS, MISSOURI

NEW YORK
HARCOURT, BRACE AND COMPANY
1940

PRINTED IN THE U.S.A.

PREFACE

In preparing this edition of the five plays of Shakespeare most commonly read in secondary schools the first consideration was to avoid overediting the text. Experience has proved that pupils take no interest in variant readings and other controversial points about Shakespeare and his work, nor would they derive any profit from such study. In teaching Shakespeare the first thought surely must be to stimulate in pupils a desire to read the text of the plays with the same eagerness displayed in reading novels and short stories. This cannot be done by surrounding the text with a vast paraphernalia of scholarship that is of value only to teachers and for advanced study in colleges.

In small single-play texts the editorial apparatus bulks so large that pupils get an exaggerated idea of its importance, causing them to feel discouraged in tackling a piece of writing that evidently requires so much more work to appreciate than a novel or a short story. In these single-play volumes much of this editorial work is duplicated over and over again, producing an intellectual weariness common to all repetition. With all the essential Shakespeare material brought together in one book which features the plays themselves, it is hoped that both teachers and pupils will find this text an agreeable as well as a profitable tool with which to work.

No effort has been made to supplant the teacher by editorial machinery. It was designed first of all to help the pupils make easy and adequate preparation for class work, leaving the teacher free to teach Shakespeare and not textual commentary. The notes are confined to explanations of the most important variations from modern usage and brief interpretations of a few passages of unusual difficulty. Pupils do not like to fuss around with a glossary, nor do they show any eagerness to search for notes at the end of a book; consequently all notes are placed at the bottom of the page. With the few necessary notes on the same page with the text, and with an unabridged dictionary at hand, the pupil has all the textual needs for understanding the play and preparing to recite on it.

The questions also are intended to aid the pupil in understanding the play. If he works out a reasonable number of them before coming to class he is in a fair way of being prepared to respond intelligently to whatever method of instruction the teacher may employ. It is the feeling of the editor that the lists of questions should not be formally used in class except perhaps as part of the written work. Many of the questions will be found suitable for long or short assignments in composition, but for actual classroom discussion, interesting to pupils and teachers alike, nothing can take the place of the spontaneity that comes from an understanding of the text by the pupils combined with the enthusiasm of the teacher.

The interpretative note appended to each play is purposely incomplete, designed merely to give the pupil a peep into the richest part of the treasure-house that he is exploring. Intensive work of this nature is best adapted to the higher grades, and every teacher will know what is best fitted to his particular problem.

The Introduction contains material not heretofore included in school texts. None of it is difficult to understand, because it is almost entirely informational, and much of it is interesting in itself. The study of Shakespeare as part of a larger study of the drama, not only of the English but of all drama, goes a long way in dissipating the myth that his genius is of such superhuman magnitude that only by hard mental labor can it be appreciated. To show Shakespeare's humanity, considerable attention is given him as a working playwright among fellow workers engaged in the theatrical business of his day.

Breaking up the Introduction into small units enables the teacher to use such sections as may fall within the province of his needs or desires. At no time should it be regarded other than as a subsidiary to the main topic of the course — Shakespeare and the drama. In the lower grades especially the introductory matter should not be stressed, with the exception of the parts that bear directly on Shakespeare.

It is the editor's hope, however, that all the material of this Introduction is presented in a way that is neither too difficult nor too abstruse for the comprehension and enjoyment of the secondary school mind. Since by far the larger number of students never pass beyond the secondary school, it seems only fair that they should have access to information that is part of an educated person's mental equipment. Surely a study of the drama in all its phases, historical and otherwise, is a not inconsiderable item in the story of the advance of the human mind, and no one phase is more significant than that of Shakespeare.

CONTENTS

LIST OF ILLUSTRATIONS

FIVE PLAYS OF SHAKESPEARE

INTRODUCTION

SHAKESPEARE'S ENGLAND

BETWEEN England and France is the English Channel. No other geographical fact has played so important a rôle in determining the individual destiny of the " tight little island." Early in his dramatic career Shakespeare patriotically gave expression to this feature of his country:

> This precious stone set in the silver sea,
> Which serves it in the office of a wall,
> Or as a moat defensive to a house,
> Against the envy of less happier lands, —
> This blessed plot, this earth, this realm, this England.
>
> *Richard II*

The difficulties of transporting an army across this narrow but unfriendly bit of water helped to convince Julius Caesar in 55 B.C. that the conquest of Britain ought to be postponed. The great movements of the Continent, political and otherwise, always hesitated on the southern shore of the Channel, keeping the finest fruits of the Renaissance out of England until the reign of Elizabeth. A timely storm on this same Channel in 1588 helped to make sure that the country of Shakespeare was to remain definitely Protestant. What it prevented in the Great War of 1914 staggers the imagination.

No period in the history of mankind saw changes greater than those of the fifteenth and sixteenth centuries. With the shackles of ignorance struck off by the spirit of the Renaissance, in England finally as well as on the Continent, man began to take an active interest in himself and his world; fostered by such humanists as Petrarch, Erasmus, and Sir Thomas More, learning became an honorable avocation, and with it all came the realization that while this might not be the best possible world, it at least was the only one of which

1

we were absolutely certain, and it was up to us to make the best of it.

But the blight of ignorance and bigotry that had lain heavily on man throughout the Middle Ages was not lifted in a day. For a long time knowledge remained the luxury of the few, until at last man's spirit of eager inquiry led to those discoveries and inventions which mark the real beginnings of our modern world. When Shakespeare was born the art of printing had been established in England for less than a hundred years. Most people still believed that the sun revolved around the earth, although Copernicus and succeeding scientists were pointing toward the truth. The mysterious secrets of the Seven Seas were being bared by the adventurous curiosity and the incredible courage of the early explorers. By the middle of the sixteenth century this restlessness of the human spirit, in England as elsewhere, was turned upon the imagination, the result of which was an outburst of literature unequaled in the history of man. Its supreme individual product was Shakespeare.

In order to picture with any accuracy at all the England of Shakespeare it is necessary to free our minds as much as possible from what we know of her today. In the middle of the sixteenth century no Englishman could boast that the sun never set on the British Empire. Wales was united to England, there were rather tenuous claims on Ireland, but Scotland was still an independent kingdom. While English explorers like the Cabots, Frobisher, Drake, and Raleigh had voyaged to America and had made nominal claims for England, it should be remembered that the first serious attempt at colonization was not made until 1607, just nine years before Shakespeare's death. India, Africa, and Australia were not even dreamt of as parts of a future empire. England was a country about the size of the state of Michigan, and its less than five million population was for the most part distributed throughout the rural sections, quite unlike its thirty-six million of today, a large percentage of which is crowded into such modern congested cities as London, Liverpool, Birmingham, Manchester.

We must also dissociate from our minds much that the progress of three hundred years has added to the advancement of civilization. Raleigh and Drake sailed the seas in vessels but little better than those of Columbus. On land the roads were uniformly bad, and the only modes of travel were on foot, on horseback, and in coaches. One of the excitements of all forms of conveyance was the possibility of being held up, one of the few things we of the twentieth century have in common with the Elizabethans.

In cities the streets were narrow and incredibly filthy. In the middle of a street was a sort of shallow trench, with pools of water here and there, and into these went most of the sewage. Garbage also was dumped into the streets and at set intervals was burned. Houses were almost equally unsanitary. Instead of carpets on the floor they had rushes strewn about. Cleaning the floors was accomplished by stirring the rushes so that the dirt went to the bottom. When the odors from filth became obnoxious the rushes were sprinkled with perfumed water. Ventilation, especially at night, was supposed to bring on rheumatism and other ailments, so it was strictly limited. It is small wonder that the dreaded plague made frequent visits.

Other living conditions were equally primitive — the matter of food, for instance, and the way it was eaten. There was far less variety than we know today, both in kinds and in preparation, the mainstays being meat, game, fish, together with bread and sweets. Potatoes were introduced from America by the early explorers. Their tables were not unlike ours, but the tableware was mostly of wood, although pewter was used by those who could afford so elegant a luxury. For plates they had wooden trenchers — that is, flat pieces of wood from which the solid food was eaten. As a boy, Shakespeare, like everybody else, ate with his fingers, but he possibly learned to use a fork before he died. Table knives had come into use in 1563, the year before Shakespeare was born, while forks came somewhat later. It is safe to assume that such newfangled notions were not generally established in a day. That eating was a messy performance is indicated by a custom at the better tables of circulating among the diners a bowl of water and a towel at frequent intervals. Do not fail to note that it was *a* bowl and *a* towel. Many different kinds of wine were consumed, and in great quantities. What Shakespeare so often calls *sack* was nothing but a cheap strong wine.

In nothing do the Elizabethans seem more ridiculous to us than in the matter of dress. From portraits in schoolbooks we get a general impression of how Queen Elizabeth, Walter

Raleigh, and Philip Sidney looked when they were dressed up. How they must have felt is not indicated. The fit of clothes, as we understand that term, seems to have been the last consideration. To conceal the real form as much as possible was the main idea, and this was achieved by the men through outrageous padding, and by the women through equally outrageous mechanical devices.

Shakespeare frequently mentions *doublet and hose*. These were the two most important garments for men. The doublet was a sort of coat, buttoned or laced in front, with slashes here and there to show the color of the lining. The sleeves, if any, were separate, and were laced to the doublet at the shoulders. The doublet extended down well over the hips, and to it were laced the hose. By *hose* we do not mean *stockings* in our sense of the word, but breeches. Trunk hose, as they were more technically called, came from the ankles to the hips, rather tight below the knees, and quite ample from there up. If the trunks were detached at the knees, the names *upper stock* and *lower stock* were used. Often high boots were worn. Both the doublet and the trunk part of the hose were cut exceedingly full and then stuffed with wool, rags, or almost anything that could be used for padding; not infrequently bran was used. There is an engaging story of a young gallant who stuffed his doublet and hose tightly with bran in order to cut a fine figure at a social function. The poor chap had the misfortune to sit on a chair adorned with a protruding nail. This punctured his breeches, and " as he turned and bowed to pay court to the ladies, the bran poured forth as from a mill that was grinding, without his perceiving it, till half his cargo was unladen on the floor." There must have been many such amusing incidents.

In those days fads in dress were usually introduced by the men. Among these was the *ruff*, that peculiar neck-gear so conspicuous in the portraits of both the men and the women of that time. Just as the doublet was the ancestor of our coat, so was the ruff the forefather of the collar. For some time the ruff had been growing in size, until in the days of Elizabeth it reached its greatest expansion, varying in depth from six inches to a foot. The use of starch, then lately introduced from Holland, made it possible to encase your neck with this stiff sort of tray, your head seeming to rest upon it. In extreme cases the ruff was so heavy that wire props were needed to keep it in place or at a fashionable elevation. Imagine the joy of eating when you had to convey your food with your fingers across this platform under your chin!

The fullness of appearance secured by the men as already described was achieved by the women with a *farthingale,* a stiff framework of wire and whalebone. This was fastened tightly around the waist. In shape it might be like a cone, or it might extend at right angles from the hips, and then straight down. The whole contraption was rigid and reached to the floor, at which point it was often more than four feet wide. Over this frame the lady placed as many petticoats as her means allowed or her fancy dictated, the outer ones slashed in order to display the colors and the richness of the cloth of the inner ones. Over all this the outer dress was finally draped, the front part being cut to show the finery and the colors of the garments underneath. The upper part of a woman's body was dressed with a tightly laced bodice corresponding somewhat to the doublet of the men, except that it was not padded. On the contrary, it fitted snugly to the body, with the neck generously exposed by those who had necks that could bear exposure. The ruff, attached to the bodice, was cut V-shape in front, unless the bodice closed. Then it resembled that of the men. Sleeves, like those of the men, were cut full above the elbows.

Shoes were of various kinds, but similar for both sexes. To show the color of the stockings it was customary to slash the shoes at the instep. Huge rosettes were a common adornment. The soles and heels were often high, especially on the women's shoes. This was less for style than for economy, for it kept the skirts out of the dirt. In the matter of shoes, as in all articles of dress, bright colors were the rage, with all possible sorts of ornamentation, including jewels.

This passion for color extended also to the hair, which in other respects, too, was worn most fantastically by both sexes. Men dyed their hair, their mustaches, and their whiskers as fancy prompted or the barbers dictated. Wigs of different colors were fashionable among the men and the women, and it was nothing unusual to see a man one day with red whiskers and the next with black. A woman might appear at a ball one night with a yellow wig, and next day be seen at a court reception with a gray one. Queen Elizabeth at one time reveled in the possession of eighty of these disguises, although everybody knew that she had red hair. Painting the face was as common as it is today, with the variation that men were equally guilty.

Fashions then, as now, were carried to the greatest extremes by the upper and wealthier leisure classes. Then, as now, these were aped by the lower and poorer working classes as their means allowed. The general trend was always the same.

SHAKESPEARE'S LONDON

The London of today has retained practically none of its Elizabethan landmarks. The fire of 1666 did a complete job. What we do know is culled mainly from contemporary sources, such as books and old prints, fortunately numerous enough to give us a fair idea how the city looked and what it was like when Shakespeare lived in it.

In the sixteenth century London was the great center of English life, even more so than it is in this twentieth century. As now, it was the largest city in England, but by our modern standards of size it was small, boasting a population of about 200,000, a city smaller than Louisville, or Denver, or Rochester, or Seattle. In the City proper — that is, the part of London under the jurisdiction of the Corporation — there were only half that number of people, the rest living in the immediate suburbs. The technical term " City " is retained to the present day, and its corporate limits are the same as in the time of Shakespeare. Roughly speaking, it includes the business section of the modern city, geographically only a small part of London. It is over this district that the Lord Mayor of London has sway, but the office is hardly more than a picturesque relic of the past. During the period of the Elizabethan drama, however, the Corporation of the City was immensely powerful and exercised considerable influence on the development of the drama, as we shall see later.

Shakespeare's London was still enclosed on three sides by the old medieval walls. As in all cities, the streets were narrow and filthy and the houses crowded closely together. The top stories projected over those immediately below, so that the streets were narrowest at the top. From the highest window it was often possible to shake hands with your neighbor across the street. During the day the streets were noisy, not from traffic only, but from the cries of every variety of peddler and county of Warwick, about eighty miles from London, and off the main highways. In Shakespeare's day it had a population of about 2000; today it has about five times that number. Unlike London, the town of Shakespeare's birth retains many of its old landmarks almost unchanged. When the boy Shakespeare trudged unwillingly to school he passed from Henley Street to High Street, on through Chapel Street, past the Guild Hall to the Edward VI Grammar School on Church Street, with perhaps a look of longing toward the Avon, down Chapel Lane. The Guild Hall and the school remain substantially the same as they were in the sixteenth century, and the streets just mentioned bear their old names; although they are wider than in former days, and certainly much cleaner. Most of the houses are modern, but a number of old cross-timbered buildings manage to give an Elizabethan flavor to these streets and others in Stratford.

The town of Stratford shared in all the vicissitudes of the times, such as regular visitations of the plague, due to unsanitary conditions; frequent fires due to the primitive methods of constructing houses (without chimneys, for instance); and destructive floods through inability to control the Avon. From the town records it is evident that the local corporation made desperate attempts to remedy these recurring disasters, with but little success. The government of Stratford was of the paternal order; that is, the corporation regulated everything for everybody, from your politics to the kind of clothes you wore. There were ordinances to curb and punish every vice and every misdemeanor possible to a citizen. Property owners were fined if they allowed too much filth to accumulate in front of their houses, so we might imagine that the streets were cleaner than in London, were it not for evidence to the contrary. Shakespeare's father, himself a member of the corporation, was once fined for this offense. As today, there seems to have been the same gulf between the making of a law and its enforcement. We also know that the corporation frowned severely on obstreperous servants, loafing apprentices, persons who swore, unmuzzled dogs, and the innocent pigs that wished to enjoy a carefree life on the dirty streets. For scolding women a ducking-stool was kept well oiled. If you "got fresh" to a town officer you spent three days and nights in the public stocks. If you were a poor workman you could patronize the alehouses, of which there were thirty, only at stated hours. The hours for playing bowls were also regulated by law, and if you failed to go to church at least once a month you were liable to a fine of twenty pounds. All of which goes to show that there must have been some excitement in the life of the sixteenth century.

Today Stratford is a neat and attractive town whose chief business is Shakespeare. Through the Shakespeare Memorial Association everything that can possibly have had any connection with the great poet and his time is being carefully preserved. The two houses on Henley Street, in one of which Shakespeare was born, have been restored to look approximately like their Elizabethan selves. New Place, Shakespeare's last home, was spitefully demolished in 1759, but the site under the same name is now a small public park. On the right bank of the Avon stands the Shakespeare Memorial Theater, a modern structure, part of which is used as a library and museum. To the theater there is now attached a theatrical company that gives at least two short seasons of Shakespeare plays annually. A short distance from the theater, on the same side of the Avon, is Trinity Church, in which Shakespeare was baptized and in which he is buried. Some miles beyond Stratford is the hamlet of Shottery, where Shakespeare courted and all too easily won the fair Anne Hathaway. The cottage is still there, one of the most beautiful specimens of its kind in all England.

The Association and the town have left nothing undone to make the Shakespeare memorials accessible to the public, and this, together with the natural attractiveness of Stratford itself, accounts for the thousands of visitors that flock to it every year.

SHAKESPEARE

In a biographical sketch of William Shakespeare it is possible to record only a few facts that are absolutely authentic, and these few are for the most part quite prosaic. In the sixteenth and the seventeenth centuries there were no newspapers with special writers like those of our day, whose chief business it is to keep the public informed about every detail in the life of a successful dramatist, usually presented in a gossipy vein, to attract the widest attention. In Shakespeare's day there was no demand for that sort of thing, or for any kind of biography except that of a few prominent men active chiefly in politics and diplomacy. But meager as the facts about Shakespeare are, they are less so than those of any other Elizabethan dramatist, with the possible exception of Ben Jonson.

The undoubtedly valid sources of information about Shakespeare are the official entry of the date of his baptism, his grave, and a monument in the church in Stratford; the publication of a few poems over his name; a number of direct references to him by enemies and friends in his profession; the mention of his name among the members of the Burbage company of actors and producers; and numerous legal documents, pertaining chiefly to property both in London and in Stratford, records of lawsuits that involved either himself or some of his friends, and his will. Of the intimate personal details that make the subject of a biography live before our eyes there are none. In the case of Shakespeare this is all the more regrettable because of the extraordinary richness of his work, a richness that surely must have had some counterpart in his individual life. Not a single bit of manuscript has been preserved, and the only examples of his handwriting are a few signatures.

The poet's father, John Shakespeare, was a prosperous merchant in Stratford, dealing mostly in the agricultural products of the surrounding country, such as grain, hay, hides, and wool. His wealth and prestige in the community had been considerably increased by his marriage to Mary Arden, the daughter of a well-to-do farmer near Stratford. That John Shakespeare took a lively interest in local affairs is shown by the various public offices with which his fellow citizens honored him. In quick succession he had been ale-taster, bailiff, and so on to Chief Alderman in 1571. As bailiff he gave official sanction and entertainment to several companies of players in 1568. There were six children, of whom William was the third, the oldest of the four boys.

We do not even have an exact record of the date of Shakespeare's birth, but in the official registry of Trinity Church his baptism is entered opposite the date April 26, 1564. As it was customary to baptize infants a few days after birth, the date may fairly be given as April 23. After his death a tradition grew up that Shakespeare had died on the anniversary of

his birth, and as the Stratford monument definitely gives
April 23 as the date of his death, the matter may be considered
closed.

As the son of an important and wealthy man, the boy undoubtedly attended the Edward VI Grammar School on Church
Street, a good local free school, still standing and still used as
a school.   Here the course of instruction was vastly different
from that of the schools of our day.   There was little reading,
writing, and arithmetic as we understand them, and none of
the many frills that adorn the curriculum of a modern school.
The study of Latin was not only considered fundamental to
sound training, it was almost the only study.   French was
also taught in the Stratford school, and possibly Greek.

Although Shakespeare spent only six years in school, there
is every reason to believe that he made good use of his time,
or was forced to do so by his teachers.   In a number of plays
there is evidence of his knowledge of Latin, particularly in
Love's Labor's Lost, his earliest comedy, in which he undoubtedly makes fun of his own school days, quoting many
phrases from a well known Latin textbook.   In a much later
play, *Henry V,* he uses a great deal of French, but that language he may have acquired in London while living with a
French family.

By the year 1577 John Shakespeare had become involved
in commercial difficulties to such an extent that he took his
son out of school and put him to work, no doubt in his own
establishment.   What the nature of Shakespeare's life was
during the next five years can only be imagined.   That he
shared in the normal activities of boyhood is beyond question,
for he was only thirteen when he left school.   What was there
for a boy to do in the sixteenth century country town?   Fortunately Shakespeare himself informs us through many hints
in his plays.   In the early ones are references to rustic
sports, such as top-spinning, quoits, leapfrog, hockey, prisoner's
base, ninepins, football, and others not so well known to us.
More grown-up sports that he must have witnessed were falconry and bowls, from both of which he has drawn so many
figures that it is fair to assume that as a young man he also
knew those from personal experience.   There were fields and
woods for hunting, streams in which to fish, and, more attractive still, there were in the vicinity of Stratford some
large estates of landed gentry whose game preserves offered

temptations for poaching, especially to the venturesome town boys. Shakespeare was probably no better than the rest, although the story about a particular poaching exploit is without proof.

Athletic "meets" were common, and there were many church festivals that had special celebrations aside from their religious aspect. Miracle plays and Morality plays he must have seen frequently, both in Stratford and in the surrounding villages, and before he left home dramatic performances by companies of strolling players were nothing unusual. It seems, therefore, that boys in the days of Shakespeare did not have such a dull time after all, lacking only the automobile, the movies, and baseball.

The astonishing amount of accurate general knowledge that Shakespeare possessed must have been acquired through a natural gift of close observation coupled with an unusually retentive memory, while no small part of his genius consisted in his ability to use this storehouse of information at will. Throughout his plays there is abundant evidence of his early experiences around and about Stratford, including intimate acquaintance with persons of all types, from the patrons of his father's business to the tapsters in the alehouses and the old wives versed in the folklore of the country. No doubt he also read whatever books were available in the village.

When a young man reaches the age of eighteen he begins to have ambitions beyond the activities just described, but what Shakespeare's were we have no way of telling. That he chafed under the restrictions of small-town life is certain, but whether he had already made up his mind to seek his fortune in London we can only conjecture. It would have been nothing unusual, of course. Possibly an ambition to enter upon a theatrical career was stimulated by his contact with the companies that visited Stratford, some of whose members he met intimately because of his father's official connection with them. While he was a mere boy at the time, it is likely that when the same companies revisited the town the members would look up their old friends.

At any rate, in 1582 Shakespeare took the most effective way of temporarily blocking whatever ambition he may have had. He got married. His bride, Anne Hathaway from the neighboring hamlet of Shottery, was eight years his senior. Of her we know but little, although it is a safe guess that, as befitted her years, she was of a practical housewifely turn, and when their first child was born in 1583 she may have insisted that her husband begin to settle down to some definite career. When two years later twins were added to the none too happy household, she may have become more insistent. All that we really know is that most of Shakespeare's early married life was unhappy, and in 1586 he quietly left Stratford.

Again there is a gap in the record of his life. Whether he went straight to London, or whether he " adventured around " for some years, we do not know. But in 1592 a contemporary dramatist, Robert Greene, died in London and left an unpublished manuscript in which there were nasty digs at Shakespeare, showing that he was already known in dramatic circles as an author, or at least as an adapter of plays for the stage. In April, 1593, Shakespeare published his poem *Venus and Adonis,* the manuscript of which had probably been circulated among his friends, according to a custom of the day. This poem, together with *Lucrece,* 1594, are the only two works of Shakespeare that were legitimately published over his name during his lifetime.

How and when Shakespeare became connected with the theater is again a matter of conjecture. If, as already hinted, he had made friends with some of the actors who had visited Stratford, it would be natural enough for the young stranger in the big city to look these up and consult them about the possibility of getting a job. In this way he may have secured a minor position as general factotum around the theater; and about this there are many traditions which need not concern us here. We do know definitely that by 1592 he was doing important work in The Theater, built in 1576 by James Burbage. This was one of the two foremost theaters in London and is discussed elsewhere in this Introduction.

Shakespeare began his theatrical career humbly enough in the Burbage company, at that time under the patronage of the powerful Earl of Leicester, first as a call boy, then as a super, and finally as an actor of small parts. Playgoing was the most popular amusement in London, and the various companies were kept busy supplying the demand for new plays. Everybody around a theater was active in producing, writing new plays, revising old ones, including such as had failed. It was in the latter capacities that Shakespeare first showed what he could do in adapting drama for performance on the stage. Before long he was the most valuable member of the company. Factotum, super, actor, reviser, adapter, and finally writer of original plays, all in an incredibly short time, sums up the beginning of the career of the greatest of all dramatists.

From this point on the life of Shakespeare as we know it is barely more than a record of his dramatic work, for the details of how he spent his time when not in the theater, or writing for it, are as meager as those of his Stratford days. We know that he remained with the Burbage company permanently, that up to 1612 he averaged two original plays a year, that he must have helped to revise and rewrite many others, and that his contemporary fame increased with the years. He continued to act when occasion demanded it, but always in small parts. Tradition says that among such parts were the Ghost in *Hamlet* and Adam in *As You Like It,* and there is definite record of his taking a part in one of Ben Jonson's plays. While he was not a leading actor, it seems that he was good enough to be among those specially summoned on different occasions to play before royalty or some nobleman. In time he became a stockholder in the company and part manager; no doubt he always was his own stage director. Unlike many men of high artistic genius, Shakespeare was both thrifty and sensible in a business way. As his finances prospered he began to invest in property, both in Stratford and in London. It is worth noting, also, that among the first things he did when he began to have money was to help straighten out the tangled finances of his father.

During these London years he must have associated familiarly with many men connected with the theaters, some of whom have left records in one way or another of their respect and affection for their fellow craftsman, notably Ben Jonson, who wrote for another company and who was Shakespeare's greatest rival in the drama of the day. Shakespeare was likewise intimate with men prominent in walks of life other than that of the theater, including members of the nobility. Among his earliest London friends was the Earl of Southampton, whose name is forever connected with the problem of the *Sonnets,* a discussion of which is not in place here. Unquestionably Shakespeare had a likable personality and was much in demand socially. As all theatrical performances took place in the afternoon, he was free in the evening either to visit his friends or to hobnob familiarly with his cronies at the Mermaid Tavern. He probably was a good listener and learned much from the talk of his friends, to be used later in his plays. There was also a publishing " boom " in those days, and that Shakespeare was not indifferent to the enormous output of books is shown abundantly in his work.

It is customary to divide the plays into four groups: (1) his early work, which includes *Romeo and Juliet* and *Richard III*; (2) his maturing work, including the great comedies, among them *The Merchant of Venice* and *As You Like It*, the English chronicle plays, as well as *Julius Caesar*; (3) his mature work, including the great tragedies of *Hamlet* and *Macbeth*; (4) his quieter comedies, like *The Tempest* and *The Winter's Tale*, both written in 1611, just before he finally left London.

Shakespeare was not quite fifty years old when he decided to retire from the theater. Whether he felt tired out, or whether he was in bad health, or whether he at last had a feeling of homesickness for the scenes of his boyhood, we do not know. He returned to Stratford in 1612, and remained there, with probably infrequent trips to London to look after his interests. During the height of his career he had not visited his home often, but he always had kept in touch with it more or less. On the death of his father he had inherited the two houses on Henley Street. For his own home he had bought New Place, and altogether he was regarded by his fellow towns-men as a man of substance, even though that substance had been acquired in the theater, an institution regarded as dis-reputable by the constantly growing Puritanic sentiment of the time.

Shakespeare no doubt found the life of a country gentleman attractive. As far as we know, he did little writing after his retirement. The unfinished play of *Henry VIII* was perhaps his last work before he left London, and he let that be com-pleted by some one else. Of his family life during these last years in Stratford we know as little as of the early days, ex-cept that he was much attached to his daughter Susanna and her husband, Dr. John Hall. To them he willed most of his property and charged them with the care of his wife. In April, 1616, Shakespeare was taken suddenly ill, and died on the twenty-third.

THE DRAMA

TO SEE A PLAY

It is not likely that any one who reads this Introduction has never seen a play. It is equally unlikely that he does not enjoy plays, even though they be only the movies. Many people, unfortunately, often go to a theater or a movie, not to see the play so much as some heavily " starred " actor or actress; the play itself is quite secondary. This, of course, is all wrong in its emphasis. Unless a play is adequate the actor is helpless, although it is true that a weak play is sometimes made possible by good acting. Only the kind of play that has staying qualities is to be considered here.

What is a play? In a general way, everybody knows — it is nothing but a story presented on a stage, and part of the reason for the tremendous popularity of plays lies in the universal love of a story. In any story there are characters who do things, or have things done to them, creating some sort of entanglement, followed by a definite outcome. But that is not by any means all. The author must arouse sympathetic interest in the characters first of all, either through what they are or by what they do. If the characters themselves are not interesting we care little for what they do, unless there is immediate stress on the entanglement — the plot, in other words — and this is so intimately bound up with character that in an interesting story it all comes back to that. In prose fiction the author is able to mingle his presentation of character with a description of the surrounding circumstances; he can take his time to make clear the details both of the setting and of the plot so that the reader's imagination easily follows the trend of the story, always assuming that it is interestingly done. There must be a struggle of some kind against opposing forces, and this comes out happily or brings disaster. The simplest kind of struggle is the hero-heroine-villain type, the first example of which is laid in the Garden of Eden. Always there must be emotional response on the part of the reader, and when all these elements are artistically combined, a story affords satisfying entertainment in the best sense of the term.

In a play the purpose is intrinsically the same, that of entertainment; the material is similar in its elements, but the method of presentation is vastly different. As in prose fiction, there must be a real story, but the dramatist must exercise severe repression and careful selection in the details — the high spots, as it were. He has at most only two hours and a half in which to tell his story, and his way of telling it is fundamentally different. In a play the author bears in mind that actors impersonate his characters, the action is real and visible on the stage, and the dialogue audible and equally real. He is addressing himself to the eye and the ear of the audience. Instead of descriptions of persons and setting, all has to be seen by the eye in the costumes of the characters and the way the scene is set on the stage. Information necessary for the audience must be conveyed through this setting, or through the conversation and action of the characters. In a well constructed play most of this information should be suggested rather than directly indicated. For instance, if the setting shows a street scene, and it is important to know where it is supposed to be, one character might say to another, "What are you doing on Fifth Avenue?" A New York audience might recognize the street without that hint, but one in Gopher Prairie might not. In the earlier drama, when scenery was limited, a sign was sometimes hung in a conspicuous spot, "Street in Verona." In the theaters of today this casual sort of information is usually given on programs, if at all, and the dramatist is free to concentrate his efforts on telling the audience an interesting story.

TO READ A PLAY

It is possible that some who read this book have never before read a play. There are plenty of regular theatergoers who never think of reading a play. Plays are made to be seen on a stage in a theater, they may say, and they are right, as we have noted. On the other hand, the world's greatest plays happen also to be fine literature. It is that quality which has preserved them for posterity. To the student of literature the Greek, the French, the German, the Elizabethan, and all other drama of the past would be practically unknown today had it not had more than mere acting possibilities. The plays would still be of interest historically, but certainly none of them would be required in school courses.

A play that makes a hit in the theater today is likely to be outmoded tomorrow. This is true of the literary play as well

as that of theatrical appeal only. Greek plays are sometimes
revived in colleges, and, in recent years a few translations have
been given before large audiences in certain open-air theaters;
the French plays of Molière, Racine, and Corneille are regularly performed in France under state patronage, but rarely in
translation outside of schools; and of the Elizabethan plays
the regular theater patron hears of none besides a few of
Shakespeare's. And even for Shakespeare it is not always
easy to find audiences. The five plays in this volume are
produced with some frequency in this country, especially
Hamlet and *The Merchant of Venice*. There have been recent revivals of *Othello* and *Romeo and Juliet*. But every
school includes Shakespeare in its courses; at least four plays
are listed in the college entrance requirements; and every
college offers courses in Shakespeare, either directly or as
part of the work in the drama, historical or otherwise. In
the world's literature Shakespeare continues to be the
greatest single figure, and this is the case because his works
rank even higher as literary masterpieces than as merely act-
able plays.

To read a play with real enjoyment is much more difficult
than to see it produced on the stage. Accustomed to enjoy a
play through the ear and the eye, the inexperienced reader,
eager chiefly for the story, dashes ahead too fast, and presently
finds himself all tangled up. The chances are that he will
want to throw the play aside and take up his favorite magazine, which is so much easier to read. How, then, is one to
read a play with real pleasure, the same kind of pleasure that
he gets out of a magazine story?

To begin with, you should read over carefully the list of
characters and note their relationship to each other, if any,
and their place in the scale of things. In Shakespeare the
dramatis personae are always grouped according to rank,
kings, dukes, and such coming first. You will not remember
much of this list, but a preliminary glance facilitates reference
later. Beginning with the scene of action, indicated in the
stage directions, you should begin to use your eyes, bearing
in mind that a play is addressed to the eye, but now it must
be the inner eye, that of the imagination. In other words, you
must visualize not only the scenes but the characters, how
they are dressed, how they talk, what they do, the gestures
they make, and their changing positions on the stage as they

go through the action. At the same time you should be able to hear them speak the lines just as if you were present at an actual stage performance. If you can read aloud, so much the better. All this may seem a large order, but after reading several plays conscientiously in this manner you will be surprised at the ease with which it can be done and the genuine pleasure you get out of it.

Take *Julius Caesar*, for example. Glance over the list of thirty-five characters and do not be appalled at the number. From your experience in the theater you will know that only a few of them can take leading parts. From the stage directions, and more particularly from the actual text, construct the scene in your mind's eye. " Rome. A Street." How do you see that? Imagine how a modern stage would be set for the opening of this play. Would the street be narrow or wide? What kind of houses would you see? How would the tribunes and commoners be dressed? What would be their relative positions on the stage? What difference in their manner of speaking? For contrast, try to imagine how all this was done in an Elizabethan production, hints of which appear elsewhere. A good cyclopedia contains pictures of costumes of all ages and times, and you will find the article " Costume " exceedingly interesting in itself. As you read along in the play be sure to fix the characters in your mind, turning to the list if you are in doubt as to who's who. Before you reach the end of the first act you will know all the important ones. Always keep visualizing the action. Follow the actors as they move about the stage and recite their lines, and before long you will have forgotten that you ever thought a play difficult to read.

HISTORICAL SUMMARY

THE GREEK DRAMA. Drama is so distinctive a form of art that it is of interest to trace briefly its origins and to follow its trend until it reached its culminating point in the Age of Shakespeare. The beginning of any art is more or less spontaneous; that is, a new form appears without a definitely conscious effort on anybody's part to create something new. Usually this new thing springs from the development of a germ that had its origin elsewhere. Among the Greeks of the sixth century B.C., or earlier, the sporadic germ that later was to evolve into the drama happened to lie in the crude cere-

THE AVON AND ITS BRIDGES AT MODERN STRATFORD

ANNE HATHAWAY'S COTTAGE AT SHOTTERY NEAR STRATFORD

the shouts of apprentices who hoped to entice customers to their shops. Fights between apprentices of rival houses were not uncommon and sometimes led to regular street riots. A popular sport along the streets was to hoot at all strangers, especially foreigners. Although the streets were poorly lighted, and wayfarers were in danger of attack, there seems to have been considerable night life. This we know chiefly from city ordinances which made some attempts to keep the nights from being too hideous.

After all, what was one to do with his leisure time in old London? There were few books and no magazines. Even had there been more books and some magazines, there would have been comparatively few to enjoy them, for reading was still an accomplishment of the elect only. Libraries, museums, and art galleries were unknown. The houses were not comfortable enough to lure a person into spending much more time in them than was necessary to eat and to sleep. Consequently many hours were spent outdoors, or at least away from home.

The center of city life was St. Paul's Cathedral, both within the building itself, and more so in the surrounding yard. It was to St. Paul's that you went when you had nothing in particular to do — to promenade, to meet friends, to buy books, or to hang around the taverns, which were both numerous and thriving here as everywhere else in the city. This was old St. Paul's, which from its hill dominated the city more conspicuously than its modern namesake. It was the largest building in the city, and looked larger than it really was, because of the smallness of London. While there were many churches, the large monasteries of an earlier day were gradually being either entirely dismantled or turned to other uses. Parts of at least two of them, Blackfriars and Whitefriars, were eventually used as theaters. An added reason for the great popularity of the inns was that many of them opened their yards for the production of plays. More will be said about them later.

On the south side of the city was the Thames, at that time perhaps more fascinating as a thoroughfare than it is today. The river was crowded with traffic. There was considerable foreign commerce, and boats from strange lands, together with the sailors who manned them, must have added to the interest and picturesqueness common to all busy waterfronts. The amusement attractions of Southwark, on the Surrey side of the Thames, gave employment to many rivermen, who ferried across all who wished to avoid the crowded bridge. These rowboats were really the taxis of their day, for they carried passengers up and down the river as well as across.

London Bridge was in those days the only bridge across the Thames. Narrow to begin with, it was made narrower by the houses and shops that lined both sides, with the exception of a small space in the middle. The Bridge was the center of the pin trade; otherwise its chief attraction lay in the south tower, whose battlements afforded a last resting-place for the heads of traitors. Executions were public in those days, and people generally took a day off to attend them. Later they no doubt found a further thrill in seeing the heads stuck on long pikes and draped along the bridge-tower battlements.

There was much activity in sports and games. Hunting, fishing, bowling, archery, falconry, cockfighting, bull and bear baiting — all were popular, both in town and country. All kinds of gambling flourished. That Shakespeare was familiar with all of these popular diversions is proved by the many apt figures and parallelisms that adorn his style. The Elizabethans were superstitious, believing in ghosts, witches, fairies, and magic of all sorts. Astrology, the " science " by means of which your destiny is determined by the stars, was consulted by persons in every rank of society. It is on record that on one occasion the Queen herself sent for an astrologer to relieve her from a toothache. Another favorite trick science was alchemy, pursued in the phantom hope that base metals could be transmuted into gold, if only the " philosopher's stone " could be found! This particular fraud was ridiculed by Ben Jonson in his farcical comedy *The Alchemist*. If by any chance you had to pass a haunted spot at night, to sheer off the ghost all you had to do was to wear your doublet inside out. Many of these superstitions are used in plays by Shakespeare and other Elizabethan dramatists, and before you laugh scornfully at them you might remember that every superstition mentioned has believers in this sophisticated twentieth century of ours.

STRATFORD–ON–AVON

The general characteristics of the large city and of the people who lived in it repeated themselves in the smaller communities. Typical of these was Stratford-on-Avon, in the

monial of the worship of the god Dionysus, the most univer-
sally popular of all the Greek gods. Perhaps you have never
heard of Dionysus. He does not appear in the galaxy that
brightens the pages of Homer — Zeus, Pallas Athena, Posei-
don, Hephaestus, Aphrodite, and the rest. Among all classes
of people in ancient Greece the belief in these higher gods was
rather conventional; they were the celestial aristocrats, accepted in much the same manner as the social aristocracy.
Both had presumably always existed, and that was all there
was to that.

On the other hand, Dionysus, who did not dwell on high
Olympus, stood for something more nearly human, something
they could really understand because it was intimately personal to themselves. Primarily he was the god of wine. It
was he who tempered the sun and the rain to insure a good
season for grapes; it was he who guaranteed weather satis-
factory for gathering the ripened fruit; it was he who presided
over the wine press; and, finally, it was he who stood by as
they eagerly opened last year's wine casks. To the Greeks a
successful grape season spelled prosperity, just as a fine wheat
crop does with us. So Dionysus came to symbolize nearly all
the good things of life, especially those that concerned mere
physical well-being. Small wonder, then, that the Greeks
should worship him sincerely and joyously.

In remote times this worship was extremely simple. In a
field or in the market place they erected a rude altar on which
a goat was placed for sacrifice, a priest of Dionysus officiating.
The whole community was present, but immediately around
the altar was grouped a band of rustic singers who shared with
the priest the more formal part of the ceremony. This chorus,
as it was called, was in charge of a leader, who might impersonate the god and tell about his adventures. Of these there
were many, most of them already known to the crowd of
villagers that formed the audience, but a clever leader could
readily fabricate new adventures for the delight of the crowd.
The members of the chorus might imagine themselves satyrs,
mythical creatures half man and half goat, who were supposed
to be congenial companions of the merry god. The serious
part of the ceremony was the actual sacrifice of the goat, ac-
companied or followed by a choral hymn chanted in honor of
the god. When this sacred part of the rites was over the
chorus, and no doubt the surrounding villagers, burst out in

gleeful song. The celebration now became something of a riot, with much drinking and rough horseplay.

Long before there was any thought of the drama, the terms for its general classification were used in this old worship of Dionysus, *tragedy* or goat-song, sung after the death of the goat, and *comedy*, the song of the villagers. The general sense of those terms applies to our modern conception of comedy and tragedy. The songs themselves were also called *dithyrambs*, but they were not yet drama; there was *playing* but not *acting*, using those words in their fundamental sense, not synonymously, as we do today. The word *drama* comes from a Greek verb which means *to act*, and so far there had been nothing in the worship of Dionysus that could be construed as acting. The dithyrambs were chanted in recitative fashion between the leader and his chorus, not unlike parts of modern church services, but in that recitative lay the germ of the drama.

The first step forward in the direction of real drama was made when the leader addressed himself to a particular individual in the chorus, and that individual responded, instead of the whole chorus. For instance, suppose that the leader, impersonating Dionysus, was telling one of his adventures. It would be a most natural thing to go through some action to make his story more vivid. A member of the chorus, taking up the story, might also indulge in impromptu action. If the two supplemented each other in dialogue and action to make a continuous story, there was drama.

This theory of how dramatic performances began may seem rather fanciful, but it is based on the conjectures of scholars who have searched minutely for every bit of evidence that Greek literature and archeology have so far disclosed. For confirming details the reader must look in books other than this.

With the germ of the drama isolated, it is not essential to our purpose to go into elaborate details of its development. Suffice it to say that its development was rapid, and we are concerned here only with its Golden Age in the fifth century B.C. One thing to remember is that Greek drama always retained some religious significance. Plays were given only in connection with three of the four yearly festivals in honor of Dionysus, and the development of the Greek theater was directly along the lines laid by the more primitive manner of

THE BANKSIDE, SHOWING THE THEATERS
(From Visscher's Map of London, 1616)

LONDON BRIDGE

(Note the Pikes with Traitors' Skulls on the Southern Tower. From Visscher's Map of London, 1616)

worship. The subject matter of the plays, however, ceased
to concern the actions of Dionysus. With the growth of the
Athenian national spirit, and the great tests to which it was
put in the dramatic crises of its history, especially the struggle
with Persia, there was new matter for drama. The writers of
plays also found additional material in the stories, mythical
and otherwise, that had become part of the tradition of the
race. Audiences were usually familiar with the story that was
to be rendered, and they looked for their entertainment in the
way it was presented and the poetic form in which it was
written.

As just stated, plays were given only as part of the worship
of Dionysus at festivals regularly dedicated to him, the most
important of which was the so-called Greater Dionysia celebrated in Athens in March. The production of plays was
competitive, under the direction of government officials chosen
by lot. These examined all the plays submitted and determined their fitness to be entered into competition. Each com-
petitor had to submit at least four plays, and the work of only
three poets was produced at a given festival. Once a play was
entered, the poet's first task was to secure a chorus. Technically this was allotted by the first or second Archon of Athens
from a body of men trained by the state, so that all the poet
had to do was to adapt it to his particular play. Wealthy
citizens competed for the privilege of providing the costumes
and other accessories for the play, and a first place in that was
an honor second only to the prize-winning play.

For a dramatist, the highest reward was to win a first prize.
This was in itself of trifling actual value, but a successful poet
received substantial monetary reward through special grants
from the state, quite aside from the prize. The actors also
were paid by the state, but of these there need not have been
many. The largest number required in any play was four;
usually there were only three, and in the earlier tragedies only
two, not counting the chorus and other supernumeraries. The
actors were elaborately costumed and wore masks with huge
mouthpieces that may have served as megaphones, so that the
remotest part of the audience could hear distinctly, for Greek
plays depended for their effect more on the ear than on the
eye. On the stage there was little action, as we understand
that term. All the terrible events that form the chief subjects
of Greek tragedy were supposed to take place behind the

scenes, the actors narrating them so effectively that the audience responded as if the deeds had taken place before their eyes.

We spoke just now of a stage, but in all likelihood the classic Greek drama had no stage in our modern sense, merely a *logium,* or speaking-place. All Greek theaters were open-air structures, built preferably on a hillside that offered a natural amphitheater. In shape they were nearly a complete circle. The lower tier of seats consisted of boxes in which sat the officers of state, while the best box was reserved for the priest of Dionysus. The circular ground space was called the *orchestra,* always occupied by the chorus, and used by the actors if needed. In the center of the orchestra was the altar of Dionysus. The *logium,* or speaking-place, was backed by the *scene,* originally a tent (the word *scene* is the Greek for tent), but later in the more substantial theaters it was a hut, with two or three doors. It was in front of this that most of the action took place. If there was any sort of stage it must have been narrow and quite low, so that the actors could step off and on without any difficulty. On both sides of the hut were entrances used by the audience when it came in, and by the actors and chorus for passing on and off the stage. Along the front of the *scene* was a colonnade from the top of which could come a " voice from above," such as that of a god.

In the last fifty years a number of these ancient theaters have been dug up by enterprising archeologists. You will find it of real interest to look up pictures of some of them, especially that of the Theater of Dionysus at Athens, a vast structure that could accommodate 30,000 people. Such enormous crowds were possible because going to the theater was a patriotic as well as a religious duty, and the price of admission of any one lacking it was paid by the government.

The classic Greek drama of the fifth century B.C. is the one rival to challenge the Elizabethans for supremacy in this form of art. Of this Greek drama we have the work of only four dramatists with a total of forty-two plays among them, thirty-one tragedies and eleven comedies. Shakespeare alone wrote thirty-seven plays. There were of course many more dramatists among the Greeks, as contemporary references show, but all their work has been lost with the exception of brief extracts quoted by other writers.

It is possible here to give only the barest facts about the Greek dramatists. The earliest was Aeschylus (525–456 B.C.), who is said to have written seventy tragedies, twenty-eight of which received first prize. Of the seven that remain the *Agamemnon* is the most readable. The hero of this play is the same Agamemnon whom you know as the leader of the Greeks against Troy as told in the *Iliad*. In this play we learn what happens to him when he returns to his native Sparta. The greatest of the Greek dramatists was Sophocles (495–405 B.C.). He wrote over one hundred plays, all lost but seven, of which the *Antigone* is the best. But all of his plays are of the highest order, and the *Electra* is especially interesting in connection with the purposes of this volume because Sophocles treated the motive of revenge in a way that at once suggests *Hamlet*. In late years the *Electra* has been performed in English many times in this country by Miss Margaret Anglin. Euripides (480–406 B.C.), the last of the great Greek playwrights, wrote seventy-five or more tragedies, of which seventeen are still extant. It is difficult to say which is his best, but for modern readers the *Alcestis* is certainly the most interesting, although it is not strictly a tragedy; it is rather a tragi-comedy, in which death is cheated by a most unusual trick, in a way not unlike that in *The Merchant of Venice*.

All Greek tragedy is permeated with the idea of Nemesis, or an avenging Fate, which brings disaster and death to persons of high degree, usually kings and princes. According to Greek beliefs, this overpowering Fate governed the destinies of the universe, and to struggle against it was useless. In tragedies the characters recognize their helplessness, but in spite of that, being human, they do struggle, mainly in an effort to propitiate the gods in whose hands lay the administering of fate; but even the gods themselves were more or less bound by this same sinister Necessity, as it was sometimes called, and had to obey certain inexorable laws which demanded punishment for crimes even though committed innocently. An angry Fate demanded punishment not only of those directly implicated in a crime, but often of members of their families also. Besides, punishment was to be inflicted not according to human laws, but according to what to the Greeks was moral law. For instance, if a father was killed it was the moral duty of the oldest son to take vengeance upon the murderer.

How complicated this scheme of vengeance might become

is illustrated by the great trilogy dealing with the Oedipus story as told by Sophocles. The *Antigone,* already mentioned, is one of these. But for more concrete illustration we may take the story of Orestes, used by all three writers. In the *Agamemnon* of Aeschylus, Clytemnestra, the wife, in order to cover up wrongdoing of her own, helped to kill her victorious husband immediately after he returned from Troy. This was an especially despicable crime, but worse was to follow. Orestes, the only son, was too young to undertake the revenge, so he was spirited away by his older sister Electra to let him mature sufficiently for the necessary deed, the killing of the murderer of his father, who happened to be his mother. Many years elapse, and Electra despairs of the return of her brother, but during all this time she has lived with only one thought, that her mother must be killed for her part in the death of her father. Just as she is planning to do the deed herself Orestes returns and in short order kills his mother. Electra is unquestionably the greatest single figure in Greek tragedy, especially as presented by Sophocles, from whose play the summary was made. But the death of Clytemnestra does not mean a happy ending for Orestes. The death of his father is avenged, but in its accomplishment a son has murdered his mother, and a relentless Fate demands that for this he too must die. However, the avenging Furies, whose duty it was to keep pursuing Orestes, were foiled for once by the direct interposition of the gods, and the hero's life is spared.

Greek comedy is usually given a threefold division, Old, Middle, and New. Of the Old Comedy the greatest figure is that of Aristophanes (448–385 B.C.). He is the only one of whose plays any remain. Aristophanes was an active dramatist for forty years, and is credited with fifty-four comedies, of which eleven have survived. Satire of contemporary life in Athens was the chief note in all his plays. He was an unsparing critic of everything and everybody, his favorite method being that of personal ridicule. In *The Frogs* he mercilessly lampoons Euripides, while in *The Clouds* he does the same for Socrates. Aristophanes was exceedingly clever in devising funny situations, with dialogue to match. The two plays mentioned are quite readable today.

All that we know of the Middle Comedy is that the unbounded freedom of the Old Comedy was considerably softened and that the chorus, still important in the plays of

Aristophanes, entirely disappeared. The New Comedy carried these changes still further; instead of a constant fling of biting satire, comedies began to have plots taken from everyday life, for the most part love stories. No complete plays of either the Middle or the New Comedy have been found, but from fragments of the latter it is evident that certain stock characters had become favorites demanded by audiences, such as the *old man,* often a father, who is easily fooled; the *spendthrift son*; and the *parasite,* a sort of tricky servant who lent his wits to whoever paid the most for them.

The name of Menander (third century B.C.) has always been the one most intimately connected with the final flourish of the Greek drama, but until recently he was known mainly through the adaptations of his work by Roman writers. Within the last twenty years excavations in Egypt have brought to light numerous fragments, some of them large enough to give a fair idea of his work. The remarkable discoveries of 1924 and 1925 offer the hope that further excavations may eventually give us complete plays not only by Menander, but by his contemporaries as well.

THE ROMAN DRAMA. The history of the Roman drama we know only in the sketchiest way. Beyond the fact that there had been early plays we know nothing about them that is of consequence here. But when the Romans conquered the Greeks the literature of Greece conquered the Romans. In the third century B.C., with the passing of the Greek drama, a Roman writer, Plautus (254–184 B.C.), adapted or paraphrased the comedies of Menander and possibly other dramatists popular at the time. All the plays of Plautus are of the type described in connection with the New Comedy. In spite of the obvious imitation of the Greeks, Plautus nevertheless displayed a lively sense of plot and inventiveness, much of which a modern reader still finds humorous. In his *Miles Gloriosus* (*The Boastful Soldier*) he created a type of character that became much liked by English dramatists, and will be mentioned again. Less original was Terence (185–159 B.C.), who was content to follow his Greek models closely, but his work is written in a much more finished style. His best play is *Andria.*

The only other writer of plays in ancient Rome was the philosopher Seneca (4 B.C.–65 A.D.), who wrote tragedies, nine of which are available today. It is generally supposed that Seneca's plays were never performed, but they are nevertheless interesting in a survey of the drama because they hark back to the classic period of the Greeks. Much of his material he drew from Sophocles and Euripides, and full of horrors as the work of those writers was, the Roman philosopher outdid them, so much so that he is sometimes called the father of the " blood and thunder " play. In general, he followed his prototypes in not having much bloodshed on the stage, but there is a great deal of ranting in his effort to produce thrills. In the first English tragedies Seneca was used as a model.

From the poverty of the Roman drama we might infer that the people were averse to amusement, but such was by no means the case. They craved entertainment, but Roman civilization was vastly different from Greek and demanded something much stronger than mere literary plays. Their favorite diversion was a spectacle in the arena. Here gladiators fought to a finish in the most literal sense of the word; condemned criminals were given the privilege of executing themselves in struggles with wild animals; and in the course of time Christians were thrown into the arena to be killed and devoured by beasts. For amusement of this kind there were always enormous crowds, just as there are for prize fights and football games. Naturally the Christians hated and opposed these shows, an opposition that they carried eventually against public performances of every sort. When the Roman Empire became officially Christian, the drama and the contests in the arena were put under the ban, and by the fifth century the only acting was that of wandering ballad-singers and dancers, who at times gave theatrical performances. But even these poor derelicts of a dying profession were relentlessly persecuted by the church, though never entirely suppressed. As it happened, these stray waifs kept alive a feeling for the art of acting throughout the Middle Ages, and it became the fate of the church to have to resort to a variation of this proscribed art of the drama for its own preservation, or at least its rejuvenation.

THE REVIVAL OF THE DRAMA IN THE MIDDLE AGES. As the ancient Greek drama had its origin in the ceremonial around the altar of the god Dionysus in the sixth century B.C., so the modern drama began in connection with the service of the medieval Christian church in the tenth century of our era, or earlier; as the ancient drama was snuffed out by the Christian church of the fifth century, so the Elizabethan drama came to an end in 1642, when the Puritans closed the theaters. It is a most interesting example of history repeating itself.

Before we condemn the church authorities of the Roman Empire we might remember that they no doubt had good reasons for their action, just as the Puritans had in a later day. Throughout those dark centuries between the fifth and the fifteenth the mass of people was densely ignorant and prone to yield to the most primitive instincts in its conduct. To curb these instincts and at the same time maintain a religious life among the people became the chief duty of the priests. Outside of the church only a few could read and write. In the course of time the modern languages began to develop, but the church service remained uniformly Latin. To keep its hold upon the people the machinery of this service became more and more histrionic; that is, it was made to appeal to the ear and the eye, even though the sense of the words remained hidden. There was the mass with its elaborate ceremonial, the priests ornately garbed as they went through the picturesque ritual; the chants, the prayers, even the confessional — all had strong touches of the dramatic. Since there was little intellect to which to appeal, the priests were justified in substituting symbolism, or whatever else was serviceable in driving home the great truths of Christianity.

However, it is likely that in the long run many people became apathetic even to this method, and as the influence of the church showed signs of waning there must have been some authorities who analyzed the situation correctly; perhaps quite unconsciously it may have occurred to some one that confidence and piety could be best maintained among the people if they were given the Bible in a way that they could understand it. As practically no one could read the Bible, nor understand the language of the church service, the great scriptural stories had ceased to mean anything. But the church had the remedy in its own hands, that of still further elaborating its service and ritual by graphic representation of the more important events in the life of Christ.

It had long been customary to celebrate the Christmas and Easter festivals by special chants and processions, with crude attempts to represent a manger or a tomb in the choir. From this feature sprang what are called the " liturgical plays," not really plays, but merely dramatic emphasis on parts of the church service. These liturgical plays are also called " dramatic tropes," the best known being those that were used at Easter. As they always begin with " Quem quaeritis in sepulchro " they are named the *Quem quaeritis* tropes. The following example shows how simple the words were; in fact, it is evident from the stage directions that the words constitute the less important element in the trope. In many other examples of tropes the directions are much fuller than in this one. The translation is made from a Latin version of the tenth century, originally found in the cathedral of Winchester. It is one of the oldest of such manuscripts in England.

The Angel after Christ's resurrection:
Whom are you seeking in the sepulcher, O Christian ones?

The response of the holy women:
The crucified Jesus of Nazareth, O heavenly one!

The Angel in a consoling voice:
He is not here, he has risen as he foretold;
Go, carry the tidings that he has risen, saying:

The Chant of the holy women and all the priests:
Alleluia! The Lord has risen today.
The strong lion, Christ the Son of God, give thanks unto God, eia!

The Angel speaks:
Come and see the place where the Lord was laid, Alleluia! Alleluia!

The Angel speaks again:
Go quickly and tell the disciples that the Lord has risen, Alleluia!   Alleluia!

The women with one accord sing joyously:
The Lord has risen from the sepulcher,
He who hung on the cross for us, Alleluia!

This trope seems almost too short to be effective, but as the words were chanted the phrases could be drawn out at length, with repetitions, as is not uncommon in chants. No doubt there was a good deal of ceremony as the priests, dressed in white, entered in procession to take their places near the sepulcher in which a cross had been buried on Good Friday. Other points to be noted are: the setting was in the choir; the women's parts were taken by priests; and the words were in Latin. You can easily see from the example how little it mattered in what language the words were chanted, for the scene of the action in front of the open tomb and the stage directions carefully followed were sufficient guaranty that the congregation would not miss the dramatic significance of so simple a rendering of the great central dogma of the Christian church. These innovations in the church festivals were first introduced on the Continent, but by the ninth century they were already in frequent use in England. As the popularity of tropes increased, their scope was widened, and before long these liturgical expansions were supplemented by real drama in the form of Miracle plays. The discussion that follows is limited to those of England, although it should be remembered that they originated on the Continent.

Miracle Plays. In a Miracle play the story is taken literally from the Bible, or from the life of some saint; the characters are therefore real human beings with the exception of those that are supernatural; and a Miracle play was given definitely for a religious or moral purpose, that of driving home the meaning of the stories in the Bible. It will be well to grasp fully the elements of this definition in order to prevent confusion with another form of play presently to be defined.

For a long time the Miracle plays were given in the church, by priests, with the full sanction of the church authorities, just like the dramatic tropes of which they were an outgrowth. The Latin of the older form gave way to the vernacular; that is, in England they were written in English, in France in French, and so on. As in the tropes, the Christmas and Easter stories were elaborated into Miracle plays, but the word " miracle " in the sense used here does not imply the supernatural; it was merely a technical term. Any Bible story was legitimate matter for a Miracle play, but naturally those which supplied strong themes were the favorites, at least in the earlier plays.

With the increase in the number of stories portrayed the " properties " became more cumbersome, and the productions were moved from the choir to the nave, then to the outside of the church, and finally to the public square. In the meanwhile the expense of giving these plays had increased to such an extent that the town guilds helped to support them. For a time they were still nominally in the hands of the church, but eventually the guilds took them over entirely. Elements that were not in the Bible also crept into the plays, and in the course of time the church once more frowned upon the drama.

An interesting illustration of how elaborate the productions had become by the thirteenth century is afforded by a play based on the story of Adam and Eve, part of the stage directions for the final scene being as follows: " Then shall come the devil and three or four devils with him, carrying in their hands chains and iron fetters, which they shall put on the necks of Adam and Eve. And some shall push and others pull them to hell; and hard by hell shall be other devils ready to meet them, who shall hold high revel at their fall. And certain other devils shall point them out as they come, and shall snatch them up and carry them into hell; and there shall they make a great smoke arise, and call aloud to each other with glee in their hell, and clash their pots and kettles, that they may be heard without. And after a little delay the devils shall come out and run about the stage; but some shall remain in hell."

In England, as elsewhere, Miracle plays were grouped in cycles; that is, in series of plays which told the main events of the Bible from the creation of man to the Judgment Day. There are four great English cycles, named after the places in which the copies were found, York, Chester, Wakefield, and Coventry; but there were a number of smaller cycles scattered throughout the country. It is probable that few towns of any size did not have Miracle plays, either of their own devising or given by traveling companies. By the fourteenth century these plays had lost much of their strictly religious nature and were frankly looked to for entertainment, the final purpose of all drama. Instead of being given only at Christmas and Easter, the play season was shifted to Corpus Christi Day or Whitsuntide, when the weather was suitable for performances outdoors.

As already stated, the production of plays was now entirely in the hands of the various trade guilds, each guild making itself responsible for at least one play, supplying both equip-

ment and actors. The main item in the equipment was the
" pageant " and the necessary properties to go with it. A
" pageant " was a wagon on which a small stage was built,
usually a two-decker, with the lower section to be used as a
dressing-room and container of properties, and the top providing the actual stage. For illustration we may use a cycle performance at York. For this it was necessary to equip forty-
eight pageants, that being the number of short plays in that
cycle. The performance began by apprentices drawing the first
pageant to a spot previously announced, very likely some conspicuous corner which could accommodate a large crowd. In
medieval towns no one place was capable of holding all the
people who flocked to these shows, so a number of stations
were designated where each pageant repeated its performance.

The York cycle could be given in a single day, but in order
to see the whole show you had to be at the first station at
half-past four in the morning. At that time the first pageant
stopped and gave its play of *Creation*. That done, it moved
on to its next station while the second pageant was drawn up
to take its place, and so on until near dusk, when the forty-
eighth individual production completed the cycle with the
Judgment Day.

While the Miracle plays followed the Bible stories quite
literally in their main essentials, it was nevertheless not considered bad form to introduce bits of action here and there
to enliven the entertainment. In the Adam play already mentioned we can feel sure that the superabundance of devils in-
spired more laughter than fear. In *The Deluge* the wife of
Noah not only roundly scolds that magnificent dreamer, but
emphasizes her remarks by cuffing him. Even today it is
thought funny when, on the stage or in your neighbor's back
yard, a wife beats her husband. But the most remarkable
divergence from Bible authority is found in *The Second
Shepherds' Play*, dealing nominally with the Nativity, but laid
mainly in England. The shepherds, instead of watching for
the star, spend most of their time in detecting Mak, a local
disreputable fellow, as a sheep-stealer, and punishing him by
a toss in a blanket. The favor with which episodes of this
type were received by audiences helped to point the way
toward the next step forward in the drama, that of character
development, for which there had been but little opportunity
in the Miracle plays, bound as they were to the Bible story.

The Morality Play. The Miracle plays emphasized religious instruction as it was found in Bible stories. The Morality play also was consciously didactic, as the name indicates, and its themes were drawn from the teachings of the Bible, but the point of emphasis lay in the presentation of the moral or lesson. The characters were abstractions personified — Virtue, Vice, Mankind, Everyman, and so on. Otherwise they differed but little from the Miracle play, either in structure or in method of performance. The cycles were much smaller, and instead of using pageants, it became a not uncommon practice to play them on fixed stages, placed at intervals in the market place. This seems also to have been done with smaller groups of Miracle plays, and not infrequently both types were given in inn yards. The earliest Morality plays were called *Paternosters,* on the theory that the separate clauses of the Lord's Prayer were antidotes to the deadly sins. The constant theme of the Moralities was the struggle between Vice and Virtue, as it is clearly stated in a fourteenth century reference to the York *Paternosters*: " All manner of vices and sins were held up to scorn and the virtues were held up to praise." An early development of the Morality play was the element of satire, usually embodied in the character of Vice, whose part was similar to that of the devil in Miracle plays, including the humorous touch.

The Morality play is really a form of allegory, a type of story exceedingly popular all over Europe from the thirteenth century on. In France the most famous allegory was the *Roman de la Rose,* of the fourteenth century, a metrical romance that brought every other form of literature under its allegorical influence, including the drama. Through the Morality plays allegory was brought to that large part of the medieval public that was unable to read. The most famous Morality play in English is *Everyman,* quite readable to this day even from a modern point of view, and presentable on the stage. It was, in fact, played to large audiences in England and America in the early years of the twentieth century. Other titles of extant Moralities are *The Castle of Perseverance, Mind, Will and Understanding,* and *Mankind.* In passing, it may be noted that of both Miracle and Morality plays the authors are unknown.

Interludes, etc. Other forms of entertainment during the era preceding that of the regular drama were puppet shows, brought from Italy; dumb shows, or pantomimes, as we call them; and pageants in our modern sense of spectacular shows. The two latter had definite bearing on the later drama, including Shakespeare. But the more immediate connecting link between the medieval drama and that of the Elizabethan was the Interlude. While the Interlude retained many of the earmarks of the Morality, it nevertheless made a great stride forward in being more human. By the fifteenth century it was characterized by satire and humor, less caustic than that of the Morality play, with the instruction idea still behind it nominally, but with the entertainment feature predominant. Interludes were commonly given indoors, usually as part of the entertainment at banquets of the rich or the noble.

The Interlude most readable today is *The Foure PP's*, written by John Heywood, who wrote many plays during the reign of Henry VIII. The title of this play is taken from the initial letter in the names of the four chief characters, a Pardoner, a 'Poticary, a Palmer, and a Peddler. They happen to meet on their travels, and decide to amuse themselves by seeing who could tell the greatest lie, the Peddler to be the judge. The 'Poticary and the Pardoner tell colossal " whoppers " in connection with their immediate professions, the Pardoner's story being especially lively and well told. Then the Palmer, in a few calm words, makes the statement that in his travels he has met half a million women, but not one of them ever lost her temper. You can imagine to whom the Peddler awarded the victory.

THE REGULAR DRAMA. In spite of the almost universal vogue of the types of plays discussed in the preceding section, it is amazing how little direct connection they had with the regular English drama born about the middle of the sixteenth century. While many incidental features were carried over, the new drama sprang more directly from the spirit of the age, discussed in another part of this Introduction. The Revival of Learning was chiefly the revival of the study of the Greek and Latin classics, including the drama. In schools it had long been customary to give plays, but now, with Plautus and Terence in the curriculum, part of the instruction in Latin was to present their plays as written, then to write and present imitations in the same language. From this it was an easy transition to give translations, and finally English imitations of the Latin originals.

It is not difficult to imagine that among schoolboys (we hear nothing of schoolgirls) comedy would be more attractive than tragedy; and so comedy developed first. Nicholas Udall (1505–1556), a schoolmaster, wrote the first regular English comedy. He was an Oxford graduate, a fine Latin scholar, and an excellent teacher. His *Ralph Roister Doister* may have been written for production in his own school, which was either Eton, where he was headmaster until 1541, or Westminster, where he occupied a similar position after 1553. The date of the play is unknown. It may have been written as early as 1541, but it was probably not produced until the later date. The play was imitated from the *Miles Gloriosus* (*The Boastful Soldier*) of Plautus, but the setting is English. Much of the fun of the play is distinctly of the slapstick variety, but the characters of Ralph and his parasite Mathew Merrygreek are well delineated. *Gammer Gurton's Needle*, by William Stevenson, shows less dependence upon the Latin. It was produced by the author at Cambridge about the same time that Udall was staging his play. The scene is laid in the country, and the action consists of a succession of farcical episodes, often with little or no relation to each other. The plot, such as it is, has to do with the search for Gammer (Dame) Gurton's lost needle, and the surprise ending is worthy of O. Henry. Much of the humor springs from the broad rustic dialogue, the character Hodge being the first " stage rube " in the English drama.

The first regular English tragedy was *Gorboduc*, written in 1562 by Thomas Norton and Thomas Sackville. It was first produced before Queen Elizabeth. The story is taken from Geoffrey of Monmouth's *History of the British Kings*, but the manner of treatment is distinctly that of Seneca. The many murders take place off stage, and are then related in long speeches in blank verse, here used for the first time in English drama. The theme resembles that of *King Lear*, in this instance a father dividing his kingdom between his two sons Ferrex and Porrex. There is an Argument and a Chorus, and in the final acts, after all the main characters have been killed, the play becomes almost a Morality, showing the ills that come upon a kingdom when civil wars arise and the entire royal family is slain.

Other early tragedies were Preston's *Cambises* (1569), and *Appius and Virginia* (1563), by R. B., both noted for their extravagant ranting dialogue and abuse of alliteration. For instance, a character in the latter play says, " O curst and cruel cankered churl, O carl unnatural! " There were of course many other plays, both comedies and tragedies.

The Predecessors of Shakespeare. The men whose work in the drama is briefly to be discussed here were not predecessors in point of time so much as in the nature of their plays. The sort of thing they did was largely experimental in a new and popular form of art that was destined to be carried to its highest development by Shakespeare.

John Lyly (1554–1606) was the oldest of a group of college-trained men who turned to literature when they settled down in London. They were termed the " university wits," the latter word being understood to mean men who made their living by their brains. In Elizabethan times literature generally offered the poorest kind of reward because there was no way of marketing its products. There were no magazines, the nearest equivalent to them being the cheap pamphlet, from which the publisher derived the chief benefit. But there were publishers and printers, and after all they had to have something to print and publish. Ordinarily they either hired writers to do a specific piece of work, or paid a small sum outright. With the growing demand for plays there arose an opportunity for writers hitherto undreamt of, and to this they turned as eagerly as writers in a later day turned to the movie scenario.

Lyly differed in certain respects from his contemporaries in the drama. In the first place, he led a cleaner life. He was never poor in the same sense that the others were, because he had a paying position as manager of the children of St. Paul's and of the Blackfriars Chapel, through which he gained much valuable experience as a producer, both of his own plays and those of others. Furthermore, his plays were written to be produced at court, and he never had to depend upon a fickle public. In a way this was a handicap because it limited the scope of his work. Not only did he have to exercise care in his choice of subject, but he had to make sure that each of his plays contained some flattering personal reference to the Queen, either as a person or as a sovereign. Between 1580 and 1591 Lyly wrote eight plays, all comedies, of which *Campaspe,* the earliest, is the best. The others are *Sapho and Phao, Gallathea, Endimion, Midas, Mother Bombie, Love's Metamorphosis,* and *The Woman in the Moone.*

While Lyly's style was artificial, as we might expect from the author of that ridiculously extravagant novel *Euphues,* he nevertheless made important contributions to the drama. His themes were always romantic, but for his strongest effects he depended on clever dialogue, usually in prose and full of puns; there was clever repartee; while his subplots rarely had much to do with the main plot, he succeeded in keeping their characters, usually smart pages and low comedy types, from being tedious; and he was the first to introduce incidental lyrics. Allegory and pageantry were freely used. All of these romantic devices were adopted by other playwrights, including Shakespeare.

George Peele (1558–97), like Lyly, was an Oxford man. With an excellent education and neither money nor a profession, he came to London, where he lived a profligate and spendthrift life. Writing plays seemed to be about the readiest way to make easy money, so Peele became a dramatist. He wrote only comedies, the most important of which is *The Arraignment of Paris,* in part written in blank verse of an unusually high order. His *Old Wives' Tale,* in addition to being interesting in itself, also has the distinction of having given Milton the idea for *Comus.* Peele had an excellent sense of humor and a genuinely poetic imagination, but riotous living kept him from completely developing his talents and shortened his life.

Robert Greene (1558–92) received his university training at Cambridge, with an honorary M.A. later from Oxford. He was proud of his degree from the two universities, but, like Peele, he did not know what to do with his education. He must have had some money, for he traveled extensively on the Continent, especially in Italy and Spain, from both of which countries he drew material for plays later. Eventually he drifted to London and engaged in writing. Besides plays Greene wrote novels, short stories, and numerous pamphlets, some of them bitterly personal, both against himself and against others. From his own statements we learn that his life in London resembled that of Peele, and while in moments of repentance he may have exaggerated his faults, it is certain that his miserably wretched death was hastened by over-indulgence in all the vices of the day.

AN ELIZABETHAN LADY

AN ELIZABETHAN GENTLEMAN

As in the case of Peele, we wonder at the surprising quality
of his romantic comedies, not only at their cleanness, but at
a literary art practiced under the debasing conditions of his
life. Greene is the first English dramatist who created women
characters both charming and true to human nature. Shakespeare alone surpassed him in this, and it must be remembered
that he had Greene's examples before him. In his two best
comedies, *Friar Bacon and Friar Bungay* and *James the
Fourth,* we find women of this type. He had an elegance of
diction equal to that of Peele, and his plays are much more
rapid in action than any produced in England before his time.
However, like Peele, he had difficulty in making his main and
subplots have coherent connection. But Greene was an important figure in the drama, and both Marlowe and Shakespeare borrowed freely from their unhappy contemporary.

Thomas Kyd (1558–94) is the only one of the five predecessors of Shakespeare here discussed who had no university
connections, and almost nothing is known of him except that
he was of a gloomy disposition and that he seemed to like
being considered mysterious. But in the history of the Elizabethan drama he has the distinction of having originated a type
of tragedy that proved the most generally popular throughout
the period, the revenge play. *The Spanish Tragedy,* written
in 1582, is the only extant play that can with certainty be
credited to Kyd.

It is likely, however, that he may have written the lost early
Hamlet which Shakespeare used in creating his own masterpiece of the same name. Into that problem we need not go,
but a reading of *The Spanish Tragedy* shows clearly how
much Shakespeare was indebted to his predecessor. In these
revenge plays, as in the old Greek tragedies, the idea of revenge is regarded as a moral duty. In Kyd's play the theme
is the revenge of a father for the death of his son; in *Hamlet*
it is the revenge of a son for the death of his father. A
parallel reading of these two plays shows remarkable similarity
in the technical devices employed to keep the action from
sagging. It is no slur on Shakespeare to say that in his play
he simply wrote the best of a type that happened to be particularly in demand. All this is aside from the poetry, the
characterization, and the philosophy of life in *Hamlet,* in
none of which *The Spanish Tragedy* offers ground for comparison.

The last and greatest of the forerunners was Christopher Marlowe (1564–93), the son of a Canterbury shoemaker. Like the rest of the " university wits," Marlowe had a splendid education, begun at the King's School in Canterbury, and completed at Cambridge. At the university he had made friends who helped him to establish connections with the best social and literary groups in London when he went to that city for a career. Unfortunately he had tastes not unlike those of Greene and Peele, of whom he was probably a boon companion at times. Aside from his literary work the most certain fact known about Marlowe is that he was killed in a saloon fight before he was thirty.

The work of Marlowe, extraordinary as it was in itself, was at least equally so in its influence upon contemporary and later drama. That he took his dramatic art seriously is shown by his determination to improve upon the style of his fellow-dramatists. In the short prologue to *Tamburlaine*, Part I (1587), in almost contemptuous terms, he tells his audience explicitly what he intends to do.

> From jigging veins of rhyming mother-wits,
> And such conceits as clownage keeps in pay,
> We'll lead you to the stately tent of war,
> Where you shall hear the Scythian Tamburlaine,
> Threatening the world with high astounding terms,
> And scourging kingdoms with his conquering sword.

This prologue is a fair example of " Marlowe's mighty line," and the theme he announces is of heroic proportions. While blank verse had been used before, as we have seen, it had always been highly stilted in those plays that had been produced under the classical influence. Marlowe broke this up by varying his meters and having the sense flow on from one line into the other instead of making each practically a complete unit. In spite of the condemnation of the critics of the day, in spite of the ranting and bombast in many of the speeches of this first play, the " high astounding terms " found immediate favor with the patrons of the theater, and *Tamburlaine*, played by the foremost tragedian of the stage, Edward Alleyn, who was nearly seven feet tall, remained a favorite on the boards throughout this period.

Besides the two parts of *Tamburlaine*, each five acts long,

Marlowe wrote three other tragedies, *Dr. Faustus*, *The Jew of Malta*, and *Edward II*. With the exception of the last, Marlowe's plays have little plot. They consist rather of a series of dramatic episodes or scenes, all centered about the hero. Many of them are extravagant, and not seldom fantastic. His heroes are really villains, each one possessed with an insatiable lust for power, but in the long run encountering a relentless fate that brings him to disaster and death. In Tamburlaine we have a Scythian shepherd who wants to be emperor of the world; the learned Dr. Faustus craves knowledge and sells his soul to the devil in order to learn the hidden mysteries of heaven and hell; the Jew of Malta thinks that money will buy everything; in *Edward II* the arch villain is not the king but Mortimer, a haughty baron who, in spirit, is much like Tamburlaine, defying his fate to the last. There is no humor in Marlowe's plays, and he paid slight attention to the portrayal of women except in *Edward II*.

It is to be noted finally that the works of these five predecessors of Shakespeare were incorrigibly romantic, both the tragedies and the comedies. Those who adhered to the classical models and style fell by the wayside, and it took a Ben Jonson (1573–1637) to restore the older type to temporary life. The age itself was romantic, and Shakespeare by temperament and inclination aligned himself with the prevailing tendency of the day.

It is not uncommon for students to approach the study of Shakespeare with a peculiar sort of dread, almost tantamount to prejudice. He is admittedly held up as the supreme god of literature, even by those who have never read him, and students subconsciously have a tendency to feel that his work must be beyond their powers of appreciation. Quite the contrary is the fact. No one need hesitate to undertake the reading and study of one who so intimately portrayed humanity and its ideals, even though he did it with a supremacy that remains unapproached. In life he was as human as any of us, a journeyman in his profession, withal a genius, but doing his daily work like the rest of us. If you think of him from that angle, as a stage hand in a theater, a tinkerer of plays, and finally as a playwright working among fellow craftsmen, you will begin to be in a frame of mind really and honestly to enjoy Shakespeare. Furthermore, if you study him in conjunction with the work of those men whom we have just discussed, you will find that he did nothing other than what they were doing, only he did it vastly better.

The Elizabethan Theater. *The Playhouses.* When Shakespeare arrived in London, about 1586, two theaters for the public production of plays were already in operation, and a third was probably under construction. All three were erected in the " liberties," that is, just outside the city limits where the Corporation of the City had no jurisdiction. The City authorities were continuously hostile to play production, and no public theaters were built in London until after the Restoration in 1660. However, this does not mean that no plays were given in the proscribed area, for the inn yards were used in London as elsewhere in the land. Because of their quadrangular shape they were well adapted for giving plays, and in spite of all the laws and regulations that the Corporation could make, there was usually a way of getting around them, chiefly through a royal permit, or that of a court favorite whom the Corporation did not venture to oppose.

The first playhouse was The Theater, built in 1576 by James Burbage, a carpenter by trade and an actor by profession. It was located in Shoreditch to the north of the city. As all later theaters conformed in their general outlines to the plan of The Theater, what is said here may be applied to the rest, with the exceptions noted. The first theater was a polygon in shape, but the interior effect was circular. The building was of wood, three stories high, each story forming a gallery for the spectators. The central part of the building, called the yard or " pit," was open to the sky, but the galleries were protected by a roof. Each of the galleries had seats, but in the pit there was standing room only. Other details of the interior will be described in connection with the stage.

The second theater was the Curtain, erected in 1577, and not far away from The Theater. It probably owed its name to the street on which it stood, Curtain Close; at any rate the name had nothing to do with a stage curtain, an accessory then unknown. While Burbage did not build this second theater, he nevertheless controlled it through a lease, quite in the manner of theatrical producers of today. As Shakespeare was never connected with any stage enterprises other than those of the Burbage company, his early plays must have been performed in one or both of these theaters.

The most formidable rival of Burbage was Philip Henslowe, who built his first playhouse, the Rose, in 1588, on the Bankside. This was a name given to the south bank of the Thames, a section of London given over to all sorts of amusements, both good and bad, such as bear-baiting, bull-baiting, cock-fighting, and every kind of gambling device then in operation; in short, everything forbidden by the Corporation was freely carried on here. Naturally, there were many inns and taverns, with all their adjuncts. In plain English, the Bankside was the " tough " section of London. The public flocked across the river in great numbers, and Henslowe displayed his usual business acumen when he selected this place for his theater. The Rose saw the production of many famous plays, among them Greene's *Friar Bacon and Friar Bungay,* Kyd's *The Spanish Tragedy,* and Marlowe's *Jew of Malta,* the chief parts of all of them being in the hands of Edward Alleyn.

In 1594 the Swan theater was built, also on the Bankside. A new company had been organized for this venture under the patronage of Lord Pembroke, and great things were expected, but most of what we know about this playhouse has little to do with the drama.

When the Burbage leasehold on the site of The Theater expired the old house was torn down, and with its timbers a new building was put up on the Bankside in 1599 and called the Globe. This was Shakespeare's theater, and in it most, if not all, of his greatest plays were produced. The Globe stood on or near the spot occupied today by Barclay's brewery.

As a moment's digression it may be not uninteresting to recall other literary associations of this immediate section of London. Not far from the brewery is the supposed site of the Tabard Inn, that " gentil hostelrye " from which Chaucer's pilgrims set out for Canterbury on a morning in April some two hundred years before Shakespeare. Hereabouts John Bunyan preached his forbidden doctrines, Goldsmith hung out his shingle as a doctor in the vain hope of patients, and Bill Sykes ingloriously ended his career on the near-by docks. Here, too, was the famous Marshalsea prison in which the father of Dickens " did time " for debt, and not far away still stands part of the George Inn where Mr. Pickwick first met Sam Weller.

Henslowe built two more theaters, the Fortune in 1600, square in shape, and the Hope in 1613. His company, headed by Edward Alleyn, continued to be the only formidable rival of the Burbage-Shakespeare combination, producing, among others, the plays of Ben Jonson, the dramatist next in importance to Shakespeare. A playhouse that seems to have been entirely independent of both companies was the Red Bull, erected in 1605, but it has no connection with our immediate subject.

The Blackfriars, 1596, was not a public theater, and although it was within the city limits, it did not come under the jurisdiction of the Corporation. It differed from all the others because it had a roof. It was used by different companies at various times when the weather was bad and during the winter months.

The Stage. When you enter the well lighted theater of today the stage is almost entirely concealed by a curtain. You know that presently the lights will be turned off in the auditorium at the same time that the footlights flare up. You know that behind this curtain the stage is set with scenery and whatever other properties may be essential to the introduction of the play. The rise and fall of the curtain indicate the divisions of the play into acts and scenes. The action on the stage is arranged to be viewed from one side only, that toward the audience. One of the first lessons of an actor is to watch his positions and moves on the stage, as well as his part of the dialogue, so that he will be acting and talking at the audience.

In the Elizabethan theater a far different situation confronted the audience. The stage was open on three sides, projecting into the pit, and acting had to take into consideration that there was audience on three sides, not to mention that undesirable part which sat on the stage. There was nothing that resembled our modern curtain, and the projecting part of the stage was practically bare and entirely visible to the gathering audience. This was the main or outer stage, on which most of the action took place. About a third of the way from the front, and set in well from the sides, were two pillars which supported a roof over the rear part of the main stage. These must often have proved a nuisance, and there seems to have been some attempt in later theaters to support this roof in a different way.

At the rear of the outer stage was a curtain, behind which was an inner stage, much smaller than the other, and two doors, one on each side. The doors led to the tiring-rooms, as they were called. Above these two doors were curtained windows, and over the inner stage a balcony, also curtained. All curtains were drawn to the side and not up, as they are in our theaters. In the tiring-rooms stage properties were kept. They could also be used as dressing-rooms and for entrances and exits. The inner stage was used for scenes which called for a cave, as in *The Tempest,* or a study, as in *Dr. Faustus,* or a play within a play, as in *Hamlet,* or a soldier's tent, as in *Julius Caesar,* or some other kind of interior, like the forest home of the Duke in *As You Like It.*

The balcony might indicate the walls of a city or a castle, as the opening scene in *Hamlet,* or any scene that called for an elevation. There are famous balcony scenes in *Romeo and Juliet* and *Richard III.* Above the balcony was a " hut " which served various practical purposes, such as providing means for ascent or descent of deities, or whatever other mechanical device might be called for by the play. From it a flag was flown to indicate a performance that afternoon. In the floor were trapdoors, and this was true also of the inner and outer stages. The stage properties were limited to the minimum essentials, such as chairs and tables. There was no painted movable scenery, nothing like the " picture " stage of today.

The pit part of the audience had to stand, or bring chairs, or rent them. This was the cheapest place in the theater, the price being one penny. The seats in the galleries cost about two shillings, while the " sports " who wished to display themselves by sitting on the stage paid half a crown, the equivalent of more than a dollar in our money. All performances were in the afternoon, and if any lighting was necessary, on the inner stage, for instance, wax candles were used. Footlights were not needed and consequently unknown.

As stated earlier, in order to read a play appreciatively it is necessary to visualize the setting, the position of the actors on the stage, and the various changes and movements required by the action. In modern printed plays the authors usually give comprehensive stage directions to help the reader, but in the Elizabethan drama such things were unknown because plays were not written to be read. The stage accessories being limited, the audience had to use its imagination. The context of the spoken lines, helped out by such properties as could be

easily moved on and off the stage, must have sufficed. To us
an Elizabethan performance would seem crude indeed, and it
is difficult to figure out just how plays as elaborate as Shakespeare's could have been presented with any degree of success.

But the doors, windows, inner stage, balcony, hut, and outer
stage, together with the few properties, must have served for
all kinds of presentation needs. The Forest of Arden in
As You Like It was concealed by the curtain to the inner
stage. It was easy enough to indicate these forest scenes by
drawing the curtain. But there must have been trees on the
outer stage for Orlando's verses, and no doubt some representation of a tree was conveniently placed without being in
the way for other scenes. Or he may have used the pillars.
He comes in and posts his paper on a tree, saying, " Hang
there, my verse," and later in the same speech he says, " These
trees shall be my books." Perhaps that was enough for an
imaginative Elizabethan audience; at any rate it was impossible, without painted scenery, to have enough trees on the
stage to give the effect of a forest elsewhere than on the inner
stage, and that was reserved for the Duke Senior's scenes.

By close examination of the text it will be noticed that the
words of a character often convey details of setting, and not
infrequently suggest action distinctly fitted to harmonize with
the stage limitations. It was essential, for instance, that a
playwright indicate in some way the entrances and exits, especially at the end of a scene or an act, there being no curtain.
Not only that; the stage had to be cleared for what was
to follow, for there were no intermissions of any kind between
scenes or acts, merely an empty stage for a few moments. For
illustration, recall how the body of Polonius is disposed of in
Hamlet, and how at the end of the last act the stage is cleared
of dead bodies. With all the crudenesses of Elizabethan
staging and acting, it was considered bad theatrical form for
characters who had died or been killed on the stage to come
to life, get up, and walk off stage.

The Actors. The Elizabethan drama was distinctly a masculine affair. There were comparatively few feminine parts,
and no actresses to play even those few. Throughout this
whole period the charming women found in many of the plays
were always portrayed by young men or boys. And curiously
enough this masculine side of the drama is emphasized by the
many feminine rôles which call for a woman disguised as a

man. One wonders how sufficient dramatic illusion was achieved in a part like Rosalind in *As You Like It*, for example, a handsome brilliant young woman, played by a boy who had to disguise himself to resemble a young woman in masculine garb. Others in Shakespeare are Portia, Nerissa, and Jessica in *The Merchant of Venice,* Imogen in *Cymbeline,* and Viola in *Twelfth Night.*

The actors who achieved earliest widespread fame were the clowns, acrobats, and jesters. For such as these, light comedy parts were prepared as soon as the legitimate or regular drama came into being. We have seen how farcical acting dates back to the Miracle plays, the Morality plays, and the Interludes, such as Mak in *The Second Shepherd's Play,* Noah's wife in *The Deluge,* the devil, and the Vice. Low comedy parts often called for singing and dancing. In Shakespeare's day the two actors best known for such parts were Richard Tarleton and William Kemp, the first famous for his jig dancing, and the other for both jigging and morris dancing, those being the popular dances. These two comedians were connected at one time or another with the large producing companies, Kemp having been for a considerable period a regular member of the Burbage company. Among the parts that Kemp is known to have played was that of Launcelot Gobbo in *The Merchant of Venice.* Much of their fun on the stage was impromptu, and that it was sometimes abused is shown in *Hamlet,* Act II, ii, 42. That this abuse is not unknown today is attested by action in London in 1925 barring players from introducing matter into their parts not called for by the play. Other comedians were Robert Wilson, John Singer, and Thomas Pope, the last named being one of the famous clowns in the Burbage company.

The instant success of the work of Marlowe was due in part to the remarkable acting of Edward Alleyn, unquestionably the greatest tragedian of the day. He had been a boy actor in one of the children's companies, but as early as 1586, about the time Shakespeare came to London, Alleyn was already a member of a regular company. His tall stature gave him a striking appearance, and this, together with a remarkable voice, made him an admirable actor for such parts as Tamburlaine and the Jew of Malta. As the son-in-law and partner of the thrifty Henslowe, Alleyn became wealthy. In spite of his profession, which was not highly regarded by many people, he became a respected, public-spirited citizen; he was sincerely religious and always charitable. Before his death he established a college at Dulwich, his home, and this school is still in existence.

Alleyn's greatest rival on the stage was Richard Burbage, who, as the son of James Burbage, was naturally brought up in the theatrical business of his father. He was probably more versatile than Alleyn, for he had to play a greater variety of parts as the interpreter of most of the famous Shakespeare rôles, not to mention others. Among the many parts that we definitely know of by contemporary reference is that of Hamlet, a rôle that is still the ambition of every serious actor. He appeared also in comedies, but only in the more serious parts, such as, perhaps, Jaques in *As You Like It*.

We have discussed the stage and its accessories, and a few of the more important actors, but we have not yet seen how they looked on the stage and how they acted their parts. Today, when *Julius Caesar* is produced, the actors dress according to the styles in vogue at the time when the story was supposed to take place. The mechanics in the opening scene look like the workmen of the first century B.C.; the tribunes and others of the higher classes wear the toga characteristic of a Roman gentleman. From books on ancient Rome, or from pictures and statues in your school or local museum, you can see what these costumes were like. But in Shakespeare's time the great Julius and others of rank trod the boards resplendent in doublet and hose, aping the styles of the courtiers of Queen Elizabeth. From Henslowe's *Diary* it appears that the costuming of a play was one of the most expensive items in figuring the cost of production, just as it is now. He listed the minutest details, and we can find out how much it cost to provide Tamburlaine with a coat with copper lace and breeches of a vivid red velvet. The Queen in *Hamlet* and Portia in *The Merchant of Venice* came on the stage dressed in the voluminous style of Queen Elizabeth herself.

One of the difficulties confronting both playwright and actor was stage " business," that is, things to do to break the monotony of mere spoken lines. Certain stock traditions developed for certain kinds of scenes. Great emotion, for instance, was frequently indicated by falling to the ground. Long soliloquies, like those of Hamlet, were given some slight offset by the character reading a book. Of this particular custom there are fifty-one examples in the plays of the period. Skilled comedians varied their acts by improvised byplay. But in the long run the success of a play depended on the spoken lines. These had to be both intelligible in themselves and indicative of the action, the setting of the story, and the proper leads for entrances and exits. In short, all the information necessary for the understanding of a play had to be "put across" by the actors. That helps to account for the long single speeches and the soliloquies. As in most of the greater plays the lines were in blank verse, an actor had a full-sized job in properly enunciating those lines.

The Audience. The discomforts of the theater necessitated quick action. Two hours was a long time for a restless audience to watch a play, but as there was hardly any change of scenery, the action went right on from one act into the next. The audience was made up of all classes, mostly men and boys. A few women were always to be found, but in the early days they wore masks so that they would not be recognized; later there were more women. The new habit of smoking was not barred within the theater, it seems, but this was not so bad after all, because the playhouses were roofless. The theater was tremendously popular with a large part of the general public, just as it is today. At the beginning of the seventeenth century, however, there was a growing number of persons in England unfavorable to play-acting, chiefly the Puritans; the rest of the public was amusement-mad.

On the stage no farce could be too strong nor tragedy too violent. This was in accordance with the life and the ideals of the day. Wars had been common. Fighting and killing were even more common than they are today. Amusement tastes had been in part formed by the bloody scenes in the bear pits. Executions of criminals were public and drew enormous crowds who watched them in a holiday spirit. Small wonder, then, that the audiences gaped with joy at scenes depicting horrors in the raw. They liked funeral processions, battles, ghosts, insane persons, deep-dyed villainy, the torturing of victims before they were killed. The thrill was the thing! Gory weapons dripping blood, the exhibition of dead bodies on the stage, murderers smearing their hands in the blood of their victims, much talk about death and murders, were some of the stage devices to produce that thrill. And the professional murderers found scattered throughout the

Elizabethan drama are strictly in a class by themselves. Compared to them, Jesse James was an amateur and the automobile bandits of today mere beginners. And do not forget that characters of this type were frequent in plays because the audiences wanted them there.

Shakespeare wrote his plays to be presented to audiences who paid money to see them. To get those audiences he had to cater to their likes, as any other dramatist has to do, so we need not be surprised to find many horror scenes. *Titus Andronicus* opens with a graveyard scene and a funeral procession. That was good drama, and graveyards are not unusual in Shakespeare and his contemporaries. In *Hamlet* we find the supreme example of that sort of thing, with a grave being dug, the diggers in merry talk as they throw skulls and human bones lightly out; the hero waxing philosophic as he gruesomely fingers a skull; a funeral procession of a suicide; and finally a fight in a grave over the body of the heroine. In the final scene of *Romeo and Juliet* there is the inside of a tomb with the body of the heroine plainly visible; there is a fight, a murder, a suicide, the coming to life of the seeming dead body, and another suicide. A tragedy was a failure unless it had plenty of deaths and killings on the stage, not behind the scenes as in the Greek drama. *Titus Andronicus* tops the list with eleven; *Richard III* is a close second with ten. In *Macbeth* there are seven, in *Hamlet* six, and in *Julius Caesar* five.

But in spite of all this, the theater was the most decent place of entertainment to be found. It must be remembered that the general public was uneducated and lacked the means of becoming educated, through the limited number of schools. As we have stated earlier in the Introduction, there were few mediums of entertainment — no libraries, no magazines, no daily papers, no illustrated supplements and comic strips, no public dancing-halls, no cabarets, practically nothing except the bear pits and similar primitive amusements. If people craved something to stimulate the imagination the only place to go was to the theater.

In view of what has just been said of tastes, likes and dislikes, it is really extraordinary that an audience so uncultured as that in the days of Elizabeth, should have flocked to plays like those of Shakespeare and the other playwrights of the time. After all, their delight in blood-and-thunder scenes was only incidental; they demanded with them a story interestingly told and well acted. Far the larger part of the audience did not know the story of *Julius Caesar* when it was first produced. Some few might have read it in North's *Plutarch*, or remembered a crude earlier play, but that number was small. Even the English history plays told stories new to most people in the audience. But the Elizabethans kept on going to these plays, — sufficient proof that they liked them; and it is an unquestionable fact that the drama, quite aside from its amusement feature, constituted an educational factor the value of which is impossible to estimate.

Theatrical Companies. There were many companies of players throughout the era of the Elizabethan drama, two of which have been frequently mentioned in this Introduction: that originally organized by James Burbage under the patronage of the Earl of Leicester, and continued by Richard and Cuthbert Burbage, together with Shakespeare and other actors, and the one organized by Philip Henslowe, generally known as the Lord Admiral's Men. By having as patrons men powerful politically or favorites at court, the companies avoided certain legal tangles to which they would have been liable, for under the statutes the actors were regarded as their patron's servants. This gave them a status in the law entirely different from that of professional players. But the two companies were often involved in legal controversies, not with each other, but in the hundred and one possible other contacts, such as leases, building contracts, unpaid bills, and the division of profits. The only reason why these legal snarls are of interest is that through them much of the history of the companies is recorded.

More is known of the Henslowe company than of the other, because Henslowe was a shrewd business man as well as a competent producer, and he kept a minute record of all his transactions. This record is extant and goes under the title of Henslowe's *Diary*. It is the best, and almost the only, authority for the stage history of the period. It covers a period of six years, 1594–1600. Among other things, it shows costs of production, gives hints of prices paid for stage properties and costumes, and receipts at the box office; above all it gives documentary proof of the popularity of plays. To illustrate the last statement the year June 15, 1594, to June 28, 1595, may be taken. In this year Henslowe put on thirty-eight plays, twenty-one of which were new. Of the seventeen old ones the most popular were those of Marlowe, already in the repertory of Alleyn. The company played almost every day for eleven months, exclusive of Sundays, and fifty-one Marlowe performances are listed, the first part of *Tamburlaine* leading with fourteen. Of the twenty-one new plays practically none have survived.

From these facts it is obvious that theatrical companies were exceedingly busy organizations. For one company to stage twenty-one new plays was in itself no slight task. Compare that with the record of a modern successful producer. If he launches half a dozen ventures a year he is considered plucky, and unless a play has a long run it is thought a failure. When he has decided to produce a certain play he invests a small fortune in order to make it go. As in the days of Henslowe, many of course fail and are heard of no more. Others have long runs, sometimes for years, whereas in the Elizabethan age a play was successful if it could be kept in a company's repertory and given several times a week or a month.

The Burbage-Shakespeare company had a continuous organization from 1576 until the closing of the theaters in 1642, and easily outranked all rivals in the number of theaters it owned or controlled, the number and quality of its actors, the genius of its playwrights, and the money it made. Besides having the sole rights to everything that Shakespeare wrote, this company also produced some of Ben Jonson's plays, and much of the work of such others as Thomas Dekker, Beaumont and Fletcher, Massinger, and Webster.

The companies were small, rarely exceeding twelve, not taking into consideration those that played small parts, and supers. Wherever possible, parts were doubled; that is, one actor took more than one part. In *Julius Caesar*, for instance, Casca is never again heard of after the death of Caesar, and the actor who took that part was free to take another which had not yet been introduced. In writing plays an author had to give some attention to the company which was to play them. While there was much rivalry between the companies, it seems that sometimes they collaborated, for there is a record of Edward Alleyn playing with the Burbage company.

Two other companies may be mentioned, both made up of children, that is, boys. These were taken from the choir boys of St. Paul's and the Chapel Royal, all no doubt recruited from various boys' schools. These companies were popular for a time at least, as is shown in Hamlet's talk with the players, but it is likely that they seldom performed in the strictly public theaters. Henslowe definitely mentions them in connection with Blackfriars. As stated elsewhere, after the middle of the sixteenth century the acting of plays in schools became quite common, and boys with trained singing voices must have made desirable boy actors. Edward Alleyn had once been a choir boy.

The Theaters and the Law. The ancient Greek theater, functioning as a state institution, had few contacts with the law. Whatever regulation was needed came from within. One of the things best known of the Roman drama is its suppression by law. When play-acting was revived through the medieval church there again was no need for regulation except that which the church authorities themselves saw fit to impose. But as soon as the production of plays passed out of the hands of the church into those of the trade guilds, the drama laid itself open to the law like any other institution.

Today every civilized country has laws defining what may or may not be produced on the stage, and theaters, as buildings, must likewise conform to legally set specifications. The new problems that arose out of the movies have already become the subjects of laws in every one of our states, many of which have some sort of censorship. One group of movie producers has its own gilt-edged official to look things over in order to prevent legal conflicts. In this country there are almost annual flurries of sentiment in favor of legal censorship for all plays, but up to the present nothing much has been accomplished except the appointment of committees. England has had an official censor practically since the days of Henry VII, and today no play can be produced in that country without his approval. That this official is more than a rubber stamp was proved as recently as 1925, when an American play with a long New York run was definitely turned down.

It is of interest to see the relation between the drama and the law from the accession of Elizabeth in 1558 to the closing of the theaters in 1642. When Elizabeth became queen, England was anything but a united country. Politics and religion were almost interchangeable terms, a state of affairs which was the direct heritage from her predecessors on the throne. Many powerful nobles were Catholic, and at least half the population.

Elizabeth wisely chose to pursue a middle course that would offend neither side, but without compromising her position as a real sovereign. It so happened that the beginnings of the regular drama and the opening of her reign took place at about the same time, and as early as 1559 she issued her first proclamation pertaining to plays.

This first proclamation prescribed how plays were to be licensed, the gist of which was that no play could be given anywhere in England unless authorized by the proper local authorities, such as mayors, bailiffs, or any others acting under royal authority. This of course was something different from censorship, but in this same edict two things were specifically declared barred from plays — matters of religion and those pertaining to the government. In general, those ideas underlay all the many laws and edicts made from that time on. The mere fact of such laws having to be made shows how prevalent was the tendency not to follow them.

Plays were absolutely forbidden on Sundays, during Lent, and when the plague was bad. In London no public theaters were allowed at any time before 1660, but that law was evaded by giving plays in inn yards, or at the Blackfriars, and in a few lesser houses which came under the same rules as the playhouses without the City because of special liberties granted earlier. But the Corporation maintained a watchful eye, and all during this era fought the theatrical and dramatic interests at every possible turn.

During the reign of Henry VII a Master of the Revels had been created, his duties being confined to court entertainments. In the course of time this officer became also the censor and licenser of plays. Among the items open to censorship during the reign of Elizabeth were profanity, immorality, religion, and such political ideas as might be considered seditious. Heavy fees were exacted from both companies and individual players, the money so obtained being applied to various public charities. In addition to that, each company had to pay weekly fees to the Master of Revels himself, ranging from five shillings to three pounds, making that office worth while financially. Sometimes a Master of Revels, being human, was open to bribery, and by means of private fees certain plays were allowed that should have been barred according to the laws.

That all regulations pertaining to theaters and plays were constantly violated is proved by the court records. It seemed

difficult to determine where one authority stopped and the
other began. A royal decree always was superior to any law,
and companies licensed directly by the queen or any of her
accredited lords were hard to stop from doing what they
wanted as long as they exercised some restraint. But during
the first half of the seventeenth century certain conditions
arose in England that neither royalty nor its lords could control. This was the rising tide of puritanism and its accom-
panying spirit of revolution. In 1642 the Puritans were sufficiently strong in Parliament to put through an ordinance to
the effect " that while these sad causes and set times of humili-
ation do continue, publick stage-plays shall cease and be for-
borne." When the war was over there were attempts to revive
the giving of plays, but the Puritans, now in full control,
ordered the police to break up all such performances and
arrest the actors. So persistent were some of the theaters that
a new law was made in 1648 which provided that the inside of
every theater was to be stripped bare, and that was done.

After all, the important thing to note in so brief a study of
the drama and theatrical conditions in the Age of Shakespeare
is that there was tremendous activity in the writing and producing of plays, that in spite of many adverse outer conditions,
such as the prevalence of the plague, the growth of puritanic
ideals, and the passing of hostile laws, the art of the theater
developed into the foremost intellectual and literary activity
of the time, the sum total of the result being an era equaled
only by that of the Age of Pericles both in amount and quality
of dramatic production.

A TYPICAL ELIZABETHAN STAGE

(From Albright's *Shaksperian Stage*, by permission of the author and
the Columbia University Press)

JULIUS CAESAR

DRAMATIS PERSONAE

JULIUS CAESAR.

OCTAVIUS CAESAR ⎫ triumvirs after
MARCUS ANTONIUS ⎬ the death of
M. AEMILIUS LEPIDUS ⎭ Julius Caesar.

CICERO ⎫
PUBLIUS ⎬ senators.
POPILIUS LENA ⎭

MARCUS BRUTUS ⎫
CASSIUS ⎪
CASCA ⎪
TREBONIUS ⎬ conspirators
LIGARIUS ⎪ against
DECIUS BRUTUS ⎪ Julius Caesar.
METELLUS CIMBER ⎪
CINNA ⎭

FLAVIUS and MARULLUS, tribunes.

ARTEMIDORUS of Cnidos, a teacher of Rhetoric.

A Soothsayer.

CINNA, a poet. Another Poet.

LUCILIUS ⎫
TITINIUS ⎪
MESSALA ⎬ friends to Brutus
Young CATO ⎪ and Cassius.
VOLUMNIUS ⎭

VARRO ⎫
CLITUS ⎪
CLAUDIUS ⎬ servants to Brutus.
STRATO ⎪
LUCIUS ⎪
DARDANIUS ⎭

PINDARUS, servant to Cassius.

CALPURNIA, wife to Caesar.

PORTIA, wife to Brutus.

Senators, Citizens, Guards, Attendants, &c.

SCENE: *Rome; the neighborhood of Sardis; the neighborhood of Philippi.*

ACT I

SCENE I. *Rome. A street.*

Enter FLAVIUS, MARULLUS, *and certain Commoners.*

Flav. Hence! home, you idle creatures, get you home!
Is this a holiday? What! know you not,
Being mechanical, you ought not walk
Upon a laboring day without the sign
Of your profession? Speak, what trade art thou?
First Com. Why, sir, a carpenter.
Mar. Where is thy leather apron and thy rule?
What dost thou with thy best apparel on?
You, sir, what trade are you? 9
Sec. Com. Truly, sir, in respect of a fine workman, I am but, as you would say, a cobbler.

Dramatis personae: persons of the play. Pronounced drăm'-à-tĭs pēr-sō' nē. 3. **mechanical:** mechanics, laborers. 4. **sign of your profession:** working clothes. 10. **in respect of:** in comparison with. 11. **cobbler:** a bungling workman as well as a mender of shoes. This whole punning passage was funny to the Elizabethan audience.

Mar. But what trade art thou? answer me directly.

Sec. Com. A trade, sir, that, I hope, I may use with a safe
conscience; which is, indeed, sir, a mender of bad soles.

Mar. What trade, thou knave? thou naughty knave, what
trade?

Sec. Com. Nay, I beseech you, sir, be not out with me;
yet, if you be out, sir, I can mend you.

Mar. What meanest thou by that? Mend me, thou saucy
fellow!   21

Sec. Com. Why, sir, cobble you.

Flav. Thou art a cobbler, art thou?

Sec. Com. Truly, sir, all that I live by is with the awl. I
meddle with no tradesmen's matters, nor women's matters, but
with awl. I am, indeed, sir, a surgeon to old shoes; when they
are in great danger, I re-cover them. As proper men as ever
trod upon neat's leather have gone upon my handiwork.   30

Flav. But wherefore art not in thy shop today?
Why dost thou lead these men about the streets?

Sec. Com. Truly, sir, to wear out their shoes, to get myself
into more work. But, indeed, sir, we make holiday, to see
Caesar and to rejoice in his triumph.

Mar. Wherefore rejoice? What conquest brings he home?
What tributaries follow him to Rome,
To grace in captive bonds his chariot-wheels?
You blocks, you stones, you worse than senseless things!   40
O you hard hearts, you cruel men of Rome,
Knew you not Pompey? Many a time and oft
Have you climbed up to walls and battlements,
To towers and windows, yea, to chimney-tops,
Your infants in your arms, and there have sat
The livelong day, with patient expectation,
To see great Pompey pass the streets of Rome;
And when you saw his chariot but appear,
Have you not made an universal shout,
That Tiber trembled underneath her banks,   50
To hear the replication of your sounds
Made in her concave shores?

29. **proper:** handsome. 35. **his triumph:** Caesar's fifth and last, to celebrate his victory over Pompey's sons at Munda, Spain, March 17, 45 B.C.
For the purposes of the play Shakespeare shoves the date ahead one year.
42. **Pompey:** Pompey the Great (106–48 B.C.), Caesar's greatest rival, treach-
erously murdered in Egypt after his defeat at Pharsalia. 51. **replication:**
echo.

And do you now put on your best attire?
And do you now cull out a holiday?
And do you now strew flowers in his way
That comes in triumph over Pompey's blood?
Be gone!
Run to your houses, fall upon your knees,
Pray to the gods to intermit the plague
That needs must light on this ingratitude.   60
   Flav. Go, go, good countrymen, and, for this fault,
Assemble all the poor men of your sort;
Draw them to Tiber banks, and weep your tears
Into the channel, till the lowest stream
Do kiss the most exalted shores of all.
                     [Exeunt all the Commoners.
See, whether their basest metal be not moved;
They vanish tongue-tied in their guiltiness.
Go you down that way towards the Capitol;
This way will I. Disrobe the images,
If you do find them decked with ceremonies.   70
   Mar. May we do so?
You know it is the feast of Lupercal.
   Flav. It is no matter; let no images
Be hung with Caesar's trophies. I'll about,
And drive away the vulgar from the streets;
So do you too, where you perceive them thick.
These growing feathers plucked from Caesar's wing
Will make him fly an ordinary pitch,
Who else would soar above the view of men
And keep us all in servile fearfulness.   *[Exeunt.*

56. **Pompey's blood:** that of his sons, one of whom was killed at Munda.
69. **images:** statues and busts of Caesar.   70. **ceremonies:** decorations.
72. **Lupercal:** festival in honor of **Lupercus Februus,** god of fertility, held Feb.
15; hence **February.** 75. **vulgar:** common people. 78. **pitch:** a term in
falconry, meaning the highest point reached by the falcon in pursuit of its prey.

Scene II. *A public place.*

Flourish. Enter Caesar; Antony, *for the course;* Calpurnia,
Portia, Decius, Cicero, Brutus, Cassius, *and* Casca;
a great crowd following, among them a Soothsayer.

Caes. Calpurnia!
Casca. Peace, ho! Caesar speaks.
Caes. Calpurnia!
Cal. Here, my lord.
Caes. Stand you directly in Antonius' way,
When he doth run his course. Antonius!
Ant. Caesar, my lord?
Caes. Forget not, in your speed, Antonius,
To touch Calpurnia; for our elders say,
The barren, touched in this holy chase,
Shake off their sterile curse.
Ant. I shall remember:
When Caesar says, " Do this," it is performed. 10
Caes. Set on; and leave no ceremony out.

[*Flourish.*

Sooth. Caesar!
Caes. Ha! who calls?
Casca. Bid every noise be still; peace yet again!
Caes. Who is it in the press that calls on me?
I hear a tongue, shriller than all the music,
Cry " Caesar! " Speak; Caesar is turned to hear.
Sooth. Beware the ides of March.
Caes. What man is that?
Bru. A soothsayer bids you beware the ides of March.
Caes. Set him before me; let me see his face. 20
Cas. Fellow, come from the throng; look upon Caesar.
Caes. What say'st thou to me now? Speak once again.
Sooth. Beware the ides of March.
Caes. He is a dreamer; let us leave him. Pass.

[*Sennet. Exeunt all except Brutus and Cassius.*

Cas. Will you go see the order of the course?
Bru. Not I.

Stage direction: **flourish:** blare of music. **Antony, for the course:** Antony
was a priest of Lupercus. At this festival the priests ran naked through the
streets, touching certain women to void off the " sterile curse " mentioned by
Caesar in line 8. 17. **ides of March:** March 15. 24. **sennet:** trumpets sound-
ing a march as persons of importance go on or off the stage.

 Cas. I pray you, do.
 Bru. I am not gamesome; I do lack some part
Of that quick spirit that is in Antony.
Let me not hinder, Cassius, your desires;   30
I'll leave you.
 Cas. Brutus, I do observe you now of late;
I have not from your eyes that gentleness
And show of love as I was wont to have.
You bear too stubborn and too strange a hand
Over your friend that loves you.
 Bru.   Cassius,
Be not deceived. If I have veiled my look,
I turn the trouble of my countenance
Merely upon myself. Vexed I am
Of late with passions of some difference,   40
Conceptions only proper to myself,
Which give some soil perhaps to my behaviors;
But let not therefore my good friends be grieved —
Among which number, Cassius, be you one —
Nor construe any further my neglect,
Than that poor Brutus, with himself at war,
Forgets the shows of love to other men.
 Cas. Then, Brutus, I have much mistook your passion;
By means whereof this breast of mine hath buried
Thoughts of great value, worthy cogitations.   50
Tell me, good Brutus, can you see your face?
 Bru. No, Cassius; for the eye sees not itself
But by reflection, by some other things.
 Cas. 'Tis just;
And it is very much lamented, Brutus,
That you have no such mirrors as will turn
Your hidden worthiness into your eye,
That you might see your shadow. I have heard,
Where many of the best respect in Rome,
Except immortal Caesar, speaking of Brutus   60
And groaning underneath this age's yoke,
Have wished that noble Brutus had his eyes.

 28. **gamesome:** fond of sports. 40. **of some difference:** Cassius was married to the sister of Brutus, and jealous of his brother-in-law's success in politics. In this speech Shakespeare clearly indicates the chief note in the character of Brutus, that of reflective thoughtfulness, turned at this point on Caesar's ambitions. 59. **of the best respect:** most highly respected. 60. **immortal Caesar:** a subtle hint by Cassius to find out how far he might go with Brutus.

Bru.   Into what dangers would you lead me, Cassius,
That you would have me seek into myself
For that which is not in me?
 Cas.   Therefore, good Brutus, be prepared to hear;
And since you know you cannot see yourself
So well as by reflection, I, your glass,
Will modestly discover to yourself
That of yourself which you yet know not of.   70
And be not jealous on me, gentle Brutus;
Were I a common laugher, or did use
To stale with ordinary oaths my love
To every new protester; if you know
That I do fawn on men and hug them hard
And after scandal them, or if you know
That I profess myself in banqueting
To all the rout, then hold me dangerous. [*Flourish, and shout.*
 Bru.   What means this shouting? I do fear, the people
Choose Caesar for their king.
 Cas.   Ay, do you fear it?   80
Then must I think you would not have it so.
 Bru.   I would not, Cassius; yet I love him well.
But wherefore do you hold me here so long?
What is it that you would impart to me?
If it be aught toward the general good,
Set honor in one eye and death i' the other,
And I will look on both indifferently;
For let the gods so speed me as I love
The name of honor more than I fear death.
 Cas.   I know that virtue to be in you, Brutus, 90
As well as I do know your outward favor.
Well, honor is the subject of my story.
I cannot tell what you and other men
Think of this life; but, for my single self,
I had as lief not be as live to be
In awe of such a thing as I myself.
I was born free as Caesar; so were you;
We both have fed as well, and we can both
Endure the winter's cold as well as he;
For once, upon a raw and gusty day,   100

 63. **dangers:** this answer encourages Cassius to go on. 71. **jealous:** suspicious. 72. **laugher:** joker. 73. **to stale:** to make cheap. 76. **scandal them:** slander them. 91. **favor:** appearance.

The troubled Tiber chafing with her shores,
Caesar said to me, " Darest thou, Cassius, now
Leap in with me into this angry flood,
And swim to yonder point? " Upon the word,
Accoutered as I was, I plungéd in
And bade him follow; so indeed he did.
The torrent roared, and we did buffet it
With lusty sinews, throwing it aside
And stemming it with hearts of controversy;
But ere we could arrive the point proposed,   110
Caesar cried, " Help me, Cassius, or I sink! "
I, as Aeneas, our great ancestor,
Did from the flames of Troy upon his shoulder
The old Anchises bear, so from the waves of Tiber
Did I the tired Caesar. And this man
Is now become a god, and Cassius is
A wretched creature and must bend his body,
If Caesar carelessly but nod on him.
He had a fever when he was in Spain,
And when the fit was on him, I did mark   120
How he did shake: 'tis true, this god did shake.
His coward lips did from their color fly,
And that same eye whose bend doth awe the world
Did lose his luster; I did hear him groan.
Ay, and that tongue of his that bade the Romans
Mark him and write his speeches in their books,
Alas, it cried, " Give me some drink, Titinius,"
As a sick girl. Ye gods, it doth amaze me
A man of such a feeble temper should
So get the start of the majestic world   130
And bear the palm alone.   [Shout. Flourish.
   Bru. Another general shout!
I do believe that these applauses are
For some new honors that are heaped on Caesar.
   Cas. Why, man, he doth bestride the narrow world
Like a Colossus, and we petty men
Walk under his huge legs and peep about
To find ourselves dishonorable graves.
Men at some time are masters of their fates;
The fault, dear Brutus, is not in our stars,   140

129. **temper:** temperament. 140. **stars:** belief in astrology was common
in Shakespeare's day.

But in ourselves, that we are underlings.
Brutus and Caesar: what should be in that " Caesar " ?
Why should that name be sounded more than yours?
Write them together, yours is as fair a name;
Sound them, it doth become the mouth as well;
Weigh them, it is as heavy; conjure with 'em,
" Brutus " will start a spirit as soon as " Caesar."
Now, in the names of all the gods at once,
Upon what meat doth this our Caesar feed,
That he is grown so great?   Age, thou art shamed!   150
Rome, thou hast lost the breed of noble bloods!
When went there by an age, since the great flood,
But it was famed with more than with one man?
When could they say till now, that talked of Rome,
That her wide walls encompassed but one man?
Now is it Rome indeed and room enough,
When there is in it but one only man.
O, you and I have heard our fathers say,
There was a Brutus once that would have brooked
The eternal devil to keep his state in Rome   160
As easily as a king.
    Bru.   That you do love me, I am nothing jealous;
What you would work me to, I have some aim.
How I have thought of this and of these times,
I shall recount hereafter; for this present,
I would not, so with love I might entreat you,
Be any further moved.   What you have said
I will consider; what you have to say
I will with patience hear, and find a time
Both meet to hear and answer such high things.   170
Till then, my noble friend, chew upon this:
Brutus had rather be a villager
Than to repute himself a son of Rome
Under these hard conditions as this time
Is like to lay upon us.
    Cas.   I am glad that my weak words
Have struck but thus much show of fire from Brutus.
    Bru.   The games are done and Caesar is returning.

156. **Rome indeed:** In Shakespeare's day **Rome** and **room** were pronounced
nearly alike.   159. **Brutus once:** Lucius Junius Brutus, an ancient Roman
patriot, who led the revolt which expelled the last of the Tarquin kings and
established the republic.   The Marcus Brutus of the play believed himself a
descendant.   160. **eternal:** infernal.   162. **nothing jealous:** not doubtful.

Cas. As they pass by, pluck Casca by the sleeve;
And he will, after his sour fashion, tell you   180
What hath proceeded worthy note today.

Reënter CAESAR *and his Train.*

Bru. I will do so. But, look you, Cassius,
The angry spot doth glow on Caesar's brow,
And all the rest look like a chidden train.
Calpurnia's cheek is pale; and Cicero
Looks with such ferret and such fiery eyes
As we have seen him in the Capitol,
Being crossed in conference by some senators.
    Cas. Casca will tell us what the matter is.
    Caes. Antonius!   190
    Ant. Caesar?
    Caes. Let me have men about me that are fat,
Sleek-headed men and such as sleep o' nights.
Yond Cassius has a lean and hungry look;
He thinks too much; such men are dangerous.
    Ant. Fear him not, Caesar; he's not dangerous;
He is a noble Roman and well given.
    Caes. Would he were fatter! But I fear him not.
Yet if my name were liable to fear,
I do not know the man I should avoid   200
So soon as that spare Cassius. He reads much;
He is a great observer and he looks
Quite through the deeds of men; he loves no plays,
As thou dost, Antony; he hears no music;
Seldom he smiles, and smiles in such a sort
As if he mocked himself and scorned his spirit
That could be moved to smile at any thing.
Such men as he be never at heart's ease
Whiles they behold a greater than themselves,
And therefore are they very dangerous.   210
I rather tell thee what is to be feared
Than what I fear; for always I am Caesar.
Come on my right hand, for this ear is deaf,
And tell me truly what thou think'st of him.
        [*Sennet. Exeunt Caesar and all his Train, but Casca.*
    Casca. You pulled me by the cloak; would you speak with
me?
    Bru. Ay, Casca; tell us what hath chanced today,
That Caesar looks so sad.

Casca. Why, you were with him, were you not?

Bru. I should not then ask Casca what had chanced. 219

Casca. Why, there was a crown offered him; and being offered him, he put it by with the back of his hand, thus; and then the people fell a-shouting.

Bru. What was the second noise for?

Casca. Why, for that too.

Cas. They shouted thrice; what was the last cry for?

Casca. Why, for that too.

Bru. Was the crown offered him thrice?

Casca. Ay, marry, was 't, and he put it by thrice, every time gentler than other, and at every putting-by mine honest neighbors shouted.   231

Cas. Who offered him the crown?

Casca. Why, Antony.

Bru. Tell us the manner of it, gentle Casca.

Casca. I can as well be hanged as tell the manner of it. It was mere foolery; I did not mark it. I saw Mark Antony offer him a crown — yet 'twas not a crown neither, 'twas one of these coronets — and, as I told you, he put it by once; but, for all that, to my thinking, he would fain have had it. Then he offered it to him again; then he put it by again; but, to my thinking, he was very loath to lay his fingers off it. And then he offered it the third time; he put it the third time by; and still as he refused it, the rabblement hooted and clapped their chopped hands and threw up their sweaty nightcaps and uttered such a deal of stinking breath because Caesar refused the crown that it had almost choked Caesar; for he swounded and fell down at it; and for mine own part, I durst not laugh, for fear of opening my lips and receiving the bad air.   252

Cas. But, soft, I pray you; what, did Caesar swound?

Casca. He fell down in the market-place, and foamed at mouth, and was speechless.

Bru. 'Tis very like; he hath the falling sickness.

Cas. No, Caesar hath it not; but you and I
And honest Casca, we have the falling sickness.

Casca. I know not what you mean by that; but, I am sure, Caesar fell down. If the ragtag people did not clap him and

---

229. **marry:** a form of Christian oath " By the Virgin Mary." Shakespeare here, as often, does not bother about histórical accuracy, the words of Cassius being spoken 44 years *before Christ.* An error of this kind is called an *anachronism.* Watch for others in this play.

hiss him, according as he pleased and displeased them, as they use to do the players in the theater, I am no true man.

Bru.   What said he when he came unto himself?   264

Casca.   Marry, before he fell down, when he perceived the common herd was glad he refused the crown, he plucked me ope his doublet and offered them his throat to cut. An I had been a man of occupation, if I would not have taken him at a word, I would I might go to hell among the rogues. And so he fell. When he came to himself again, he said, if he had done or said any thing amiss, he desired their worships to think it was his infirmity. Three or four wenches, where I stood, cried, " Alas, good soul! " and forgave him with all their hearts. But there's no heed to be taken of them; if Caesar had stabbed their mothers, they would have done no less.

Bru.   And after that, he came, thus sad, away?

Casca.   Ay.   280

Cas.   Did Cicero say any thing?

Casca.   Ay, he spoke Greek.

Cas.   To what effect?

Casca.   Nay, an I tell you that, I'll ne'er look you i' the face again; but those that understood him smiled at one another and shook their heads; but, for mine own part, it was Greek to me. I could tell you more news too. Marullus and Flavius, for pulling scarfs off Caesar's images, are put to silence. Fare you well. There was more foolery yet, if I could remember it.   291

Cas.   Will you sup with me tonight, Casca?

Casca.   No, I am promised forth.

Cas.   Will you dine with me tomorrow?

Casca.   Ay, if I be alive and your mind hold and your dinner worth the eating.

Cas.   Good; I will expect you.

Casca.   Do so.   Farewell, both.   [*Exit.*

Bru.   What a blunt fellow is this grown to be!
He was quick mettle when he went to school.

Cas.   So is he now in execution   301
Of any bold or noble enterprise,
However he puts on this tardy form.
This rudeness is a sauce to his good wit,
Which gives men stomach to digest his words

287. **Greek to me:** unintelligible.   300. **quick mettle:** lively spirit.

With better appetite.
  Bru. And so it is. For this time I will leave you;
Tomorrow, if you please to speak with me,
I will come home to you; or, if you will,
Come home to me, and I will wait for you.   310
  Cas. I will do so; till then, think of the world.
           [Exit Brutus.

Well, Brutus, thou art noble; yet, I see,
Thy honorable metal may be wrought
From that it is disposed; therefore it is meet
That noble minds keep ever with their likes;
For who so firm that cannot be seduced?
Caesar doth bear me hard, but he loves Brutus.
If I were Brutus now and he were Cassius,
He should not humor me. I will this night,
In several hands, in at his windows throw,   320
As if they came from several citizens,
Writings all tending to the great opinion
That Rome holds of his name; wherein obscurely
Caesar's ambition shall be glanced at;
And after this let Caesar seat him sure;
For we will shake him, or worse days endure.   *[Exit.*

Scene III. *The same. A street.*

Thunder and lightning. Enter, from opposite sides, Casca,
with his sword drawn, and Cicero.

  Cic. Good even, Casca; brought you Caesar home?
Why are you breathless? and why stare you so?
  Casca. Are you not moved, when all the sway of earth
Shakes like a thing unfirm? O Cicero,
I have seen tempests, when the scolding winds
Have rived the knotty oaks, and I have seen
The ambitious ocean swell and rage and foam,
To be exalted with the threatening clouds;
But never till tonight, never till now,

311. **think of the world:** consider the present state of things. 313. **metal:** spirit. **Metal** and **mettle** have the same meaning in Shakespeare. 314. **bear me hard:** does not like me. 315. **he:** probably Brutus.
A month elapses after Scene ii, but there was nothing to indicate the fact to the audience. 3. **sway of earth:** the established order of government.

Did I go through a tempest dropping fire.   10
Either there is a civil strife in heaven,
Or else the world, too saucy with the gods,
Incenses them to send destruction.
   Cic. Why, saw you any thing more wonderful?
   Casca. A common slave — you know him well by sight —
Held up his left hand, which did flame and burn
Like twenty torches joined, and yet his hand,
Not sensible of fire, remained unscorched.
Besides — I ha' not since put up my sword —
Against the Capitol I met a lion,   20
Who glared upon me, and went surly by,
Without annoying me; and there were drawn
Upon a heap a hundred ghastly women,
Transforméd with their fear, who swore they saw
Men all in fire walk up and down the streets.
And yesterday the bird of night did sit
Even at noon-day upon the market-place,
Hooting and shrieking. When these prodigies
Do so conjointly meet, let not men say
" These are their reasons; they are natural; "   30
For, I believe, they are portentous things
Unto the climate that they point upon.
   Cic. Indeed, it is a strange-disposéd time;
But men may construe things after their fashion,
Clean from the purpose of the things themselves.
Comes Caesar to the Capitol tomorrow?
   Casca. He doth; for he did bid Antonius
Send word to you he would be there tomorrow.
   Cic. Good night then, Casca; this disturbéd sky   39
Is not to walk in.
   Casca.   Farewell, Cicero.   [*Exit Cicero.*

Enter CASSIUS.

   Cas. Who's there?
   Casca.   A Roman.
   Cas.   Casca, by your voice.
   Casca. Your ear is good. Cassius, what night is this?
   Cas. A very pleasing night to honest men.
   Casca. Who ever knew the heavens menace so?
   Cas. Those that have known the earth so full of faults.

     12. **saucy:** impudent. 32. **climate:** region.

For my part, I have walked about the streets,
Submitting me unto the perilous night,
And, thus unbracéd, Casca, as you see,
Have bared my bosom to the thunder-stone;
And when the cross blue lightning seemed to open   50
The breast of heaven, I did present myself
Even in the aim and very flash of it.
    Casca. But wherefore did you so much tempt the heavens?
It is the part of men to fear and tremble,
When the most mighty gods by tokens send
Such dreadful heralds to astonish us.
    Cas. You are dull, Casca, and those sparks of life
That should be in a Roman you do want,
Or else you use not. You look pale and gaze
And put on fear and cast yourself in wonder,   60
To see the strange impatience of the heavens;
But if you would consider the true cause
Why all these fires, why all these gliding ghosts,
Why birds and beasts from quality and kind,
Why old men fool and children calculate,
Why all these things change from their ordinance
Their natures and preforméd faculties
To monstrous quality, why, you shall find
That Heaven hath infused them with these spirits,
To make them instruments of fear and warning
Unto some monstrous state.   71
Now could I, Casca, name to thee a man
Most like this dreadful night,
That thunders, lightens, opens graves, and roars
As doth the lion in the Capitol,
A man no mightier than thyself or me
In personal action, yet prodigious grown
And fearful, as these strange eruptions are.
    Casca. 'Tis Caesar that you mean; is it not, Cassius?
    Cas. Let it be who it is; for Romans now   80
Have thews and limbs like to their ancestors;
But, woe the while! our fathers' minds are dead,
And we are governed with our mothers' spirits;
Our yoke and sufferance show us womanish.
    Casca. Indeed, they say the senators tomorrow

48. **unbraced:** his doublet unlaced. On the Elizabethan stage Romans
were dressed in the current English fashions. See Introduction. 67. **pre-
formed:** preordained.

Mean to establish Caesar as a king;
And he shall wear his crown by sea and land,
In every place, save here in Italy.
  Cas. I know where I will wear this dagger then;
Cassius from bondage will deliver Cassius.
Therein, ye gods, you make the weak most strong;
Therein, ye gods, you tyrants do defeat;
Nor stony tower, nor walls of beaten brass,
Nor airless dungeon, nor strong links of iron,
Can be retentive to the strength of spirit;
But life, being weary of these worldly bars,
Never lacks power to dismiss itself.
If I know this, know all the world besides,
That part of tyranny that I do bear
I can shake off at pleasure.   *[Thunder still.*
  Casca.   So can I;   100
So every bondman in his own hand bears
The power to cancel his captivity.
  Cas. And why should Caesar be a tyrant then?
Poor man! I know he would not be a wolf,
But that he sees the Romans are but sheep;
He were no lion, were not Romans hinds.
Those that with haste will make a mighty fire
Begin it with weak straws: what trash is Rome,
What rubbish and what offal, when it serves
For the base matter to illuminate   110
So vile a thing as Caesar! But, O grief,
Where hast thou led me? I perhaps speak this
Before a willing bondman; then I know
My answer must be made. But I am armed,
And dangers are to me indifferent.
  Casca. You speak to Casca, and to such a man
That is no fleering telltale. Hold, my hand.
Be factious for redress of all these griefs,
And I will set this foot of mine as far
As who goes farthest.
  Cas.   There's a bargain made.   120
Now know you, Casca, I have moved already
Some certain of the noblest-minded Romans
To undergo with me an enterprise

---

118. **Be factious:** get up a faction or party.

Of honorable dangerous consequence;
And I do know, by this, they stay for me
In Pompey's porch; for now, this fearful night,
There is no stir or walking in the streets;
And the complexion of the element
In favor's like the work we have in hand,
Most bloody, fiery, and most terrible.   130
   Casca. Stand close awhile, for here comes one in haste.
   Cas. 'Tis Cinna; I do know him by his gait;
He is a friend.

Enter CINNA.

           Cinna, where haste you so?
   Cin. To find out you. Who's that? Metellus Cimber?
   Cas. No, it is Casca; one incorporate
To our attempts. Am I not stayed for, Cinna?
   Cin. I am glad on 't. What a fearful night is this!
There's two or three of us have seen strange sights.
   Cas. Am I not stayed for? tell me.
   Cin.   Yes, you are.
O Cassius, if you could   140
But win the noble Brutus to our party —
   Cas. Be you content. Good Cinna, take this paper,
And look you lay it in the praetor's chair,
Where Brutus may but find it; and throw this
In at his window; set this up with wax
Upon old Brutus' statue. All this done,
Repair to Pompey's porch, where you will find us.
Is Decius Brutus and Trebonius there?
   Cin. All but Metellus Cimber; and he's gone
To seek you at your house. Well, I will hie,   150
And so bestow these papers as you bade me.
   Cas. That done, repair to Pompey's theater. [*Exit Cinna.*
Come, Casca, you and I will yet ere day
See Brutus at his house. Three parts of him
Is ours already, and the main entire
Upon the next encounter yields him ours.
   Casca. O, he sits high in all the people's hearts;
And that which would appear offence in us,
His countenance, like richest alchemy,

---

126. **Pompey's porch:** portico of Pompey's theater. 129. **In favor:** in
appearance. 137. **I am glad on 't:** " I am glad that Casca is of our party."
146. **old Brutus:** the Brutus mentioned in Sc. ii, l. 159.

Will change to virtue and to worthiness.   160
  Cas.   Him and his worth and our great need of him
You have right well conceited.   Let us go,
For it is after midnight; and ere day
We will awake him and be sure of him.   [*Exeunt.*

ACT II

Scene I.   *Rome.   Brutus' orchard.*

Enter Brutus.

  Bru.   What, Lucius, ho!
I cannot, by the progress of the stars,
Give guess how near to day.   Lucius, I say!
I would it were my fault to sleep so soundly.
When, Lucius, when?   Awake, I say!   What, Lucius!

Enter Lucius.

  Luc.   Called you, my lord?
  Bru.   Get me a taper in my study, Lucius.
When it is lighted, come and call me here.
  Luc.   I will, my lord.   [*Exit.*
  Bru.   It must be by his death; and for my part,   10
I know no personal cause to spurn at him,
But for the general.   He would be crowned:
How that might change his nature, there's the question.
It is the bright day that brings forth the adder;
And that craves wary walking.   Crown him? — that; —
And then, I grant, we put a sting in him,
That at his will he may do danger with.
The abuse of greatness is, when it disjoins
Remorse from power; and, to speak truth of Caesar,
I have not known when his affections swayed   20
More than his reason.   But 'tis a common proof,
That lowliness is young ambition's ladder,
Whereto the climber-upward turns his face;
But when he once attains the upmost round,

---

162. **conceited:** conceived.
  Stage direction: **orchard:** garden.   12. **general:** public.   19. **remorse:**
pity.   20. **affections:** feelings.

He then unto the ladder turns his back,
Looks in the clouds, scorning the base degrees
By which he did ascend. So Caesar may.
Then, lest he may, prevent. And, since the quarrel
Will bear no color for the thing he is,
Fashion it thus; that what he is, augmented,   30
Would run to these and these extremities;
And therefore think him as a serpent's egg
Which, hatched, would, as his kind, grow mischievous,
And kill him in the shell.

Reënter LUCIUS.

Luc. The taper burneth in your closet, sir.
Searching the window for a flint, I found
This paper, thus sealed up; and, I am sure,
It did not lie there when I went to bed.
                           [Gives him the letter.
Bru. Get you to bed again; it is not day.
Is not tomorrow, boy, the ides of March?   40
Luc. I know not, sir.
Bru. Look in the calendar, and bring me word.
Luc. I will, sir.   *[Exit.*
Bru. The exhalations whizzing in the air
Give so much light that I may read by them.
                     [Opens the letter and reads.
" Brutus, thou sleep'st; awake, and see thyself.
Shall Rome, &c. Speak, strike, redress!
Brutus, thou sleep'st: awake! "
Such instigations have been often dropped
Where I have took them up.   50
" Shall Rome, &c." Thus must I piece it out:
Shall Rome stand under one man's awe? What, Rome?
My ancestors did from the streets of Rome
The Tarquin drive, when he was called a king.
" Speak, strike, redress! " Am I entreated
To speak and strike? O Rome, I make thee promise;
If the redress will follow, thou receivest
Thy full petition at the hand of Brutus!

26. **base degrees:** lower rungs of a ladder. 29. **bear no color:** cannot be
made plausible. Brutus admits that he has no reason to oppose Caesar for
what he now is, but for what he is likely to become in the near future. 44.
exhalations: meteors; here probably flashes of lightning.

Reënter Lucius.

Luc. Sir, March is wasted fourteen days.
                              [*Knocking within.*
  Bru. 'Tis good.   Go to the gate; somebody knocks.   60
                              [*Exit Lucius.*
Since Cassius first did whet me against Caesar,
I have not slept.
Between the acting of a dreadful thing
And the first motion, all the interim is
Like a phantasma, or a hideous dream:
The genius and the mortal instruments
Are then in council; and the state of man,
Like to a little kingdom, suffers then
The nature of an insurrection.

Reënter Lucius.

  Luc. Sir, 'tis your brother Cassius at the door,   70
Who doth desire to see you.
  Bru.   Is he alone?
  Luc. No, sir, there are moe with him.
  Bru.   Do you know them?
  Luc. No, sir; their hats are plucked about their ears,
And half their faces buried in their cloaks,
That by no means I may discover them
By any mark of favor.
  Bru.   Let 'em enter.   [*Exit Lucius.*
They are the faction.   O conspiracy,
Shamest thou to show thy dangerous brow by night,
When evils are most free?   O, then by day
Where wilt thou find a cavern dark enough   80
To mask thy monstrous visage?   Seek none, conspiracy;
Hide it in smiles and affability;
For if thou path, thy native semblance on,
Not Erebus itself were dim enough
To hide thee from prevention.

66. **genius, etc.**: the soul and the bodily organs.   70. **brother**: brother-
in-law.   72. **moe**: more.   76. **favor**: feature.   83. **path**: walk.   85. **from
prevention**: from discovery.

Enter the conspirators, CASSIUS, CASCA, DECIUS, CINNA,
        METELLUS CIMBER, *and* TREBONIUS.

   Cas. I think we are too bold upon your rest.
Good morrow, Brutus; do we trouble you?
   Bru. I have been up this hour, awake all night.
Know I these men that come along with you?
   Cas. Yes, every man of them, and no man here   90
But honors you; and every one doth wish
You had but that opinion of yourself
Which every noble Roman bears of you.
This is Trebonius.
   Bru.   He is welcome hither.
   Cas. This, Decius Brutus.
   Bru.   He is welcome too.
   Cas. This, Casca; this, Cinna; and this, Metellus Cimber.
   Bru. They are all welcome.
What watchful cares do interpose themselves
Betwixt your eyes and night?
   Cas. Shall I entreat a word?   100
                 [*Brutus and Cassius whisper.*
   Dec. Here lies the east; doth not the day break here?
   Casca. No.
   Cin. O, pardon, sir, it doth; and yon gray lines
That fret the clouds are messengers of day.
   Casca. You shall confess that you are both deceived.
Here, as I point my sword, the sun arises,
Which is a great way growing on the south,
Weighing the youthful season of the year.
Some two months hence up higher toward the north
He first presents his fire; and the high east   110
Stands, as the Capitol, directly here.
   Bru. Give me your hands all over, one by one.
   Cas. And let us swear our resolution.
   Bru. No, not an oath! If not the face of men,
The sufferance of our souls, the time's abuse, —
If these be motives weak, break off betimes,
And every man hence to his idle bed;
So let high-sighted tyranny range on,
Till each man drop by lottery. But if these,

---

  115. **sufferance:** sufferings. 118. **high-sighted:** with lofty arrogant
looks. 119. **by lottery:** by chance.

As I am sure they do, bear fire enough   120
To kindle cowards and to steel with valor
The melting spirits of women, then, countrymen,
What need we any spur but our own cause,
To prick us to redress? what other bond
Than secret Romans, that have spoke the word,
And will not palter? and what other oath
Than honesty to honesty engaged,
That this shall be, or we will fall for it?
Swear priests and cowards and men cautelous,
Old feeble carrions and such suffering souls   130
That welcome wrongs; unto bad causes swear
Such creatures as men doubt; but do not stain
The even virtue of our enterprise,
Nor the insuppressive mettle of our spirits,
To think that or our cause or our performance
Did need an oath; when every drop of blood
That every Roman bears, and nobly bears,
Is guilty of a several bastardy,
If he do break the smallest particle
Of any promise that hath passed from him.   140
 Cas. But what of Cicero? Shall we sound him?
I think he will stand very strong with us.
 Casca. Let us not leave him out.
 Cin.   No, by no means.
 Met. O, let us have him, for his silver hairs
Will purchase us a good opinion
And buy men's voices to commend our deeds.
It shall be said, his judgment ruled our hands;
Our youths and wildness shall no whit appear,
But all be buried in his gravity.
 Bru. O, name him not; let us not break with him;   150
For he will never follow any thing
That other men begin.
 Cas.   Then leave him out.
 Casca. Indeed he is not fit.
 Dec. Shall no man else be touched but only Caesar?
 Cas. Decius, well urged. I think it is not meet,
Mark Antony, so well beloved of Caesar,
Should outlive Caesar. We shall find of him

126. **palter:** say one thing and mean another. 129. **cautelous:** tricky or
deceitful. 135. **to think:** by thinking. 150. **break with:** inform him.
157. **of him:** in him.

A shrewd contriver; and, you know, his means,
If he improve them, may well stretch so far
As to annoy us all; which to prevent,   160
Let Antony and Caesar fall together.
    Bru. Our course will seem too bloody, Caius Cassius,
To cut the head off and then hack the limbs,
Like wrath in death and envy afterwards;
For Antony is but a limb of Caesar.
Let us be sacrificers, but not butchers, Caius.
We all stand up against the spirit of Caesar,
And in the spirit of men there is no blood;
O, that we then could come by Caesar's spirit,
And not dismember Caesar! But, alas,   170
Caesar must bleed for it! And, gentle friends,
Let's kill him boldly, but not wrathfully;
Let's carve him as a dish fit for the gods,
Not hew him as a carcass fit for hounds;
And let our hearts, as subtle masters do,
Stir up their servants to an act of rage,
And after seem to chide 'em. This shall make
Our purpose necessary and not envious;
Which so appearing to the common eyes,
We shall be called purgers, not murderers.   180
And for Mark Antony, think not of him;
For he can do no more than Caesar's arm
When Caesar's head is off.
    Cas.   Yet I fear him;
For in the ingrafted love he bears to Caesar —
    Bru. Alas, good Cassius, do not think of him.
If he love Caesar, all that he can do
Is to himself, take thought and die for Caesar;
And that were much he should; for he is given
To sports, to wildness and much company.
    Treb. There is no fear in him; let him not die;   190
For he will live, and laugh at this hereafter. [*Clock strikes*.
    Bru. Peace! count the clock.
    Cas.   The clock hath stricken three
    Treb. 'Tis time to part.
    Cas.   But it is doubtful yet,
Whether Caesar will come forth today, or no;

164. **envy:** malice. 187. **take thought:** grieve. 190. **no fear:** nothing to
fear. 192. **clock:** there were no striking clocks in ancient Rome.

For he is superstitious grown of late,
Quite from the main opinion he held once
Of fantasy, of dreams and ceremonies.
It may be, these apparent prodigies,
The unaccustomed terror of this night,
And the persuasion of his augurers,   200
May hold him from the Capitol today.
   Dec. Never fear that. If he be so resolved,
I can o'ersway him; for he loves to hear
That unicorns may be betrayed with trees,
And bears with glasses, elephants with holes,
Lions with toils and men with flatterers;
But when I tell him he hates flatterers,
He says he does, being then most flattered.
Let me work;
For I can give his humor the true bent,   210
And I will bring him to the Capitol.
   Cas. Nay, we will all of us be there to fetch him.
   Bru. By the eighth hour; is that the uttermost?
   Cin. Be that the uttermost, and fail not then.
   Met. Caius Ligarius doth bear Caesar hard,
Who rated him for speaking well of Pompey.
I wonder none of you have thought of him.
   Bru. Now, good Metellus, go along by him.
He loves me well, and I have given him reasons;
Send him but hither, and I'll fashion him.   220
   Cas. The morning comes upon 's. We'll leave you, Brutus.
And, friends, disperse yourselves; but all remember
What you have said, and show yourselves true Romans.
   Bru. Good gentlemen, look fresh and merrily;
Let not our looks put on our purposes,
But bear it as our Roman actors do,
With untired spirits and formal constancy:
And so good morrow to you every one.
                                    [*Exeunt all but Brutus.*
Boy! Lucius! Fast asleep? It is no matter;
Enjoy the honey-heavy dew of slumber.   230
Thou hast no figures nor no fantasies,
Which busy care draws in the brains of men;
Therefore thou sleep'st so sound.

196. **main:** firm. 205. **glasses:** mirrors. 210. **humor:** disposition.
227. **formal constancy:** dignified and self-possessed.

Enter PORTIA.

Por.   Brutus, my lord!
Bru. Portia, what mean you? wherefore rise you now?
It is not for your health thus to commit
Your weak condition to the raw cold morning.
    Por. Nor for yours neither. You've ungently, Brutus,
Stole from my bed; and yesternight, at supper,
You suddenly arose, and walked about,
Musing and sighing, with your arms across,   240
And when I asked you what the matter was,
You stared upon me with ungentle looks;
I urged you further; then you scratched your head,
And too impatiently stamped with your foot;
Yet I insisted, yet you answered not,
But, with an angry wafture of your hand,
Gave sign for me to leave you. So I did,
Fearing to strengthen that impatience
Which seemed too much enkindled, and withal
Hoping it was but an effect of humor,   250
Which sometimes hath his hour with every man.
It will not let you eat, nor talk, nor sleep,
And could it work so much upon your shape
As it hath much prevailed on your condition,
I should not know you, Brutus. Dear my lord,
Make me acquainted with your cause of grief.
    Bru. I am not well in health, and that is all.
    Por. Brutus is wise, and, were he not in health,
He would embrace the means to come by it.
    Bru. Why, so I do. Good Portia, go to bed.
    Por. Is Brutus sick? and is it physical   261
To walk unbraced and suck up the humors
Of the dank morning? What, is Brutus sick,
And will he steal out of his wholesome bed,
To dare the vile contagion of the night
And tempt the rheumy and unpurgéd air
To add unto his sickness? No, my Brutus;
You have some sick offence within your mind,
Which, by the right and virtue of my place,
I ought to know of; and, upon my knees,   270
I charm you, by my once-commended beauty,

250. **humor:** caprice. 261. **physical:** healthful. 262. **humors:** moisture.
266. **rheumy:** damp, causing rheumatism.

By all your vows of love and that great vow
Which did incorporate and make us one,
That you unfold to me, yourself, your half,
Why you are heavy, and what men tonight
Have had resort to you; for here have been
Some six or seven, who did hide their faces
Even from darkness.
 Bru.   Kneel not, gentle Portia.
 Por. I should not need, if you were gentle Brutus.
Within the bond of marriage, tell me, Brutus,
Is it excepted I should know no secrets   281
That appertain to you? Am I yourself
But, as it were, in sort or limitation,
To keep with you at meals, comfort your bed,
And talk to you sometimes? Dwell I but in the suburbs
Of your good pleasure? If it be no more,
Portia is Brutus' harlot, not his wife.
 Bru. You are my true and honorable wife,
As dear to me as are the ruddy drops
That visit my sad heart.   290
 Por. If this were true, then should I know this secret.
I grant I am a woman; but withal
A woman that Lord Brutus took to wife.
I grant I am a woman; but withal
A woman well reputed, Cato's daughter.
Think you I am no stronger than my sex,
Being so fathered and so husbanded?
Tell me your counsels, I will not disclose 'em.
I have made strong proof of my constancy,
Giving myself a voluntary wound   300
Here, in the thigh; can I bear that with patience,
And not my husband's secrets?
 Bru.   O ye gods,
Render me worthy of this noble wife! [*Knocking within.*
Hark, hark! one knocks. Portia, go in awhile;
And by and by thy bosom shall partake
The secrets of my heart.
All my engagements I will construe to thee,
All the charactery of my sad brows;
Leave me with haste. [*Exit Portia.*] Lucius, who's that
  knocks?

308. **charactery:** lines of thought.

Reënter LUCIUS *with* LIGARIUS.

Luc. Here is a sick man that would speak with you. 310
Bru. Caius Ligarius, that Metellus spake of.
Boy, stand aside. Caius Ligarius! how?
Lig. Vouchsafe good morrow from a feeble tongue.
Bru. O, what a time have you chose out, brave Caius,
To wear a kerchief! Would you were not sick!
Lig. I am not sick, if Brutus have in hand
Any exploit worthy the name of honor.
Bru. Such an exploit have I in hand, Ligarius,
Had you a healthful ear to hear of it.
Lig. By all the gods that Romans bow before,   320
I here discard my sickness! Soul of Rome!
Brave son, derived from honorable loins!
Thou, like an exorcist, hast conjured up
My mortified spirit. Now bid me run,
And I will strive with things impossible;
Yea, get the better of them. What's to do?
Bru. A piece of work that will make sick men whole.
Lig. But are not some whole that we must make sick?
Bru. That must we also. What it is, my Caius,
I shall unfold to thee, as we are going   330
To whom it must be done.
Lig.   Set on your foot,
And with a heart new-fired I follow you,
To do I know not what; but it sufficeth
That Brutus leads me on.
Bru.   Follow me, then.   [*Exeunt.*

SCENE II. *Caesar's house.*

Thunder and lightning. Enter CAESAR *in his nightgown.*

Caes. Nor heaven nor earth have been at peace tonight:
Thrice hath Calpurnia in her sleep cried out,
" Help, ho! they murder Caesar! " Who's within?

324. **mortified:** dead.

Enter a Servant.

Serv. My lord?
Caes. Go bid the priests do present sacrifice
And bring me their opinions of success.
   Serv. I will, my lord.   [*Exit.*

Enter CALPURNIA.

   Cal. What mean you, Caesar? Think you to walk forth?
You shall not stir out of your house today.
   Caes. Caesar shall forth. The things that threatened
      me   10
Ne'er looked but on my back; when they shall see
The face of Caesar, they are vanished.
   Cal. Caesar, I never stood on ceremonies,
Yet now they fright me. There is one within,
Besides the things that we have heard and seen,
Recounts most horrid sights seen by the watch.
A lioness hath whelpéd in the streets;
And graves have yawned, and yielded up their dead;
Fierce fiery warriors fought upon the clouds,
In ranks and squadrons and right form of war,
Which drizzled blood upon the Capitol;   21
The noise of battle hurtled in the air,
Horses did neigh, and dying men did groan,
And ghosts did shriek and squeal about the streets.
O Caesar! these things are beyond all use,
And I do fear them.
   Caes.   What can be avoided
Whose end is purposed by the mighty gods?
Yet Caesar shall go forth; for these predictions
Are to the world in general as to Caesar.
   Cal. When beggars die, there are no comets seen;   30
The heavens themselves blaze forth the death of princes.
   Caes. Cowards die many times before their deaths;
The valiant never taste of death but once.
Of all the wonders that I yet have heard,
It seems to me most strange that men should fear;
Seeing that death, a necessary end,
Will come when it will come.

   5. **present:** immediate.   6. **success:** result.   13. **never stood on ceremonies:** took no stock in auguries.

Reënter Servant.

What say the augurers?
Serv. They would not have you to stir forth today.
Plucking the entrails of an offering forth,
They could not find a heart within the beast.   40
Caes. The gods do this in shame of cowardice;
Caesar should be a beast without a heart,
If he should stay at home today for fear.
No, Caesar shall not; Danger knows full well
That Caesar is more dangerous than he.
We are two lions littered in one day,
And I the elder and more terrible;
And Caesar shall go forth.
Cal.   Alas, my lord,
Your wisdom is consumed in confidence.
Do not go forth today; call it my fear   50
That keeps you in the house, and not your own.
We'll send Mark Antony to the senate house;
And he shall say you are not well today:
Let me, upon my knee, prevail in this.
Caes. Mark Antony shall say I am not well;
And, for thy humor, I will stay at home.

Enter DECIUS.

Here's Decius Brutus, he shall tell them so.
Dec. Caesar, all hail! good morrow, worthy Caesar;
I come to fetch you to the senate house.
Caes. And you are come in very happy time,
To bear my greeting to the senators   61
And tell them that I will not come today.
Cannot, is false, and that I dare not, falser;
I will not come today. Tell them so, Decius.
Cal. Say he is sick.
Caes.   Shall Caesar send a lie?
Have I in conquest stretched mine arm so far,
To be afeared to tell graybeards the truth?
Decius, go tell them Caesar will not come.
Dec. Most mighty Caesar, let me know some cause,
Lest I be laughed at when I tell them so.   70
Caes. The cause is in my will; I will not come;
That is enough to satisfy the senate.

But for your private satisfaction,
Because I love you, I will let you know:
Calpurnia here, my wife, stays me at home.
She dreamt tonight she saw my statua,
Which, like a fountain with an hundred spouts,
Did run pure blood; and many lusty Romans
Came smiling, and did bathe their hands in it;
And these does she apply for warnings, and portents,   80
And evils imminent; and on her knee
Hath begged that I will stay at home today.
  Dec. This dream is all amiss interpreted;
It was a vision fair and fortunate.
Your statue spouting blood in many pipes,
In which so many smiling Romans bathed,
Signifies that from you great Rome shall suck
Reviving blood, and that great men shall press
For tinctures, stains, relics and cognizance.
This by Calpurnia's dream is signified.   90
  Caes. And this way have you well expounded it.
  Dec. I have, when you have heard what I can say;
And know it now. The senate have concluded
To give this day a crown to mighty Caesar.
If you shall send them word you will not come,
Their minds may change. Besides, it were a mock
Apt to be rendered, for some one to say,
" Break up the senate till another time,
When Caesar's wife shall meet with better dreams."
If Caesar hide himself, shall they not whisper,
" Lo, Caesar is afraid " ?   101
Pardon me, Caesar; for my dear dear love
To your proceeding bids me tell you this;
And reason to my love is liable.
  Caes. How foolish do your fears seem now, Calpurnia!
I am ashaméd I did yield to them.
Give me my robe, for I will go.

Enter PUBLIUS, BRUTUS, LIGARIUS, METELLUS, CASCA,
TREBONIUS, *and* CINNA.

And look where Publius is come to fetch me.
  Pub. Good morrow, Caesar.
  Caes.   Welcome, Publius.

89. **cognizance:** badges of honor (from heraldry).

What, Brutus, are you stirred so early too?   110
Good morrow, Casca. Caius Ligarius,
Caesar was ne'er so much your enemy
As that same ague which has made you lean.
What is 't o'clock?
    Bru.   Caesar, 'tis strucken eight.
    Caes. I thank you for your pains and courtesy.

Enter ANTONY.

See! Antony, that revels long o' nights,
Is notwithstanding up. Good morrow, Antony.
    Ant. So to most noble Caesar.
    Caes.   Bid them prepare within;
I am to blame to be thus waited for.
Now, Cinna; now, Metellus; what, Trebonius!
I have an hour's talk in store for you;   121
Remember that you call on me today.
Be near me, that I may remember you.
    Treb. Caesar, I will; [*aside*] and so near will I be,
That your best friends shall wish I had been further.
    Caes. Good friends, go in, and taste some wine with me;
And we, like friends, will straightway go together.
    Bru. [*Aside*] That every like is not the same, O Caesar,
The heart of Brutus yearns to think upon!   [*Exeunt.*

SCENE III. *A street near the Capitol.*

Enter ARTEMIDORUS, *reading a paper.*

    Art. " Caesar, beware of Brutus; take heed of Cassius;
come not near Casca; have an eye to Cinna; trust not Trebonius; mark well Metellus Cimber; Decius Brutus loves thee
not; thou hast wronged Caius Ligarius. There is but one
mind in all these men, and it is bent against Caesar. If thou
beest not immortal, look about you; security gives way to
conspiracy. The mighty gods defend thee! Thy lover,
                                    " ARTEMIDORUS."

Here will I stand till Caesar pass along,   11
And as a suitor will I give him this.

129. **yearns:** grieves. 6. **security:** feeling of security.

My heart laments that virtue cannot live
Out of the teeth of emulation.
If thou read this, O Caesar, thou mayst live;
If not, the Fates with traitors do contrive.   [*Exit.*

SCENE IV.   *Another part of the same street, before the house
of Brutus.*

Enter PORTIA *and* LUCIUS.

Por. I prithee, boy, run to the senate house;
Stay not to answer me, but get thee gone.
Why dost thou stay?
Luc.   To know my errand, madam.
Por. I would have had thee there, and here again,
Ere I can tell thee what thou shouldst do there.
O constancy, be strong upon my side,
Set a huge mountain 'tween my heart and tongue!
I have a man's mind, but a woman's might.
How hard it is for women to keep counsel!
Art thou here yet?
Luc.   Madam, what should I do?   10
Run to the Capitol, and nothing else?
And so return to you, and nothing else?
Por. Yes, bring me word, boy, if thy lord look well,
For he went sickly forth; and take good note
What Caesar doth, what suitors press to him.
Hark, boy! what noise is that?
Luc. I hear none, madam.
Por.   Prithee, listen well;
I heard a bustling rumor, like a fray,
And the wind brings it from the Capitol.
Luc. Sooth, madam, I hear nothing.   20

Enter the Soothsayer.

Por. Come hither, fellow; which way hast thou been?
Sooth. At mine own house, good lady.
Por. What is 't o'clock?
Sooth.   About the ninth hour, lady.
Por. Is Caesar yet gone to the Capitol?

Sc. iii. 14. **emulation:** jealous rivalry.   Sc. iv. 6. **constancy:** self-posses-
sion. 18. **rumor:** noise.

Sooth.   Madam, not yet; I go to take my stand,
To see him pass on to the Capitol.
  Por.   Thou hast some suit to Caesar, hast thou not?
  Sooth.   That I have, lady; if it will please Caesar
To be so good to Caesar as to hear me,
I shall beseech him to befriend himself.   30
  Por.   Why, know'st thou any harm's intended towards him?
  Sooth.   None that I know will be, much that I fear may
        chance.
Good morrow to you.   Here the street is narrow;
The throng that follows Caesar at the heels,
Of senators, of praetors, common suitors,
Will crowd a feeble man almost to death.
I'll get me to a place more void, and there
Speak to great Caesar as he comes along.   [*Exit.*
  Por.   I must go in.   Ay, me, how weak a thing
The heart of woman is!   O Brutus,   40
The heavens speed thee in thine enterprise!
Sure, the boy heard me.   Brutus hath a suit
That Caesar will not grant.   O, I grow faint.
Run, Lucius, and commend me to my lord;
Say I am merry.   Come to me again,
And bring me word what he doth say to thee.
                                          [*Exeunt severally.*

ACT III

Scene I.   *Rome.   Before the Capitol; the Senate sitting
                above.*

A crowd of people; among them Artemidorus *and the* Sooth-
      sayer.   *Flourish.   Enter* Caesar, Brutus, Cassius,
      Casca, Decius, Metellus, Trebonius, Cinna, Antony,
      Lepidus, Popilius, Publius, *and others.*

  Caes.   [*To the Soothsayer*] The ides of March are come.
  Sooth.   Ay, Caesar; but not gone.
  Art.   Hail, Caesar! read this schedule.
  Dec.   Trebonius doth desire you to o'erread,

42. **hath a suit:** spoken to the boy, to cover up her previous words.

At your leisure, this his humble suit.
   Art. O Caesar, read mine first; for mine's a suit
That touches Caesar nearer. Read it, great Caesar.
    Caes. What touches us ourself shall be last served.
    Art. Delay not, Caesar; read it instantly.
    Caes. What, is the fellow mad?
    Pub.   Sirrah, give place.   10
    Cas. What, urge you your petitions in the street?
Come to the Capitol.

    Caesar *goes up to the Senate House, the rest following.*

    Pop. I wish your enterprise today may thrive.
    Cas. What enterprise, Popilius?
    Pop.   Fare you well.
                         [Advances to Caesar.
    Bru. What said Popilius Lena?
    Cas. He wished today our enterprise might thrive.
I fear our purpose is discovered.
    Bru. Look, how he makes to Caesar; mark him.
    Cas. Casca, be sudden, for we fear prevention.
Brutus, what shall be done? If this be known,
Cassius or Caesar never shall turn back,   21
For I will slay myself.
    Bru.   Cassius, be constant;
Popilius Lena speaks not of our purposes;
For, look, he smiles, and Caesar doth not change.
    Cas. Trebonius knows his time; for, look you, Brutus,
He draws Mark Antony out of the way.
                  [Exeunt Antony and Trebonius.
    Dec. Where is Metellus Cimber? Let him go,
And presently prefer his suit to Caesar.
    Bru. He is addressed; press near and second him.
    Cin. Casca, you are the first that rears your hand.   30
    Caes. Are we all ready? What is now amiss
That Caesar and his senate must redress?
    Met. Most high, most mighty, and most puissant Caesar,
Metellus Cimber throws before thy seat
An humble heart —   *[Kneeling.*
    Caes.   I must prevent thee, Cimber.
These couchings and these lowly courtesies

    28. **presently prefer:** offer at once. 29. **addressed:** ready.

Might fire the blood of ordinary men,
And turn pre-ordinance and first decree
Into the law of children. Be not fond
To think that Caesar bears such rebel blood   40
That will be thawed from the true quality
With that which melteth fools; I mean, sweet words,
Low-crooked court'sies and base spaniel-fawning.
Thy brother by decree is banishèd;
If thou dost bend and pray and fawn for him,
I spurn thee like a cur out of my way.
Know, Caesar doth not wrong, nor without cause
Will he be satisfied.

    Met. Is there no voice more worthy than my own,
To sound more sweetly in great Caesar's ear   50
For the repealing of my banished brother?

    Bru. I kiss thy hand, but not in flattery, Caesar;
Desiring thee that Publius Cimber may
Have an immediate freedom of repeal.

    Caes. What, Brutus!

    Cas.   Pardon, Caesar; Caesar, pardon!
As low as to thy foot doth Cassius fall,
To beg enfranchisement for Publius Cimber.

    Caes. I could be well moved, if I were as you;
If I could pray to move, prayers would move me;
But I am constant as the northern star,   60
Of whose true-fixed and resting quality
There is no fellow in the firmament.
The skies are painted with unnumbered sparks,
They are all fire and every one doth shine;
But there's but one in all doth hold his place.
So in the world; 'tis furnished well with men,
And men are flesh and blood, and apprehensive;
Yet in the number I do know but one
That unassailable holds on his rank,
Unshaked of motion; and that I am he,   70
Let me a little show it, even in this:
That I was constant Cimber should be banished,
And constant do remain to keep him so.

    Cin. O Caesar —

    Caes. Hence! wilt thou lift up Olympus?

39. **fond:** foolish.   51. **repealing:** recalling.   70. **that I am he:** this arrogant speech is not in accordance with Caesar's real character, but for dramatic purposes it helps to clear the conscience of Brutus.

Dec.   Great Caesar —
Caes.   Doth not Brutus bootless kneel?
Casca.   Speak, hands, for me!
          [*Casca first, then the other Conspirators and*
                              Marcus Brutus stab Caesar.
Caes.   *Et tu, Brute!* Then fall, Caesar!   [*Dies.*
Cin.   Liberty! Freedom! Tyranny is dead!
Run hence, proclaim, cry it about the streets.
   Cas.   Some to the common pulpits, and cry out,   80
" Liberty, freedom, and enfranchisement! "
   Bru.   People and senators, be not affrighted;
Fly not; stand still; ambition's debt is paid.
   Casca.   Go to the pulpit, Brutus.
   Dec.   And Cassius too.
   Bru.   Where's Publius?
   Cin.   Here, quite confounded with this mutiny.
   Met.   Stand fast together, lest some friend of Caesar's
Should chance —
   Bru.   Talk not of standing. Publius, good cheer;
There is no harm intended to your person,   90
Nor to no Roman else. So tell them, Publius.
   Cas.   And leave us, Publius; lest that the people,
Rushing on us, should do your age some mischief.
   Bru.   Do so: and let no man abide this deed,
But we the doers.

                  Reënter TREBONIUS.

Cas.   Where is Antony?
   Tre.   Fled to his house amazed.
Men, wives and children stare, cry out and run
As it were doomsday.
   Bru.   Fates, we will know your pleasures.
That we shall die, we know; 'tis but the time
And drawing days out, that men stand upon.
   Cas.   Why, he that cuts off twenty years of life   101
Cuts off so many years of fearing death.
   Bru.   Grant that, and then is death a benefit;
So are we Caesar's friends, that have abridged
His time of fearing death. Stoop, Romans, stoop,
And let us bathe our hands in Caesar's blood
Up to the elbows, and besmear our swords;

80. **pulpits:** elevated speaking-places in the forum.   94. **abide:** be responsible for.   100. **stand upon:** bother about.

Then walk we forth, even to the market-place,
And, waving our red weapons o'er our heads,
Let's all cry, " Peace, freedom and liberty! "   110
  Cas. Stoop, then, and wash. How many ages hence
Shall this our lofty scene be acted over
In states unborn and accents yet unknown!
  Bru. How many times shall Caesar bleed in sport,
That now on Pompey's basis lies along
No worthier than the dust!
  Cas.   So oft as that shall be,
So often shall the knot of us be called
The men that gave their country liberty.
  Dec. What, shall we forth?
  Cas.   Ay, every man away.
Brutus shall lead; and we will grace his heels   120
With the most boldest and best hearts of Rome.

Enter a Servant.

  Bru. Soft! who comes here? A friend of Antony's.
  Serv. Thus, Brutus, did my master bid me kneel;
Thus did Mark Antony bid me fall down;
And being prostrate, thus he bade me say:
Brutus is noble, wise, valiant, and honest;
Caesar was mighty, bold, royal, and loving;
Say I love Brutus, and I honor him;
Say I feared Caesar, honored him and loved him.
If Brutus will vouchsafe that Antony   130
May safely come to him, and be resolved
How Caesar hath deserved to lie in death,
Mark Antony shall not love Caesar dead
So well as Brutus living; but will follow
The fortunes and affairs of noble Brutus
Thorough the hazards of this untrod state
With all true faith. So says my master Antony.
  Bru. Thy master is a wise and valiant Roman;
I never thought him worse.
Tell him, so please him come unto this place,
He shall be satisfied; and, by my honor,   141
Depart untouched.
  Serv.   I'll fetch him presently.   [*Exit.*

115. **Pompey's basis:** base of Pompey's statue. 131. **resolved:** informed.
136. **untried state:** the untried political policies now inaugurated.

Bru. I know that we shall have him well to friend.
Cas. I wish we may; but yet have I a mind
That fears him much; and my misgiving still
Falls shrewdly to the purpose.
    Bru. But here comes Antony.

Reënter ANTONY.

                                   Welcome, Mark Antony.
    Ant. O mighty Caesar! dost thou lie so low?
Are all thy conquests, glories, triumphs, spoils,
Shrunk to this little measure?   Fare thee well.
I know not, gentlemen, what you intend,   151
Who else must be let blood, who else is rank;
If I myself, there is no hour so fit
As Caesar's death's hour, nor no instrument
Of half that worth as those your swords, made rich
With the most noble blood of all this world.
I do beseech ye, if you bear me hard,
Now, whilst your purpled hands do reek and smoke,
Fulfil your pleasure.   Live a thousand years,
I shall not find myself so apt to die;   160
No place will please me so, no mean of death,
As here by Caesar, and by you cut off,
The choice and master spirits of this age.
    Bru. O Antony, beg not your death of us.
Though now we must appear bloody and cruel,
As, by our hands and this our present act,
You see we do, yet see you but our hands
And this the bleeding business they have done.
Our hearts you see not; they are pitiful;
And pity to the general wrong of Rome —   170
As fire drives out fire, so pity pity —
Hath done this deed on Caesar. For your part,
To you our swords have leaden points, Mark Antony;
Our arms, in strength of malice, and our hearts
Of brothers' temper, do receive you in
With all kind love, good thoughts, and reverence.
    Cas. Your voice shall be as strong as any man's
In the disposing of new dignities.
    Bru. Only be patient till we have appeased

---

146. **my misgiving, etc.:** my suspicions usually turn into certainties. 152.
rank: too full of blood. 159. **live:** if I live. 160. **apt:** ready.

The multitude, beside themselves with fear,   180
And then we will deliver you the cause,
Why I, that did love Caesar when I struck him,
Have thus proceeded.
    Ant.   I doubt not of your wisdom.
Let each man render me his bloody hand:
First, Marcus Brutus, will I shake with you;
Next, Caius Cassius, do I take your hand;
Now, Decius Brutus, yours; now yours, Metellus;
Yours, Cinna; and, my valiant Casca, yours;
Though last, not least in love, yours, good Trebonius.
Gentlemen all — alas, what shall I say?   190
My credit now stands on such slippery ground,
That one of two bad ways you must conceit me,
Either a coward or a flatterer.
That I did love thee, Caesar, O, 'tis true:
If then thy spirit look upon us now,
Shall it not grieve thee dearer than thy death,
To see thy Antony making his peace,
Shaking the bloody fingers of thy foes,
Most noble! in the presence of thy corse?
Had I as many eyes as thou hast wounds,   200
Weeping as fast as they stream forth thy blood,
It would become me better than to close
In terms of friendship with thine enemies.
Pardon me, Julius! Here wast thou bayed, brave hart;
Here didst thou fall; and here thy hunters stand,
Signed in thy spoil, and crimsoned in thy lethe.
O world, thou wast the forest to this hart;
And this, indeed, O world, the heart of thee.
How like a deer, strucken by many princes,
Dost thou here lie!   210
    Cas.   Mark Antony —
    Ant.   Pardon me, Caius Cassius:
The enemies of Caesar shall say this;
Then, in a friend, it is cold modesty.
    Cas.   I blame you not for praising Caesar so;
But what compact mean you to have with us?
Will you be pricked in number of our friends;
Or shall we on, and not depend on you?

192. **conceit:** think of. 196. **dearer:** more deeply. 204. **bayed:** brought
to bay. 206. **lethe:** violent death. 213. **modesty:** moderation. 216. **pricked:**
marked.

Ant.   Therefore I took your hands, but was, indeed,
Swayed from the point, by looking down on Caesar.
Friends am I with you all and love you all,   220
Upon this hope, that you shall give me reasons
Why and wherein Caesar was dangerous.
   Bru.   Or else were this a savage spectacle.
Our reasons are so full of good regard
That were you, Antony, the son of Caesar,
You should be satisfied.
   Ant.   That's all I seek;
And am moreover suitor that I may
Produce his body to the market-place;
And in the pulpit, as becomes a friend,
Speak in the order of his funeral.   230
   Bru.   You shall, Mark Antony.
   Cas.   Brutus, a word with you.
[*Aside to Bru.*] You know not what you do. Do not consent
That Antony speak in his funeral.
Know you how much the people may be moved
By that which he will utter?
   Bru.   By your pardon.
I will myself into the pulpit first,
And show the reason of our Caesar's death.
What Antony shall speak, I will protest
He speaks by leave and by permission,
And that we are contented Caesar shall   240
Have all true rites and lawful ceremonies.
It shall advantage more than do us wrong.
   Cas.   I know not what may fall; I like it not.
   Bru.   Mark Antony, here, take you Caesar's body.
You shall not in your funeral speech blame us,
But speak all good you can devise of Caesar,
And say you do't by our permission;
Else shall you not have any hand at all
About his funeral. And you shall speak
In the same pulpit whereto I am going,   250
After my speech is ended.
   Ant.   Be it so;
I do desire no more.

218. **therefore:** for that purpose.   224. **good regard:** worthy of consideration.   230. **order:** ceremony.   231. **you shall:** Giving Antony permission to
speak was Brutus' second mistake in policy.   The first was when he opposed his
death.   Cassius was much the shrewder politician.

Bru. Prepare the body then, and follow us.
[*Exeunt all but Antony.*

Ant. O, pardon me, thou bleeding piece of earth,
That I am meek and gentle with these butchers!
Thou art the ruins of the noblest man
That ever lived in the tide of times.
Woe to the hand that shed this costly blood!
Over thy wounds now do I prophesy —   259
Which, like dumb mouths, do ope their ruby lips,
To beg the voice and utterance of my tongue —
A curse shall light upon the limbs of men;
Domestic fury and fierce civil strife
Shall cumber all the parts of Italy;
Blood and destruction shall be so in use
And dreadful objects so familiar
That mothers shall but smile when they behold
Their infants quartered with the hands of war;
All pity choked with custom of fell deeds;
And Caesar's spirit, ranging for revenge,   270
With Ate by his side come hot from hell,
Shall in these confines with a monarch's voice
Cry " Havoc," and let slip the dogs of war;
That this foul deed shall smell above the earth
With carrion men, groaning for burial.

Enter a Servant.

You serve Octavius Caesar, do you not?
Serv. I do, Mark Antony.
Ant. Caesar did write for him to come to Rome.
Serv. He did receive his letters, and is coming;
And bid me say to you by word of mouth —   280
O Caesar! —   [*Seeing the body.*
Ant. Thy heart is big, get thee apart and weep.
Passion, I see, is catching; for mine eyes,
Seeing those beads of sorrow stand in thine,
Began to water. Is thy master coming?
Serv. He lies tonight within seven leagues of Rome.
Ant. Post back with speed, and tell him what hath chanced.
Here is a mourning Rome, a dangerous Rome,
No Rome of safety for Octavius yet;

254. Antony's soliloquy reveals his real state of mind and gives a clue to
what is to follow.   271. **Ate:** goddess of revenge.   274. **Havoc:** a command
that no quarter was to be given.

Hie hence, and tell him so. Yet, stay awhile;   290
Thou shalt not back till I have borne this corse
Into the market-place. There shall I try,
In my oration, how the people take
The cruel issue of these bloody men;
According to the which, thou shalt discourse
To young Octavius of the state of things.
Lend me your hand.   [*Exeunt with Caesar's body.*

SCENE II. *The Forum.*

Enter BRUTUS *and* CASSIUS, *and a throng of* Citizens.

Citizens. We will be satisfied; let us be satisfied.
Bru. Then follow me, and give me audience, friends.
Cassius, go you into the other street,
And part the numbers.
Those that will hear me speak, let 'em stay here;
Those that will follow Cassius, go with him;
And public reasons shall be rendered
Of Caesar's death.
First Cit.   I will hear Brutus speak.
Sec. Cit. I will hear Cassius; and compare their reasons,
When severally we hear them rendered.   10
          [*Exit Cassius, with some of the Citizens.*
                    Brutus goes into the pulpit.
Third Cit. The noble Brutus is ascended. Silence!
Bru. Be patient till the last.
Romans, countrymen, and lovers! hear me for my cause, and
be silent, that you may hear; believe me for mine honor, and
have respect to mine honor, that you may believe; censure me
in your wisdom, and awake your senses, that you may the
better judge. If there be any in this assembly, any dear
friend of Caesar's, to him I say, that Brutus' love to Caesar
was no less than his. If then that friend demand why Brutus
rose against Caesar, this is my answer: Not that I loved
Caesar less, but that I loved Rome more. Had you rather
Caesar were living and die all slaves, than that Caesar were
dead, to live all free men? As Caesar loved me, I weep for

This scene is the most dramatic in the play. Its effectiveness depends upon
the acting of the mob as well as the rendering of the speeches. 13. **lovers:** an
intensive term for friends. 16. **censure:** judge

him; as he was fortunate, I rejoice at it; as he was valiant, I
honor him; but, as he was ambitious, I slew him.   There is
tears for his love; joy for his fortune; honor for his valor;
and death for his ambition.   Who is here so base that would
be a bondman?   If any, speak; for him have I offended.   Who
is here so rude that would not be a Roman?   If any, speak,
for him have I offended.   Who is here so vile that will not
love his country?   If any, speak; for him have I offended.
I pause for a reply.   37

All.   None, Brutus, none.

Bru.   Then none have I offended.   I have done no more to
Caesar than you shall do to Brutus.   The question of his death
is enrolled in the Capitol; his glory not extenuated, wherein
he was worthy, nor his offences enforced, for which he suffered
death.

Enter ANTONY *and others, with* CAESAR'S *body.*

Here comes his body, mourned by Mark Antony; who, though
he had no hand in his death, shall receive the benefit of his
dying, a place in the commonwealth; as which of you shall
not?   With this I depart — that, as I slew my best lover for
the good of Rome, I have the same dagger for myself, when it
shall please my country to need my death.   52

All.   Live, Brutus! live, live!

First Cit.   Bring him with triumph home unto his house.

Sec. Cit.   Give him a statue with his ancestors.

Third Cit.   Let him be Caesar.

Fourth Cit.   Caesar's better parts
Shall be crowned in Brutus.

First Cit.   We'll bring him to his house
With shouts and clamors.

Bru.   My countrymen —

Sec. Cit.   Peace, silence!   Brutus speaks.

First Cit.   Peace, ho!

Bru.   Good countrymen, let me depart alone,
And, for my sake, stay here with Antony.   61
Do grace to Caesar's corpse, and grace his speech
Tending to Caesar's glories; which Mark Antony,
By our permission, is allowed to make.
I do entreat you, not a man depart,
Save I alone, till Antony have spoke.   [*Exit.*

40. **question:** reason.

First Cit. Stay, ho! and let us hear Mark Antony.
Third Cit. Let him go up into the public chair;
We'll hear him. Noble Antony, go up.   69
Ant. For Brutus' sake, I am beholding to you.
                              [*Goes into the pulpit.*
Fourth Cit. What does he say of Brutus?
Third Cit.   He says, for Brutus' sake,
He finds himself beholding to us all.
Fourth Cit. 'Twere best he speak no harm of Brutus here.
First Cit. This Caesar was a tyrant.
Third Cit.   Nay, that's certain:
We are blest that Rome is rid of him.
Sec. Cit. Peace! let us hear what Antony can say.
Ant. You gentle Romans —
Citizens.   Peace, ho! let us hear him.
Ant. Friends, Romans, countrymen, lend me your ears!
I come to bury Caesar, not to praise him.
The evil that men do lives after them;   80
The good is oft interréd with their bones;
So let it be with Caesar. The noble Brutus
Hath told you Caesar was ambitious;
If it were so, it was a grievous fault,
And grievously hath Caesar answered it.
Here, under leave of Brutus and the rest —
For Brutus is an honorable man;
So are they all, all honorable men —
Come I to speak in Caesar's funeral.
He was my friend, faithful and just to me;   90
But Brutus says he was ambitious;
And Brutus is an honorable man.
He hath brought many captives home to Rome,
Whose ransoms did the general coffers fill;
Did this in Caesar seem ambitious?
When that the poor have cried, Caesar hath wept;
Ambition should be made of sterner stuff:
Yet Brutus says he was ambitious;
And Brutus is an honorable man.
You all did see that on the Lupercal   100
I thrice presented him a kingly crown,
Which he did thrice refuse. Was this ambition?
Yet Brutus says he was ambitious;

79. **bury:** the Romans burned their dead.

And, sure, he is an honorable man.
I speak not to disprove what Brutus spoke,
But here I am to speak what I do know.
You all did love him once, not without cause;
What cause withholds you then, to mourn for him?
O judgment! thou art fled to brutish beasts,
And men have lost their reason. Bear with me;   110
My heart is in the coffin there with Caesar,
And I must pause till it come back to me.

    First Cit. Methinks there is much reason in his say-
ings.

    Sec. Cit. If thou consider rightly of the matter,
Caesar has had great wrong.

    Third Cit.   Has he, masters?
I fear there will a worse come in his place.

    Fourth Cit. Marked ye his words? He would not take
      the crown;
Therefore 'tis certain he was not ambitious.

    First Cit. If it be found so, some will dear abide it.

    Sec. Cit. Poor soul! his eyes are red as fire with weep-
      ing.   120

    Third Cit. There's not a nobler man in Rome than Antony.

    Fourth Cit. Now mark him, he begins again to speak.

    Ant. But yesterday the word of Caesar might
Have stood against the world; now lies he there,
And none so poor to do him reverence.
O masters, if I were disposed to stir
Your hearts and minds to mutiny and rage,
I should do Brutus wrong, and Cassius wrong,
Who, you all know, are honorable men.
I will not do them wrong; I rather choose   130
To wrong the dead, to wrong myself and you,
Than I will wrong such honorable men.
But here's a parchment with the seal of Caesar;
I found it in his closet; 'tis his will.
Let but the commons hear this testament —
Which, pardon me, I do not mean to read —
And they would go and kiss dead Caesar's wounds
And dip their napkins in his sacred blood,
Yea, beg a hair of him for memory,
And, dying, mention it within their wills,   140

138. **napkins:** handkerchiefs.

Bequeathing it as a rich legacy
Unto their issue.

    Fourth Cit. We'll hear the will. Read it, Mark Antony.

    All. The will, the will! we will hear Caesar's will.

    Ant. Have patience, gentle friends, I must not read it;
It is not meet you know how Caesar loved you.
You are not wood, you are not stones, but men;
And, being men, hearing the will of Caesar,
It will inflame you, it will make you mad.
'Tis good you know not that you are his heirs;
For, if you should, O, what would come of it!   150

    Fourth Cit. Read the will; we will hear it, Antony;
You shall read us the will, Caesar's will.

    Ant. Will you be patient? Will you stay awhile?
I have o'ershot myself to tell you of it.
I fear I wrong the honorable men
Whose daggers have stabbed Caesar; I do fear it.

    Fourth Cit. They were traitors; honorable men!

    All. The will! the testament!

    Sec. Cit. They were villains, murderers.
The will! read the will.   160

    Ant. You will compel me, then, to read the will?
Then make a ring about the corpse of Caesar,
And let me show you him that made the will.
Shall I descend? and will you give me leave?

    Several Cit. Come down.

    Sec. Cit. Descend.

    Third Cit. You shall have leave. [*Antony comes down.*

    Fourth Cit. A ring; stand round.

    First Cit. Stand from the hearse, stand from the body.

    Sec. Cit. Room for Antony, most noble Antony.   170

    Ant. Nay, press not so upon me; stand far off.

    Several Cit. Stand back; room; bear back!

    Ant. If you have tears, prepare to shed them now.
You all do know this mantle; I remember
The first time ever Caesar put it on.
'Twas on a summer's evening, in his tent,
That day he overcame the Nervii.
Look, in this space ran Cassius' dagger through;
See what a rent the envious Casca made;

---

    177. **Nervii:** a telling reference to Caesar's most famous victory. 179. **envious:** malicious.

Through this the well-belovéd Brutus stabbed;
And as he plucked his curséd steel away,   181
Mark how the blood of Caesar followed it,
As rushing out of doors, to be resolved
If Brutus so unkindly knocked, or no;
For Brutus, as you know, was Caesar's angel.
Judge, O you gods, how dearly Caesar loved him!
This was the most unkindest cut of all;
For when the noble Caesar saw him stab,
Ingratitude, more strong than traitors' arms,
Quite vanquished him. Then burst his mighty heart;   190
And, in his mantle muffling up his face,
Even at the base of Pompey's statua,
Which all the while ran blood, great Caesar fell.
O, what a fall was there, my countrymen!
Then I, and you, and all of us fell down,
Whilst bloody treason flourished over us.
O, now you weep; and, I perceive, you feel
The dint of pity. These are gracious drops.
Kind souls, what, weep you when you but behold
Our Caesar's vesture wounded? Look you here,
Here is himself, marred, as you see, with traitors.   201
    First Cit. O piteous spectacle!
    Sec. Cit. O noble Caesar!
    Third Cit. O woeful day!
    Fourth Cit. O traitors, villains!
    First Cit. O most bloody sight!
    Sec. Cit. We will be revenged.
    All. Revenge! About! Seek! Burn! Fire!
Kill! Slay! Let not a traitor live!
    Ant. Stay, countrymen.   210
    First Cit. Peace there! hear the noble Antony.
    Sec. Cit. We'll hear him, we'll follow him, we'll die with
him.
    Ant. Good friends, sweet friends, let me not stir you up
To such a sudden flood of mutiny.
They that have done this deed are honorable.
What private griefs they have, alas, I know not,
That made them do it; they are wise and honorable,
And will, no doubt, with reasons answer you.
I come not, friends, to steal away your hearts.

198. dint: effect.

I am no orator, as Brutus is;   221
But, as you know me all, a plain blunt man,
That love my friend; and that they know full well
That gave me public leave to speak of him;
For I have neither wit, nor words, nor worth,
Action, nor utterance, nor the power of speech,
To stir men's blood; I only speak right on.
I tell you that which you yourselves do know;
Show you sweet Caesar's wounds, poor poor dumb mouths,
And bid them speak for me.   But were I Brutus,   230
And Brutus Antony, there were an Antony
Would ruffle up your spirits and put a tongue
In every wound of Caesar that should move
The stones of Rome to rise and mutiny.
    All.   We'll mutiny.
    First Cit.   We'll burn the house of Brutus.
    Third Cit.   Away, then! come, seek the conspirators.
    Ant.   Yet hear me, countrymen; yet hear me speak.
    All.   Peace, ho! Hear Antony. Most noble Antony!
    Ant.   Why, friends, you go to do you know not what.   240
Wherein hath Caesar thus deserved your loves?
Alas, you know not; I must tell you, then.
You have forgot the will I told you of.
    All.   Most true. The will! Let's stay and hear the will.
    Ant.   Here is the will, and under Caesar's seal.
To every Roman citizen he gives,
To every several man, seventy-five drachmas.
    Sec. Cit.   Most noble Caesar!   We'll revenge his death.
    Third Cit.   O royal Caesar!
    Ant.   Hear me with patience.   250
    All.   Peace, ho!
    Ant.   Moreover, he hath left you all his walks,
His private arbors and new-planted orchards,
On this side Tiber; he hath left them you,
And to your heirs forever, common pleasures,
To walk abroad, and recreate yourselves.
Here was a Caesar! When comes such another?
    First Cit.   Never, never. Come, away, away!
We'll burn his body in the holy place,
And with the brands fire the traitors' houses.
Take up the body.   261

      247. **seventy-five drachmas:** about fifteen dollars.

Sec. Cit. Go fetch fire.
Third Cit. Pluck down benches.
Fourth Cit. Pluck down forms, windows, any thing.
                              [*Exeunt Citizens with the body.*
Ant. Now let it work. Mischief, thou art afoot,
Take thou what course thou wilt!

Enter a Servant.

                              How now; fellow!
Serv. Sir, Octavius is already come to Rome.
Ant. Where is he?
Serv. He and Lepidus are at Caesar's house.
Ant. And thither will I straight to visit him;
He comes upon a wish. Fortune is merry,   271
And in this mood will give us any thing.
Serv. I heard him say, Brutus and Cassius
Are rid like madmen through the gates of Rome.
Ant. Belike they had some notice of the people,
How I had moved them. Bring me to Octavius.   [*Exeunt.*

SCENE III. *A street.*

Enter CINNA *the poet.*

Cin. I dreamt tonight that I did feast with Caesar,
And things unluckily charge my fantasy.
I have no will to wander forth of doors,
Yet something leads me forth.

Enter Citizens.

First Cit. What is your name?
Sec. Cit. Whither are you going?
Third Cit. Where do you dwell?
Fourth Cit. Are you a married man or a bachelor?
Sec. Cit. Answer every man directly.   10
First Cit. Ay, and briefly.
Fourth Cit. Ay, and wisely.
Third Cit. Ay, and truly, you were best.
Cin. What is my name? Whither am I going? Where do
I dwell? Am I a married man or a bachelor? Then, to

        264. **forms:** benches.   1. **tonight:** he means last night.

answer every man directly and briefly, wisely and truly:
wisely I say, I am a bachelor.

Sec. Cit. That's as much as to say, they are fools that
marry. You'll bear me a bang for that, I fear. Proceed;
directly.   21

Cin. Directly, I am going to Caesar's funeral.

First Cit. As a friend or an enemy?

Cin. As a friend.

Sec. Cit. That matter is answered directly.

Fourth Cit. For your dwelling — briefly.

Cin. Briefly, I dwell by the Capitol.

Third Cit. Your name, sir, truly.

Cin. Truly, my name is Cinna.

First Cit. Tear him to pieces; he's a conspirator.   31

Cin. I am Cinna the poet, I am Cinna the poet.

Fourth Cit. Tear him for his bad verses, tear him for his
bad verses.

Cin. I am not Cinna the conspirator.

Fourth Cit. It is no matter, his name's Cinna; pluck but
his name out of his heart, and turn him going.   39

Third Cit. Tear him, tear him! Come, brands, ho! fire-
brands. To Brutus', to Cassius'; burn all. Some to Decius'
house, and some to Casca's; some to Ligarius'. Away, go!

[*Exeunt.*

ACT IV

SCENE I.   *A house in Rome.*

ANTONY, OCTAVIUS, *and* LEPIDUS, *seated at a table.*

Ant. These many, then, shall die; their names are pricked.

Oct. Your brother too must die; consent you, Lepidus?

Lep. I do consent —

Oct.   Prick him down, Antony.

Lep. Upon condition Publius shall not live,
Who is your sister's son, Mark Antony.

Ant. He shall not live; look, with a spot I damn him.
But, Lepidus, go you to Caesar's house;
Fetch the will hither, and we shall determine

20. **bear:** receive.

How to cut off some charge in legacies.
    Lep. What, shall I find you here?   10
    Oct. Or here, or at the Capitol.   *[Exit Lepidus.*
    Ant. This is a slight unmeritable man,
Meet to be sent on errands; is it fit,
The threefold world divided, he should stand
One of the three to share it?
    Oct.   So you thought him;
And took his voice who should be pricked to die,
In our black sentence and proscription.
    Ant. Octavius, I have seen more days than you;
And though we lay these honors on this man,
To ease ourselves of divers slanderous loads,   20
He shall but bear them as the ass bears gold,
To groan and sweat under the business,
Either led or driven, as we point the way;
And having brought our treasure where we will,
Then take we down his load, and turn him off,
Like to the empty ass, to shake his ears,
And graze in commons.
    Oct.   You may do your will;
But he's a tried and valiant soldier.
    Ant. So is my horse, Octavius; and for that
I do appoint him store of provender.   30
It is a creature that I teach to fight,
To wind, to stop, to run directly on,
His corporal motion governed by my spirit.
And, in some taste, is Lepidus but so;
He must be taught and trained and bid go forth;
A barren-spirited fellow; one that feeds
On abjects, orts and imitations,
Which, out of use and staled by other men,
Begin his fashion. Do not talk of him,
But as a property. And now, Octavius,   40
Listen great things. Brutus and Cassius
Are levying powers; we must straight make head;
Therefore let our alliance be combined,
Our best friends made, our means stretched;
And let us presently go sit in council,
How covert matters may be best disclosed,
And open perils surest answeréd.

   14. **threefold world:** Europe, Asia, and Africa.   37. **abjects, etc.:** cast-off
things, fragments, and imitations.   40. **property:** stage property.

Oct. Let us do so; for we are at the stake,
And bayed about with many enemies;
And some that smile have in their hearts, I fear,   50
Millions of mischiefs.   [*Exeunt.*

Scene II. *Camp near Sardis. Before Brutus' tent.*

Drum.   Enter Brutus, Lucilius, Lucius, *and* Soldiers;
Titanius *and* Pindarus *meeting them.*

Bru. Stand, ho!
Lucil. Give the word, ho! and stand.
Bru. What now, Lucilius! is Cassius near?
Lucil. He is at hand; and Pindarus is come
To do you salutation from his master.
Bru. He greets me well. Your master, Pindarus,
In his own change, or by ill officers,
Hath given me some worthy cause to wish
Things done, undone; but, if he be at hand,
I shall be satisfied.
   Pin.   I do not doubt   10
But that my noble master will appear
Such as he is, full of regard and honor.
Bru. He is not doubted. A word, Lucilius:
How he received you, let me be resolved.
Lucil. With courtesy and with respect enough;
But not with such familiar instances,
Nor with such free and friendly conference,
As he hath used of old.
   Bru.   Thou hast described
A hot friend cooling. Ever note, Lucilius,
When love begins to sicken and decay,   20
It useth an enforcéd ceremony.
There are no tricks in plain and simple faith;
But hollow men, like horses hot at hand,
Make gallant show and promise of their mettle;
But when they should endure the bloody spur,
They fall their crests, and, like deceitful jades,
Sink in the trial. Comes his army on?

48. **at the stake:** like the bear in the popular Elizabethan sport of bear-
baiting.   The bear was tied to a stake and the dogs were set on him.
    7. **change:** change in disposition. 16. **instances:** proofs. 23. **hot at hand:**
hard to hold back.

Lucil.   They mean this night in Sardis to be quartered;
The greater part, the horse in general,
Are come with Cassius.

Bru.   Hark! he is arrived.   30

[*Low march within.*

March gently on to meet him.

Enter Cassius *and his powers.*

Cas.   Stand, ho!
Bru.   Stand, ho!   Speak the word along.
First Sol.   Stand!
Sec. Sol.   Stand!
Third Sol.   Stand!
Cas.   Most noble brother, you have done me wrong.
Bru.   Judge me, you gods! wrong I mine enemies?
And, if not so, how should I wrong a brother?
Cas.   Brutus, this sober form of yours hides wrongs;   40
And when you do them —
Bru.   Cassius, be content;
Speak your griefs softly; I do know you well.
Before the eyes of both our armies here,
Which should perceive nothing but love from us,
Let us not wrangle.   Bid them move away;
Then in my tent, Cassius, enlarge your griefs,
And I will give you audience.
Cas.   Pindarus,
Bid our commanders lead their charges off
A little from this ground.
Bru.   Lucilius, do you the like; and let no man   50
Come to our tent till we have done our conference.
Let Lucius and Titinius guard our door.   [*Exeunt.*

Scene III.   *Brutus' tent.*

Enter Brutus *and* Cassius.

Cas.   That you have wronged me doth appear in this:
You have condemned and noted Lucius Pella
For taking bribes here of the Sardians;
Wherein my letters, praying on his side,
Because I knew the man, were slighted off.
Bru.   You wronged yourself to write in such a case.

Cas.   In such a time as this it is not meet
That every nice offence should bear his comment.
   Bru.   Let me tell you, Cassius, you yourself
Are much condemned to have an itching palm;
To sell and mart your offices for gold   11
To undeservers.
   Cas.   I an itching palm!
You know that you are Brutus that speaks this,
Or, by the gods, this speech were else your last.
   Bru.   The name of Cassius honors this corruption,
And chastisement doth therefore hide his head.
   Cas.   Chastisement!
   Bru.   Remember March, the ides of March remember:
Did not great Julius bleed for justice' sake?
What villain touched his body, that did stab,   20
And not for justice?   What, shall one of us,
That struck the foremost man of all this world
But for supporting robbers, shall we now
Contaminate our fingers with base bribes,
And sell the mighty space of our large honors
For so much trash as may be graspéd thus?
I had rather be a dog, and bay the moon,
Than such a Roman.
   Cas.   Brutus, bait not me;
I'll not endure it.   You forget yourself,
To hedge me in; I am a soldier, I,   30
Older in practice, abler than yourself
To make conditions.
   Bru.   Go to; you are not, Cassius.
   Cas.   I am.
   Bru.   I say you are not.
   Cas.   Urge me no more, I shall forget myself;
Have mind upon your health, tempt me no farther.
   Bru.   Away, slight man!
   Cas.   Is 't possible?
   Bru.   Hear me, for I will speak.
Must I give way and room to your rash choler?
Shall I be frighted when a madman stares?   40
   Cas.   O ye gods, ye gods! must I endure all this?
   Bru.   All this! ay, more.   Fret till your proud heart break;

This is one of the most famous scenes in Shakespeare.   8. **nice:** trifling;
his: its.   37. **health:** safety.

Go show your slaves how choleric you are,
And make your bondmen tremble. Must I budge?
Must I observe you?   Must I stand and crouch
Under your testy humor?   By the gods,
You shall digest the venom of your spleen,
Though it do split you; for, from this day forth,
I'll use you for my mirth, yea, for my laughter,
When you are waspish.
    Cas.   Is it come to this?   50
    Bru. You say you are a better soldier:
Let it appear so; make your vaunting true,
And it shall please me well. For mine own part,
I shall be glad to learn of noble men.
    Cas. You wrong me every way; you wrong me, Brutus;
I said, an elder soldier, not a better:
Did I say " better " ?
    Bru.   If you did, I care not.
    Cas. When Caesar lived, he durst not thus have moved
me.
    Bru. Peace, peace! you durst not so have tempted him.
    Cas. I durst not!   60
    Bru. No.
    Cas. What, durst not tempt him!
    Bru.   For your life you durst not.
    Cas. Do not presume too much upon my love;
I may do that I shall be sorry for.
    Bru. You have done that you should be sorry for.
There is no terror, Cassius, in your threats,
For I am armed so strong in honesty
That they pass by me as the idle wind,
Which I respect not. I did send to you
For certain sums of gold, which you denied me;
For I can raise no money by vile means.   71
By heaven, I had rather coin my heart,
And drop my blood for drachmas, than to wring
From the hard hands of peasants their vile trash
By any indirection. I did send
To you for gold to pay my legions,
Which you denied me. Was that done like Cassius?
Should I have answered Caius Cassius so?
When Marcus Brutus grows so covetous,

    45. **observe:** i.e., must I be subservient to you? 75. **indirection:** crook-
edness.

To lock such rascal counters from his friends,   80
Be ready, gods, with all your thunderbolts;
Dash him to pieces!
    Cas.   I denied you not.
    Bru. You did.
    Cas. I did not.   He was but a fool that brought
My answer back.   Brutus hath rived my heart.
A friend should bear his friend's infirmities,
But Brutus makes mine greater than they are.
    Bru. I do not, till you practice them on me.
    Cas. You love me not.
    Bru.   I do not like your faults.
    Cas. A friendly eye could never see such faults.   90
    Bru. A flatterer's would not, though they do appear
As huge as high Olympus.
    Cas. Come, Antony, and young Octavius, come,
Revenge yourselves alone on Cassius,
For Cassius is aweary of the world;
Hated by one he loves; braved by his brother;
Checked like a bondman; all his faults observed,
Set in a notebook, learned, and conned by rote,
To cast into my teeth.   O, I could weep
My spirit from mine eyes!   There is my dagger,   100
And here my naked breast; within, a heart
Dearer than Plutus' mine, richer than gold.
If that thou be'st a Roman, take it forth;
I, that denied thee gold, will give my heart.
Strike, as thou didst at Caesar; for, I know,
When thou didst hate him worst, thou lovedst him better
Than ever thou lovedst Cassius.
    Bru.   Sheathe your dagger.
Be angry when you will, it shall have scope;
Do what you will, dishonor shall be humor.
O Cassius, you are yokéd with a lamb   110
That carries anger as the flint bears fire;
Who, much enforcéd, shows a hasty spark,
And straight is cold again.
    Cas.   Hath Cassius lived
To be but mirth and laughter to his Brutus,
When grief, and blood ill-tempered, vexeth him?
    Bru. When I spoke that, I was ill-tempered too.

80. **counters:** round pieces of metal used in counting. Here **rascal counters** means worthless money.

Cas. Do you confess so much?   Give me your hand.

Bru. And my heart too.

Cas.   O Brutus!

Bru.   What's the matter?

Cas. Have not you love enough to bear with me,
When that rash humor which my mother gave me   120
Makes me forgetful?

Bru. Yes, Cassius; and, from henceforth,
When you are over-earnest with your Brutus,
He'll think your mother chides, and leave you so.

Poet. [*Within*] Let me go in to see the generals;
There is some grudge between 'em, 'tis not meet
They be alone.

Lucil. [*Within*] You shall not come to them.

Poet. [*Within*] Nothing but death shall stay me.

Enter Poet, *followed by* LUCILIUS, TITINIUS, *and* LUCIUS.

Cas. How now! what's the matter?

Poet. For shame, you generals! what do you mean?   130
Love, and be friends, as two such men should be;
For I have seen more years, I'm sure, than ye.

Cas. Ha, ha! how vilely doth this cynic rhyme!

Bru. Get you hence, sirrah; saucy fellow, hence!

Cas. Bear with him, Brutus; 'tis his fashion.

Bru. I'll know his humor, when he knows his time.
What should the wars do with these jigging fools?
Companion, hence!

Cas.   Away, away, be gone!   [*Exit Poet.*

Bru. Lucilius and Titinius, bid the commanders
Prepare to lodge their companies tonight.   140

Cas. And come yourselves, and bring Messala with you
Immediately to us.   [*Exeunt Lucilius and Titinius.*

Bru. Lucius, a bowl of wine!   [*Exit Lucius.*

Cas. I did not think you could have been so angry.

Bru. O Cassius, I am sick of many griefs.

Cas. Of your philosophy you make no use,
If you give place to accidental evils.

Bru. No man bears sorrow better.   Portia is dead.

Cas. Ha! Portia!

Bru. She is dead.

Cas. How 'scaped I killing when I crossed you so?   150

120. **rash humor:** quick temper.   138. **companion:** fellow.

O insupportable and touching loss!
Upon what sickness?
   Bru.   Impatient of my absence,
And grief that young Octavius with Mark Antony
Have made themselves so strong, — for with her death
That tidings came, — with this she fell distract,
And, her attendants absent, swallowed fire.
   Cas. And died so?
   Bru.   Even so.
   Cas.   O ye immortal gods!

       Reënter Lucius, *with wine and taper.*

   Bru. Speak no more of her. Give me a bowl of wine.
In this I bury all unkindness, Cassius.
   Cas. My heart is thirsty for that noble pledge.   160
Fill, Lucius, till the wine o'erswell the cup;
I cannot drink too much of Brutus' love.
   Bru. Come in, Titinius!   *[Exit Lucius.*

       Reënter Titinius, *with* Messala.

                 Welcome, good Messala.
Now sit we close about this taper here,
And call in question our necessities.
   Cas. Portia, art thou gone?
   Bru.   No more, I pray you.
Messala, I have here receivéd letters,
That young Octavius and Mark Antony
Come down upon us in a mighty power,
Bending their expedition toward Philippi.   170
   Mes. Myself have letters of the selfsame tenor.
   Bru. With what addition?
   Mes. That by proscription and bills of outlawry,
Octavius, Antony, and Lepidus,
Have put to death an hundred senators.
   Bru. Therein our letters do not well agree;
Mine speak of seventy senators that died
By their proscriptions, Cicero being one.
   Cas. Cicero one!
   Mes.   Cicero is dead,
And by that order of proscription.   180
Had you your letters from your wife, my lord?
   Bru. No, Messala.

Mes.   Nor nothing in your letters writ of her?

Bru.   Nothing, Messala.

Mes.   That, methinks, is strange.

Bru.   Why ask you?   Hear you aught of her in yours?

Mes.   No, my lord.

Bru.   Now, as you are a Roman, tell me true.

Mes.   Then like a Roman bear the truth I tell:

For certain she is dead, and by strange manner.

Bru.   Why, farewell, Portia.   We must die, Messala.   190

With meditating that she must die once,

I have the patience to endure it now.

Mes.   Even so great men great losses should endure.

Cas.   I have as much of this in art as you,

But yet my nature could not bear it so.

Bru.   Well, to our work alive.   What do you think

Of marching to Philippi presently?

Cas.   I do not think it good.

Bru.   Your reason?

Cas.   This it is: 199

'Tis better that the enemy seek us.

So shall he waste his means, weary his soldiers,

Doing himself offence; whilst we, lying still,

Are full of rest, defence, and nimbleness.

Bru.   Good reasons must, of force, give place to better.

The people 'twixt Philippi and this ground

Do stand but in a forced affection,

For they have grudged us contribution.

The enemy, marching along by them,

By them shall make a fuller number up,

Come on refreshed, new-added, and encouraged;

From which advantage shall we cut him off,   210

If at Philippi we do face him there,

These people at our back.

Cas.   Hear me, good brother.

Bru.   Under your pardon.   You must note beside,

That we have tried the utmost of our friends,

Our legions are brimful, our cause is ripe.

The enemy increaseth every day;

We, at the height, are ready to decline.

There is a tide in the affairs of men,

Which, taken at the flood, leads on to fortune;

Omitted, all the voyage of their life

Is bound in shallows and in miseries.)
On such a full sea are we now afloat;
And we must take the current when it serves,
Or lose our ventures.
    Cas.   Then, with your will, go on;
We'll along ourselves, and meet them at Philippi.
    Bru. The deep of night is crept upon our talk,
And nature must obey necessity;
Which we will niggard with a little rest.
There is no more to say?
    Cas.   No more. Good night.
Early tomorrow will we rise, and hence.   230
    Bru. Lucius! [*Enter Lucius.*] My gown.
               [*Exit Lucius.*] Farewell, good Messala;
Good night, Titinius. Noble, noble Cassius,
Good night, and good repose.
    Cas.   O my dear brother!
This was an ill beginning of the night.
Never come such division 'tween our souls!
Let it not, Brutus.
    Bru.   Every thing is well.
    Cas. Good night, my lord.
    Bru.   Good night, good brother.
    Tit. Mes. Good night, Lord Brutus.
    Bru.   Farewell, every one.
            [*Exeunt all but Brutus.*

        Reënter Lucius, *with the gown.*

Give me the gown. Where is thy instrument?
    Luc. Here in the tent.
    Bru.   What, thou speak'st drowsily? 240
Poor knave, I blame thee not; thou art o'erwatched.
Call Claudius and some other of my men;
I'll have them sleep on cushions in my tent.
    Luc. Varro and Claudius!
        Enter Varro *and* Claudius.
    Var. Calls my lord?
    Bru. I pray you, sirs, lie in my tent and sleep;
It may be I shall raise you by and by
On business to my brother Cassius.
    Var. So please you, we will stand and watch your pleasure.

        228. **niggard:** indulge sparingly.

Bru. I will not have it so: lie down, good sirs;   250
It may be I shall otherwise bethink me.
Look, Lucius, here's the book I sought for so;
I put it in the pocket of my gown.

> [*Var. and Clau. lie down.*

Luc. I was sure your lordship did not give it me.
Bru. Bear with me, good boy, I am much forgetful.
Canst thou hold up thy heavy eyes awhile,
And touch thy instrument a strain or two?
Luc. Ay, my lord, an't please you.
Bru.   It does, my boy.
I trouble thee too much, but thou art willing.
Luc. It is my duty, sir.   260
Bru. I should not urge thy duty past thy might;
I know young bloods look for a time of rest.
Luc. I have slept, my lord, already.
Bru. It was well done; and thou shalt sleep again;
I will not hold thee long. If I do live,
I will be good to thee. [*Music, and a song.*
This is a sleepy tune. O murderous slumber,
Lay'st thou thy leaden mace upon my boy,
That plays thee music? Gentle knave, good night;   269
I will not do thee so much wrong to wake thee.
If thou dost nod, thou break'st thy instrument;
I'll take it from thee; and, good boy, good night.
Let me see, let me see; is not the leaf turned down
Where I left reading? Here it is, I think.

Enter the Ghost of Caesar.

How ill this taper burns! Ha! who comes here?
I think it is the weakness of mine eyes
That shapes this monstrous apparition.
It comes upon me. Art thou any thing?
Art thou some god, some angel, or some devil,
That makest my blood cold and my hair to stare?
Speak to me what thou art.   281
Ghost. Thy evil spirit, Brutus.
Bru. Why comest thou?
Ghost. To tell thee thou shalt see me at Philippi.
Bru. Well; then I shall see thee again?

241. **knave:** boy.   275. **taper:** In Shakespeare's day lights were supposed to grow dim with the approach of a ghost. 280. **stare:** stand on end.

Ghost. Ay, at Philippi.

Bru. Why, I will see thee at Philippi, then. [*Exit Ghost.*
Now I have taken heart thou vanishest.
Ill spirit, I would hold more talk with thee.
Boy, Lucius! Varro! Claudius! Sirs, awake!   290
Claudius!

Luc. The strings, my lord, are false.

Bru. He thinks he still is at his instrument.
Lucius, awake!

Luc. My lord?

Bru. Didst thou dream, Lucius, that thou so criedst out?

Luc. My lord, I do not know that I did cry.

Bru. Yes, that thou didst. Didst thou see any thing?

Luc. Nothing, my lord.

Bru. Sleep again, Lucius. Sirrah Claudius! [*To Var.*]
Fellow thou, awake!   301

Var. My lord?

Clau. My lord?

Bru. Why did you so cry out, sirs, in your sleep?

Var. Clau. Did we, my lord?

Bru.   Ay. Saw you any thing?

Var. No, my lord, I saw nothing.

Clau.   Nor I, my lord.

Bru. Go and commend me to my brother Cassius;
Bid him set on his powers betimes before,
And we will follow.

Var. Clau. It shall be done, my lord.   [*Exeunt.*

ACT V

Scene I. *The plains of Philippi.*

Enter Octavius, Antony, *and their* army.

Oct. Now, Antony, our hopes are answeréd.
You said the enemy would not come down,
But keep the hills and upper regions;
It proves not so: their battles are at hand;
They mean to warn us at Philippi here,
Answering before we do demand of them.

4. **battles:** armies; battle lines.

Ant. Tut, I am in their bosoms, and I know
Wherefore they do it. They could be content
To visit other places, and come down
With fearful bravery, thinking by this face   10
To fasten in our thoughts that they have courage;
But 'tis not so.

Enter a Messenger.

Mess.   Prepare you, generals.
The enemy comes on in gallant show;
Their bloody sign of battle is hung out,
And something to be done immediately.
Ant. Octavius, lead your battle softly on,
Upon the left hand of the even field.
Oct. Upon the right hand I; keep thou the left.
Ant. Why do you cross me in this exigent?   19
Oct. I do not cross you; but I will do so.   [*March.*

Drum. Enter Brutus, Cassius, *and their* army; Lucilius,
Titinius, Messala, *and others.*

Bru. They stand, and would have parley.
Cas. Stand fast, Titinius; we must out and talk.
Oct. Mark Antony, shall we give sign of battle?
Ant. No, Caesar, we will answer on their charge.
Make forth; the generals would have some words.
Oct. Stir not until the signal.
Bru. Words before blows; is it so, countrymen?
Oct. Not that we love words better, as you do.
Bru. Good words are better than bad strokes, Octavius.
Ant. In your bad strokes, Brutus, you give good words; 30
Witness the hole you made in Caesar's heart,
Crying " Long live! hail, Caesar! "
Cas.   Antony,
The posture of your blows are yet unknown;
But for your words, they rob the Hybla bees, ˙
And leave them honeyless.
Ant.   Not stingless too.
Bru. O, yes, and soundless too;
For you have stol'n their buzzing, Antony,
And very wisely threat before you sting.

---

10. **fearful:** cowardly. 20. **will do so:** will do as I said. This gives an
excellent touch of the character of Octavius. 34. **Hybla:** a town in Sicily
noted for its bees.

Ant. Villains, you did not so, when your vile daggers
Hacked one another in the sides of Caesar.   40
You showed your teeth like apes, and fawned like hounds,
And bowed like bondmen, kissing Caesar's feet;
Whilst damnéd Casca, like a cur, behind
Struck Caesar on the neck. O you flatterers!

Cas. Flatterers! Now, Brutus, thank yourself;
This tongue had not offended so today,
If Cassius might have ruled.

Oct. Come, come, the cause! If arguing make us sweat,
The proof of it will turn to redder drops.
Look!   50
I draw a sword against conspirators;
When think you that the sword goes up again?
Never, till Caesar's three and thirty wounds
Be well avenged; or till another Caesar
Have added slaughter to the sword of traitors.

Bru. Caesar, thou canst not die by traitors' hands,
Unless thou bring'st them with thee.

Oct.   So I hope;
I was not born to die on Brutus' sword.

Bru. O, if thou wert the noblest of thy strain,
Young man, thou couldst not die more honorable.   60

Cas. A peevish schoolboy, worthless of such honor,
Joined with a masker and a reveler!

Ant. Old Cassius still!

Oct.   Come, Antony, away!
Defiance, traitors, hurl we in your teeth.
If you dare fight today, come to the field;
If not, when you have stomachs.
                         [*Exeunt Octavius, Antony, and their army.*

Cas. Why, now, blow wind, swell billow and swim bark!
The storm is up, and all is on the hazard.

Bru. Ho, Lucilius! hark, a word with you.

Lucil. [*Standing forth*]   My lord?
                         [*Brutus and Lucilius converse apart.*

Cas. Messala!

Mes. [*Standing forth*] What says my general?

Cas. Messala.   71
This is my birthday; as this very day
Was Cassius born. Give me thy hand, Messala.

---

66. **stomachs:** courage.

Be thou my witness that against my will,
As Pompey was, am I compelled to set
Upon one battle all our liberties.
You know that I held Epicurus strong
And his opinion; now I change my mind,
And partly credit things that do presage.
Coming from Sardis, on our former ensign   80
Two mighty eagles fell, and there they perched,
Gorging and feeding from our soldiers' hands;
Who to Philippi here consorted us.
This morning are they fled away and gone;
And in their steads do ravens, crows, and kites,
Fly o'er our heads and downward look on us,
As we were sickly prey.   Their shadows seem
A canopy most fatal, under which
Our army lies, ready to give up the ghost.
  Mes.   Believe not so.
  Cas.   I but believe it partly;
For I am fresh of spirit and resolved
To meet all perils very constantly.
  Bru.   Even so, Lucilius.
  Cas.   Now, most noble Brutus,
The gods today stand friendly, that we may,
Lovers in peace, lead on our days to age!
But since the affairs of men rest still incertain,
Let's reason with the worst that may befall.
If we do lose this battle, then is this
The very last time we shall speak together.
What are you then determined to do?   100
  Bru.   Even by the rule of that philosophy
By which I did blame Cato for the death
Which he did give himself, I know not how,
But I do find it cowardly and vile,
For fear of what might fall, so to prevent
The time of life: arming myself with patience
To stay the providence of some high powers
That govern us below.
  Cas.   Then, if we lose this battle,
You are contented to be led in triumph
Thorough the streets of Rome?   110

77. **Epicurus:** a Greek philosopher who held that pleasure was the chief
end in life. Brutus was a Stoic and believed that self-denial was the supreme
virtue. 80. **former:** foremost. 92. **constantly:** firmly.

Bru. No, Cassius, no. Think not, thou noble Roman,
That ever Brutus will go bound to Rome;
He bears too great a mind. But this same day
Must end that work the ides of March begun;
And whether we shall meet again I know not.
Therefore our everlasting farewell take.
Forever, and forever, farewell, Cassius!
If we do meet again, why, we shall smile;
If not, why then, this parting was well made.
    Cas. Forever, and forever, farewell, Brutus!
If we do meet again, we'll smile indeed;   121
If not, 'tis true this parting was well made.
    Bru. Why, then, lead on. O, that a man might know
The end of this day's business ere it come!
But it sufficeth that the day will end,
And then the end is known. Come, ho! away!   [*Exeunt.*

SCENE II.   *The same. The field of battle. Alarum.*

Enter BRUTUS *and* MESSALA.

Bru. Ride, ride, Messala, ride, and give these bills
Unto the legions on the other side.   [*Loud alarum.*
Let them set on at once; for I perceive
But cold demeanor in Octavius' wing,
And sudden push gives them the overthrow.
Ride, ride, Messala: let them all come down.   [*Exeunt.*

SCENE III.   *Another part of the field.*

Alarums.   Enter CASSIUS *and* TITINIUS.

Cas. O, look, Titinius, look, the villains fly!
Myself have to mine own turned enemy:
This ensign here of mine was turning back;
I slew the coward, and did take it from him.
    Tit. O Cassius, Brutus gave the word too early;
Who, having some advantage on Octavius,

Sc. ii. 1. **bills:** dispatches.
    Sc. iii. 2. **enemy:** the flag-bearer referred to in the following line. 3. **ensign:** flag-bearer and flag. 4. **it:** flag.

Took it too eagerly. His soldiers fell to spoil,
Whilst we by Antony are all enclosed.

Enter Pindarus.

 Pin. Fly further off, my lord, fly further off;
Mark Antony is in your tents, my lord;   10
Fly, therefore, noble Cassius, fly far off.
 Cas. This hill is far enough. Look, look, Titinius;
Are those my tents where I perceive the fire?
 Tit. They are, my lord.
 Cas.   Titinius, if thou lovest me,
Mount thou my horse, and hide thy spurs in him,
Till he have brought thee up to yonder troops,
And here again; that I may rest assured
Whether yond troops are friend or enemy.
 Tit. I will be here again, even with a thought. [*Exit.*
 Cas. Go, Pindarus, get higher on that hill;
My sight was ever thick; regard Titinius,   21
And tell me what thou notest about the field.
          [*Pindarus ascends the hill.*
This day I breathéd first; time is come round,
And where I did begin, there shall I end;
My life is run his compass. Sirrah, what news?
 Pin. [*Above*] O my lord!
 Cas. What news?
 Pin. [*Above*] Titinius is encloséd round about
With horsemen, that make to him on the spur;
Yet he spurs on. Now they are almost on him.
Now, Titinius! Now some light. O, he lights too. 31
He's ta'en. [*Shout.*] And, hark! they shout for joy.
 Cas. Come down, behold no more.
O, coward that I am, to live so long,
To see my best friend ta'en before my face!

Pindarus *descends.*

Come hither, sirrah.
In Parthia did I take thee prisoner;
And then I swore thee, saving of thy life,
That whatsoever I did bid thee do,
Thou shouldst attempt it. Come now, keep thine oath; 40
Now be a freeman; and with this good sword,
That ran through Caesar's bowels, search this bosom.

Stand not to answer; here, take thou the hilts;
And, when my face is covered, as 'tis now,
Guide thou the sword. [*Pindarus stabs him.*]   Caesar, thou
    art revenged,
Even with the sword that killed thee.   [*Dies.*
    Pin. So, I am free; yet would not so have been,
Durst I have done my will. O Cassius,
Far from this country Pindarus shall run,   49
Where never Roman shall take note of him.   [*Exit.*

                Reënter TITINIUS *with* MESSALA.

    Mes. It is but change, Titinius; for Octavius
Is overthrown by noble Brutus' power,
As Cassius' legions are by Antony.
    Tit. These tidings will well comfort Cassius.
    Mes. Where did you leave him?
    Tit.   All disconsolate,
With Pindarus his bondman, on this hill.
    Mes. Is not that he that lies upon the ground?
    Tit. He lies not like the living. O my heart!
    Mes. Is not that he?
    Tit.   No, this was he, Messala,
But Cassius is no more. O setting sun,   60
As in thy red rays thou dost sink to night,
So in his red blood Cassius' day is set;
The sun of Rome is set! Our day is gone;
Clouds, dews, and dangers come; our deeds are done!
Mistrust of my success hath done this deed.
    Mes. Mistrust of good success hath done this deed.
O hateful error, melancholy's child,
Why dost thou show to the apt thoughts of men
The things that are not? O error, soon conceived,
Thou never comest unto a happy birth,   70
But kill'st the mother that engendered thee!
    Tit. What, Pindarus! Where art thou, Pindarus?
    Mes. Seek him, Titinius, whilst I go meet
The noble Brutus, thrusting this report
Into his ears; I may say, thrusting it;
For piercing steel and darts envenomed
Shall be as welcome to the ears of Brutus
As tidings of this sight.
    Tit.   Hie you, Messala,

And I will seek for Pindarus the while.   [*Exit Messala.*
Why didst thou send me forth, brave Cassius?   80
Did I not meet thy friends? and did not they
Put on my brows this wreath of victory,
And bid me give it thee?   Didst thou not hear their shouts?
Alas, thou hast misconstrued every thing!
But, hold thee, take this garland on thy brow;
Thy Brutus bid me give it thee, and I
Will do his bidding.   Brutus, come apace,
And see how I regarded Caius Cassius.
By your leave, gods! — this is a Roman's part.
Come, Cassius' sword, and find Titinius' heart.   [*Kills himself.*

Alarum.   Reënter MESSALA, *with* BRUTUS, *young* CATO,
STRATO, VOLUMNIUS, *and* LUCILIUS.

Bru.   Where, where, Messala, doth his body lie?   91
Mes.   Lo, yonder, and Titinius mourning it.
Bru.   Titinius' face is upward.
Cato.   He is slain.
Bru.   O Julius Caesar, thou art mighty yet!
Thy spirit walks abroad, and turns our swords
In our own proper entrails.   [*Low alarums.*
Cato.   Brave Titinius!
Look, whether he have not crowned dead Cassius!
Bru.   Are yet two Romans living such as these?
The last of all the Romans, fare thee well!
It is impossible that ever Rome   100
Should breed thy fellow.   Friends, I owe more tears
To this dead man than you shall see me pay.
I shall find time, Cassius, I shall find time.
Come, therefore, and to Thasos send his body;
His funerals shall not be in our camp,
Lest it discomfort us.   Lucilius, come;
And come, young Cato; let us to the field.
Labeo and Flavius, set our battles on.
'Tis three o'clock; and, Romans, yet ere night
We shall try fortune in a second fight.   [*Exeunt.*

SCENE IV. *Another part of the field.*

Alarum.   Enter fighting, Soldiers *of both armies; then*
BRUTUS, *young* CATO, LUCILIUS, *and others.*

Bru. Yet, countrymen, O, yet hold up your heads!
Cato. What bastard doth not?   Who will go with me?
I will proclaim my name about the field.
I am the son of Marcus Cato, ho!
A foe to tyrants, and my country's friend;
I am the son of Marcus Cato, ho!
Bru. And I am Brutus, Marcus Brutus, I;
Brutus, my country's friend; know me for Brutus!   [*Exit.*
Lucil. O young and noble Cato, art thou down?
Why, now thou diest as bravely as Titinius;   10
And mayst be honored, being Cato's son.
First Sold. Yield, or thou diest.
Lucil.   Only I yield to die:
There is so much that thou wilt kill me straight;
                                        [*Offering money.*
Kill Brutus, and be honored in his death.
First Sold. We must not.   A noble prisoner!
Sec. Sold. Room, ho!   Tell Antony, Brutus is ta'en.
First Sold. I'll tell the news.   Here comes the general.

Enter ANTONY.

Brutus is ta'en, Brutus is ta'en, my lord.
Ant. Where is he?
Lucil. Safe, Antony; Brutus is safe enough.
I dare assure thee that no enemy   21
Shall ever take alive the noble Brutus;
The gods defend him from so great a shame!
When you do find him, or alive or dead,
He will be found like Brutus, like himself.
Ant. This is not Brutus, friend; but, I assure you,
A prize no less in worth.   Keep this man safe;
Give him all kindness; I had rather have
Such men my friends than enemies.   Go on,
And see whether Brutus be alive or dead;   30
And bring us word unto Octavius' tent
How every thing is chanced.   [*Exeunt.*

The second fight actually took place twenty days later, but for dramatic
purposes Shakespeare combined them.   12. **Only I yield:** I yield only to die.
32. **is chanced:** has turned out.

Scene V. *Another part of the field.*

Enter Brutus, Dardanius, Clitus, Strato, *and* Volumnius.

  Bru. Come, poor remains of friends, rest on this rock.
  Cli. Statilius showed the torch-light, but, my lord,
He came not back. He is or ta'en or slain.
  Bru. Sit thee down, Clitus; slaying is the word;
It is a deed in fashion. Hark thee, Clitus.   [*Whispers.*
  Cli. What, I, my lord? No, not for all the world.
  Bru. Peace then! no words.
  Cli.   I'll rather kill myself.
  Bru. Hark thee, Dardanius.   [*Whispers.*
  Dar.   Shall I do such a deed?
  Cli. O Dardanius!
  Dar. O Clitus!   10
  Cli. What ill request did Brutus make to thee?
  Dar. To kill him, Clitus. Look, he meditates.
  Cli. Now is that noble vessel full of grief,
That it runs over even at his eyes.
  Bru. Come hither, good Volumnius; list a word.
  Vol. What says my lord?
  Bru.   Why, this, Volumnius:
The ghost of Caesar hath appeared to me
Two several times by night; at Sardis once,
And, this last night, here in Philippi fields.
I know my hour is come.
  Vol.   Not so, my lord.   20
  Bru. Nay, I am sure it is, Volumnius.
Thou seest the world, Volumnius, how it goes;
Our enemies have beat us to the pit.   [*Low alarums.*
It is more worthy to leap in ourselves,
Than tarry till they push us. Good Volumnius,
Thou know'st that we two went to school together;
Even for that our love of old, I prithee,
Hold thou my sword-hilts, whilst I run on it.
  Vol. That's not an office for a friend, my lord.
                                  [*Alarum still.*
  Cli. Fly, fly, my lord; there is no tarrying here.   30
  Bru. Farewell to you; and you; and you, Volumnius.
Strato, thou hast been all this while asleep;
Farewell to thee too, Strato. Countrymen,
My heart doth joy that yet in all my life

I found no man but he was true to me.
I shall have glory by this losing day
More than Octavius and Mark Antony
By this vile conquest shall attain unto.
So fare you well at once; for Brutus' tongue
Hath almost ended his life's history.   40
Night hangs upon mine eyes; my bones would rest,
That have but labored to attain this hour.
                    [*Alarum.   Cry within, " Fly, fly, fly! "*
   Cli.   Fly, my lord, fly.
   Bru.   Hence!   I will follow.
                    [*Exeunt Clitus, Dardanius, and Volumnius.*
I prithee, Strato, stay thou by thy lord.
Thou art a fellow of a good respect;
Thy life hath had some smatch of honor in it.
Hold then my sword, and turn away thy face,
While I do run upon it.   Wilt thou, Strato?
   Stra.   Give me your hand first.   Fare you well, my lord.
   Bru.   Farewell, good Strato.   [*Runs on his sword.*]
Caesar, now be still;   50
I killed not thee with half so good a will.   [*Dies.*

   Alarum.   Retreat.   Enter Octavius, Antony, Messala,
                    Lucilius, *and the* army.

   Oct.   What man is that?
   Mes.   My master's man.   Strato, where is thy master?
   Stra.   Free from the bondage you are in, Messala;
The conquerors can but make a fire of him;
For Brutus only overcame himself,
And no man else hath honor by his death.
   Lucil.   So Brutus should be found.   I thank thee, Brutus,
That thou hast proved Lucilius' saying true.
   Oct.   All that served Brutus, I will entertain them.   60
Fellow, wilt thou bestow thy time with me?
   Stra.   Ay, if Messala will prefer me to you.
   Oct.   Do so, good Messala.
   Mes.   How died my master, Strato?
   Stra.   I held the sword, and he did run on it.
   Mes.   Octavius, then take him to follow thee,
That did the latest service to my master.

   45. **respect:** reputation. 60. **entertain:** receive. 62. **prefer:** recommend.

Ant. This was the noblest Roman of them all.
All the conspirators save only he
Did that they did in envy of great Caesar;　　　　　70
He only, in a general honest thought
And common good to all, made one of them.
His life was gentle, and the elements
So mixed in him that Nature might stand up
And say to all the world, " This was a man! "
　Oct. According to his virtue let us use him,
With all respect and rites of burial.
Within my tent his bones tonight shall lie,
Most like a soldier, ordered honorably.
So call the field to rest; and let's away,　　　　　80
To part the glories of this happy day.　　　　[*Exeunt.*

81. **to part:** divide.

INTERPRETATIVE NOTE

The story of the death of Julius Caesar was popular with the Elizabethans, and a number of plays on the subject had appeared before
1601, when Shakespeare wrote the play we know today. In form it is
like his chronicle plays; that is, plays taken more or less literally from
actual history. In *Julius Caesar* the dramatist follows his authority
with remarkable fidelity, drawing on Plutarch's *Lives* of Caesar, Antony,
and Brutus. Many of Plutarch's actual expressions, as they are to be
found in the later edition of North's translation (1595), are used by
Shakespeare. On the other hand, the speech of Brutus and that of
Antony are not given in Plutarch at all, but merely the statement that
they made speeches. The quarrel scene in the last act is also almost
wholly Shakespeare's. The amplification of these three episodes shows
how clear was the author's sense of dramatic values, for these scenes
have always been the most popular with audiences and actors alike.

The student who has formed his ideals of Caesar from the *Commentaries* will have to readjust them when he tries to appreciate Shakespeare's play. In the *Commentaries* Caesar is a successful man of action,
and that holds true until his last triumph. In the play he is the successful man at home, receiving the highest honors that the public could
bestow, but remaining unsatisfied. For the general status of affairs in
the Roman Republic at this time the student must consult his history.
It is too long a story to go into here. Suffice it to say that Caesar
and his immediate admirers must have felt that the old ideals of the
republic were at so low an ebb that a *coup d'état* might be successfully
carried out. At any rate, Caesar was ambitious to be king in name as
well as in fact, and that weak human foible constitutes the motive of
one part of the play.

On the other hand, the senatorial party, headed by such men as
Brutus, Cassius, and Cicero, stood for the republic. Of the three,
Cicero has practically no part in the play, so that the element of
struggle is provided for chiefly by Brutus and Cassius. The characters
of these two men Shakespeare has portrayed in no uncertain terms.
Brutus is a scholar, a philosopher, and a thinker rather than a man of
action; his character is irreproachable, and he has been honored by high
office. Cassius, too, is a scholar and a student of philosophy, but where
Brutus had followed the Stoics, who presented the more serious reflec-
tions on life, Cassius was an Epicurean, although by no means deceived
by their maxim, " Eat, drink, and be merry, for tomorrow ye die." He
was serious enough, but personally selfish and politically ambitious. As
a politician he had been unsuccessful, in the main, largely through his
personality, and a known tendency toward trickery. He mouthed
republican ideals beautifully enough to deceive Brutus and the rest, but
Shakespeare took care that the reader was not equally deceived.

The nominal hero, Caesar, appears in only three short scenes of the
play, and in each Shakespeare emphasized what was undoubtedly his
weakest trait, the desire to be named king. It was easy for Brutus and
Cassius to get a following. Besides certain malcontents who had personal grudges against Caesar, there were such swashbucklers as Casca,

the type that is easily stirred by street-corner orators and the waving
of the flag, without understanding exactly what is going on. It is
Casca who delivers the first blow. Then he is heard of no more.
Brutus gave the final thrust, and with the death of Caesar fondly hoped
that Caesarism was dead also.

Up to this point the character of Brutus has been the dominating
force. Without him the conspiracy could never have functioned. That
was one reason why Cassius had resorted to every possible trick to get
him into the plot. That Cassius was justified is proved by Brutus'
speech in the forum. This remarkable bit of high-minded patriotism
rang so true that the fickle mob was carried away by it momentarily,
but the true situation in Rome develops when Mark Antony, with
studied eloquence, inflames the mob by appealing to their motives of
selfish gain. Small wonder that Brutus and Cassius fled precipitately.

The struggle now nominally becomes one of revenge for the death of
Caesar. How patriotic the revengers are is shown by the cold-blooded
scene at the opening of Act IV, in which they plan a division of the
spoils before there really are any. The forces of Brutus and Cassius
have to be defeated, and the scene in Brutus' tent leaves no doubt in
the reader's mind as to the outcome. Their cause is foreordained to
defeat because republican ideals in Rome are dead, and the time is at
hand for a capable and diplomatic leader to step in and grasp absolute
power. This man was Octavius, later known as Augustus.

QUESTIONS

I. i.

1. Does this scene make a lively opening? Comment.
2. In Shakespeare's day puns were popular on the stage. Are they now?
3. What hints do you note about Caesar?
4. For full effect, the speech of Marullus should be read aloud.

I. ii.

1. What first impression do you get of Caesar? of Antony?
2. This scene affords a key to the characters of Brutus and Cassius. Study it carefully.
3. What does Brutus mean by being " with himself at war "?
4. Why is Cassius so long-winded in making his point to Brutus?
5. How does Brutus unconsciously encourage him to go on?
6. What else, during this conversation, helps Cassius?
7. Does Cassius' plea for equality ring true, or does it smack of political jealousy?
8. Write out in detail Caesar's estimate of Cassius.
9. How does Casca impress you?
10. What plot elements do you find so far?

I. iii.

1. What interesting contrast between Casca and Cicero?
2. How does Cassius work on Casca?
3. What was Cassius' theory about suicide? Was he sincere?

4. Why was Cassius so eager to have Brutus join the conspirators?
5. What elements of plot struggle are becoming evident?

II. i.

1. In your own words, what is Brutus' summing up of the situation as to Caesar?
2. How does it compare with that of Cassius?
3. Note Brutus' estimate of Cicero.
4. Read aloud Brutus' speech, lines 162–83, and carefully note the points.
5. Why does Cassius yield on the question of not killing Antony?
6. Does Portia deserve the full confidence of her husband?
7. Why was this one circumstance withheld from her?

II. ii.

1. How does Calpurnia compare with Portia? Be definite.
2. Did Decius present a good argument for Caesar's going to the Capitol?
3. Is there anything of plot value in this scene?

II. iii.

1. What of dramatic value in this scene?
2. Was Artemidorus a person of consequence in Rome?

II. iv.

1. Why is Portia so distracted?
2. Had Brutus kept his promise of confiding fully in her? Be definite.

III. i.

1. How does Artemidorus defeat his own purpose?
2. Note what traits of Caesar are stressed in this scene.
3. What is the connection of Publius Cimber with the action?
4. Visualize the action on the stage as the conspirators gradually close in on Caesar.
5. Who stabbed Caesar first? last?
6. How do you see the action on the stage after the stabbing?
7. How did the conspirators announce " Peace, freedom and liberty " ?
8. Do you think the method effective? Comment.
9. After Caesar's death, what occupies chief place in the mind of Brutus? Cassius? Explain.
10. With the death of Caesar, Mark Antony becomes one of the important characters.
11. Who is the cleverer politician, Cassius or Antony?
12. What prophecy does Antony make?
13. Sum up your estimate of Antony from the latter part of the scene.
14. What new plot angle is suggested by the mention of Octavius?
15. Do " the people " receive any consideration from the leaders? Explain.

III. ii.

1. Read the speech of Brutus aloud. What qualities in it carried the mob with him?

2. This is one of the two great scenes in the play. Note the important part played by the mob.
3. Antony's speech makes good reciting. What qualities make it so?
4. The mob had been entirely with Brutus. How does Antony at first court their sympathies?
5. Is there anything theatrical about Antony's manner?
6. How is the mob finally swung over entirely? Comment.
7. What does Antony say about his own oratory? Comment.
8. Why did Antony's words have an effect on the mob different from that of Brutus'? Be definite.
9. What is your own feeling as to the relative merits of the two speeches?
10. Why does he say that Octavius " comes upon a wish " ? How does he say it?
11. At this point, are your sympathies with Antony or with Brutus? Explain.

III. iii.

1. What does this scene contribute to the action of the play?
2. State concisely how the various elements of the plot stand at the end of this act.

IV. i.

1. Caesar is dead, but Caesarism lives. How can you verify that statement from this scene?
2. Explain what is meant by " Caesarism."
3. How does Antony's first remark in this scene compare with his eloquence in the previous act?
4. Do you find it necessary to readjust your estimate of Antony?
5. Who shows up the worse, Antony or Octavius? Explain.

IV. ii.

1. Give a brief general statement of what has happened since the death of Caesar.
2. Do you note any changes in Brutus? Think twice before you answer.

IV. iii.

1. Apply question 2 of the previous scene to all of Scene iii.
2. This is the best scene of the play. Argue for or against that statement.
3. Select some of the more interesting details of the quarrel, and comment.
4. Was the accusation against Cassius probably true?
5. Why does Cassius " endure all this " from Brutus?
6. What had Cassius really said, " elder " or " better " ? In either case, was he right?
7. What was the real basis of the quarrel? How was it patched?
8. How had Brutus received the news of Portia's death? Why is Cassius so astonished at the news?
9. Lines 218–21 are famous. Learn them.
10. Why does Cassius give in so readily to the battle plan of Brutus?

11. What is the dramatic significance of the ghost?
12. Once more, how did Brutus show up in this scene? Cassius?

V. i.

1. What do you note in the relationship between Antony and Octavius?
2. These military scenes are difficult to play. How do you picture them?
3. What does Cassius mean by lines 45–47?
4. What character does Cassius give Antony at this point? Do you recall a similar reference to Antony earlier in the play?
5. What did Antony mean by " Old Cassius still " ?
6. Is the farewell scene effective? Comment.

V. ii.

1. Is any dramatic purpose served by this short scene?

V. iii.

1. The action speeds up. Note carefully all its twists and turns.
2. From the apparent action of Titinius, as reported by Pindarus, was Cassius justified in his conclusions? Comment.
3. What had really happened to Titinius?
4. Did Cassius earlier in the play refer to suicide?
5. Why did Titinius kill himself? Why was it " a Roman's part " ?
6. Why should Brutus call Cassius " the last of all the Romans " ?
7. What is your final estimate of Cassius?

V. iv.

1. Does Lucilius really want to be killed? Explain.
2. Why does he impersonate Brutus?

V. v.

1. Describe briefly the last moments of Brutus.
2. As a revolutionist and a soldier, what two great mistakes can you lay against him? Be specific.
3. From the point of view of idealism, contrast him with Cassius and Antony.
4. In your own words, why does Antony call him " the noblest Roman of them all " ?
5. How many deaths in this play? Compare with other Shakespeare tragedies you have read.
6. In your opinion, who is the real hero of this play? Be prepared to defend your answer.

THE MERCHANT OF VENICE

DRAMATIS PERSONAE

THE DUKE OF VENICE.
THE PRINCE OF MOROCCO \ suitors to
THE PRINCE OF ARRAGON / Portia.
ANTONIO, a merchant of Venice.
BASSANIO, his friend, suitor likewise
   to Portia.
SALANIO \
SALARINO | friends to Antonio and
GRATIANO } Bassanio.
SALERIO /
LORENZO, in love with Jessica.
SHYLOCK, a rich Jew.
TUBAL, a Jew, his friend.

LAUNCELOT GOBBO, the clown,
   servant to Shylock.
OLD GOBBO, father to Launcelot.
LEONARDO, servant to Bassanio.
BALTHASAR \
STEPHANO } servants to Portia.
PORTIA, a rich heiress.
NERISSA, her waiting-maid.
JESSICA, daughter to Shylock.
Magnificoes of Venice, Officers of
   the Court of Justice, Jailer,
   Servants to Portia, and other
   Attendants.

SCENE: *Partly at Venice, and partly at Belmont, the seat of Portia, on
the Continent.*

ACT I

SCENE I. *Venice. A street.*

Enter ANTONIO, SALARINO, *and* SALANIO.

Ant. In sooth, I know not why I am so sad.
It wearies me; you say it wearies you;
But how I caught it, found it, or came by it,
What stuff 'tis made of, whereof it is born,
I am to learn;
And such a want-wit sadness makes of me,
That I have much ado to know myself.
   Salar. Your mind is tossing on the ocean;
There, where your argosies with portly sail,
Like signiors and rich burghers on the flood,   10
Or, as it were, the pageants of the sea,
Do overpeer the petty traffickers,
That curtsy to them, do them reverence,
As they fly by them with their woven wings.
   Salan. Believe me, sir, had I such venture forth,
The better part of my affections would

1. **sad:** serious. 9. **argosies:** merchant ships, contrasted with **petty
traffickers** in l. 12. 16. **affections:** feelings.

Be with my hopes abroad. I should be still
Plucking the grass to know where sits the wind,
Peering in maps for ports and piers and roads;
And every object that might make me fear   20
Misfortune to my ventures, out of doubt
Would make me sad.
   Salar.   My wind cooling my broth
Would blow me to an ague, when I thought
What harm a wind too great at sea might do.
I should not see the sandy hourglass run,
But I should think of shallows and of flats,
And see my wealthy Andrew docked in sand,
Vailing her high-top lower than her ribs
To kiss her burial. Should I go to church
And see the holy edifice of stone,   30
And not bethink me straight of dangerous rocks,
Which touching but my gentle vessel's side,
Would scatter all her spices on the stream,
Enrobe the roaring waters with my silks,
And, in a word, but even now worth this,
And now worth nothing? Shall I have the thought
To think on this, and shall I lack the thought
That such a thing bechanced would make me sad?
But tell not me; I know, Antonio
Is sad to think upon his merchandise.   40
   Ant. Believe me, no. I thank my fortune for it,
My ventures are not in one bottom trusted,
Nor to one place; nor is my whole estate
Upon the fortune of this present year:
Therefore my merchandise makes me not sad.
   Salar. Why, then you are in love.
   Ant.   Fie, fie!
   Salar. Not in love neither? Then let us say you are sad
Because you are not merry; and 'twere as easy
For you to laugh and leap and say you are merry,
Because you are not sad. Now, by two-headed Janus,   50
Nature hath framed strange fellows in her time:
Some that will evermore peep through their eyes
And laugh like parrots at a bagpiper,
And other of such vinegar aspect

19. **roads:** harbors.   27. **Andrew:** name of an imaginary ship.   28. **vailing:** lowering.   50. **Janus:** god of gates, represented as facing in opposite directions.

That they'll not show their teeth in way of smile,
Though Nestor swear the jest be laughable.

Enter BASSANIO, LORENZO, *and* GRATIANO.

Salan. Here comes Bassanio, your most noble kinsman,
Gratiano and Lorenzo. Fare ye well;
We leave you now with better company.
Salar. I would have stayed till I had made you merry, 60
If worthier friends had not prevented me.
Ant. Your worth is very dear in my regard.
I take it, your own business calls on you
And you embrace the occasion to depart.
Salar. Good morrow, my good lords.
Bass. Good signiors both, when shall we laugh? say, when?
You grow exceeding strange. Must it be so?
Salar. We'll make our leisures to attend on yours.
                    [*Exeunt Salarino and Salanio.*
Lor. My Lord Bassanio, since you have found Antonio,
We two will leave you; but at dinner-time,   70
I pray you, have in mind where we must meet.
Bass. I will not fail you.
Gra. You look not well, Signior Antonio;
You have too much respect upon the world.
They lose it that do buy it with much care.
Believe me, you are marvelously changed.
Ant. I hold the world but as the world, Gratiano;
A stage where every man must play a part,
And mine a sad one.
Gra.   Let me play the fool!
With mirth and laughter let old wrinkles come,
And let my liver rather heat with wine   81
Than my heart cool with mortifying groans.
Why should a man, whose blood is warm within,
Sit like his grandsire cut in alabaster?
Sleep when he wakes and creep into the jaundice
By being peevish? I tell thee what, Antonio —
I love thee, and it is my love that speaks —
There are a sort of men whose visages

56. **Nestor:** the oldest of the wise men among the Greeks before Troy.
61. **prevented:** been ahead of me. 67. **grow exceeding strange:** act like
strangers. 70. **dinner-time:** between eleven and twelve in the morning.
74. **respect upon:** regard for. 79. **fool:** professional jester. 81. **liver:**
thought to be the seat of the emotions.

Do cream and mantle like a standing pond,
And do a wilful stillness entertain,   90
With purpose to be dressed in an opinion
Of wisdom, gravity, profound conceit,
As who should say, " I am Sir Oracle,
And when I ope my lips let no dog bark! "
O my Antonio, I do know of these
That therefore only are reputed wise
For saying nothing, when, I am very sure,
If they should speak, would almost damn those ears
Which, hearing them, would call their brothers fools.
I'll tell thee more of this another time;   100
But fish not, with this melancholy bait,
For this fool gudgeon, this opinion.
Come, good Lorenzo. Fare ye well awhile;
I'll end my exhortation after dinner.

   Lor.   Well, we will leave you then till dinner-time:
I must be one of these same dumb wise men,
For Gratiano never lets me speak.

   Gra.   Well, keep me company but two years moe,
Thou shalt not know the sound of thine own tongue.

   Ant.   Farewell! I'll grow a talker for this gear.   110

   Gra.   Thanks, i' faith, for silence is only commendable
In a neat's tongue dried and a maid not vendible.
                    [*Exeunt Gratiano and Lorenzo.*

   Ant.   Is that any thing now?

   Bass.   Gratiano speaks an infinite deal of nothing, more
than any man in all Venice. His reasons are as two grains of
wheat hid in two bushels of chaff: you shall seek all day ere
you find them, and when you have them, they are not worth
the search.

   Ant.   Well, tell me now what lady is the same
To whom you swore a secret pilgrimage   120
That you today promised to tell me of?

   Bass.   'Tis not unknown to you, Antonio,
How much I have disabled mine estate,
By something showing a more swelling port
Than my faint means would grant continuance.
Nor do I now make moan to be abridged
From such a noble rate; but my chief care

90. **wilful, etc.:** purposely remain silent.   91. **opinion:** reputation.   102. **gudgeon:** a stupid worthless fish.   110. **gear:** matter.   124. **showing, etc.:** living more expensively.   126. **to be abridged:** to cut down.

Is to come fairly off from the great debts
Wherein my time something too prodigal
Hath left me gaged. To you, Antonio,   130
I owe the most, in money and in love,
And from your love I have a warranty
To unburden all my plots and purposes
How to get clear of all the debts I owe.

    Ant. I pray you, good Bassanio, let me know it;
And if it stand, as you yourself still do,
Within the eye of honor, be assured,
My purse, my person, my extremest means,
Lie all unlocked to your occasions.

    Bass. In my school-days, when I had lost one shaft, 140
I shot his fellow of the selfsame flight
The selfsame way with more adviséd watch,
To find the other forth, and by adventuring both
I oft found both. I urge this childhood proof,
Because what follows is pure innocence.
I owe you much, and, like a wilful youth,
That which I owe is lost; but if you please
To shoot another arrow that self way
Which you did shoot the first, I do not doubt,
As I will watch the aim, or to find both   150
Or bring your latter hazard back again
And thankfully rest debtor for the first.

    Ant. You know me well, and herein spend but time
To wind about my love with circumstance;
And out of doubt you do me now more wrong
In making question of my uttermost
Than if you had made waste of all I have.
Then do but say to me what I should do
That in your knowledge may by me be done,
And I am prest unto it; therefore, speak.   160

    Bass. In Belmont is a lady richly left;
And she is fair and, fairer than that word,
Of wondrous virtues. Sometimes from her eyes
I did receive fair speechless messages.
Her name is Portia, nothing undervalued
To Cato's daughter, Brutus' Portia.
Nor is the wide world ignorant of her worth,

---

139. **still:** always. 145. **innocence:** foolishness. 154. **circumstance:**
roundabout talk. 160. **prest unto:** ready to do it.

For the four winds blow in from every coast
Renownéd suitors, and her sunny locks
Hang on her temples like a golden fleece,   170
Which makes her seat of Belmont Colchos' strand,
And many Jasons come in quest of her.
O my Antonio, had I but the means
To hold a rival place with one of them,
I have a mind presages me such thrift,
That I should questionless be fortunate!
  Ant. Thou know'st that all my fortunes are at sea;
Neither have I money nor commodity
To raise a present sum. Therefore go forth;
Try what my credit can in Venice do: 180
That shall be racked, even to the uttermost,
To furnish thee to Belmont, to fair Portia.
Go, presently inquire, and so will I,
Where money is, and I no question make
To have it of my trust or for my sake.   [*Exeunt.*

Scene II. *Belmont. A room in* Portia's *house.*

Enter Portia *and* Nerissa.

  Por. By my troth, Nerissa, my little body is aweary of
this great world.

  Ner. You would be, sweet madam, if your miseries were
in the same abundance as your good fortunes are; and yet,
for aught I see, they are as sick that surfeit with too much as
they that starve with nothing. It is no mean happiness, therefore, to be seated in the mean. Superfluity comes sooner by
white hairs, but competency lives longer.   10

  Por. Good sentences and well pronounced.

  Ner. They would be better, if well followed.

  Por. If to do were as easy as to know what were good to
do, chapels had been churches and poor men's cottages princes'
palaces. It is a good divine that follows his own instructions;
I can easier teach twenty what were good to be done, than be
one of the twenty to follow mine own teaching. The brain
may devise laws for the blood, but a hot temper leaps o'er a

170. **golden fleece:** for the story of Jason and the Golden Fleece see
cyclopedia. 175. **presages, etc.:** promises success. 178. **commodity:** merchandise. 181. **racked:** stretched.
  9. **in the mean:** neither rich nor poor. 11. **sentences:** maxims.

cold decree; such a hare is madness the youth, to skip o'er the meshes of good counsel the cripple.   But this reasoning is not in the fashion to choose me a husband.   O me, the word " choose " !   I may   neither choose whom I would nor refuse whom I dislike; so is the will of a living daughter curbed by the will of a dead father.   Is it not hard, Nerissa, that I cannot choose one nor refuse none?   29

Ner.   Your father was ever virtuous, and holy men at their death have good inspirations; therefore the lottery, that he hath devised in these three chests of gold, silver, and lead, whereof who chooses his meaning chooses you, will, no doubt, never be chosen by any rightly but one who shall rightly love. But what warmth is there in your affection towards any of these princely suitors that are already come?

Por.   I pray thee, over-name them; and as thou namest them, I will describe them; and, according to my description, level at my affection.

Ner.   First, there is the Neapolitan prince.

Por.   Ay, that's a colt indeed, for he doth nothing but talk of his horse; and he makes it a great appropriation to his own good parts, that he can shoe him himself.   I am much afeard my lady his mother played false with a smith.

Ner.   Then there is the County Palatine.   49

Por.   He doth nothing but frown, as who should say, " If you will not have me, choose "; he hears merry tales and smiles not.   I fear he will prove the weeping philosopher when he grows old, being so full of unmannerly sadness in his youth. I had rather be married to a death's-head with a bone in his mouth than to either of these.   God defend me from these two!

Ner.   How say you by the French lord, Monsieur Le Bon?

Por.   God made him, and therefore let him pass for a man. In truth, I know it is a sin to be a mocker; but, he! why, he hath a horse better than the Neapolitan's, a better bad habit of frowning than the Count Palatine; he is every man in no man; if a throstle sing, he falls straight a-capering.   He will fence with his own shadow.   If I should marry him, I should marry twenty husbands.   If he would despise me, I would forgive him, for if he love me to madness, I shall never requite him.   70

---

42. **level at:** pass judgment on.   46. **appropriation:** addition.   51. **choose:** do as you please.   53. **weeping philosopher:** Heraclitus (500 B.C.).

Ner. What say you, then, to Falconbridge, the young baron of England?

Por. You know I say nothing to him, for he understands not me, nor I him. He hath neither Latin, French, nor Italian, and you will come into the court and swear that I have a poor pennyworth in the English. He is a proper man's picture, but, alas, who can converse with a dumb-show? How oddly he is suited! I think he bought his doublet in Italy, his round hose in France, his bonnet in Germany and his behavior everywhere.

Ner. What think you of the Scottish lord, his neighbor?

Por. That he hath a neighborly charity in him, for he borrowed a box of the ear of the Englishman and swore he would pay him again when he was able. I think the Frenchman became his surety and sealed under for another.

Ner. How like you the young German, the Duke of Saxony's nephew?   91

Por. Very vilely in the morning, when he is sober, and most vilely in the afternoon, when he is drunk. When he is best, he is a little worse than a man, and when he is worst, he is little better than a beast. An the worst fall that ever fell, I hope I shall make shift to go without him.

Ner. If he should offer to choose, and choose the right casket, you should refuse to perform your father's will, if you should refuse to accept him.

Por. Therefore, for fear of the worst, I pray thee, set a deep glass of Rhenish wine on the contrary casket, for if the devil be within and that temptation without, I know he will choose it. I will do any thing, Nerissa, ere I'll be married to a sponge.

Ner. You need not fear, lady, the having any of these lords. They have acquainted me with their determinations; which is, indeed, to return to their home and to trouble you with no more suit, unless you may be won by some other sort than your father's imposition depending on the caskets.   115

Por. If I live to be as old as Sibylla, I will die as chaste as Diana, unless I be obtained by the manner of my father's will. I am glad this parcel of wooers are so reasonable, for there is not one among them but I dote on his very absence, and I pray God grant them a fair departure.

76. **proper:** handsome. 98. **casket:** jewel box. 116. **Sibylla:** a Roman prophetess to whom Apollo allotted as many years of life as she could hold grains of sand in her hand.

Ner. Do you not remember, lady, in your father's time, a Venetian, a scholar and a soldier, that came hither in company of the Marquis of Montferrat?

Por. Yes, yes, it was Bassanio; as I think, he was so called.

Ner. True, madam. He, of all the men that ever my foolish eyes looked upon, was the best deserving a fair lady. 131

Por. I remember him well, and I remember him worthy of thy praise.

Enter a Serving-man.

How now! what news?

Serv. The four strangers seek for you, madam, to take their leave; and there is a forerunner come from a fifth, the Prince of Morocco, who brings word the prince his master will be here tonight. 139

Por. If I could bid the fifth welcome with so good a heart as I can bid the other four farewell, I should be glad of his approach. If he have the condition of a saint and the complexion of a devil, I had rather he should shrive me than wive me.

Come, Nerissa. Sirrah, go before.

Whiles we shut the gates upon one wooer, another knocks at the door. [*Exeunt.*

SCENE III. *Venice. A public place.*

Enter BASSANIO *and* SHYLOCK.

Shy. Three thousand ducats; well.

Bass. Ay, sir, for three months.

Shy. For three months; well.

Bass. For the which, as I told you, Antonio shall be bound.

Shy. Antonio shall become bound; well.

Bass. May you stead me? Will you pleasure me? Shall I know your answer?

Shy. Three thousand ducats for three months and Antonio bound. 10

Bass. Your answer to that.

Shy. Antonio is a good man.

Bass. Have you heard any imputation to the contrary?

Shy. Oh, no, no, no, no! My meaning in saying he is a good man is to have you understand me that he is sufficient.

1. **ducat:** about one dollar. 6. **stead:** help.

Yet his means are in supposition: he hath an argosy bound to
Tripolis, another to the Indies; I understand, moreover, upon
the Rialto, he hath a third at Mexico, a fourth for England,
and other ventures he hath, squandered abroad. But ships
are but boards, sailors but men: there be land-rats and water-
rats, water-thieves and land-thieves, I mean pirates, and then
there is the peril of waters, winds and rocks. The man is,
notwithstanding, sufficient. Three thousand ducats; I think
I may take his bond.

Bass. Be assured you may.   29

Shy. I will be assured I may; and, that I may be assured,
I will bethink me. May I speak with Antonio?

Bass. If it please you to dine with us.

Shy. Yes, to smell pork; to eat of the habitation which
your prophet the Nazarite conjured the devil into. I will buy
with you, sell with you, talk with you, walk with you, and so
following, but I will not eat with you, drink with you, nor
pray with you. What news on the Rialto? Who is he comes
here?   40

Enter ANTONIO.

Bass. This is Signior Antonio.

Shy. [*Aside*] How like a fawning publican he looks!
I hate him for he is a Christian,
But more for that in low simplicity
He lends out money gratis and brings down
The rate of usance here with us in Venice.
If I can catch him once upon the hip,
I will feed fat the ancient grudge I bear him.
He hates our sacred nation, and he rails,
Even there where merchants most do congregate,   50
On me, my bargains and my well-won thrift,
Which he calls interest. Curséd be my tribe,
If I forgive him!

Bass.   Shylock, do you hear?

Shy. I am debating of my present store,
And, by the near guess of my memory,
I cannot instantly raise up the gross
Of full three thousand ducats. What of that?

20. **in supposition:** in doubt because not at hand. 22. **Rialto:** the Exchange. 23. **squandered:** scattered. 42. **fawning:** cringing as though to
court favor. 42. **publican:** Roman tax collector, hated by Jews. Of course
Antonio does not "fawn." 46. **usance:** interest. In Shakespeare's day it
was still considered wicked to take interest for money lent.

Tubal, a wealthy Hebrew of my tribe,
Will furnish me. But soft! how many months
Do you desire? [*To Ant.*] Rest you fair, good signior;   60
Your worship was the last man in our mouths.
   Ant. Shylock, although I neither lend nor borrow
By taking nor by giving of excess,
Yet, to supply the ripe wants of my friend,
I'll break a custom. Is he yet possessed
How much ye would?
   Shy.   Ay, ay, three thousand ducats.
   Ant. And for three months.
   Shy. I had forgot; three months; you told me so.
Well then, your bond; and let me see; but hear you;
Methought you said you neither lend nor borrow
Upon advantage.
   Ant.   I do never use it.   71
   Shy. When Jacob grazed his uncle Laban's sheep —
This Jacob from our holy Abram was,
As his wise mother wrought in his behalf,
The third possessor; ay, he was the third —
   Ant. And what of him? did he take interest?
   Shy. No, not take interest, not, as you would say,
Directly interest. Mark what Jacob did.
When Laban and himself were compromised
That all the eanlings which were streaked and pied   80
Should fall as Jacob's hire, the ewes, being rank,
In the end of autumn turned to the rams,
And, when the work of generation was
Between these woolly breeders in the act,
The skilful shepherd peeled me certain wands
And, in the doing of the deed of kind,
He stuck them up before the fulsome ewes,
Who then conceiving did in eaning time
Fall parti-colored lambs, and those were Jacob's.
This was a way to thrive, and he was blest: 90
And thrift is blessing, if men steal it not.
   Ant. This was a venture, sir, that Jacob served for;
A thing not in his power to bring to pass,
But swayed and fashioned by the hand of Heaven.
Was this inserted to make interest good?
Or is your gold and silver ewes and rams?

                80. **eanlings:** newborn lambs.

Shy.   I cannot tell; I make it breed as fast.
But note me, signior.
    Ant.   Mark you this, Bassanio,
The devil can cite Scripture for his purpose.
An evil soul producing holy witness   100
Is like a villain with a smiling cheek,
A goodly apple rotten at the heart.
O what a goodly outside falsehood hath!
    Shy.   Three thousand ducats; 'tis a good round sum.
Three months from twelve; then, let me see; the rate —
    Ant.   Well, Shylock, shall we be beholding to you?
    Shy.   Signior Antonio, many a time and oft
In the Rialto you have rated me
About my moneys and my usances.
Still have I borne it with a patient shrug,   110
For sufferance is the badge of all our tribe.
You call me misbeliever, cutthroat dog,
And spit upon my Jewish gaberdine,
And all for use of that which is mine own.
Well then, it now appears you need my help.
Go to, then; you come to me, and you say,
"Shylock, we would have moneys," you say so;
You, that did void your rheum upon my beard
And foot me as you spurn a stranger cur
Over your threshold; moneys is your suit.   120
What should I say to you?   Should I not say,
"Hath a dog money?   Is it possible
A cur can lend three thousand ducats?"   Or
Shall I bend low and in a bondman's key,
With bated breath and whispering humbleness,
Say this:
"Fair sir, you spit on me on Wednesday last;
You spurned me such a day; another time
You called me dog; and for these courtesies
I'll lend you thus much moneys"?   130
    Ant.   I am as like to call thee so again,
To spit on thee again, to spurn thee too.
If thou wilt lend this money, lend it not
As to thy friends; for when did friendship take
A breed for barren metal of his friend?

108. **rated:** berated.   111. **sufferance:** endurance.   113. **gaberdine:** loose
outer cloak.   118. **void, etc.:** spit.

But lend it rather to thine enemy,
Who, if he break, thou mayst with better face
Exact the penalty.
    Shy.   Why, look you, how you storm!
I would be friends with you and have your love,
Forget the shames that you have stained me with,   140
Supply your present wants and take no doit
Of usance for my moneys, and you'll not hear me.
This is kind I offer.
    Bass.   This were kindness.
    Shy.   This kindness will I show.
Go with me to a notary, seal me there
Your single bond; and, in a merry sport,
If you repay me not on such a day,
In such a place, such sum or sums as are
Expressed in the condition, let the forfeit
Be nominated for an equal pound   150
Of your fair flesh, to be cut off and taken
In what part of your body pleaseth me.
    Ant.   Content, i' faith; I'll seal to such a bond
And say there is much kindness in the Jew.
    Bass.   You shall not seal to such a bond for me;
I'll rather dwell in my necessity.
    Ant.   Why, fear not, man; I will not forfeit it.
Within these two months, that's a month before
This bond expires, I do expect return
Of thrice three times the value of this bond.   160
    Shy.   O father Abram, what these Christians are
Whose own hard dealings teaches them suspect
The thoughts of others! Pray you, tell me this:
If he should break his day, what should I gain
By the exaction of the forfeiture?
A pound of man's flesh taken from a man
Is not so estimable, profitable neither,
As flesh of muttons, beefs, or goats. I say,
To buy his favor, I extend this friendship.
If he will take it, so; if not, adieu;   170
And, for my love, I pray you wrong me not.
    Ant.   Yes, Shylock, I will seal unto this bond.
    Shy.   Then meet me forthwith at the notary's;

   141. **doit**: a coin worth one-quarter cent. 146. **single bond**: guaranteed
by the maker only.

Give him direction for this merry bond,
And I will go and purse the ducats straight,
See to my house, left in the fearful guard
Of an unthrifty knave, and presently
I will be with you.
    Ant. Hie thee, gentle Jew.   [*Exit Shylock.*
The Hebrew will turn Christian; he grows kind.
    Bass. I like not fair terms and a villain's mind.   180
    Ant. Come on; in this there can be no dismay;
My ships come home a month before the day.   [*Exeunt.*

ACT II

Scene I. *Belmont. A room in* Portia's *house.*

Flourish of cornets. Enter the Prince of Morocco *and his
    train;* Portia, Nerissa, *and others attending.*

    Mor. Mislike me not for my complexion,
The shadowed livery of the burnished sun,
To whom I am a neighbor and near bred.
Bring me the fairest creature northward born,
Where Phoebus' fire scarce thaws the icicles,
And let us make incision for your love,
To prove whose blood is reddest, his or mine.
I tell thee, lady, this aspect of mine
Hath feared the valiant. By my love, I swear
The best-regarded virgins of our clime   10
Have loved it too. I would not change this hue,
Except to steal your thoughts, my gentle queen.
    Por. In terms of choice I am not solely led
By nice direction of a maiden's eyes;
Besides, the lottery of my destiny
Bars me the right of voluntary choosing.
But if my father had not scanted me
And hedged me by his wit, to yield myself
His wife who wins me by that means I told you,
Yourself, renownèd prince, then stood as fair   20
As any comer I have looked on yet
For my affection.

    Flourish: a few notes on a horn to indicate the entrance or exit of persons
of importance.

Mor.   Even for that I thank you.
Therefore, I pray you, lead me to the caskets
To try my fortune. By this scimitar
That slew the Sophy and a Persian prince
That won three fields of Sultan Solyman,
I would outstare the sternest eyes that look,
Outbrave the heart most daring on the earth,
Pluck the young sucking cubs from the she-bear,
Yea, mock the lion when he roars for prey,   30
To win thee, lady. But, alas the while!
If Hercules and Lichas play at dice
Which is the better man, the greater throw
May turn by fortune from the weaker hand.
So is Alcides beaten by his page;
And so may I, blind fortune leading me,
Miss that which one unworthier may attain,
And die with grieving.
Por.   You must take your chance,
And either not attempt to choose at all
Or swear before you choose, if you choose wrong
Never to speak to lady afterward   41
In way of marriage; therefore be advised.
Mor. Nor will not. Come, bring me unto my chance.
Por. First, forward to the temple. After dinner
Your hazard shall be made.
Mor.   Good fortune then!
To make me blest or cursed'st among men.

[*Cornets, and exeunt.*

SCENE II. *Venice. A street.*

Enter LAUNCELOT.

Laun. Certainly my conscience will serve me to run from
this Jew my master. The fiend is at mine elbow and tempts
me, saying to me, " Gobbo, Launcelot Gobbo, good Launcelot,"
or " good Gobbo," or " Good Launcelot Gobbo, use your legs,
take the start, run away." My conscience says, "No; take
heed, honest Launcelot; take heed, honest Gobbo," or, as
aforesaid, " Honest Launcelot Gobbo, do not run; scorn running with thy heels." Well, the most courageous fiend bids me

35. **Alcides:** Hercules.   43. **Nor will not:** i.e., will not be " advised," or
cautious.

pack. " Via! " says the fiend; " away! " says the fiend; " for
the heavens, rouse up a brave mind," says the fiend, " and
run."   Well, my conscience, hanging about the neck of my
heart, says very wisely to me, " My honest friend Launcelot,
being an honest man's son," or rather an honest woman's son;
for, indeed, my father did something smack, something grow
to, he had a kind of taste; well, my conscience says, " Launcelot, budge not."   " Budge," says the fiend.   " Budge not,"
says my conscience.   " Conscience," say I, " you counsel
well."   " Fiend," say I, " you counsel well."   To be ruled by
my conscience, I should stay with the Jew my master, who,
God bless the mark, is a kind of devil; and, to run away from
the Jew, I should be ruled by the fiend, who, saving your
reverence, is the devil himself.   Certainly the Jew is the very
devil incarnal; and, in my conscience, my conscience is but
a kind of hard conscience, to offer to counsel me to stay with
the Jew.   The fiend gives the more friendly counsel.   I will
run, fiend; my heels are at your command; I will run.   33

Enter Old Gobbo, *with a basket.*

Gob.   Master young man, you, I pray you, which is the
way to master Jew's?

Laun.   [*Aside*] O heavens, this is my true-begotten father!
who, being more than sand-blind, high-gravel blind, knows me
not.   I will try confusions with him.

Gob.   Master young gentleman, I pray you, which is the
way to master Jew's?   41

Laun.   Turn up on your right hand at the next turning, but
at the next turning of all, on your left; marry, at the very
next turning, turn of no hand, but turn down indirectly to the
Jew's house.

Gob.   By God's sonties, 'twill be a hard way to hit.   Can
you tell me whether one Launcelot, that dwells with him, dwell
with him or no?   49

Laun.   Talk you of young Master Launcelot? [*Aside*] Mark
me now; now will I raise the waters.   Talk you of young
Master Launcelot?

Gob.   No master, sir, but a poor man's son.   His father,
though I say it, is an honest exceeding poor man, and, God be
thanked, well to live.

Part of the humor of this scene lies in the extraordinary misuse of words by
both father and son.   Most of them are self-evident.   38. **sand-blind:** half-
blind.   39. **confusions:** conclusions.   44. **marry:** by Mary, a mild oath
common in Shakespeare.   47. **sonties:** saints.

Laun.   Well, let his father be what a' will, we talk of young Master Launcelot.

Gob.   Your worship's friend and Launcelot, sir.

Laun.   But I pray you, ergo, old man, ergo, I beseech you, talk you of young Master Launcelot?   60

Gob.   Of Launcelot, an 't please your mastership.

Laun.   Ergo, Master Launcelot. Talk not of Master Launcelot, father; for the young gentleman, according to Fates and Destinies and such odd sayings, the Sisters Three and such branches of learning, is indeed deceased, or, as you would say in plain terms, gone to heaven.

Gob.   Marry, God forbid! The boy was the very staff of my age, my very prop.   70

Laun.   Do I look like a cudgel or a hovelpost, a staff or a prop? Do you know me, father?

Gob.   Alack the day, I know you not, young gentleman; but, I pray you, tell me, is my boy, God rest his soul, alive or dead?

Laun.   Do you not know me, father?

Gob.   Alack, sir, I am sand-blind; I know you not.

Laun.   Nay, indeed, if you had your eyes, you might fail of the knowing me. It is a wise father that knows his own child. Well, old man, I will tell you news of your son. Give me your blessing; truth will come to light; murder cannot be hid long; a man's son may, but at the length truth will out.

Gob.   Pray you, sir, stand up. I am sure you are not Launcelot, my boy.

Laun.   Pray you, let's have no more fooling about it, but give me your blessing. I am Launcelot, your boy that was, your son that is, your child that shall be.   91

Gob.   I cannot think you are my son.

Laun.   I know not what I shall think of that; but I am Launcelot, the Jew's man, and I am sure Margery your wife is my mother.

Gob.   Her name is Margery, indeed. I'll be sworn, if thou be Launcelot, thou art mine own flesh and blood. Lord worshiped might he be! what a beard hast thou got! Thou hast got more hair on thy chin than Dobbin my fill-horse has on his tail.   101

---

59. **ergo:** therefore. 64. **father:** used here as a familiar term for old man. In l. 72 it is used literally. 100. **fill-horse:** shaft-horse. Old Gobbo was feeling the back of his son's head, Launcelot having waggishly knelt backward for his father's blessing.

Laun. It should seem, then, that Dobbin's tail grows backward. I am sure he had more hair of his tail than I have of my face when I last saw him.

Gob. Lord, how art thou changed! How dost thou and thy master agree? I have brought him a present. How 'gree you now?

Laun. Well, well: but, for mine own part, as I have set up my rest to run away, so I will not rest till I have run some ground. My master's a very Jew. Give him a present! give him a halter. I am famished in his service; you may tell every finger I have with my ribs. Father, I am glad you are come; give me your present to one Master Bassanio, who, indeed, gives rare new liveries. If I serve not him, I will run as far as God has any ground. O rare fortune! here comes the man. To him, father; for I am a Jew, if I serve the Jew any longer.

Enter Bassanio, *with* Leonardo *and other followers.*

Bass. You may do so; but let it be so hasted that supper be ready at the farthest by five of the clock. See these letters delivered; put the liveries to making, and desire Gratiano to come anon to my lodging.   [*Exit a Servant.*

Laun. To him, father.

Gob. God bless your worship!

Bass. Gramercy! wouldst thou aught with me?

Gob. Here's my son, sir, a poor boy —   129

Laun. Not a poor boy, sir, but the rich Jew's man; that would, sir, as my father shall specify —

Gob. He hath a great infection, sir, as one would say, to serve —

Laun. Indeed, the short and the long is, I serve the Jew, and have a desire, as my father shall specify —

Gob. His master and he, saving your worship's reverence, are scarce cater-cousins —   139

Laun. To be brief, the very truth is that the Jew, having done me wrong, doth cause me, as my father, being, I hope, an old man, shall frutify unto you —

Gob. I have here a dish of doves that I would bestow upon your worship, and my suit is —

Laun. In very brief, the suit is impertinent to myself, as

108. **set up my rest:** staked my all. 139. **scarce cater-cousins:** not on intimate terms. 142. **frutify:** Launcelot's variation for "specify."

your worship shall know by this honest old man; and, though
I say it, though old man, yet poor man, my father.

Bass. One speak for both. What would you?

Laun. Serve you, sir.   151

Gob. That is the very defect of the matter, sir.

Bass. I know thee well; thou hast obtained thy suit.
Shylock thy master spoke with me this day,
And hath preferred thee, if it be preferment
To leave a rich Jew's service, to become
The follower of so poor a gentleman.

Laun. The old proverb is very well parted between my
master Shylock and you, sir: you have the grace of God, sir,
and he hath enough.

Bass. Thou speak'st it well. Go, father, with thy son. 161
Take leave of thy old master and inquire
My lodging out. Give him a livery
More guarded than his fellows'; see it done.

Laun. Father, in. I cannot get a service, no; I have
ne'er a tongue in my head. Well, if any man in Italy have
a fairer table which doth offer to swear upon a book, I shall
have good fortune. Go to, here's a simple line of life! Here's
a small trifle of wives! Alas, fifteen wives is nothing; eleven
widows and nine maids is a simple coming-in for one man.
And then to 'scape drowning thrice, and to be in peril of my
life with the edge of a featherbed; here are simple scapes.
Well, if Fortune be a woman, she's a good wench for this gear.
Father, come; I'll take my leave of the Jew in the twinkling
of an eye.   [*Exeunt Launcelot and Old Gobbo.*

Bass. I pray thee, good Leonardo, think on this:
These things being bought and orderly bestowed,
Return in haste, for I do feast tonight   180
My best-esteemed acquaintance. Hie thee, go.

Leon. My best endeavors shall be done herein.

Enter GRATIANO.

Gra. Where is your master?

Leon.   Yonder, sir, he walks. [*Exit.*

Gra. Signior Bassanio!

Bass. Gratiano!

---

164. **guarded:** trimmed. 167. **table:** the palm of his hand. Through the
rest of this speech Launcelot is reading his own fortune by the lines of his hand,
and finds that fortune exceedingly good!

Gra. I have a suit to you.

Bass. You have obtained it.

Gra. You must not deny me; I must go with you to Belmont.

Bass. Why, then you must. But hear thee, Gratiano:
Thou art too wild, too rude and bold of voice —
Parts that become thee happily enough   191
And in such eyes as ours appear not faults;
But where thou art not known, why, there they show
Something too liberal. Pray thee, take pain
To allay with some cold drops of modesty
Thy skipping spirit, lest through thy wild behavior
I be misconstrued in the place I go to
And lose my hopes.

Gra. Signior Bassanio, hear me:
If I do not put on a sober habit,   199
Talk with respect and swear but now and then,
Wear prayer-books in my pocket, look demurely,
Nay more, while grace is saying, hood mine eyes
Thus with my hat, and sigh and say " Amen,"
Use all the observance of civility,
Like one well studied in a sad ostent
To please his grandam, never trust me more.

Bass. Well, we shall see your bearing.

Gra. Nay, but I bar tonight: you shall not gauge me
By what we do tonight.

Bass. No, that were pity.
I would entreat you rather to put on   210
Your boldest suit of mirth, for we have friends
That purpose merriment. But fare you well!
I have some business.

Gra. And I must to Lorenzo and the rest;
But we will visit you at supper-time.   [*Exeunt.*

SCENE III. *The same. A room in* SHYLOCK'S *house.*

Enter JESSICA *and* LAUNCELOT.

Jes. I am sorry thou wilt leave my father so.
Our house is hell, and thou, a merry devil,
Didst rob it of some taste of tediousness.
But fare thee well, there is a ducat for thee;

205. **sad ostent:** serious look.

And, Launcelot, soon at supper shalt thou see
Lorenzo, who is thy new master's guest.
Give him this letter; do it secretly;
And so farewell. I would not have my father
See me in talk with thee.   9
   Laun. Adieu! tears exhibit my tongue. Most beautiful
pagan, most sweet Jew! if a Christian did not play the knave
and get thee, I am much deceived. But, adieu! These foolish
drops do something drown my manly spirit. Adieu.
   Jes. Farewell, good Launcelot.   [*Exit Launcelot.*
Alack, what heinous sin is it in me
To be ashamed to be my father's child!
But though I am a daughter to his blood,
I am not to his manners. O Lorenzo,
If thou keep promise, I shall end this strife,   20
Become a Christian and thy loving wife.   [*Exit.*

SCENE IV. *The same. A street.*

Enter GRATIANO, LORENZO, SALARINO, *and* SALANIO.

   Lor. Nay, we will slink away in supper-time,
Disguise us at my lodging and return,
All in an hour.
   Gra. We have not made good preparation.
   Salar. We have not spoke us yet of torch-bearers.
   Salan. 'Tis vile, unless it may be quaintly ordered,
And better in my mind not undertook.
   Lor. 'Tis now but four o'clock; we have two hours
To furnish us.

Enter LAUNCELOT, *with a letter.*

Friend Launcelot, what's the news?
   Laun. An it shall please you to break up this, it shall seem
to signify.   11
   Lor. I know the hand; in faith, 'tis a fair hand;
And whiter than the paper it writ on
Is the fair hand that writ.
   Gra.   Love-news, in faith.
   Laun. By your leave, sir.

Sc. iii. 10. **exhibit:** Launcelot was saying " Tears speak for me."
Sc. iv. 6. **quaintly:** skilfully. 10. **break up:** break open.

Lor. Whither goest thou?

Laun. Marry, sir, to bid my old master the Jew to sup
tonight with my new master the Christian.

Lor. Hold, here, take this. Tell gentle Jessica
I will not fail her; speak it privately. Go. [*Exit Launcelot.*
Gentlemen,
Will you prepare you for this masque tonight?
I am provided of a torch-bearer.

Salar. Ay, marry, I'll be gone about it straight.

Salan. And so will I.

Lor.   Meet me and Gratiano
At Gratiano's lodging some hour hence.

Salar. 'Tis good we do so.   [*Exeunt Salar. and Salan.*

Gra. Was not that letter from fair Jessica?

Lor. I must needs tell thee all. She hath directed   30
How I shall take her from her father's house,
What gold and jewels she is furnished with,
What page's suit she hath in readiness.
If e'er the Jew her father come to heaven,
It will be for his gentle daughter's sake;
And never dare misfortune cross her foot,
Unless she do it under this excuse,
That she is issue to a faithless Jew.
Come, go with me; peruse this as thou goest.
Fair Jessica shall be my torch-bearer.   [*Exeunt.*

SCENE V. *The same. Before* SHYLOCK'S *house.*

Enter SHYLOCK *and* LAUNCELOT.

Shy. Well, thou shalt see, thy eyes shall be thy judge,
The difference of old Shylock and Bassanio. —
What, Jessica! — Thou shalt not gormandize,
As thou hast done with me, — what, Jessica! —
And sleep and snore, and rend apparel out; —
Why, Jessica, I say!

Laun.   Why, Jessica!

Shy. Who bids thee call? I do not bid thee call.

---

23. **masque:** a spectacular play, but here the word has rather the sense of
"carnival." 37. **she:** refers to misfortune, here personified. 38. **faithless:**
unbelieving.
3. **What:** an exclamation of impatience when calling some one. 5. **rend:**
wear.

Laun. Your worship was wont to tell me that I could do
nothing without bidding.

Enter JESSICA.

Jes. Call you? What is your will?   10
Shy. I am bid forth to supper, Jessica.
There are my keys. But wherefore should I go?
I am not bid for love; they flatter me;
But yet I'll go in hate, to feed upon
The prodigal Christian. Jessica, my girl,
Look to my house. I am right loath to go.
There is some ill a-brewing towards my rest,
For I did dream of money-bags tonight.
Laun. I beseech you, sir, go. My young master doth
expect your reproach.   20
Shy. So do I his.
Laun. And they have conspired together. I will not say
you shall see a masque; but if you do, then it was not for
nothing that my nose fell a-bleeding on Black Monday last at
six o'clock i' the morning, falling out that year on Ash Wednes-
day was four year, in the afternoon.
Shy. What, are there masques? Hear you me, Jessica.
Lock up my doors; and when you hear the drum
And the vile squealing of the wry-necked fife,   30
Clamber not you up to the casements then,
Nor thrust your head into the public street
To gaze on Christian fools with varnished faces,
But stop my house's ears, I mean my casements.
Let not the sound of shallow foppery enter
My sober house. By Jacob's staff, I swear,
I have no mind of feasting forth tonight;
But I will go. Go you before me, sirrah;
Say I will come.
Laun. I will go before, sir. Mistress, look out at window,
for all this: 41
     There will come a Christian by,
     Will be worth a Jewess' eye.   [*Exit.*
Shy. What says that fool of Hagar's offspring, ha?
Jes. His words were " Farewell, mistress "; nothing else.
Shy. The patch is kind enough, but a huge feeder;

18. **tonight:** last night. In l. 37 it is used in the modern sense. 46.
patch: fool.

Snail-slow in profit, and he sleeps by day
More than the wild-cat; drones hive not with me;
Therefore I part with him, and part with him
To one that I would have him help to waste   50
His borrowed purse. Well, Jessica, go in.
Perhaps I will return immediately.
Do as I bid you; shut doors after you;
Fast bind, fast find;
A proverb never stale in thrifty mind.   [*Exit.*

   Jes. Farewell; and if my fortune be not crost,
I have a father, you a daughter, lost.   [*Exit.*

Scene VI. *The same.*

Enter Gratiano *and* Salarino, *masqued.*

   Gra. This is the penthouse under which Lorenzo
Desired us to make stand.
   Salar.   His hour is almost past.
   Gra. And it is marvel he out-dwells his hour,
For lovers ever run before the clock.
   Salar. O, ten times faster Venus' pigeons fly
To seal love's bonds new-made, than they are wont
To keep obligéd faith unforfeited!
   Gra. That ever holds. Who riseth from a feast
With that keen appetite that he sits down?
Where is the horse that doth untread again   10
His tedious measures with the unbated fire
That he did pace them first? All things that are,
Are with more spirit chased than enjoyed.
How like a younker or a prodigal
The scarféd bark puts from her native bay,
Hugged and embracéd by the strumpet wind,
How like the prodigal doth she return,
With over-weathered ribs and ragged sails,
Lean, rent and beggared by the strumpet wind!
   Salar. Here comes Lorenzo; more of this hereafter.   20

1. **penthouse:** a sloping roof extending from a wall.   5. **Venus' pigeons:**
in mythology the goddess of love's chariot was drawn by pigeons.   7. **pledged:**
obliged.   14. **younker:** youngster.   15. **scarped bark:** boat decorated with
pennants.

Enter Lorenzo.

Lor. Sweet friends, your patience for my long abode;
Not I, but my affairs, have made you wait.
When you shall please to play the thieves for wives,
I'll watch as long for you then.   Approach;
Here dwells my father Jew. Ho! who's within?

Enter Jessica, *above, in boy's clothes.*

Jes. Who are you? Tell me, for more certainty,
Albeit I'll swear that I do know your tongue.
Lor. Lorenzo and thy love.
Jes. Lorenzo, certain, and my love indeed,
For who love I so much? And now who knows
But you, Lorenzo, whether I am yours?   31
Lor. Heaven and thy thoughts are witness that thou art.
Jes. Here, catch this casket; it is worth the pains.
I am glad 'tis night, you do not look on me,
For I am much ashamed of my exchange.
But love is blind and lovers cannot see
The pretty follies that themselves commit;
For if they could, Cupid himself would blush
To see me thus transforméd to a boy.
Lor. Descend, for you must be my torch-bearer.   40
Jes. What, must I hold a candle to my shames?
They in themselves, good sooth, are too too light.
Why, 'tis an office of discovery, love;
And I should be obscured.
Lor.   So are you, sweet,
Even in the lovely garnish of a boy.
But come at once;
For the close night doth play the runaway,
And we are stayed for at Bassanio's feast.
Jes. I will make fast the doors, and gild myself
With some more ducats, and be with you straight.   50
                                              [*Exit above.*
Gra. Now, by my hood, a Gentile and no Jew.
Lor. Beshrew me but I love her heartily;
For she is wise, if I can judge of her,
And fair she is, if that mine eyes be true,
And true she is as she hath proved herself,

43. **office, etc.**: a torchbearer's duty is to show the way, and I ought to
remain obscured.

And therefore, like herself, wise, fair and true,
Shall she be placéd in my constant soul.

Enter JESSICA, *below.*

What, art thou come? On, gentlemen; away!
Our masquing mates by this time for us stay.
                         [*Exit with Jessica and Salarino.*

Enter ANTONIO.

  Ant. Who's there?   60
  Gra. Signior Antonio!
  Ant. Fie, fie, Gratiano! where are all the rest?
'Tis nine o'clock; our friends all stay for you.
No masque tonight; the wind is come about;
Bassanio presently will go aboard.
I have sent twenty out to seek for you.
  Gra. I am glad on 't. I desire no more delight
Than to be under sail and gone tonight.   [*Exeunt.*

SCENE VII. *Belmont. A room in* PORTIA'S *house.*

Flourish of cornets. Enter PORTIA, *with the* PRINCE OF
MOROCCO, *and their trains.*

  Por. Go draw aside the curtains and discover
The several caskets to this noble prince.
Now make your choice.
  Mor. The first, of gold, who this inscription bears,
" Who chooseth me shall gain what many men desire ";
The second, silver, which this promise carries,
" Who chooseth me shall get as much as he deserves;"
This third, dull lead, with warning all as blunt,
" Who chooseth me must give and hazard all he hath."
How shall I know if I do choose the right?   10
  Por. The one of them contains my picture, prince:
If you choose that, then I am yours withal.
  Mor. Some god direct my judgment! Let me see;
I will survey the inscriptions back again.
What says this leaden casket?
" Who chooseth me must give and hazard all he hath."
Must give: for what? for lead? hazard for lead?
This casket threatens. Men that hazard all
Do it in hope of fair advantages;

A golden mind stoops not to shows of dross;   20
I'll then nor give nor hazard aught for lead.
What says the silver with her virgin hue?
" Who chooseth me shall get as much as he deserves."
As much as he deserves!   Pause there, Morocco,
And weigh thy value with an even hand.
If thou be'st rated by thy estimation,
Thou dost deserve enough; and yet enough
May not extend so far as to the lady;
And yet to be afeared of my deserving
Were but a weak disabling of myself.   30
As much as I deserve!   Why, that's the lady.
I do in birth deserve her, and in fortunes,
In graces and in qualities of breeding;
But more than these, in love I do deserve.
What if I strayed no further, but chose here?
Let's see once more this saying graved in gold:
" Who chooseth me shall gain what many men desire."
Why, that's the lady; all the world desires her;
From the four corners of the earth they come
To kiss this shrine, this mortal-breathing saint;
The Hyrcanian deserts and the vasty wilds   41
Of wide Arabia are as throughfares now
For princes to come view fair Portia.
The watery kingdom, whose ambitious head
Splits in the face of heaven, is no bar
To stop the foreign spirits, but they come,
As o'er a brook, to see fair Portia.
One of these three contains her heavenly picture.
Is 't like that lead contains her?   'Twere damnation
To think so base a thought.   It were too gross
To rib her cerecloth in the obscure grave.   51
Or shall I think in silver she's immured,
Being ten times undervalued to tried gold?
O sinful thought!   Never so rich a gem
Was set in worse than gold.   They have in England
A coin that bears the figure of an angel
Stamped in gold, but that's insculped upon;
But here an angel in a golden bed
Lies all within.   Deliver me the key.

50–51. **too gross, etc.:** lead is too coarse to contain even her corpse.
53. **ten times undervalued:** silver was only one-tenth the value of gold.
57. **insculped upon:** engraved on the outside.

Here do I choose, and thrive I as I may! 60
  Por. There, take it, prince; and if my form lie there,
Then I am yours.

> [*He unlocks the golden casket.*

  Mor.   O hell! what have we here?
A carrion Death, within whose empty eye
There is a written scroll! I'll read the writing.
[*Reads*] " All that glisters is not gold;
          Often have you heard that told.
          Many a man his life hath sold
          But my outside to behold.
          Gilded tombs do worms infold,
          Had you been as wise as bold, 70
          Young in limbs, in judgment old,
          Your answer had not been inscrolled.
          Fare you well; your suit is cold."

    Cold, indeed; and labor lost:
        Then, farewell, heat, and welcome, frost!
Portia, adieu. I have too grieved a heart
To take a tedious leave; thus losers part.

> [*Exit with his train. Flourish of cornets.*

  Por. A gentle riddance. Draw the curtains, go.
Let all of his complexion choose me so.   [*Exeunt.*

SCENE VIII. *Venice. A street.*

Enter SALARINO *and* SALANIO.

  Salar. Why, man, I saw Bassanio under sail.
With him is Gratiano gone along;
And in their ship I am sure Lorenzo is not.
  Salan. The villain Jew with outcries raised the duke,
Who went with him to search Bassanio's ship.
  Salar. He came too late, the ship was under sail;
But there the duke was given to understand
That in a gondola were seen together
Lorenzo and his amorous Jessica.
Besides, Antonio certified the duke 10
They were not with Bassanio in his ship.
  Salan. I never heard a passion so confused,

63. **carrion Death:** skull.

So strange, outrageous, and so variable,
As the dog Jew did utter in the streets:
" My daughter!   O my ducats!   O my daughter!
Fled with a Christian!   O my Christian ducats!
Justice! the law! my ducats, and my daughter!
A sealed bag, two sealed bags of ducats,
Of double ducats, stolen from me by my daughter!
And jewels, two stones, two rich and precious stones,   20
Stolen by my daughter!   Justice! find the girl;
She hath the stones upon her, and the ducats."
  Salar.   Why, all the boys in Venice follow him,
Crying, his stones, his daughter, and his ducats.
  Salan.   Let good Antonio look he keep his day,
Or he shall pay for this.
  Salar.   Marry, well remembered.
I reasoned with a Frenchman yesterday,
Who told me, in the narrow seas that part
The French and English, there miscarried
A vessel of our country richly fraught.   30
I thought upon Antonio when he told me;
And wished in silence that it were not his.
  Salan.   You were best to tell Antonio what you hear;
Yet do not suddenly, for it may grieve him.
  Salar.   A kinder gentleman treads not the earth.
I saw Bassanio and Antonio part;
Bassanio told him he would make some speed
Of his return; he answered: " Do not so;
Slubber not business for my sake, Bassanio,
But stay the very riping of the time;   40
And for the Jew's bond which he hath of me,
Let it not enter in your mind of love.
Be merry, and employ your chiefest thoughts
To courtship and such fair ostents of love
As shall conveniently become you there."
And even there, his eye being big with tears,
Turning his face, he put his hand behind him,
And with affection wondrous sensible
He wrung Bassanio's hand; and so they parted.
  Salan.   I think he only loves the world for him.   50
I pray thee, let us go and find him out

27. **reasoned:** talked.   28. **narrow seas:** English Channel.   39. **slubber:**
perform carelessly.   44. **ostents:** displays.   48. **sensible:** sensitive.

And quicken his embracéd heaviness
With some delight or other.
Salar.   Do we so.   [*Exeunt.*

Scene IX.   *Belmont.   A room in* Portia's *house.*

Enter Nerissa *with a* Servitor.

Ner.   Quick, quick, I pray thee; draw the curtain straight.
The Prince of Arragon hath ta'en his oath,
And comes to his election presently.

Flourish of cornets.   Enter the Prince of Arragon, Portia,
and their trains.

Por.   Behold, there stand the caskets, noble prince.
If you choose that wherein I am contained,
Straight shall our nuptial rites be solemnized;
But if you fail, without more speech, my lord,
You must be gone from hence immediately.
Ar.   I am enjoined by oath to observe three things:
First, never to unfold to any one   10
Which casket 'twas I chose; next, if I fail
Of the right casket, never in my life
To woo a maid in way of marriage;
Lastly,
If I do fail in fortune of my choice,
Immediately to leave you and be gone.
Por.   To these injunctions every one doth swear
That comes to hazard for my worthless self.
Ar.   And so have I addressed me.   Fortune now
To my heart's hope!   Gold; silver; and base lead.   20
" Who chooseth me must give and hazard all he hath."
You shall look fairer, ere I give or hazard.
What says the golden chest?   Ha! let me see:
" Who chooseth me shall gain what many men desire."
What many men desire!   That " many " may be meant
By the fool multitude, that choose by show,
Not learning more than the fond eye doth teach;
Which pries not to the interior, but, like the martlet,
Builds in the weather on the outward wall,
Even in the force and road of casualty.   30

28. **martlet:** swallow.

I will not choose what many men desire,
Because I will not jump with common spirits
And rank me with the barbarous multitudes.
Why, then to thee, thou silver treasure-house;
Tell me once more what title thou dost bear:
" Who chooseth me shall get as much as he deserves ";
And well said too; for who shall go about
To cozen fortune and be honorable
Without the stamp of merit?   Let none presume
To wear an undeservéd dignity.   40
O, that estates, degrees and offices
Were not derived corruptly, and that clear honor
Were purchased by the merit of the wearer!
How many then should cover that stand bare!
How many be commandéd that command!
How much low peasantry would then be gleaned
From the true seed of honor! and how much honor
Picked from the chaff and ruin of the times
To be new-varnished! Well, but to my choice:
" Who chooseth me shall get as much as he deserves."   50
I will assume desert. Give me a key for this,
And instantly unlock my fortunes here.

                        [*He opens the silver casket.*
  Por. Too long a pause for that which you find there.
  Ar. What's here? The portrait of a blinking idiot,
Presenting me a schedule!   I will read it.
How much unlike art thou to Portia!
How much like my hopes and my deservings!
" Who chooseth me shall have as much as he deserves."
Did I deserve no more than a fool's head?
Is that my prize? Are my deserts no better?   60
  Por. To offend, and judge, are distinct offices
And of opposéd natures.
  Ar.   What is here?
[*Reads*] " The fire seven times tried this;
            Seven times tried that judgment is,
            That did never choose amiss.
            Some there be that shadows kiss;
            Such have but a shadow's bliss.
            There be fools alive, I wis,
            Silvered o'er; and so was this.

38. cozen: cheat.   51. assume, etc.: I will assume that I deserve.   55.
schedule: document.

Take what wife you will to bed,   70
I will ever be your head.
So be gone; you are sped."

Still more fool I shall appear
By the time I linger here:
With one fool's head I came to woo,
But I go away with two.
Sweet, adieu. I'll keep my oath,
Patiently to bear my wroth.

            [*Exeunt Arragon and train.*
Por. Thus hath the candle singed the moth.
O, these deliberate fools! When they do choose,
They have the wisdom by their wit to lose.   81
    Ner. The ancient saying is no heresy,
Hanging and wiving goes by destiny.
    Por. Come, draw the curtain, Nerissa.

                Enter a Servant.

Serv. Where is my lady?
Por.   Here; what would my lord?
Serv. Madam, there is alighted at your gate
A young Venetian, one that comes before
To signify the approaching of his lord;
From whom he bringeth sensible regrets,
To wit, besides commends and courteous breath,
Gifts of rich value. Yet I have not seen   91
So likely an ambassador of love.
A day in April never came so sweet,
To show how costly summer was at hand,
As this fore-spurrer comes before his lord.
    Por. No more, I pray thee. I am half afeard
Thou wilt say anon he is some kin to thee,
Thou spend'st such high-day wit in praising him.
Come, come, Nerissa; for I long to see
Quick Cupid's post that comes so mannerly.   100
    Ner. Bassanio, lord Love, if thy will it be! [*Exeunt.*

85. **my lord:** a pleasantry in reply to the servant's "my lady." 89. **sensible regrets:** regrets that may be seen and touched: presents. 92. **likely:** likable. 98. **high-day:** holiday.

stnd unon

ACT III

Scene I. *Venice. A street.*

Enter Salanio *and* Salarino.

Salan.   Now, what news on the Rialto?

Salar.   Why, yet it lives there unchecked that Antonio hath
a ship of rich lading wrecked on the narrow seas; the Good-
wins, I think they call the place; a very dangerous flat and
fatal, where the carcasses of many a tall ship lie buried, as
they say, if my gossip Report be an honest woman of her word.

Salan.   I would she were as lying a gossip in that as ever
knapped ginger or made her neighbors believe she wept for the
death of a third husband.   But it is true, without any slips
of prolixity or crossing the plain highway of talk, that the
good Antonio, the honest Antonio —   O that I had a title
good enough to keep his name company!

Salar.   Come, the full stop.

Salan.   Ha! what sayest thou?   Why, the end is, he hath
lost a ship.

Salar.   I would it might prove the end of his losses.   21

Salan.   Let me say " Amen " betimes, lest the devil cross
my prayer, for here he comes in the likeness of a Jew.

Enter Shylock.

How, now, Shylock! what news among the merchants?

Shy.   You knew, none so well, none so well as you, of my
daughter's flight.

Salar.   That's certain.   I, for my part, knew the tailor that
made the wings she flew withal.   30

Salan.   And Shylock, for his own part, knew the bird was
fledged; and then it is the complexion of them all to leave
the dam.

Shy.   She is damned for it.

Salar.   That's certain, if the devil may be her judge.

Shy.   My own flesh and blood to rebel!

Salan.   Out upon it, old carrion!   Rebels it at these years?

Shy.   I say, my daughter is my flesh and blood.   40

Salar.   There is more difference between thy flesh and hers
than between jet and ivory; more between your bloods than

8. **knapped:** snapped.   30. **wings:** clothes.   32. **complexion:** nature.
37. **carrion:** an epithet of contempt.

there is between red wine and Rhenish. But tell us, do you
hear whether Antonio have had any loss at sea or no?

Shy. There I have another bad match. A bankrupt, a
prodigal, who dare scarce show his head on the Rialto; a
beggar, that was used to come so smug upon the mart; let
him look to his bond. He was wont to call me usurer; let
him look to his bond. He was wont to lend money for a
Christian courtesy; let him look to his bond.   51

Salar. Why, I am sure, if he forfeit, thou wilt not take his
flesh; what's that good for?

Shy. To bait fish withal. If it will feed nothing else, it
will feed my revenge. He hath disgraced me, and hindered
me half a million; laughed at my losses, mocked at my gains,
scorned my nation, thwarted my bargains, cooled my friends,
heated mine enemies; and what's his reason? I am a Jew.
Hath not a Jew eyes? Hath not a Jew hands, organs, dimen-
sions, senses, affections, passions? fed with the same food, hurt
with the same weapons, subject to the same diseases, healed
by the same means, warmed and cooled by the same winter
and summer, as a Christian is? If you prick us, do we not
bleed? If you tickle us, do we not laugh? If you poison us,
do we not die? And if you wrong us, shall we not revenge?
If we are like you in the rest, we will resemble you in that.
If a Jew wrong a Christian, what is his humility? Revenge.
If a Christian wrong a Jew, what should this sufferance be by
Christian example? Why, revenge. The villainy you teach
me, I will execute, and it shall go hard but I will better the
instruction.

Enter a Servant.

Serv. Gentlemen, my master Antonio is at his house and
desires to speak with you both.

Salar. We have been up and down to seek him.   79

Enter TUBAL.

Salan. Here comes another of the tribe; a third cannot be
matched, unless the devil himself turn Jew.

[*Exeunt Salan., Salar., and Servant.*

Shy. How now, Tubal! what news from Genoa? Hast
thou found my daughter?

Tub. I often came where I did hear of her, but cannot
find her.

72. **humility:** humanity.

Shy. Why, there, there, there, there! A diamond gone, cost me two thousand ducats in Frankfort! The curse never fell upon our nation till now; I never felt it till now. Two thousand ducats in that; and other precious, precious jewels. I would my daughter were dead at my foot, and the jewels in her ear! Would she were hearsed at my foot, and the ducats in her coffin! No news of them? Why, so; and I know not what's spent in the search. Why, thou loss upon loss! the thief gone with so much, and so much to find the thief; and no satisfaction, no revenge; nor no ill luck stirring but what lights on my shoulders; no sighs but of my breathing; no tears but of my shedding.   101

Tub. Yes, other men have ill luck too. Antonio, as I heard in Genoa —

Shy. What, what, what? Ill luck, ill luck?

Tub. Hath an argosy cast away, coming from Tripolis.

Shy. I thank God, I thank God. Is 't true, is 't true?

Tub. I spoke with some of the sailors that escaped the wreck.   110

Shy. I thank thee, good Tubal; good news, good news! Ha, ha! Where? in Genoa?

Tub. Your daughter spent in Genoa, as I heard, in one night fourscore ducats.

Shy. Thou stickest a dagger in me. I shall never see my gold again. Fourscore ducats at a sitting! Fourscore ducats!

Tub. There came divers of Antonio's creditors in my company to Venice, that swear he cannot choose but break.   120

Shy. I am very glad of it. I'll plague him; I'll torture him. I am glad of it.

Tub. One of them showed me a ring that he had of your daughter for a monkey.

Shy. Out upon her! Thou torturest me, Tubal. It was my turquoise; I had it of Leah when I was a bachelor. I would not have given it for a wilderness of monkeys.

Tub. But Antonio is certainly undone.   129

Shy. Nay, that's true, that's very true. Go, Tubal, fee me an officer; bespeak him a fortnight before. I will have the heart of him, if he forfeit; for, were he out of Venice, I can make what merchandise I will. Go, go, Tubal, and meet me at our synagogue; go, good Tubal; at our synagogue, Tubal.

[*Exeunt.*

89. **in that:** refers back to diamond.

SCENE II.   *Belmont.   A room in* PORTIA'S *house.*

Enter BASSANIO, PORTIA, GRATIANO, NERISSA, *and* Attendants.

 Por.   I pray you, tarry.   Pause a day or two
Before you hazard; for, in choosing wrong,
I lose your company; therefore forbear a while
There's something tells me, but it is not love,
I would not lose you; and you know yourself
Hate counsels not in such a quality.
But lest you should not understand me well, —
And yet a maiden hath no tongue but thought, —
I would detain you here some month or two   9
Before you venture for me.   I could teach you
How to choose right, but I am then forsworn;
So will I never be; so may you miss me;
But if you do you'll make me wish a sin,
That I had been forsworn.   Beshrew your eyes,
They have o'erlooked me and divided me;
One half of me is yours, the other half yours,
Mine own, I would say; but if mine, then yours,
And so all yours.   O, these naughty times
Put bars between the owners and their rights!
And so, though yours, not yours.   Prove it so.
Let fortune go to hell for it, not I.   21
I speak too long; but 'tis to peize the time,
To eke it and to draw it out in length,
To stay you from election.
 Bass.   Let me choose;
For as I am, I live upon the rack.
 Por.   Upon the rack, Bassanio!   Then confess
What treason there is mingled with your love.
 Bass.   None but that ugly treason of mistrust,
Which makes me fear the enjoying of my love.
There may as well be amity and life   30
'Tween snow and fire, as treason and my love.
 Por.   Ay, but I fear you speak upon the rack,
Where men enforcéd do speak anything.
 Bass.   Promise me life, and I'll confess the truth.
 Por.   Well, then, confess and live.
 Bass.   " Confess " and " love "

15. **o'erlooked:** bewitched.   22. **peize:** retard.   29. **fear the enjoying:** makes me afraid that I shall not enjoy.

Had been the very sum of my confession.
O happy torment, when my torturer
Doth teach me answers for deliverance!
But let me to my fortune and the caskets.

Por. Away, then! I am locked in one of them;   40
If you do love me, you will find me out.
Nerissa and the rest, stand all aloof.
Let music sound while he doth make his choice;
Then, if he lose, he makes a swanlike end,
Fading in music. That the comparison
May stand more proper, my eye shall be the stream
And watery deathbed for him. He may win;
And what is music then? Then music is
Even as the flourish when true subjects bow
To a new-crownéd monarch; such it is   50
As are those dulcet sounds in break of day
That creep into the dreaming bridegroom's ear
And summon him to marriage. Now he goes,
With no less presence, but with much more love,
Than young Alcides, when he did redeem
The virgin tribute paid by howling Troy
To the sea-monster. I stand for sacrifice;
The rest aloof are the Dardanian wives,
With blearéd visages, come forth to view
The issue of the exploit. Go, Hercules!   60
Live thou, I live: with much much more dismay
I view the fight than thou that makest the fray.

Music, whilst Bassanio *comments on the caskets to himself.*

SONG

Tell me where is fancy bred,
Or in the heart or in the head?
How begot, how nourishéd?
      Reply, reply.
It is engendered in the eyes,
With gazing fed; and fancy dies
In the cradle where it lies.
      Let us all ring fancy's knell;   70
I'll begin it — Ding, dong, bell.

44. **swan-like:** an old tradition that a swan sings just before it dies. 55.
Alcides: Hercules. For the story see cyclopedia. 63. **fancy:** love in the
lighter sense. This song is supposed to give the lover a vague hint.

All. Ding, dong, bell.

Bass. So may the outward shows be least themselves;
The world is still deceived with ornament.
In law, what plea so tainted and corrupt
But, being seasoned with a gracious voice,
Obscures the show of evil? In religion,
What damnéd error, but some sober brow
Will bless it and approve it with a text,
Hiding the grossness with fair ornament? 80
There is no vice so simple but assumes
Some mark of virtue on his outward parts.
How many cowards, whose hearts are all as false
As stairs of sand, wear yet upon their chins
The beards of Hercules and frowning Mars,
Who, inward searched, have livers white as milk;
And these assume but valor's excrement
To render them redoubted! Look on beauty,
And you shall see 'tis purchased by the weight;
Which therein works a miracle in nature, 90
Making them lightest that wear most of it.
So are those crispéd snaky golden locks
Which make such wanton gambols with the wind,
Upon supposéd fairness, often known
To be the dowry of a second head,
The skull that bred them in the sepulcher.
Thus ornament is but the guiléd shore
To a most dangerous sea; the beauteous scarf
Veiling an Indian beauty; in a word,
The seeming truth which cunning time puts on
To entrap the wisest. Therefore, thou gaudy gold, 101
Hard food for Midas, I will none of thee,
Nor none of thee, thou pale and common drudge
'Tween man and man; but thou, thou meager lead,
Which rather threatenest than dost promise aught,
Thy plainness moves me more than eloquence;
And here choose I. Joy be the consequence!

Por. [*Aside*] How all the other passions fleet to air,
As doubtful thoughts, and rash-embraced despair,

87. **excrement:** exterior, i.e., beard. 89. **purchased by the weight:** " drug
store " beauty. Shakespeare often scores artificial beauty. 95. **second head:**
its hair false, taken from the dead, continuing the idea of l. 89. 97. **guiled:**
treacherous. 99. **Indian beauty:** i.e., ugliness hidden by a " beauteous
scarf," in this case the golden casket. 102. **Midas:** everything he touched
turned to gold. See cyclopedia. 103. **common drudge:** i.e., silver.

And shuddering fear, and green-eyed jealousy!
O love,   111
Be moderate; allay thy ecstasy;
In measure rein thy joy; scant this excess.
I feel too much thy blessing; make it less,
For fear I surfeit.
    Bass.   What find I here?   [*Opening the leaden casket.*
Fair Portia's counterfeit!   What demigod
Hath come so near creation?   Move these eyes?
Or whether, riding on the balls of mine,
Seem they in motion?   Here are severed lips,
Parted with sugar breath; so sweet a bar   120
Should sunder such sweet friends.   Here in her hairs
The painter plays the spider and hath woven
A golden mesh to entrap the hearts of men
Faster than gnats in cobwebs.   But her eyes —
How could he see to do them?   Having made one,
Methinks it should have power to steal both his
And leave itself unfurnished.   Yet look, how far
The substance of my praise doth wrong this shadow
In underprizing it, so far this shadow
Doth limp behind the substance.   Here's the scroll,   130
The continent and summary of my fortune.
[*Reads*] " You that choose not by the view,
       Chance as fair and choose as true!
       Since this fortune falls to you,
       Be content and seek no new.
       If you be well pleased with this
       And hold your fortune for your bliss,
       Turn you where your lady is
       And claim her with a loving kiss."
A gentle scroll.   Fair lady, by your leave;   140
I come by note, to give and to receive.
Like one of two contending in a prize,
That thinks he hath done well in people's eyes,
Hearing applause and universal shout,
Giddy in spirit, still gazing in a doubt
Whether those peals of praise be his or no;
So, thrice-fair lady, stand I, even so;
As doubtful whether what I see be true,
Until confirmed, signed, ratified by you.

131. **continent:** container.

Por.   You see me, Lord Bassanio, where I stand,   150
Such as I am.   Though for myself alone
I would not be ambitious in my wish,
To wish myself much better; yet, for you
I would be trebled twenty times myself;
A thousand times more fair, ten thousand times
More rich;
That only to stand high in your account,
I might in virtues, beauties, livings, friends,
Exceed account; but the full sum of me   159
Is sum of something, which, to term in gross,
Is an unlessoned girl, unschooled, unpracticed;
Happy in this, she is not yet so old
But she may learn; happier than this,
She is not bred so dull but she can learn;
Happiest of all is that her gentle spirit
Commits itself to yours to be directed,
As from her lord, her governor, her king.
Myself and what is mine to you and yours
Is now converted.   But now I was the lord
Of this fair mansion, master of my servants,   170
Queen o'er myself; and even now, but now,
This house, these servants and this same myself
Are yours, my lord; I give them with this ring;
Which when you part from, lose, or give away,
Let it presage the ruin of your love
And be my vantage to exclaim on you.
   Bass.   Madam, you have bereft me of all words,
Only my blood speaks to you in my veins;
And there is such confusion in my powers,
As, after some oration fairly spoke   180
By a belovéd prince, there doth appear
Among the buzzing pleaséd multitude;
Where every something, being blent together,
Turns to a wild of nothing, save of joy,
Expressed and not expressed.   But when this ring
Parts from this finger, then parts life from hence;
O, then be bold to say Bassanio's dead!
   Ner.   My lord and lady, it is now our time,
That have stood by and seen our wishes prosper,
To cry, good joy.   Good joy, my lord and lady!   190

158. **livings:** possessions.   169. **converted:** turned over.

Gra.   My lord Bassanio and my gentle lady,
I wish you all the joy that you can wish;
For I am sure you can wish none from me;
And when your honors mean to solemnize
The bargain of your faith, I do beseech you,
Even at that time I may be married too.
   Bass.   With all my heart, so thou canst get a wife.
   Gra.   I thank your lordship, you have got me one.
My eyes, my lord, can look as swift as yours.
You saw the mistress, I beheld the maid;   200
You loved, I loved; for intermission
No more pertains to me, my lord, than you.
Your fortune stood upon the casket there,
And so did mine too, as the matter falls;
For wooing here until I sweat again,
And swearing till my very roof was dry
With oaths of love, at last, if promise last,
I got a promise of this fair one here
To have her love, provided that your fortune
Achieved her mistress.
   Por.   Is this true, Nerissa?   210
   Ner.   Madam, it is, so you stand pleased withal.
   Bass.   And do you, Gratiano, mean good faith?
   Gra.   Yes, faith, my lord.
   Bass.   Our feast shall be much honored in your marriage.
   Gra.   We'll play with them the first boy for a thousand
ducats.
   Ner.   What, and stake down?
   Gra.   No; we shall ne'er win at that sport, and stake
down.   220
But who comes here? Lorenzo and his infidel?
What, and my old Venetian friend Salerio?

Enter Lorenzo, Jessica, *and* Salerio, *a Messenger from*
Venice.

   Bass.   Lorenzo and Salerio, welcome hither;
If that the youth of my new interest here
Have power to bid you welcome. By your leave,
I bid my friends and countrymen,
Sweet Portia, welcome.
   Por.   So do I, my lord;

200. **maid:** not a maidservant but a companion.

They are entirely welcome.
    Lor. I thank your honor. For my part, my lord,
My purpose was not to have seen you here;   230
But meeting with Salerio by the way,
He did entreat me, past all saying nay,
To come with him along.
    Saler.   I did, my lord;
And I have reason for it. Signior Antonio
Commends him to you.   [*Gives Bassanio a letter.*
    Bass.   Ere I ope his letter,
I pray you, tell me how my good friend doth.
    Saler. Not sick, my lord, unless it be in mind;
Nor well, unless in mind. His letter there
Will show you his estate.
    Gra. Nerissa, cheer yon stranger; bid her welcome. 240
Your hand, Salerio. What's the news from Venice?
How doth that royal merchant, good Antonio?
I know he will be glad of our success;
We are the Jasons, we have won the fleece.
    Saler. I would you had won the fleece that he hath lost.
    Por. There are some shrewd contents in yon same paper,
That steals the color from Bassanio's cheek.
Some dear friend dead; else nothing in the world
Could turn so much the constitution
Of any constant man. What, worse and worse!
With leave, Bassanio; I am half yourself,   251
And I must freely have the half of anything
That this same paper brings you.
    Bass.   O sweet Portia,
Here are a few of the unpleasant'st words
That ever blotted paper! Gentle lady,
When I did first impart my love to you,
I freely told you, all the wealth I had
Ran in my veins; I was a gentleman.
And then I told you true; and yet, dear lady,
Rating myself at nothing, you shall see   260
How much I was a braggart. When I told you
My state was nothing, I should then have told you
That I was worse than nothing; for, indeed,
I have engaged myself to a dear friend,
Engaged my friend to his mere enemy,

    239. **estate:** condition. 242. **royal:** noble. 246. **shrewd:** bad. 250. **constant:** self-possessed. 265. **mere:** absolute.

To feed my means.   Here is a letter, lady;
The paper as the body of my friend,
And every word in it a gaping wound,
Issuing life-blood.   But is it true, Salerio?
Have all his ventures failed?   What, not one hit?   270
From Tripolis, from Mexico and England,
From Lisbon, Barbary and India?
And not one vessel 'scape the dreadful touch
Of merchant-marring rocks?
   Saler.   Not one, my lord.
Besides, it should appear, that if he had
The present money to discharge the Jew,
He would not take it.   Never did I know
A creature, that did bear the shape of man,
So keen and greedy to confound a man.
He plies the duke at morning and at night,   280
And doth impeach the freedom of the state,
If they deny him justice.   Twenty merchants,
The duke himself, and the magnificoes
Of greatest port, have all persuaded with him;
But none can drive him from the envious plea
Of forfeiture, of justice and his bond.
   Jes.   When I was with him I have heard him swear
To Tubal and to Chus, his countrymen,
That he would rather have Antonio's flesh
Than twenty times the value of the sum   290
That he did owe him; and I know, my lord,
If law, authority and power deny not,
It will go hard with poor Antonio.
   Por.   Is it your dear friend that is thus in trouble?
   Bass.   The dearest friend to me, the kindest man,
The best-conditioned and unwearied spirit
In doing courtesies, and one in whom
The ancient Roman honor more appears
Than any that draws breath in Italy.
   Por.   What sum owes he the Jew?   300
   Bass.   For me three thousand ducats.
   Por.   What, no more?
Pay him six thousand, and deface the bond;
Double six thousand, and then treble that,
Before a friend of this description

284. **persuaded:** argued.

Shall lose a hair through Bassanio's fault.
First go with me to church and call me wife,
And then away to Venice to your friend;
For never shall you lie by Portia's side
With an unquiet soul.   You shall have gold
To pay the petty debt twenty times over.   310
When it is paid, bring your true friend along.
My maid Nerissa and myself meantime
Will live as maids and widows.   Come, away!
For you shall hence upon your wedding-day:
Bid your friends welcome, show a merry cheer;
Since you are dear bought, I will love you dear.
But let me hear the letter of your friend.

   Bass. [*Reads*]   " Sweet Bassanio, my ships have all miscarried, my creditors grow cruel, my estate is very low, my
bond to the Jew is forfeit; and since in paying it, it is impossible I should live, all debts are cleared between you and
I, if I might but see you at my death.   Notwithstanding, use
your pleasure; if your love do not persuade you to come, let
not my letter."

   Por.   O love, dispatch all business, and be gone!

   Bass.   Since I have your good leave to go away,
   I will make haste; but, till I come again,
No bed shall o'er be guilty of my stay,   329
No rest be interposer 'twixt us twain.   [*Exeunt.*

SCENE III.   *Venice.   A street.*

Enter SHYLOCK, SALARINO, ANTONIO, *and* Jailer.

   Shy.   Jailer, look to him: tell not me of mercy;
This is the fool that lent out money gratis!
Jailer, look to him.

   Ant.   Hear me yet, good Shylock.

   Shy.   I'll have my bond; speak not against my bond.
I have sworn an oath that I will have my bond.
Thou call'dst me dog before thou hadst a cause;
But, since I am a dog, beware my fangs.
The duke shall grant me justice.   I do wonder,
Thou naughty jailer, that thou art so fond
To come abroad with him at his request.   10

   Ant.   I pray thee, hear me speak.

Shy. I'll have my bond; I will not hear thee speak.
I'll have my bond; and therefore speak no more.
I'll not be made a soft and dull-eyed fool,
To shake the head, relent, and sigh, and yield
To Christian intercessors. Follow not;
I'll have no speaking; I will have my bond.   [*Exit.*
    Salar. It is the most impenetrable cur
That ever kept with men.
    Ant.   Let him alone;
I'll follow him no more with bootless prayers.
He seeks my life; his reason well I know: 21
I oft delivered from his forfeitures
Many that have at times made moan to me;
Therefore he hates me.
    Salar.   I am sure the duke
Will never grant this forfeiture to hold.
    Ant. The duke cannot deny the course of law;
For the commodity that strangers have
With us in Venice, if it be denied,
Will much impeach the justice of his state,
Since that the trade and profit of the city   30
Consisteth of all nations. Therefore, go.
These griefs and losses have so bated me,
That I shall hardly spare a pound of flesh
Tomorrow to my bloody creditor.
Well, jailer, on. Pray God, Bassanio come
To see me pay his debt, and then I care not!   [*Exeunt.*

SCENE IV.   *Belmont.   A room in* PORTIA'S *house.*

Enter PORTIA, NERISSA, LORENZO, JESSICA, *and* BALTHASAR.

    Lor. Madam, although I speak it in your presence,
You have a noble and a true conceit
Of godlike amity; which appears most strongly
In bearing thus the absence of your lord.
But if you knew to whom you show this honor,
How true a gentleman you send relief,
How dear a lover of my lord your husband,

22. forfeitures: notes due.   27. commodity: privilege of trade.   32. bated:
fagged out.
    2. conceit: conception.   3. amity: friendship.

I know you would be prouder of the work
Than customary bounty can enforce you.

Por.   I never did repent for doing good,   10
Nor shall not now: for in companions
That do converse and waste the time together,
Whose souls do bear an equal yoke of love,
There must be needs a like proportion
Of lineaments, of manners and of spirit;
Which makes me think that this Antonio,
Being the bosom lover of my lord,
Must needs be like my lord. If it be so,
How little is the cost I have bestowed
In purchasing the semblance of my soul   20
From out the state of hellish misery!
This comes too near the praising of myself;
Therefore no more of it. Hear other things.
Lorenzo, I commit into your hands
The husbandry and manage of my house
Until my lord's return. For mine own part,
I have toward heaven breathed a secret vow
To live in prayer and contemplation,
Only attended by Nerissa here,
Until her husband and my lord's return.   30
There is a monastery two miles off;
And there will we abide. I do desire you
Not to deny this imposition;
The which my love and some necessity
Now lays upon you.

Lor.   Madam, with all my heart
I shall obey you in all fair commands.

Por.   My people do already know my mind,
And will acknowledge you and Jessica
In place of Lord Bassanio and myself.
And so farewell, till we shall meet again.   40

Lor.   Fair thoughts and happy hours attend on you!

Jes.   I wish your ladyship all heart's content.

Por.   I thank you for your wish, and am well pleased
To wish it back on you. Fare you well, Jessica.
                              [*Exeunt Jessica and Lorenzo.*

Now, Balthasar,
As I have ever found thee honest-true,

---

12. **waste:** pass. 14–15. **proportion, etc.:** similarity of appearance and character.

So let me find thee still. Take this same letter,
And use thou all the endeavor of a man
In speed to Padua: see thou render this
Into my cousin's hand, Doctor Bellario;   50
And, look, what notes and garments he doth give thee,
Bring them, I pray thee, with imagined speed
Unto the traject, to the common ferry
Which trades to Venice. Waste no time in words,
But get thee gone. I shall be there before thee.
   Balth. Madam, I go with all convenient speed.   [*Exit*
   Por. Come on, Nerissa; I have work in hand
That you yet know not of: we'll see our husbands
Before they think of us.
   Ner.   Shall they see us?
   Por. They shall, Nerissa; but in such a habit,   60
That they shall think we are accomplished
With that we lack. I'll hold thee any wager,
When we are both accoutered like young men,
I'll prove the prettier fellow of the two,
And wear my dagger with the braver grace,
And speak between the change of man and boy
With a reed voice, and turn two mincing steps
Into a manly stride, and speak of frays
Like a fine bragging youth, and tell quaint lies,
How honorable ladies sought my love,   70
Which I denying, they fell sick and died;
I could not do withal; then I'll repent,
And wish, for all that, that I had not killed them;
And twenty of these puny lies I'll tell,
That men shall swear I have discontinued school
Above a twelvemonth. I have within my mind
A thousand raw tricks of these bragging Jacks,
Which I will practice.
   Ner.   Why, shall we turn to men?
   Por. Fie, what a question's that,
If thou wert near a lewd interpreter!   80
But come, I'll tell thee all my whole device
When I am in my coach, which stays for us
At the park gate; and therefore haste away,
For we must measure twenty miles today.   [*Exeunt.*

50. **cousin:** kinsman. 52. **imagined:** the quickest possible. 53. **traject:** ferry. 69. **quaint:** clever. 72. **I could not, etc.:** couldn't help it.

SCENE V. *The same. A garden.*

Enter Launcelot *and* Jessica.

Laun. Yes, truly; for, look you, the sins of the father are to be laid upon the children; therefore, I promise ye, I fear you. I was always plain with you, and so now I speak my agitation of the matter; therefore be of good cheer, for truly I think you are damned.

Jes. I shall be saved by my husband; he hath made me a Christian.

Laun. Truly, the more to blame he; we were Christians enow before; e'en as many as could well live, one by another. This making of Christians will raise the price of hogs: if we grow all to be pork-eaters, we shall not shortly have a rasher on the coals for money.

Enter Lorenzo.

Jes. I'll tell my husband, Launcelot, what you say. Here he comes.   30

Lor. I shall grow jealous of you shortly, Launcelot, if you thus get my wife into corners.

Jes. Nay, you need not fear us, Lorenzo; Launcelot and I are out. He tells me flatly there is no mercy for me in heaven because I am a Jew's daughter; and he says you are no good member of the commonwealth, for in converting Jews to Christians, you raise the price of pork.   39

Lor. I think the best grace of wit will shortly turn into silence, and discourse grow commendable in none only but parrots. Go you! then bid them prepare for dinner.

Laun. That is done, sir; they have all stomachs.

Lor. Goodly Lord, what a wit-snapper are you! Then bid them prepare dinner.

Laun. That is done too, sir; only "cover" is the word.

Lor. Will you cover then, sir?

Laun. Not so, sir, neither; I know my duty.   59

Lor. Yet more quarreling with occasion! Wilt thou show the whole wealth of thy wit in an instant? I pray thee, understand a plain man in his plain meaning: go to thy fellows; bid

4. **agitation:** cogitation.   34. **out:** in disagreement.   52. **stomachs:** appetites.

them cover the table, serve in the meat, and we will come in
to dinner.

    Laun. For the table, sir, it shall be served in; for the
meat, sir, it shall be covered; for your coming in to dinner,
sir, why, let it be as humors and conceits shall govern. [*Exit.*

    Lor. O dear discretion, how his words are suited!   70
The fool hath planted in his memory
An army of good words; and I do know
A many fools, that stand in better place,
Garnished like him, that for a tricksy word
Defy the matter. How cheer'st thou, Jessica?
And now, good sweet, say thy opinion,
How dost thou like the Lord Bassanio's wife?

    Jes. Past all expressing. It is very meet
The Lord Bassanio live an upright life;
For, having such a blessing in his lady,   80
He finds the joys of heaven here on earth;
And if on earth he do not mean it, then
In reason he should never come to heaven.
Why, if two gods should play some heavenly match
And on the wager lay two earthly women,
And Portia one, there must be something else
Pawned with the other, for the poor rude world
Hath not her fellow.

    Lor.   Even such a husband
Hast thou of me as she is for a wife.

    Jes. Nay, but ask my opinion too of that.   90

    Lor. I will anon; first, let us go to dinner.

    Jes. Nay, let me praise you while I have a stomach.

    Lor. No, pray thee, let it serve for table-talk;
Then, howsoe'er thou speak'st, 'mong other things
I shall digest it.

    Jes.   Well, I'll set you forth.   [*Exeunt.*

ACT IV

SCENE I. *Venice. A court of justice.*

Enter the DUKE, *the Magnificoes,* ANTONIO, BASSANIO, GRA-
TIANO, SALERIO, *and others.*

Duke. What, is Antonio here?
Ant. Ready, so please your grace.
Duke. I am sorry for thee. Thou art come to answer
A stony adversary, an inhuman wretch
Uncapable of pity, void and empty
From any dram of mercy.
Ant.   I have heard
Your grace hath ta'en great pains to qualify
His rigorous course; but since he stands obdurate
And that no lawful means can carry me
Out of his envy's reach, I do oppose   10
My patience to his fury, and am armed
To suffer, with a quietness of spirit,
The very tyranny and rage of his.
Duke. Go one, and call the Jew into the court.
Saler. He is ready at the door. He comes, my lord.

Enter SHYLOCK.

Duke. Make room, and let him stand before our face.
Shylock, the world thinks, and I think so too,
That thou but lead'st this fashion of thy malice
To the last hour of act; and then 'tis thought
Thou'lt show thy mercy and remorse more strange   20
Than is thy strange apparent cruelty;
And where thou now exact'st the penalty,
Which is a pound of this poor merchant's flesh,
Thou wilt not only loose the forfeiture,
But, touched with human gentleness and love,
Forgive a moiety of the principal;
Glancing an eye of pity on his losses,
That have of late so huddled on his back,
Enow to press a royal merchant down
And pluck commiseration of his state   30
From brassy bosoms and rough hearts of flint,

20. **remorse:** pity. 21. **apparent:** seeming. 26. **moiety:** half, or at
least part.

From stubborn Turks and Tartars, never trained
To offices of tender courtesy.
We all expect a gentle answer, Jew.
   Shy. I have possessed your grace of what I purpose;
And by our holy Sabbath have I sworn
To have the due and forfeit of my bond.
If you deny it, let the danger light
Upon your charter and your city's freedom.
You'll ask me, why I rather choose to have   40
A weight of carrion flesh than to receive
Three thousand ducats. I'll not answer that;
But, say, it is my humor. Is it answered?
What if my house be troubled with a rat
And I be pleased to give ten thousand ducats
To have it baned? What, are you answered yet?
Some men there are love not a gaping pig;
Some, that are mad if they behold a cat;
                  For affection,   50
Mistress of passion, sways it to the mood
Of what it likes or loathes. Now, for your answer:
As there is no firm reason to be rendered,
Why he cannot abide a gaping pig;
Why he, a harmless necessary cat;
Why he, a woolen bagpipe; but of force
Must yield to such inevitable shame
As to offend, himself being offended;
So can I give no reason, nor I will not,
More than a lodged hate and a certain loathing
I bear Antonio, that I follow thus   61
A losing suit against him. Are you answered?
   Bass. This is no answer, thou unfeeling man,
To excuse the current of thy cruelty.
   Shy. I am not bound to please thee with my answers.
   Bass. Do all men kill the things they do not love?
   Shy. Hates any man the thing he would not kill?
   Bass. Every offence is not a hate at first.
   Shy. What, wouldst thou have a serpent sting thee twice?
   Ant. I pray you, think, you question with the Jew. 70
You may as well go stand upon the beach
And bid the main flood bate his usual height;

33. **offices:** duties. 46. **baned:** poisoned. 50. **affection:** emotion. 70. **question:** argue.

You may as well use question with the wolf
Why he hath made the ewe bleat for the lamb;
You may as well forbid the mountain pines
To wag their high tops and to make no noise,
When they are fretten with the gusts of heaven;
You may as well do any thing most hard,
As seek to soften that — than which what's harder? —
His Jewish heart. Therefore, I do beseech you,
Make no more offers, use no farther means,   81
But with all brief and plain conveniency
Let me have judgment and the Jew his will.
     Bass. For thy three thousand ducats here is six.
     Shy. If every ducat in six thousand ducats
Were in six parts and every part a ducat,
I would not draw them; I would have my bond.
     Duke. How shalt thou hope for mercy, rendering none?
     Shy. What judgment shall I dread, doing no wrong?
You have among you many a purchased slave,
Which, like your asses and your dogs and mules,   91
You use in abject and in slavish parts,
Because you bought them: shall I say to you,
Let them be free, marry them to your heirs?
Why sweat they under burthens? Let their beds
Be made as soft as yours and let their palates
Be seasoned with such viands? You will answer
" The slaves are ours." So do I answer you:
The pound of flesh, which I demand of him,
Is dearly bought; 'tis mine and I will have it.
If you deny me, fie upon your law!   101
There is no force in the decrees of Venice.
I stand for judgment! Answer: shall I have it?
     Duke. Upon my power I may dismiss this court,
Unless Bellario, a learned doctor,
Whom I have sent for to determine this,
Come here today.
     Saler.   My lord, here stays without
A messenger with letters from the doctor,
New come from Padua.
     Duke. Bring us the letters; call the messenger.   110
     Bass. Good cheer, Antonio! What, man, courage yet!
The Jew shall have my flesh, blood, bones and all,

77. **fretten:** swayed.

Ere thou shalt loose for me one drop of blood.
    Ant. I am a tainted wether of the flock,
Meetest for death. The weakest kind of fruit
Drops earliest to the ground; and so let me.
You cannot better be employed, Bassanio,
Than to live still and write mine epitaph.

       Enter NERISSA, *dressed like a lawyer's clerk.*

    Duke. Came you from Padua, from Bellario?
    Ner. From both, my lord. Bellario greets your grace. 120
                                                               [Presenting a letter.
    Bass. Why dost thou whet thy knife so earnestly?
    Shy. To cut the forfeiture from that bankrupt there.
    Gra. Not on thy sole, but on thy soul, harsh Jew,
Thou makest thy knife keen; but no metal can,
No, not the hangman's ax, bear half the keenness
Of thy sharp envy. Can no prayers pierce thee?
    Shy. No, none that thou hast wit enough to make.
    Gra. O, be thou damned, inexecrable dog!
And for thy life let justice be accused.
Thou almost makest me waver in my faith   130
To hold opinion with Pythagoras,
That souls of animals infuse themselves
Into the trunks of men. Thy currish spirit
Governed a wolf, who, hanged for human slaughter,
Even from the gallows did his fell soul fleet,
And, whilst thou lay'st in thy unhallowed dam,
Infused itself in thee; for thy desires
Are wolvish, bloody, starved and ravenous.
    Shy. Till thou canst rail the seal from off my bond,
Thou but offend'st thy lungs to speak so loud.
Repair thy wit, good youth, or it will fall   141
To cureless ruin. I stand here for law.
    Duke. This letter from Bellario doth commend
A young and learned doctor to our court.
Where is he?
    Ner.   He attendeth here hard by,
To know your answer, whether you'll admit him.
    Duke. With all my heart. Some three or four of you
Go give him courteous conduct to this place.
Meantime the court shall hear Bellario's letter.

                125. **hangman:** executioner.

Clerk. [*Reads*] " Your grace shall understand that at the receipt of your letter I am very sick; but in the instant that your messenger came, in loving visitation was with me a young doctor of Rome; his name is Balthasar. I acquainted him with the cause in controversy between the Jew and Antonio the merchant. We turned o'er many books together. He is furnished with my opinion; which, bettered with his own learning, the greatness whereof I cannot enough commend, comes with him, at my importunity, to fill up your grace's request in my stead. I beseech you, let his lack of years be no impediment to let him lack a reverend estimation; for I never knew so young a body with so old a head. I leave him to your gracious acceptance, whose trial shall better publish his commendation."

Duke. You hear the learned Bellario, what he writes:
And here, I take it, is the doctor come.

Enter Portia, *dressed like a doctor of laws.*

Give me your hand. Come you from old Bellario?
  Por. I did, my lord.
  Duke. You are welcome: take your place.
Are you acquainted with the difference   171
That holds this present question in the court?
  Por. I am informéd thoroughly of the cause.
Which is the merchant here, and which the Jew?
  Duke. Antonio and old Shylock, both stand forth.
  Por. Is your name Shylock?
  Shy.   Shylock is my name.
  Por. Of a strange nature is the suit you follow;
Yet in such rule that the Venetian law
Cannot impugn you as you do proceed.
You stand within his danger, do you not?   180
  Ant. Ay, so he says.
  Por.   Do you confess the bond?
  Ant. I do.
  Por.   Then must the Jew be merciful.
  Shy. On what compulsion must I? Tell me that.
  Por. The quality of mercy is not strained,
It droppeth as the gentle rain from heaven
Upon the place beneath. It is twice blest;
It blesseth him that gives and him that takes.

184. **strained:** forced, referring back to Shylock's " compulsion."

'Tis mightiest in the mightiest; it becomes
The thronéd monarch better than his crown;
His scepter shows the force of temporal power,
The attribute to awe and majesty,   191
Wherein doth sit the dread and fear of kings;
But mercy is above this sceptered sway;
It is enthronéd in the hearts of kings,
It is an attribute to God himself;
And earthly power doth then show likest God's
When mercy seasons justice. Therefore, Jew,
Though justice be thy plea, consider this,
That, in the course of justice, none of us   199
Should see salvation. We do pray for mercy;
And that same prayer doth teach us all to render
The deeds of mercy. I have spoke thus much
To mitigate the justice of thy plea;
Which if thou follow, this strict court of Venice
Must needs give sentence 'gainst the merchant there.
    Shy. My deeds upon my head! I crave the law,
The penalty and forfeit of my bond.
    Por. Is he not able to discharge the money?
    Bass. Yes, here I tender it for him in the court;
Yea, twice the sum. If that will not suffice,   210
I will be bound to pay it ten times o'er,
On forfeit of my hands, my head, my heart.
If this will not suffice, it must appear
That malice bears down truth. And I beseech you,
Wrest once the law to your authority;
To do a great right, do a little wrong,
And curb this cruel devil of his will.
    Por. It must not be; there is no power in Venice
Can alter a decree established.
'Twill be recorded for a precedent,   220
And many an error by the same example
Will rush into the state. It cannot be.
    Shy. A Daniel come to judgment! yea, a Daniel!
O wise young judge, how I do honor thee!
    Por. I pray you, let me look upon the bond.
    Shy. Here 'tis, most reverend doctor, here it is.
    Por. Shylock, there's thrice thy money offered thee.

215. **Wrest, etc.:** take the law into your own hands. 223. **Daniel: a** young
judge in the Apocrypha, not the Daniel of the lion's den fame.

Shy. An oath, an oath, I have an oath in heaven!
Shall I lay perjury upon my soul?
No, not for Venice.

   Por.   Why, this bond is forfeit;
And lawfully by this the Jew may claim   231
A pound of flesh, to be by him cut off
Nearest the merchant's heart. Be merciful;
Take thrice thy money; bid me tear the bond.

   Shy. When it is paid according to the tenor.
It doth appear you are a worthy judge;
You know the law, your exposition
Hath been most sound. I charge you by the law,
Whereof you are a well-deserving pillar,
Proceed to judgment. By my soul I swear   240
There is no power in the tongue of man
To alter me. I stay here on my bond.

   Ant. Most heartily I do beseech the court
To give the judgment.

   Por.   Why then, thus it is:
You must prepare your bosom for his knife.

   Shy. O noble judge! O excellent young man!

   Por. For the intent and purpose of the law
Hath full relation to the penalty,
Which here appeareth due upon the bond.

   Shy. 'Tis very true. O wise and upright judge!   250
How much more elder art thou than thy looks!

   Por. Therefore lay bare your bosom.

   Shy.   Ay, his breast;
So says the bond; doth it not, noble judge?
" Nearest his heart ": those are the very words.

   Por. It is so. Are there balance here to weigh
The flesh?

   Shy. I have them ready.

   Por. Have by some surgeon, Shylock, on your charge,
To stop his wounds lest he doth bleed to death.

   Shy. Is it so nominated in the bond?

   Por. It is not so expressed; but what of that?
Twere good you do so much for charity.   261

   Shy. I cannot find it; 'tis not in the bond.

   Por. You, merchant, have you any thing to say?

   Ant. But little; I am armed and well prepared.

255. **balance:** scales.

Give me your hand, Bassanio; fare you well!
Grieve not that I am fallen to this for you;
For herein Fortune shows herself more kind
Than is her custom. It is still her use
To let the wretched man outlive his wealth,
To view with hollow eye and wrinkled brow   270
An age of poverty; from which lingering penance
Of such misery doth she cut me off.
Commend me to your honorable wife.
Tell her the process of Antonio's end;
Say how I loved you, speak me fair in death;
And, when the tale is told, bid her be judge
Whether Bassanio had not once a love.
Repent but you that you shall lose your friend,
And he repents not that he pays your debt;
For if the Jew do cut but deep enough,   280
I'll pay it presently with all my heart.
    Bass. Antonio, I am married to a wife
Which is as dear to me as life itself;
But life itself, my wife, and all the world,
Are not with me esteemèd above thy life.
I would lose all, ay, sacrifice them all
Here to this devil, to deliver you.
    Por. Your wife would give you little thanks for that,
If she were by, to hear you make the offer.
    Gra. I have a wife, whom, I protest, I love;
I would she were in heaven, so she could   291
Entreat some power to change this currish Jew.
    Ner. 'Tis well you offer it behind her back;
The wish would make else an unquiet house.
    Shy. These be the Christian husbands. I have a daughter;
Would any of the stock of Barrabas
Had been her husband rather than a Christian!   [*Aside.*
We trifle time. I pray thee, pursue sentence.
    Por. A pound of that same merchant's flesh is thine.
The court awards it, and the law doth give it.
    Shy. Most rightful judge!   301
    Por. And you must cut this flesh from off his breast.
The law allows it, and the court awards it.
    Shy. Most learned judge! A sentence! Come, prepare!
    Por. Tarry a little; there is something else.

278. **Repent:** regret.

This bond doth give thee here no jot of blood;
The words expressly are " a pound of flesh."
Take then thy bond, take thou thy pound of flesh;
But, in the cutting it, if thou dost shed
One drop of Christian blood, thy lands and goods   310
Are, by the laws of Venice, confiscate
Unto the state of Venice.
    Gra. O upright judge! Mark, Jew: O learnéd judge!
    Shy. Is that the law?
    Por.   Thyself shalt see the act;
For, as thou urgest justice, be assured
Thou shalt have justice, more than thou desirest.
    Gra. O learned judge! Mark, Jew: a learned judge!
    Shy. I take this offer, then; pay the bond thrice
And let the Christian go.
    Bass.   Here is the money.
    Por. Soft!   320
The Jew shall have all justice. Soft! no haste:
He shall have nothing but the penalty.
    Gra. O Jew! an upright judge, a learned judge!
    Por. Therefore prepare thee to cut off the flesh.
Shed thou no blood, nor cut thou less nor more
But just a pound of flesh: if thou cut'st more
Or less than a just pound, be it but so much
As makes it light or heavy in the substance,
Or the division of the twentieth part
Of one poor scruple, nay, if the scale do turn
But in the estimation of a hair,   331
Thou diest and all thy goods are confiscate.
    Gra. A second Daniel, a Daniel, Jew!
Now, infidel, I have you on the hip.
    Por. Why doth the Jew pause? Take thy forfeiture.
    Shy. Give me my principal, and let me go.
    Bass. I have it ready for thee; here it is.
    Por. He hath refused it in the open court.
He shall have merely justice and his bond.   339
    Gra. A Daniel, still say I, a second Daniel!
I thank thee, Jew, for teaching me that word.
    Shy. Shall I not have barely my principal?
    Por. Thou shalt have nothing but the forfeiture,
To be so taken at thy peril, Jew.
    Shy. Why, then the devil give him good of it!

I'll stay no longer question.
   Por.   Tarry, Jew:
The law hath yet another hold on you.
It is enacted in the laws of Venice,
If it be proved against an alien
That by direct or indirect attempts   350
He seek the life of any citizen,
The party 'gainst the which he doth contrive
Shall seize one half his goods; the other half
Comes to the privy coffer of the state;
And the offender's life lies in the mercy
Of the duke only, 'gainst all other voice.
In which predicament, I say, thou stand'st;
For it appears, by manifest proceeding,
That indirectly and directly too
Thou hast contrived against the very life   360
Of the defendant; and thou hast incurred
The danger formerly by me rehearsed.
Down therefore and beg mercy of the duke.
   Gra. Beg that thou mayst have leave to hang thyself;
And yet, thy wealth being forfeit to the state,
Thou hast not left the value of a cord;
Therefore thou must be hanged at the state's charge.
   Duke. That thou shalt see the difference of our spirits,
I pardon thee thy life before thou ask it:
For half thy wealth, it is Antonio's;   370
The other half comes to the general state,
Which humbleness may drive unto a fine.
   Por. Ay, for the state, not for Antonio.
   Shy. Nay, take my life and all; pardon not that.
You take my house when you do take the prop
That doth sustain my house; you take my life
When you do take the means whereby I live.
   Por. What mercy can you render him, Antonio?
   Gra. A halter gratis; nothing else, for God's sake.
   Ant. So please my lord the duke and all the court 380
To quit the fine for one half of his goods,
I am content; so he will let me have
The other half in use, to render it,
Upon his death, unto the gentleman

354. **privy coffer:** treasury. 373. **not for Antonio:** i.e., Antonio's part can not be remitted by a fine.

That lately stole his daughter:
Two things provided more, that, for this favor,
He presently become a Christian;
The other, that he do record a gift,
Here in the court, of all he dies possessed,
Unto his son Lorenzo and his daughter.   390
    Duke.   He shall do this, or else I do recant
The pardon that I late pronouncéd here.
    Por.   Art thou contented, Jew?   What dost thou say?
    Shy.   I am content.
    Por.   Clerk, draw a deed of gift.
    Shy.   I pray you, give me leave to go from hence.
I am not well.   Send the deed after me,
And I will sign it.
    Duke.   Get thee gone, but do it.
    Gra.   In christening shalt thou have two godfathers:
Had I been judge, thou shouldst have had ten more,
To bring thee to the gallows, not the font.   [*Exit Shylock.*
    Duke.   Sir, I entreat you home with me to dinner.   401
    Por.   I humbly do desire your grace of pardon.
I must away this night toward Padua,
And it is meet I presently set forth.
    Duke.   I am sorry that your leisure serves you not.
Antonio, gratify this gentleman,
For, in my mind, you are much bound to him.
                   [*Exeunt Duke and his train.*
    Bass.   Most worthy gentleman, I and my friend
Have by your wisdom been this day acquitted
Of grievous penalties; in lieu whereof,   410
Three thousand ducats, due unto the Jew,
We freely cope your courteous pains withal.
    Ant.   And stand indebted, over and above,
In love and service to you evermore.
    Por.   He is well paid that is well satisfied;
And I, delivering you, am satisfied
And therein do account myself well paid.
My mind was never yet more mercenary.
I pray you, know me when we meet again.
I wish you well, and so I take my leave.   420
    Bass.   Dear sir, of force I must attempt you further.

399. **ten more:** i.e., a jury.   412. **cope:** reward.   418. **My mind, etc.:** I
had no intention of doing this for money.   421. **of force:** perforce.   421. **attempt:** urge.

Take some remembrance of us, as a tribute,
Not as a fee.   Grant me two things, I pray you,
Not to deny me, and to pardon me.

    Por.   You press me far, and therefore I will yield.
[*To Ant.*] Give me your gloves, I'll wear them for your sake;
[*To Bass.*] And, for your love, I'll take this ring from you.
Do not draw back your hand; I'll take no more;
And you in love shall not deny me this.

    Bass.   This ring, good sir, alas, it is a trifle!
I will not shame myself to give you this.   431

    Por.   I will have nothing else but only this;
And now methinks I have a mind to it.

    Bass.   There's more depends on this than on the value.
The dearest ring in Venice will I give you,
And find it out by proclamation;
Only for this, I pray you, pardon me.

    Por.   I see, sir, you are liberal in offers.
You taught me first to beg; and now methinks
You teach me how a beggar should be answered.

    Bass.   Good sir, this ring was given me by my wife;   441
And when she put it on, she made me vow
That I should neither sell nor give nor lose it.

    Por.   That scuse serves many men to save their gifts.
And if your wife be not a madwoman,
And know how well I have deserved the ring,
She would not hold out enemy for ever,
For giving it to me.   Well, peace be with you!

                    [*Exeunt Portia and Nerissa.*

    Ant.   My Lord Bassanio, let him have the ring.
Let his deservings and my love withal   450
Be valued 'gainst your wife's commandment.

    Bass.   Go, Gratiano, run and overtake him;
Give him the ring, and bring him, if thou canst,
Unto Antonio's house.   Away! make haste.   [*Exit Gratiano.*
Come, you and I will thither presently;
And in the morning early will we both
Fly toward Belmont.   Come, Antonio.   [*Exeunt.*

        427. **love:** friendship.

SCENE II.   *The same.   A street.*

Enter PORTIA *and* NERISSA.

Por.   Inquire the Jew's house out, give him this deed.
And let him sign it.   We'll away tonight
And be a day before our husbands home.
This deed will be well welcome to Lorenzo.

Enter GRATIANO.

Gra.   Fair sir, you are well o'erta'en.
My Lord Bassanio upon more advice
Hath sent you here this ring, and doth entreat
Your company at dinner.
Por.   That cannot be.
His ring I do accept most thankfully,
And so, I pray you, tell him; furthermore,   10
I pray you, show my youth old Shylock's house.
Gra.   That will I do.
Ner.   Sir, I would speak with you.
[*Aside to Por.*] I'll see if I can get my husband's ring,
Which I did make him swear to keep for ever.
Por. [*Aside to Ner.*] Thou mayst, I warrant.
We shall have old swearing
That they did give the rings away to men;
But we'll outface them, and outswear them too.
[*Aloud*] Away! make haste.   Thou know'st where I will tarry.
Ner.   Come, good sir, will you show me to this house?
                                        [*Exeunt.*

ACT V

SCENE I.   *Belmont.   Avenue to* PORTIA'S *house.*

Enter LORENZO *and* JESSICA.

Lor.   The moon shines bright.   In such a night as this,
When the sweet wind did gently kiss the trees
And they did make no noise, in such a night
Troilus methinks mounted the Troyan walls

16. **old swearing:** great swearing.
4. **Troilus:** for the proper names in this scene see cyclopedia.

And sighed his soul toward the Grecian tents,
Where Cressid lay that night.
 Jes.   In such a night
Did Thisbe fearfully o'ertrip the dew
And saw the lion's shadow ere himself
And ran dismayed away.
 Lor.   In such a night
Stood Dido with a willow in her hand   10
Upon the wild sea banks and waft her love
To come again to Carthage.
 Jes.   In such a night
Medea gathered the enchanted herbs
That did renew old Aeson.
 Lor.   In such a night
Did Jessica steal from the wealthy Jew
And with an unthrift love did run from Venice
As far as Belmont.
 Jes.   In such a night
Did young Lorenzo swear he loved her well,
Stealing her soul with many vows of faith
And ne'er a true one.
 Lor.   In such a night   20
Did pretty Jessica, like a little shrew,
Slander her love, and he forgave it her.
 Jes. I would out-night you, did nobody come;
But, hark, I hear the footing of a man.

Enter STEPHANO.

 Lor. Who comes so fast in silence of the night?
 Steph. A friend.
 Lor. A friend! what friend? Your name, I pray you,
  friend?
 Steph. Stephano is my name; and I bring word
My mistress will before the break of day
Be here at Belmont. She doth stray about   30
By holy crosses, where she kneels and prays
For happy wedlock hours.
 Lor.   Who comes with her?
 Steph. None but a holy hermit and her maid.
I pray you, is my master yet returned?
 Lor. He is not, nor we have not heard from him.
But go we in, I pray thee, Jessica,

And ceremoniously let us prepare
Some welcome for the mistress of the house.

Enter LAUNCELOT.

   Laun.   Sola, sola! wo ha, ho! sola, sola!
   Lor.   Who calls?   40
   Laun.   Sola!   Did you see Master Lorenzo?   Master Lo-
renzo, sola, sola!
   Lor.   Leave hollaing, man; here.
   Laun.   Sola! where? where?
   Lor.   Here.
   Laun.   Tell him there's a post come from my master, with
his horn full of good news.   My master will be here ere
morning.   [*Exit.*
   Lor.   Sweet soul, let's in, and there expect their coming.
And yet no matter; why should we go in?   50
My friend Stephano, signify, I pray you,
Within the house, your mistress is at hand;
And bring your music forth into the air.   [*Exit Stephano.*
How sweet the moonlight sleeps upon this bank!
Here will we sit and let the sounds of music
Creep in our ears.   Soft stillness and the night
Become the touches of sweet harmony.
Sit, Jessica.   Look how the floor of heaven
Is thick inlaid with patines of bright gold.
There's not the smallest orb which thou behold'st   60
But in his motion like an angel sings,
Still quiring to the young-eyed cherubins;
Such harmony is in immortal souls;
But whilst this muddy vesture of decay
Doth grossly close it in, we cannot hear it.

Enter Musicians.

Come, ho! and wake Diana with a hymn.
With sweetest touches pierce your mistress' ear
And draw her home with music.   [*Music.*
   Jes.   I am never merry when I hear sweet music.
   Lor.   The reason is, your spirits are attentive;   70
For do but note a wild and wanton herd,
Or race of youthful and unhandled colts,

46. **post:** messenger. 49. **expect:** await. 59. **patines of bright gold:** the
stars are compared to small discs (patines) of gold.

Fetching mad bounds, bellowing and neighing loud,
Which is the hot condition of their blood;
If they but hear perchance a trumpet sound,
Or any air of music touch their ears,
You shall perceive them make a mutual stand,
Their savage eyes turned to a modest gaze
By the sweet power of music; therefore the poet
Did feign that Orpheus drew trees, stones and floods;   80
Since nought so stockish, hard and full of rage,
But music for the time doth change his nature.
The man that hath no music in himself,
Nor is not moved with concord of sweet sounds,
Is fit for treasons, stratagems and spoils;
The motions of his spirit are dull as night
And his affections dark as Erebus.
Let no such man be trusted.   Mark the music.

Enter PORTIA *and* NERISSA.

   Por.   That light we see is burning in my hall.
How far that little candle throws his beams!   90
So shines a good deed in a naughty world.
   Ner.   When the moon shone, we did not see the candle.
   Por.   So doth the greater glory dim the less.
A substitute shines brightly as a king
Until a king be by, and then his state
Empties itself, as doth an inland brook
Into the main of waters.   Music!   Hark!
   Ner.   It is your music, madam, of the house.
   Por.   Nothing is good, I see, without respect;
Methinks it sounds much sweeter than by day.
   Ner.   Silence bestows that virtue on it, madam.   101
   Por.   The crow doth sing as sweetly as the lark
When neither is attended, and I think
The nightingale, if she should sing by day,
When every goose is cackling, would be thought
No better a musician than the wren.
How many things by season seasoned are
To their right praise and true perfection!
Peace, ho! the moon sleeps with Endymion
And would not be awaked.   [*Music ceases.*

   81. **stockish:** like a stick.   99. **without respect:** without considering the circumstances.

Lor. That is the voice, 110
Or I am much deceived, of Portia.

Por. He knows me as the blind man knows the cuckoo,
By the bad voice.

Lor. Dear lady, welcome home.

Por. We have been praying for our husbands' healths,
Which speed, we hope, the better for our words.
Are they returned?

Lor. Madam, they are not yet;
But there is come a messenger before,
To signify their coming.

Por. Go in, Nerissa;
Give order to my servants that they take
No note at all of our being absent hence; 120
Nor you, Lorenzo; Jessica, nor you. [*A tucket sounds.*

Lor. Your husband is at hand; I hear his trumpet.
We are no telltales, madam; fear you not.

Por. This night methinks is but the daylight sick;
It looks a little paler. 'Tis a day,
Such as the day is when the sun is hid.

Enter BASSANIO, ANTONIO, GRATIANO, *and their followers.*

Bass. We should hold day with the Antipodes,
If you would walk in absence of the sun.

Por. Let me give light, but let me not be light;
For a light wife doth make a heavy husband, 130
And never be Bassanio so for me.
But God sort all! You are welcome home, my lord.

Bass. I thank you, madam. Give welcome to my friend.
This is the man, this is Antonio,
To whom I am so infinitely bound.

Por. You should in all sense be much bound to him,
For, as I hear, he was much bound for you.

Ant. No more than I am well acquitted of.

Por. Sir, you are very welcome to our house.
It must appear in other ways than words, 140
Therefore I scant this breathing courtesy.

Gra. [*To Ner.*] By yonder moon I swear you do me
      wrong;
In faith, I gave it to the judge's clerk.

128. **Antipodes:** the side of the earth opposite our feet. 132. **sort:** dispose.
138. **acquitted:** rewarded.

Would he were dead that had it, for my part,
Since you do take it, love, so much at heart.

Por. A quarrel, ho, already! What's the matter?

Gra. About a hoop of gold, a paltry ring
That she did give me, whose posy was
For all the world like cutler's poetry
Upon a knife, " Love me, and leave me not."   150

Ner. What talk you of, the posy or the value?
You swore to me, when I did give it you,
That you would wear it till your hour of death
And that it should lie with you in your grave.
Though not for me, yet for your vehement oaths,
You should have been respective and have kept it.
Gave it a judge's clerk! no, God's my judge,
The clerk will ne'er wear hair on 's face that had it.

Gra. He will, an if he live to be a man.

Ner. Ay, if a woman live to be a man.   160

Gra. Now, by this hand, I gave it to a youth,
A kind of boy, a little scrubbéd boy,
No higher than thyself, the judge's clerk,
A prating boy, that begged it as a fee.
I could not for my heart deny it him.

Por. You were to blame, I must be plain with you,
To part so slightly with your wife's first gift;
A thing stuck on with oaths upon your finger
And so riveted with faith unto your flesh.
I gave my love a ring and made him swear   170
Never to part with it; and here he stands;
I dare be sworn for him he would not leave it
Nor pluck it from his finger, for the wealth
That the world masters. Now, in faith, Gratiano,
You give your wife too unkind a cause of grief.
An 'twere to me, I should be mad at it.

Bass. [*Aside*] Why, I were best to cut my left hand off
And swear I lost the ring defending it.

Gra. My Lord Bassanio gave his ring away
Unto the judge that begged it and indeed   180
Deserved it too; and then the boy, his clerk,
That took some pains in writing, he begged mine;
And neither man nor master would take aught
But the two rings.

148. **posy**: motto. 156. **respective**: careful.

Por.   What ring gave you, my lord?
Not that, I hope, which you received of me.
Bass. If I could add a lie unto a fault,
I would deny it; but you see my finger
Hath not the ring upon it; it is gone.
Por. Even so void is your false heart of truth.
By heaven, I will ne'er come in your bed   190
Until I see the ring.
Ner.   Nor I in yours.
Till I again see mine.
Bass.   Sweet Portia,
If you did know to whom I gave the ring,
If you did know for whom I gave the ring
And would conceive for what I gave the ring
And how unwillingly I left the ring,
When naught would be accepted but the ring,
You would abate the strength of your displeasure.
Por. If you had known the virtue of the ring,
Or half her worthiness that gave the ring,   200
Or your own honor to contain the ring,
You would not then have parted with the ring.
What man is there so much unreasonable,
If you had pleased to have defended it
With any terms of zeal, wanted the modesty
To urge the thing held as a ceremony?
Nerissa teaches me what to believe:
I'll die for 't but some woman had the ring.
Bass. No, by my honor, madam, by my soul,
No woman had it, but a civil doctor,   210
Which did refuse three thousand ducats of me
And begged the ring; the which I did deny him
And suffered him to go displeased away;
Even he that did uphold the very life
Of my dear friend. What should I say, sweet lady?
I was enforced to send it after him;
I was beset with shame and courtesy;
My honor would not let ingratitude
So much besmear it. Pardon me, good lady;
For, by these blessed candles of the night,   220
Had you been there, I think you would have begged
The ring of me to give the worthy doctor.

201. **contain:** retain. 210. **civil doctor:** doctor of civil law.

Por.   Let not that doctor e'er come near my house.
Since he hath got the jewel that I loved,
And that which you did swear to keep for me,
I will become as liberal as you;
I'll not deny him any thing I have.
 Ner.   Nor I his clerk; therefore be well advised
How you do leave me to mine own protection.
 Gra.   Well, do you so; let not me take him, then;
For if I do, I'll mar the young clerk's pen.
 Ant.   I am the unhappy subject of these quarrels.
 Por.   Sir, grieve not you; you are welcome notwithstanding.
 Bass.   Portia, forgive me this enforcéd wrong; 240
And, in the hearing of these many friends,
I swear to thee, even by thine own fair eyes,
Wherein I see myself —
 Por.   Mark you but that!
In both my eyes he doubly sees himself;
In each eye, one.   Swear by your double self,
And there's an oath of credit.
 Bass.   Nay, but hear me.
Pardon this fault, and by my soul I swear
I never more will break an oath with thee.
 Ant.   I once did lend my body for his wealth;
Which, but for him that had your husband's ring, 250
Had quite miscarried.   I dare be bound again,
My soul upon the forfeit, that your lord
Will never more break faith advisedly.
 Por.   Then you shall be his surety.   Give him this
And bid him keep it better than the other.
 Ant.   Here, Lord Bassanio; swear to keep this ring.
 Bass.   By heaven, it is the same I gave the doctor!
 Por.   You are all amazed.
Here is a letter; read it at your leisure;
It comes from Padua, from Bellario.
There you shall find that Portia was the doctor,
Nerissa there her clerk.   Lorenzo here 270
Shall witness I set forth as soon as you
And even but now returned; I have not yet
Entered my house.   Antonio, you are welcome;
And I have better news in store for you
Than you expect.   Unseal this letter soon;
There you shall find three of your argosies

Are richly come to harbor suddenly.
You shall not know by what strange accident
I chancéd on this letter.

    Ant.   I am dumb.

    Bass. Were you the doctor and I knew you not?   280

    Gra. Were you the clerk that is to make me watchful?

    Ner. Ay, but the clerk that never means to do it,
Unless he live until he be a man.

    Ant. Sweet lady, you have given me life and living;
For here I read for certain that my ships
Are safely come to road.

    Por.   How now, Lorenzo!
My clerk hath some good comforts too for you.

    Ner. Ay, and I'll give them him without a fee.   290
There do I give to you and Jessica,
From the rich Jew, a special deed of gift,
After his death, of all he dies possessed of.

    Lor. Fair ladies, you drop manna in the way
Of starvéd people.

    Por.   It is almost morning.
And yet I am sure you are not satisfied
Of these events at full. Let us go in;
And charge us there upon inter'gatories,
And we will answer all things faithfully.

    Gra. Let it be so: the first inter'gatory   300
That my Nerissa shall be sworn on is,
Whether till the next night she had rather stay
Or go to bed now, being two hours to day.
Well, while I live I'll fear no other thing
So sore as keeping safe Nerissa's ring.   [*Exeunt.*

305. **sore**: much.

INTERPRETATIVE NOTE

A modern dramatist would in all probability call this play *The Jew of Venice*. One reason why Shakespeare did not adopt so obvious a title was the existence of Marlowe's *Jew of Malta*, first produced in 1590, and still popular in 1596 when *The Merchant of Venice* was written. It is even possible that the success of Marlowe's play, with Edward Alleyn in the leading part, may have been partly responsible for Shakespeare's wanting to create a similar rôle for Richard Burbage in their own company. But whatever the facts may be, Shakespeare adopted a number of Marlowe's ideas, although the earlier play was a tragedy and that of Shakespeare is a comedy. Marlowe obviously attacked the Jews; his Barabas has practically no redeeming traits. Shakespeare undoubtedly meant Shylock to be a laughing stock, but he was fairer than Marlowe in that he gave his Jew redeeming qualities which must have made some appeal even to an Elizabethan audience. Nothing is more certain than that the popularity of the play today is due to its author's unerring instinct in making Shylock true to life.

In all modern productions of this play it is the character of Shylock that is featured, not as a comic figure but rather as an alien placed in tragically pathetic circumstances among people who hated his race. In Shakespeare's day it was still illegal for Jews to reside in England, although the law against them was but laxly enforced. Furthermore, only two years before this play was written the country had been violently agitated by the case of Dr. Lopez, a Spanish Jew, executed because of a supposed plot to assassinate Queen Elizabeth. To Shakespeare the Jew was made the villain of the play, not as a foil for the nominal hero Antonio, but to set off the virtues and the charm of Portia, the fascinating heiress of Belmont.

While we of today think of the play as a tragi-comedy, that is, a play in which impending tragedy is averted at the last moment, Shakespeare intended it for pure romance, with Portia as the central figure. Had he regarded it otherwise he would never have written a fifth act like the one in the play, an act that has little dramatic justification other than that of making the audience forget the essentially tragic exit of Shylock in the fourth act. *The Merchant of Venice* was written in that period of Shakespeare's work when he was producing his greatest romantic comedies, *A Midsummer-Night's Dream* having preceded it by two years, and *As You Like It* following it three years later.

The scene of *The Merchant of Venice* is technically laid in Venice, but, as in all of Shakespeare's romantic comedies, the real scene is that of a Land of Romance which never existed anywhere except in the imagination of the author. The essence of romance always is life not as it is really lived, but as we think we should like it to be. The Elizabethan audiences fed on the improbabilities of the stories much as we today do on those of the movies.

The Merchant of Venice is unusually rich in plot construction and will repay careful study from that angle. Four distinct stories are cleverly interwoven: the " bond " or " pound of flesh " story and the "caskets" story as the chief ingredients of the main plot, and the Lorenzo-Jessica story, with that of the rings serving as the material for the subplot. None of these was original with Shakespeare, with the possible exception of that of the rings; the first two had even been used in an earlier play from which Shakespeare is supposed to have borrowed freely, while the similarity of the Lorenzo-Jessica story to Marlowe's play is evident to any one who reads the two. Equally evident is the superiority of Shakespeare's genius in the way he used these various elements. It is not possible here to go into an analysis of the plot, but attention may be called to the way in which Shakespeare contrived that all four of these "motives," as they are sometimes called, come together in the climax of the play at the end of the fourth act.

Students will find it interesting to compare plays after several have been studied. In the notes and questions several pointed hints have been given, but the parallelism goes much further. In this volume you will find that in the later play of *As You Like It* the author used many devices already used in the earlier play, some of them used earlier still in such plays as *Love's Labor's Lost*, *The Two Gentlemen of Verona*, and *A Midsummer-Night's Dream*.

QUESTIONS

I. i.

1. Describe "Venice. A street" as you visualize it.
2. How do you picture the group of friends? To what class do they belong?
3. Do they vary in age? Give reasons for thinking so.
4. Why the emphasis on Antonio's sadness?
5. Are any of the suggested reasons plausible?
6. How does Gratiano impress you? His chief characteristic?
7. What do you learn of Antonio's situation?
8. Where is the first hint of plot complication? Be definite.
9. Briefly, the story of Bassanio's money troubles.
10. What do you think of his plan to recoup his fortune?
11. At the end of the scene, what do you think of Bassanio? of Antonio?
12. From hints in this scene, do you get a favorable impression of Portia?
13. Bassanio's reasons for thinking he can win Portia.
14. How is the action left in suspense?
15. State the facts which you think will have plot importance.

I. ii.

1. How does Portia's opening speech resemble that of Antonio?
2. Do you get a favorable impression of Portia? How old is she?
3. What is the dramatic purpose of this scene?
4. How does Nerissa help in bringing this out?
5. State clearly the scheme of the caskets.
6. Why did her father make such a cumbersome arrangement?
7. What remark by Nerissa has definite plot significance?
8. Just what relationship exists between Portia and Nerissa?

I. iii.

1. Is the opening line the beginning of a conversation or not? Explain.
2. What does Shylock mean by saying "Antonio is a *good* man"?
3. Give Shylock's reasons for hating Antonio. Are any justified?
4. How does Antonio's manner in this scene compare with that in the preceding?
5. Does Shylock tell the truth in lines 107–120? Explain.
6. Does Shylock really want to be friendly with Antonio?
7. Is he already thinking of his plan for revenge?
8. In your own words, state the conditions of the bond.
9. Why does Antonio not hesitate to sign it?
10. Why didn't Bassanio object more strenuously?
11. So far, who stands out more favorably, Antonio or Shylock?

II. i.

1. State your impression of the Prince of Morocco.
2. Try to visualize this scene as Shakespeare devised it.
3. Does the scene serve any purpose in the play? Explain.

II. ii.

1. This is one of the best humorous scenes in Shakespeare. Do you find it funny?
2. What makes Launcelot amusing? Name specific points from the text.
3. Shakespearean audiences were fond of such scenes. Find similar ones in the other plays in this volume.
4. Why is Gratiano introduced in this scene?

II. iii.

1. What are your first impressions of Jessica?
2. Does this scene have any plot value?

II. iv.

1. In your own words, what was Lorenzo's plan?
2. What is a "masque"?

II. v.

1. Compare Shylock's uneasiness with that of Antonio and Portia.
2. Is there an indirect reference to Antonio in this scene?

II. vi.

1. Does Gratiano's long speech confirm or modify your opinion of him?
2. Was Jessica a thief, or was she justified in helping herself?
3. What in this scene was especially enjoyable to an Elizabethan audience?
4. The several lines of action are now well started. Name them.

II. vii.

1. Consider Shakespeare's reasons for placing this scene so far from Sc. i.
2. Give the Moor's reasons for his choice.
3. Are they in line with his character?
4. How does the end of the scene help in creating suspense?

II. viii.

1. In this scene, what information necessary to the story is given?
2. Did Antonio know that Lorenzo and Jessica were on the boat? Were they?
3. What ominous plot hints are thrown out in this scene?

II. ix.

1. What oath did Portia's suitors have to take?
2. What is the dramatic value of having a second suitor make his choice?
3. How does Arragon compare with the Moor?
4. What can you say of Portia's attitude toward her suitors?
5. How does Nerissa's last speech link up with the plot?

III. i.

1. What information is given at once?
2. Contrast the moods of Shylock in this scene. How do they affect your estimate of him so far?
3. Compare lines 55–76 with *Hamlet*, II. ii., 304–323.
4. How is Shylock's spirit of revenge intensified by Tubal?
5. What special touch is given by reference to the turquoise?
6. Is this scene serious or funny? Explain.
7. How did Shakespeare probably intend it?

III. ii.

1. The Portia of this scene differs from what we saw of her before. Comment.
2. Does she seem to be " throwing herself " at Bassanio?
3. In this respect contrast her with Rosalind in *As You Like It*.
4. How does Bassanio's reasoning differ from that of his predecessors?
5. At this point, sum up your estimate of Bassanio.
6. Is anything gained dramatically by Gratiano marrying Nerissa? Explain.
7. What was Bassanio's idea of a "gentleman "?
8. How is the climax of the story prepared for by the letter?
9. Do you see any plot significance in the ring episode?
10. Does Gratiano also receive a ring? Explain.

III. iii.

1. How does this scene prepare for possible tragedy?
2. Is this a good dramatic device? Explain.
3. Contrast Antonio's attitude toward Shylock with that earlier in the play.
4. Note Shylock's reference to "mercy " and Antonio's to "law."
5. Why should Antonio long so ardently for the presence of Bassanio?

III. iv.

1. Is this scene necessary for the plot? Explain.
2. What part is most important? Most interesting in itself?
3. Contrast the latter part of this scene with the end of the first act of *As You Like It*, remembering that feminine rôles were played by boys.

III. v.

1. Apply the first two questions on Sc. iv to this scene.
2. In modern productions this scene is always omitted. Comment on this.
3. Does your interest in Launcelot, Lorenzo, and Jessica hold up? Comment.

IV. i.

1. Picture "A court of justice."
2. Comment on Antonio's attitude throughout this scene.
3. Is the Duke fittingly presented as a judge? Explain.
4. This is the big scene for the actor who plays Shylock. Try to visualize how he looked and what stage "business" he went through, noting especially the change as the action proceeds.
5. If possible, contrast the court procedure in this scene with that of an actual court of today.
6. Note the dialogue between Gratiano and Shylock. Would this interest an audience? Explain.
7. Does this prepare you for a later passage in the scene?
8. With the entrance of Portia the three women of the play have appeared in men's dress. Comment.
9. Why does Portia say "The Jew must be merciful"?
10. Portia's next speech is the most famous passage in the play. Comment.
11. Does this speech have legal value?
12. At first Portia seems to favor the Jew. Is this good drama?
13. Is the dramatic moment too long delayed?
14. Would an audience seeing the play for the first time think so?
15. Portia's remark "Tarry a little" is the dramatic climax of the play. Try to picture each of the important characters at this point.
16. Do you feel a distinct drop in the tenseness of the situation?
17. How is this reaction indicated by Gratiano?
18. Could the play easily have been turned into a tragedy at this point?
19. Comment on Portia's interpretation of the law.
20. Had she really consulted the learned Bellario? Explain.
21. Is her sentence too severe, from a modern point of view?
22. Why was there no jury?
23. Visualize the exit of Shylock.
24. Could the play properly have ended at that point? Comment.
25. Does the byplay of the rings add anything of dramatic value?

IV. ii.

1. How does this scene suggest the line of action for Act V?
2. Is the scene really important? Explain.
3. Is there any part of the plot not yet worked out?

V. i.

1. What tone is given to the story by this concluding scene?
2. On the whole, do you think that the Lorenzo-Jessica part of the story was justified dramatically?
3. What do you think of Lorenzo's comments on music?
4. Is the conclusion of the ring episode amusing to one who already knows the facts?

5. Was it important that Antonio be dragged into this scene?
6. This scene is laid at night. Does that in any way affect its spirit?
7. Are all the threads of the plot satisfactorily straightened out?
8. Do the poetry and the air of happiness in this scene effectually blot out the memory of Shylock?
9. Would anything have been gained by showing more of him?

MACBETH

DRAMATIS PERSONAE

DUNCAN, king of Scotland.
MALCOLM, } his sons.
DONALBAIN }
MACBETH } generals of the king's
BANQUO } army.
MACDUFF }
LENNOX }
ROSS }
MENTEITH } noblemen of Scotland.
ANGUS }
CAITHNESS }
FLEANCE, son to Banquo.
SIWARD, Earl of Northumberland,
general of the English forces.
Young SIWARD, his son.
SEYTON, an officer attending on
Macbeth.

Boy, son to Macduff.
An English Doctor.
A Scotch Doctor.
A Sergeant.
A Porter.
An Old Man.
LADY MACBETH.
LADY MACDUFF.
Gentlewoman attending on Lady
Macbeth.
HECATE.
Three witches.
Apparitions.

Lords, Gentlemen, Officers, Soldiers,
Murderers, Attendants, and Messengers.

SCENE: *Scotland; England.*

ACT I

SCENE I. *A desert place.*

Thunder and lightning. Enter three Witches.

First Witch. When shall we three meet again
In thunder, lightning, or in rain?
Sec. Witch. When the hurlyburly's done,
When the battle's lost and won.
Third Witch. That will be ere the set of sun.
First Witch. Where the place?
Sec. Witch.   Upon the heath.
Third Witch. There to meet with Macbeth.
First Witch. I come, Graymalkin!
Sec. Witch. Paddock calls.
Third Witch. Anon.   10
All. Fair is foul, and foul is fair:
Hover through the fog and filthy air.   [*Exeunt.*

3. **hurlyburly:** tumult. 8. **Graymalkin:** cat. 9. **paddock:** toad. The
governing spirit of a witch was supposed to be embodied in some animal.

Scene II. *A camp near Forres.*

Alarum within. Enter Duncan, Malcolm, Donalbain, Lennox, *with* Attendants, *meeting a bleeding* Sergeant.

  Dun. What bloody man is that? He can report,
As seemeth by his plight, of the revolt
The newest state.
  Mal.   This is the sergeant
Who like a good and hardy soldier fought
'Gainst my captivity. Hail, brave friend!
Say to the king the knowledge of the broil
As thou didst leave it.
  Ser.   Doubtful it stood,
As two spent swimmers, that do cling together
And choke their art. The merciless Macdonwald —
Worthy to be a rebel, for to that   10
The multiplying villainies of nature
Do swarm upon him — from the western isles
Of kerns and gallowglasses is supplied;
And fortune, on his damnéd quarrel smiling,
Showed like a rebel's wench. But all's too weak;
For brave Macbeth — well he deserves that name —
Disdaining fortune, with his brandished steel,
Which smoked with bloody execution,
Like valor's minion carved out his passage
Till he faced the slave;   20
Which ne'er shook hands, nor bade farewell to him,
Till he unseamed him from the nave to the chaps,
And fixed his head upon our battlements.
  Dun. O valiant cousin! worthy gentleman!
  Ser. As whence the sun 'gins his reflection
Shipwrecking storms and direful thunders break,
So from that spring whence comfort seemed to come
Discomfort swells. Mark, king of Scotland, mark:
No sooner justice had with valor armed
Compelled these skipping kerns to trust their heels, 30

1. **bloody:** this significant word occurs often in this play. 3. **sergeant:** a foot soldier attending a king or high officer. 9. **choke:** make useless. 10. **for to that:** because. 12. **western isles:** the Hebrides and Ireland. 13. **kerns, etc.:** light-armed and heavy-armed troops. 19. **minion:** favorite. 21. **Which:** i.e., Macbeth. 24. **cousin:** Macbeth was first cousin to Duncan, but the word was often used for any relative, and sometimes merely as a familiar term. 25. **whence:** direction from which, i.e., the east.

But the Norweyan lord surveying vantage
With furbished arms and new supplies of men
Began a fresh assault.
    Dun.   Dismayed not this
Our captains, Macbeth and Banquo?
    Ser.   Yes;
As sparrows eagles, or the hare the lion.
If I say sooth, I must report they were
As cannons overcharged with double cracks, so they
Doubly redoubled strokes upon the foe.
Except they meant to bathe in reeking wounds,
Or memorize another Golgotha,   40
I cannot tell.
But I am faint, my gashes cry for help.
    Dun. So well thy words become thee as thy wounds;
They smack of honor both. Go get him surgeons.
                   [*Exit Sergeant, attended.*
Who comes here?

                Enter Ross.

    Mal.   The worthy thane of Ross.
    Len. What a haste looks through his eyes! So should he
      look
That seems to speak things strange.
    Ross.   God save the king!
    Dun. Whence camest thou, worthy thane?
    Ross.   From Fife, great king;
Where the Norweyan banners flout the sky
And fan our people cold. Norway himself,   50
With terrible numbers,
Assisted by that most disloyal traitor
The thane of Cawdor, began a dismal conflict;
Till that Bellona's bridegroom, lapped in proof,
Confronted him with self-comparisons,
Point against point rebellious, arm 'gainst arm,
Curbing his lavish spirit; and, to conclude,
The victory fell on us.
    Dun.   Great happiness!
    Ross.   That now
Sweno, the Norways' king, craves composition;

---

31. **vantage:** opportunity. 45. **thane:** minor nobleman. 49. **flout:** insult. 54. **Bellona's bridegroom:** Mars, to whom Macbeth is compared. 54. **lapped in proof:** wrapped in perfect armor. 59. **composition:** terms of peace.

Nor would we deign him burial of his men   60
Till he disburséd at Saint Colme's inch
Ten thousand dollars to our general use.
    Dun. No more that thane of Cawdor shall deceive
Our bosom interest. Go pronounce his present death,
And with his former title greet Macbeth.
    Ross. I'll see it done.
    Dun. What he hath lost noble Macbeth hath won.
                                      [Exeunt.

SCENE III. *A heath near Forres.*

Thunder. Enter the three Witches.

    First Witch. Where hast thou been, sister?
    Sec. Witch. Killing swine.
    Third Witch. Sister, where thou?
    First Witch. A sailor's wife had chestnuts in her lap,
And munched, and munched, and munched. " Give me,"
      quoth I.
" Aroint thee, witch! " the rump-fed ronyon cries.
Her husband's to Aleppo gone, master o' the Tiger;
But in a sieve I'll thither sail,
And, like a rat without a tail,
I'll do, I'll do, and I'll do.   10
    Sec. Witch. I'll give thee a wind.
    First Witch. Thou'rt kind.
    Third Witch. And I another.
    First Witch. I myself have all the other,
And the very ports they blow,
All the quarters that they know
I' the shipman's card.
I will drain him dry as hay;
Sleep shall neither night nor day
Hang upon his penthouse lid;   20
He shall live a man forbid.
Weary se'nnights nine times nine
Shall he dwindle, peak and pine:

    61. **Saint Colme's Inch:** an island now called Inchcolm.
    2. **killing swine:** supposed to be a favorite pastime. 2. **aroint:** begone.
9. **without a tail:** Witches could assume the form of any animal, but the tail
was always lacking. 10. **do:** i.e., gnaw. 15. **blow:** i.e., to which they blow.
17. **card:** chart. 20. **penthouse:** sloping. 21. **forbid:** cursed. 23. **dwindle, etc.:** The belief was that witches, placing a wax image of a person before
a fire, caused that person's slow death as the wax melted.

Though his bark cannot be lost,
Yet it shall be tempest-tost.
Look what I have.
 Sec. Witch. Show me, show me.
 First Witch. Here I have a pilot's thumb,
Wrecked as homeward he did come.   [*Drum within.*
 Third Witch. A drum, a drum!   30
Macbeth doth come.
 All. The weird sisters, hand in hand,
Posters of the sea and land,
Thus do go about, about;
Thrice to thine and thrice to mine
And thrice again, to make up nine.
Peace! the charm's wound up.

Enter Macbeth *and* Banquo.

 Macb. So foul and fair a day I have not seen.
 Ban. How far is 't call'd to Forres? What are these
So withered and so wild in their attire,   40
That look not like the inhabitants o' the earth,
And yet are on 't? Live you? or are you aught
That man may question? You seem to understand me,
By each at once her choppy finger laying
Upon her skinny lips. You should be women,
And yet your beards forbid me to interpret
That you are so.
 Macb. Speak, if you can. What are you?
 First Witch. All hail, Macbeth! hail to thee, thane of
  Glamis!
 Sec. Witch. All hail, Macbeth! hail to thee, thane of
  Cawdor!
 Third Witch. All hail, Macbeth, that shalt be king here-
  after!   50
 Ban. Good sir, why do you start, and seem to fear
Things that do sound so fair? I' the name of truth,
Are ye fantastical, or that indeed
Which outwardly ye show? My noble partner
You greet with present grace and great prediction
Of noble having and of royal hope,
That he seems rapt withal; to me you speak not.

32. **weird**: fatal, in the sense of determining fate. 33. **posters**: rapid travelers. 35. **thrice**: three and its multiples had magic significance. 53. **fantastical**: imaginary.

If you can look into the seeds of time,
And say which grain will grow and which will not,
Speak then to me, who neither beg nor fear   60
Your favors nor your hate.

First Witch. Hail!
Sec. Witch. Hail!
Third Witch. Hail!
First Witch. Lesser than Macbeth, and greater.
Sec. Witch. Not so happy, yet much happier.
Third Witch. Thou shalt get kings, though thou be none;
So all hail, Macbeth and Banquo!
First Witch. Banquo and Macbeth, all hail!
Macb. Stay, you imperfect speakers, tell me more.   70
By Sinel's death I know I am thane of Glamis;
But how of Cawdor? The thane of Cawdor lives,
A prosperous gentleman; and to be king
Stands not within the prospect of belief,
No more than to be Cawdor. Say from whence
You owe this strange intelligence, or why
Upon this blasted heath you stop our way
With such prophetic greeting? Speak, I charge you.

                              [*Witches vanish.*

Ban. The earth hath bubbles, as the water has,
And these are of them. Whither are they vanished?   80
Macb. Into the air; and what seemed corporal melted
As breath into the wind. Would they had stayed!
Ban. Were such things here as we do speak about?
Or have we eaten on the insane root
That takes the reason prisoner?
Macb. Your children shall be kings.
Ban.   You shall be king.
Macb. And thane of Cawdor too: went it not so?
Ban. To the selfsame tune and words. Who's here?

Enter Ross *and* Angus.

Ross. The king hath happily received, Macbeth,
The news of thy success; and when he reads   90
Thy personal venture in the rebels' fight,
His wonders and his praises do contend
Which should be thine or his. Silenced with that,
In viewing o'er the rest o' the selfsame day,

71. **Sinel's death:** Sinel was Macbeth's father. 81. **corporal:** having body.

He finds thee in the stout Norweyan ranks,
Nothing afeard of what thyself didst make,
Strange images of death.   As thick as hail
Came post with post; and every one did bear
Thy praises in his kingdom's great defence,
And poured them down before him.
    Ang.   We are sent   100
To give thee from our royal master thanks;
Only to herald thee into his sight,
Not pay thee.
    Ross.   And, for an earnest of a greater honor,
He bade me, from him, call thee thane of Cawdor;
In which addition, hail, most worthy thane!
For it is thine.
    Ban.   What, can the devil speak true?
    Macb.   The thane of Cawdor lives; why do you dress me
In borrowed robes?
    Ang.   Who was the thane lives yet;
But under heavy judgment bears that life   110
Which he deserves to lose.   Whether he was combined
With those of Norway, or did line the rebel
With hidden help and vantage, or that with both
He labored in his country's wreck, I know not;
But treasons capital, confessed and proved,
Have overthrown him.
    Macb. [*Aside*] Glamis, and thane of Cawdor!
The greatest is behind. [*To Ross and Angus*] Thanks for your
        pains.
[*To Ban.*] Do you not hope your children shall be kings,
When those that gave the thane of Cawdor to me
Promised no less to them?
    Ban.   That trusted home   120
Might yet enkindle you unto the crown,
Besides the thane of Cawdor.   But 'tis strange;
And oftentimes, to win us to our harm,
The instruments of darkness tell us truths,
Win us with honest trifles, to betray 's
In deepest consequence.
Cousins, a word, I pray you.
    Macb.   [*Aside*] Two truths are told,
As happy prologues to the swelling act

      106. **addition:** title.   120. **That trusted home:** fully trusted.

Of the imperial theme. — I thank you, gentlemen.
[*Aside*] This supernatural soliciting   130
Cannot be ill, cannot be good.   If ill,
Why hath it given me earnest of success,
Commencing in truth?   I am thane of Cawdor;
If good, why do I yield to that suggestion
Whose horrid image doth unfix my hair
And make my seated heart knock at my ribs,
Against the use of nature?   Present fears
Are less than horrible imaginings:
My thought, whose murder yet is but fantastical,
Shakes so my single state of man that function
Is smothered in surmise, and nothing is   141
But what is not.
    Ban.   Look, how our partner's rapt.
    Macb. [*Aside*] If chance will have me king, why, chance
      may crown me,
Without my stir.
    Ban.   New honors come upon him,
Like our strange garments, cleave not to their mold
But with the aid of use.
    Macb.   [*Aside*] Come what come may,
Time and the hour runs through the roughest day.
    Ban.   Worthy Macbeth, we stay upon your leisure.
    Macb.   Give me your favor.   My dull brain was wrought
With things forgotten.   Kind gentlemen, your pains   150
Are registered where every day I turn
The leaf to read them.   Let us toward the king.
[*To Ban.*]   Think upon what hath chanced, and, at more time,
The interim having weighed it, let us speak
Our free hearts each to other.
    Ban.   Very gladly.
    Macb. Till then, enough.   Come, friends.   [*Exeunt.*

SCENE IV.   *Forres.   The palace.*

Flourish.   Enter DUNCAN, MALCOLM, DONALBAIN, LENNOX,
and Attendants.

    Dun. Is execution done on Cawdor?   Are not
Those in commission yet returned?

Mal.   My liege,
They are not yet come back. But I have spoke
With one that saw him die; who did report
That very frankly he confessed his treasons,
Implored your highness' pardon and set forth
A deep repentance. Nothing in his life
Became him like the leaving it; he died
As one that had been studied in his death
To throw away the dearest thing he owed,   10
As 'twere a careless trifle.
    Dun.   There's no art
To find the mind's construction in the face:
He was a gentleman on whom I built
An absolute trust.

      Enter MACBETH, BANQUO, ROSS, *and* ANGUS.

                O worthiest cousin!
The sin of my ingratitude even now
Was heavy on me. Thou art so far before
That swiftest wing of recompense is slow
To overtake thee. Would thou hadst less deserved,
That the proportion both of thanks and payment
Might have been mine! Only I have left to say,   20
More is thy due than more than all can pay.
    Macb. The service and the loyalty I owe,
In doing it, pays itself. Your highness' part
Is to receive our duties; and our duties
Are to your throne and state children and servants,
Which do but what they should, by doing every thing
Safe toward your love and honor.
    Dun.   Welcome hither:
I have begun to plant thee, and will labor
To make thee full of growing. Noble Banquo,
That hast no less deserved, nor must be known
No less to have done so, let me infold thee   31
And hold thee to my heart.
    Ban.   There if I grow,
The harvest is your own.
    Dun.   My plenteous joys,
Wanton in fulness, seek to hide themselves
In drops of sorrow. Sons, kinsmen, thanes,

12. **To find:** i.e., capable of finding.

And you whose places are the nearest, know
We will establish our estate upon
Our eldest, Malcolm, whom we name hereafter
The Prince of Cumberland; which honor must
Not unaccompanied invest him only,   40
But signs of nobleness, like stars, shall shine
On all deservers.   From hence to Inverness,
And bind us further to you.
   Macb.   The rest is labor, which is not used for you.
I'll be myself the harbinger and make joyful
The hearing of my wife with your approach;
So humbly take my leave.
   Dun.   My worthy Cawdor!
   Macb.   [*Aside*] The Prince of Cumberland!   That is a step
On which I must fall down, or else o'erleap,
For in my way it lies.   Stars, hide your fires;   50
Let not light see my black and deep desires:
The eye wink at the hand; yet let that be,
Which the eye fears, when it is done, to see.   [*Exit.*
   Dun.   True, worthy Banquo; he is full so valiant,
And in his commendations I am fed;
It is a banquet to me.   Let's after him,
Whose care is gone before to bid us welcome.
It is a peerless kinsman.   [*Flourish.   Exeunt.*

Scene V.   *Inverness.   Macbeth's castle.*

Enter Lady Macbeth, *reading a letter.*

   Lady M.   " They met me in the day of success; and I have
learned by the perfectest report, they have more in them than
mortal knowledge.   When I burned in desire to question them
further, they made themselves air, into which they vanished.
Whiles I stood rapt in the wonder of it, came missives from the
king, who all-hailed me ' Thane of Cawdor '; by which title,
before, these weird sisters saluted me, and referred me to the
coming on of time, with ' Hail, king that shalt be! '   This
have I thought good to deliver thee, my dearest partner of
greatness, that thou mightst not lose the dues of rejoicing, by
being ignorant of what greatness is promised thee.   Lay it to
thy heart, and farewell."

   42. **Inverness:** Macbeth's castle, twenty-five miles from Forres.

Glamis thou art, and Cawdor; and shalt be
What thou art promised. Yet do I fear thy nature;
It is too full o' the milk of human kindness
To catch the nearest way. Thou wouldst be great;
Art not without ambition, but without   20
The illness should attend it. What thou wouldst highly
That wouldst thou holily; wouldst not play false,
And yet wouldst wrongly win. Thou 'ldst have, great Glamis,
That which cries, " Thus thou must do, if thou have it ";
And that which rather thou dost fear to do
Than wishest should be undone. Hie thee hither,
That I may pour my spirits in thine ear,
And chastise with the valor of my tongue
All that impedes thee from the golden round,
Which fate and metaphysical aid doth seem   30
To have thee crowned withal.

Enter a Messenger.

What is your tidings?
 Mess. The king comes here tonight.
 Lady M.   Thou'rt mad to say it!
Is not thy master with him? who, were 't so,
Would have informed for preparation.
 Mess. So please you, it is true; our thane is coming.
One of my fellows had the speed of him,
Who, almost dead for breath, had scarcely more
Than would make up his message.
 Lady M.   Give him tending;
He brings great news.   *[Exit Messenger.*
      The raven himself is hoarse
That croaks the fatal entrance of Duncan   40
Under my battlements. Come, you spirits
That tend on mortal thoughts, unsex me here,
And fill me from the crown to the toe top-full
Of direst cruelty! make thick my blood;
Stop up the access and passage to remorse,
That no compunctious visitings of nature
Shake my fell purpose, nor keep peace between
The effect and it! Come to my woman's breasts,

19. **nearest way:** i.e., murder.   21. **illness:** unscrupulousness.   24. **That:** the crown.   29. **golden round:** crown.   30. **metaphysical:** supernatural. 39. **raven:** bird of ill omen.   42. **mortal:** murderous.   45. **remorse:** compassion.   46. **compunctious, etc.:** feelings of pity.

And take my milk for gall, you murdering ministers,
Wherever in your sightless substances   50
You wait on nature's mischief!   Come, thick night,
And pall thee in the dunnest smoke of hell,
That my keen knife see not the wound it makes,
Nor Heaven peep through the blanket of the dark,
To cry " Hold, hold! "

Enter MACBETH.

       Great Glamis! worthy Cawdor!
Greater than both, by the all-hail hereafter!
Thy letters have transported me beyond
This ignorant present, and I feel now
The future in the instant.
  Macb.   My dearest love,   59
Duncan comes here tonight.
  Lady M.   And when goes hence?
  Macb.   Tomorrow, as he purposes.
  Lady M.   O, never
Shall sun that morrow see!
Your face, my thane, is as a book where men
May read strange matters.   To beguile the time,
Look like the time; bear welcome in your eye,
Your hand, your tongue; look like the innocent flower,
But be the serpent under 't.   He that's coming
Must be provided for; and you shall put
This night's great business into my dispatch;
Which shall to all our nights and days to come
Give solely sovereign sway and masterdom.   71
  Macb.   We will speak further.
  Lady M.   Only look up clear;
To alter favor ever is to fear.
Leave all the rest to me.   [*Exeunt*.

 50. **sightless:** invisible.   64. **To beguile, etc.:** To deceive, you must look
natural.   73. **alter favor, etc.:** change of countenance shows fear.

Scene VI. *Before Macbeth's castle.*

Hautboys and torches. Enter Duncan, Malcolm, Donalbain, Banquo, Lennox, Macduff, Ross, Angus, *and*
  Attendants.

Dun. This castle hath a pleasant seat; the air
Nimbly and sweetly recommends itself
Unto our gentle senses.
Ban.   This guest of summer,
The temple-haunting martlet, does approve,
By his loved mansionry, that the heaven's breath
Smells wooingly here; no jutty, frieze,
Buttress, nor coign of vantage, but this bird
Hath made his pendent bed and procreant cradle.
Where they most breed and haunt, I have observed,
The air is delicate.

Enter Lady Macbeth.

Dun. See, see, our honored hostess!   10
The love that follows us sometime is our trouble,
Which still we thank as love. Herein I teach you
How you shall bid God 'ild us for your pains,
And thank us for your trouble.
Lady M.   All our service
In every point twice done and then done double
Were poor and single business to contend
Against those honors deep and broad wherewith
Your majesty loads our house; for those of old,
And the late dignities heaped up to them,
We rest your hermits.
Dun. Where's the thane of Cawdor?   20
We coursed him at the heels, and had a purpose
To be his purveyor; but he rides well;
And his great love, sharp as his spur, hath holp him
To his home before us. Fair and noble hostess,
We are your guest tonight.
Lady M.   Your servants ever
Have theirs, themselves and what is theirs in compt,

---

1. **seat:** location. 5. **mansionry:** masonry. 20. **rest your hermits:** i.e.,
we shall always pray for you. 22. **purveyor:** forerunner. 26. **compt:** readiness.

To make their audit at your highness' pleasure,
Still to return your own.
   Dun.   Give me your hand;
Conduct me to mine host. We love him highly,
And shall continue our graces towards him.   30
By your leave, hostess.   *[Exeunt.*

SCENE VII. *Macbeth's castle.*

Hautboys and torches. Enter a Sewer, *and divers* Servants
*with dishes and service, and pass over the stage. Then
enter* MACBETH.

  Macb. If it were done when 'tis done, then 'twere well
It were done quickly. If the assassination
Could trammel up the consequence, and catch
With his surcease success; that but this blow
Might be the be-all and the end-all here,
But here, upon this bank and shoal of time,
We 'ld jump the life to come. But in these cases
We still have judgment here; that we but teach
Bloody instructions, which, being taught, return
To plague the inventor. This even-handed justice   10
Commends the ingredients of our poisoned chalice
To our own lips. He's here in double trust;
First, as I am his kinsman and his subject,
Strong both against the deed; then, as his host,
Who should against his murderer shut the door,
Not bear the knife myself. Besides, this Duncan
Hath borne his faculties so meek, hath been
So clear in his great office, that his virtues
Will plead like angels, trumpet-tongued, against
The deep damnation of his taking-off;   20
And pity, like a naked newborn babe,
Striding the blast, or heaven's cherubim, horsed
Upon the sightless couriers of the air,
Shall blow the horrid deed in every eye,
That tears shall drown the wind. I have no spur
To prick the sides of my intent, but only

   Stage direction: **Sewer:** one who arranges the table. 3. **trammel up:**
tangle up, or suspend. 6. **But:** only. 7. **jump:** take chances on. 8. **that:**
so that. 10. **even-handed:** impartial. 11. **commends:** offers. 17. **faculties:** royal powers. 23. **sightless couriers:** the winds.

Vaulting ambition, which o'erleaps itself
And falls on the other.

Enter LADY MACBETH.

                    How now! what news?
  Lady M. He has almost supped. Why have you left the
    chamber?
  Macb. Hath he asked for me?
  Lady M.   Know you not he has?   30
  Macb. We will proceed no further in this business.
He hath honored me of late; and I have bought
Golden opinions from all sorts of people,
Which would be worn now in their newest gloss,
Not cast aside so soon.
  Lady M.   Was the hope drunk
Wherein you dressed yourself? Hath it slept since?
And wakes it now, to look so green and pale
At what it did so freely? From this time
Such I account thy love. Art thou afeard
To be the same in thine own act and valor   40
As thou art in desire? Wouldst thou have that
Which thou esteem'st the ornament of life,
And live a coward in thine own esteem,
Letting "I dare not" wait upon "I would,"
Like the poor cat i' the adage?
  Macb.   Prithee, peace!
I dare do all that may become a man;
Who dares do more is none.
  Lady M.   What beast was 't, then,
That made you break this enterprise to me?
When you durst do it, then you were a man;
And, to be more than what you were, you would   50
Be so much more the man. Nor time nor place
Did then adhere, and yet you would make both.
They have made themselves, and that their fitness now
Does unmake you. I have given suck, and know
How tender 'tis to love the babe that milks me:
I would, while it was smiling in my face,
Have plucked my nipple from his boneless gums,

    8. **other:** other side. 32. **bought:** acquired. 42. **ornament:** i.e., the
crown. 52. **adhere:** suit.

And dashed the brains out, had I so sworn as you
Have done to this.

   Macb.   If we should fail?

   Lady M.   We fail!
But screw your courage to the sticking-place,   60
And we'll not fail. When Duncan is asleep —
Whereto the rather shall his day's hard journey
Soundly invite him — his two chamberlains
Will I with wine and wassail so convince
That memory, the warder of the brain,
Shall be a fume, and the receipt of reason
A limbeck only. When in swinish sleep
Their drenchéd natures lie as in a death,
What cannot you and I perform upon
The unguarded Duncan? what not put upon   70
His spongy officers, who shall bear the guilt
Of our great quell?

   Macb.   Bring forth men-children only;
For thy undaunted mettle should compose
Nothing but males. Will it not be received,
When we have marked with blood those sleepy two
Of his own chamber and used their very daggers,
That they have done 't?

   Lady M.   Who dares receive it other,
As we shall make our griefs and clamor roar
Upon his death?

   Macb.   I am settled, and bend up
Each corporal agent to this terrible feat.   80
Away, and mock the time with fairest show;
False face must hide what the false heart doth know. [*Exeunt*.

---

   60. **sticking-place:** the line refers to the tuning-process of a stringed
instrument.   64. **convince:** overpower.   66. **fume:** i.e., filled with fumes.
66. **receipt of reason:** the reasoning power will be a condenser, in this case
filled with fumes.   72. **quell:** murder.   80. **corporal agent:** bodily powers.

ACT II

Scene I. *Court of Macbeth's castle.*

Enter Banquo, *and* Fleance *bearing a torch before him.*

Ban. How goes the night, boy?
Fle. The moon is down; I have not heard the clock.
Ban. And she goes down at twelve.
Fle.   I take 't, 'tis later, sir.
Ban. Hold, take my sword. There's husbandry in heaven;
Their candles are all out. Take thee that too.
A heavy summons lies like lead upon me,
And yet I would not sleep. Merciful powers,
Restrain in me the cursèd thoughts that nature
Gives way to in repose!

Enter Macbeth, *and a* Servant *with a torch.*

Give me my sword.
Who's there?   10
Macb. A friend.
Ban. What, sir, not yet at rest? The king's abed.
He hath been in unusual pleasure, and
Sent forth great largess to your offices.
This diamond he greets your wife withal,
By the name of most kind hostess; and shut up
In measureless content.
Macb.   Being unprepared,
Our will became the servant to defect;
Which else should free have wrought.
Ban.   All's well.
I dreamt last night of the three weird sisters: 20
To you they have showed some truth.
Macb.   I think not of them;
Yet, when we can entreat an hour to serve,
We would spend it in some words upon that business,
If you would grant the time.
Ban.   At your kind'st leisure.
Macb. If you shall cleave to my consent, when 'tis,

4. **husbandry:** thrift; i.e., it is cloudy. 14. **largess . . . offices:** presents to your servants. 18. **Our will, etc.:** i.e., we could not entertain as we should have liked. 25. **cleave, etc.:** agree to my wishes.

It shall make honor for you.
   Ban.   So I lose none
In seeking to augment it, but still keep
My bosom franchised and allegiance clear,
I shall be counseled.
   Macb.   Good repose the while!
   Ban.   Thanks, sir; the like to you!   30
            [Exeunt Banquo and Fleance.
   Macb.   Go bid thy mistress, when my drink is ready,
She strike upon the bell. Get thee to bed.   *[Exit Servant.*
Is this a dagger which I see before me,
The handle toward my hand? Come, let me clutch thee.
I have thee not, and yet I see thee still.
Art thou not, fatal vision, sensible
To feeling as to sight? or art thou but
A dagger of the mind, a false creation,
Proceeding from the heat-oppressèd brain?
I see thee yet, in form as palpable   40
As this which now I draw.
Thou marshal'st me the way that I was going;
And such an instrument I was to use.
Mine eyes are made the fools o' the other senses,
Or else worth all the rest; I see thee still,
And on thy blade and dudgeon gouts of blood,
Which was not so before. There's no such thing.
It is the bloody business which informs
Thus to mine eyes. Now o'er the one half-world
Nature seems dead, and wicked dreams abuse
The curtained sleep; witchcraft celebrates   51
Pale Hecate's offerings, and withered murder,
Alarumed by his sentinel, the wolf,
Whose howl's his watch, thus with his stealthy pace,
With Tarquin's ravishing strides, towards his design
Moves like a ghost. Thou sure and firm-set earth,
Hear not my steps, which way they walk, for fear
Thy very stones prate of my whereabout,
And take the present horror from the time,

---

28. **franchised:** free from guilt. 29. **counseled:** willing to discuss. 36. **sensible to feeling:** perceptible to the touch. 44. **Mine eyes, etc.:** i.e., if the dagger is not real my eyes are fooled by my imagination; if real, my eyes are worth all my other senses. 46. **dudgeon:** hilt. 51. **curtained:** beds had curtains. 52. **Hecate's offerings:** rites to the goddess of the lower regions. 59. **time:** i.e., midnight.

Which now suits with it. Whiles I threat, he lives: 60
Words to the heat of deeds too cold breath gives. [*A bell rings:*
I go, and it is done; the bell invites me.
Hear it not, Duncan; for it is a knell
That summons thee to heaven or to hell.   [*Exit.*

SCENE II. *The same.*

Enter LADY MACBETH.

Lady M. That which hath made them drunk hath made
      me bold;
What hath quenched them hath given me fire. Hark! Peace!
It was the owl that shrieked, the fatal bellman,
Which gives the stern'st good night. He is about it.
The doors are open; and the surfeited grooms
Do mock their charge with snores. I have drugged their
      possets,
That death and nature do contend about them,
Whether they live or die.
    Macb. [*Within*] Who's there? what, ho!
    Lady M. Alack, I am afraid they have awaked,   10
And 'tis not done. The attempt and not the deed
Confounds us. Hark! I laid their daggers ready;
He could not miss 'em. Had he not resembled
My father as he slept, I had done 't.

Enter MACBETH.
                                    My husband!
    Macb. I have done the deed. Didst thou not hear a noise?
    Lady M. I heard the owl scream and the crickets cry.
Did not you speak?
    Macb.   When?
    Lady M.   Now.
    Macb.   As I descended?
    Lady M. Ay.
    Macb. Hark!
Who lies i' the second chamber?
    Lady M.   Donalbain.   20
    Macb. This is a sorry sight.   [*Looking on his hands.*

3. **fatal bellman:** The night before execution, a condemned man was noti-
fied by a bellman that the execution was set for next day.   6. **possets:**
bedtime drinks made of a mixture of hot milk and ale.   11. **attempt:** if
unsuccessful we are ruined.   20. **sorry:** miserable.

Lady M. A foolish thought, to say a sorry sight.
Macb. There's one did laugh in 's sleep, and one cried
"Murder!"
That they did wake each other: I stood and heard them;
But they did say their prayers, and addressed them
Again to sleep.
Lady M.   There are two lodged together.
Macb. One cried "God bless us!" and "Amen" the other,
As they had seen me with these hangman's hands.
Listening their fear, I could not say "Amen,"
When they did say "God bless us!"
Lady M.   Consider it not so deeply.   30
Macb. But wherefore could not I pronounce "Amen"?
I had most need of blessing, and "Amen"
Stuck in my throat.
Lady M.   These deeds must not be thought
After these ways; so, it will make us mad.
Macb. Methought I heard a voice cry "Sleep no more!
Macbeth does murder sleep," the innocent sleep,
Sleep that knits up the raveled sleave of care,
The death of each day's life, sore labor's bath,
Balm of hurt minds, great nature's second course,
Chief nourisher in life's feast —
Lady M.   What do you mean?
Macb. Still it cried "Sleep no more!" to all the house: 41
"Glamis hath murdered sleep, and therefore Cawdor
Shall sleep no more; Macbeth shall sleep no more."
Lady M. Who was it that thus cried? Why, worthy thane,
You do unbend your noble strength, to think
So brainsickly of things.   Go get some water,
And wash this filthy witness from your hand.
Why did you bring these daggers from the place?
They must lie there: go carry them; and smear
The sleepy grooms with blood.
Macb.   I'll go no more.   50
I am afraid to think what I have done;
Look on 't again I dare not.
Lady M.   Infirm of purpose!
Give me the daggers.   The sleeping and the dead
Are but as pictures; 'tis the eye of childhood
That fears a painted devil.   If he do bleed,

---

27. **hangman:** any executioner.   37. **raveled:** tangled.

I'll gild the faces of the grooms withal;
For it must seem their guilt.   [*Exit. Knocking within.*
   Macb.   Whence is that knocking?
How is 't with me, when every noise appalls me?
What hands are here?   Ha! they pluck out mine eyes.
Will all great Neptune's ocean wash this blood
Clean from my hand?   No, this my hand will rather   61
The multitudinous seas incarnadine,
Making the green one red.

Reënter LADY MACBETH.

   Lady M.   My hands are of your color; but I shame
To wear a heart so white.   [*Knocking within.*]   I hear a
      knocking
At the south entry.   Retire we to our chamber:
A little water clears us of this deed.
How easy is it, then!   Your constancy
Hath left you unattended.   [*Knocking within.*]   Hark! more
      knocking.
Get on your nightgown, lest occasion call us,   70
And show us to be watchers.   Be not lost
So poorly in your thoughts.
   Macb.   To know my deed, 'twere best not know myself.
                                        [*Knocking within.*
Wake Duncan with thy knocking!   I would thou couldst!
                                        [*Exeunt.*

SCENE III.   *The same.*

Knocking within.   Enter a Porter.

   Porter.   Here's a knocking indeed!   If a man were porter
of hell-gate, he should have old turning the key.   [*Knocking
within.*]   Knock, knock, knock!   Who's there, i' the name
of Beelzebub?   Here's a farmer, that hanged himself on the
expectation of plenty.   Come in time; have napkins enow
about you; here you'll sweat for 't.   [*Knocking within.*]
Knock, knock!   Who's there, in the other devil's name?   Faith,
here's an equivocator, that could swear in both the scales against
either scale; who committed treason enough for God's sake,

---

62. **incarnadine:** make red.   68. **constancy:** firmness.
2. **have old:** have a hard time.   8. **equivocator:** deceiver.

yet could not equivocate to heaven. O, come in, equivocator. [*Knocking within.*] Knock, knock, knock! Who's there? Faith, here's an English tailor come hither, for stealing out of a French hose. Come in, tailor; here you may roast your goose. [*Knocking within.*] Knock, knock; never at quiet! What are you? But this place is too cold for hell. I'll devil-porter it no further: I had thought to have let in some of all professions that go the primrose way to the everlasting bonfire. [*Knocking within.*] Anon, anon! I pray you, remember the porter. [*Opens the gate.*

Enter MACDUFF *and* LENNOX.

Macd. Was it so late, friend, ere you went to bed,
That you do lie so late?
Port. Faith, sir, we were carousing till the second cock: and drink, sir, is a great provoker.
Macd. I believe drink gave thee the lie last night. 41
Port. That it did, sir, i' the very throat on me. But I requited him for his lie; and, I think, being too strong for him, though he took up my legs sometime, yet I made a shift to cast him.
Macd. Is thy master stirring?

Enter MACBETH.

Our knocking has awaked him; here he comes.
Len. Good morrow, noble sir.
Macb.   Good morrow, both.
Macd. Is the king stirring, worthy thane?
Macb.   Not yet.
Macd. He did command me to call timely on him. 51
I have almost slipped the hour.
Macb.   I'll bring you to him.
Macd. I know this is a joyful trouble to you;
But yet 'tis one.
Macb. The labor we delight in physics pain.
This is the door.
Macd.   I'll make so bold to call,
For 'tis my limited service. [*Exit.*
Len. Goes the king hence today?

---

23. **primrose:** easy. 27. **second cock:** about three in the morning. 55. **physics:** cures.

Macb.   He does: he did appoint so.
Len. The night has been unruly: where we lay,
Our chimneys were blown down; and, as they say,   60
Lamentings heard i' the air; strange screams of death,
And prophesying with accents terrible
Of dire combustion and confused events
New hatched to the woeful time.   The obscure bird
Clamored the livelong night; some say, the earth
Was feverous and did shake.
Macb.   'Twas a rough night.
Len. My young remembrance cannot parallel
A fellow to it.

Reënter MACDUFF.

Macd. O horror, horror, horror! Tongue nor heart
Cannot conceive nor name thee!
Macb.⎫   What's the matter?   70
Len. ⎭
Macd. Confusion now hath made his masterpiece!
Most sacrilegious murder hath broke ope
The Lord's anointed temple, and stole thence
The life o' the building!
Macb.   What is 't you say?   The life?
Len. Mean you his majesty?
Macd. Approach the chamber, and destroy your sight
With a new Gorgon.   Do not bid me speak;
See, and then speak yourselves.
[Exeunt Macbeth and Lennox.
Awake, awake!
Ring the alarum-bell.   Murder and treason!
Banquo and Donalbain! Malcolm! awake!   80
Shake off this downy sleep, death's counterfeit,
And look on death itself!   Up, up, and see
The great doom's image!   Malcolm!   Banquo!
As from your graves rise up, and walk like sprites,
To countenance this horror!   Ring the bell.   [*Bell rings.*

Enter LADY MACBETH.

Lady M. What's the business,
That such a hideous trumpet calls to parley
The sleepers of the house?   Speak, speak!

63. **combustion:** tumult. 64. **obscure bird:** owl. 83. **great doom's image:**
a sight like that of the end of the world.

Macd.   O gentle lady,
'Tis not for you to hear what I can speak;
The repetition, in a woman's ear,   90
Would murder as it fell.

Enter BANQUO.

　　　　　　　　　O Banquo, Banquo,
Our royal master's murdered!
　　Lady M.   Woe, alas!
What, in our house?
　　Ban.   Too cruel anywhere.
Dear Duff, I prithee, contradict thyself,
And say it is not so.

Reënter MACBETH *and* LENNOX, *with* ROSS.

　　Macb. Had I but died an hour before this chance,
I had lived a blessed time; for, from this instant,
There's nothing serious in mortality.
All is but toys: renown and grace is dead;
The wine of life is drawn, and the mere lees
Is left this vault to brag of.   101

Enter MALCOLM *and* DONALBAIN.

　　Don. What is amiss?
　　Macb.   You are, and do not know 't:
The spring, the head, the fountain of your blood
Is stopped; the very source of it is stopped.
　　Macd. Your royal father's murdered.
　　Mal.   O, by whom?
　　Len. Those of his chamber, as it seemed, had done 't.
Their hands and faces were all badged with blood;
So were their daggers, which unwiped we found
Upon their pillows.
They stared, and were distracted; no man's life   110
Was to be trusted with them.
　　Macb. O, yet I do repent me of my fury,
That I did kill them.
　　Macd.   Wherefore did you so?
　　Macb. Who can be wise, amazed, temperate and furious,
Loyal and neutral, in a moment? No man.

　　96. **chance:** happening. 98. **serious in mortal:** worth while in life. 107.
badged: smeared.

The expedition of my violent love
Outrun the pauser, reason. Here lay Duncan,
His silver skin laced with his golden blood,
And his gashed stabs looked like a breach in nature
For ruin's wasteful entrance; there, the murderers,   120
Steeped in the colors of their trade, their daggers
Unmannerly breeched with gore. Who could refrain,
That had a heart to love, and in that heart
Courage to make 's love known?
  Lady M.   Help me hence, ho!
  Macd. Look to the lady.
  Mal. [*Aside to Don.*] Why do we hold our tongues,
That most may claim this argument for ours?
  Don. [*Aside to Mal.*] What should be spoken here, where
    our fate,
Hid in an auger-hole, may rush, and seize us?
Let's away;
Our tears are not yet brewed.
  Mal. [*Aside to Don.*] Nor our strong sorrow
Upon the foot of motion.
  Ban.   Look to the lady: 131
        [*Lady Macbeth is carried out.*
And when we have our naked frailties hid,
That suffer in exposure, let us meet,
And question this most bloody piece of work,
To know it further. Fears and scruples shake us.
In the great hand of God I stand; and thence
Against the undivulged pretence I fight
Of treasonous malice.
  Macd.   And so do I.
  All.   So all.
  Macb. Let's briefly put on manly readiness,
And meet i' the hall together.
  All.   Well contented.
     [*Exeunt all but Malcolm and Donalbain.*
  Mal. What will you do? Let's not consort with them; 141
To show an unfelt sorrow is an office
Which the false man does easy. I'll to England.
  Don. To Ireland, I; our separated fortune

 122. **breeched:** completely covered. 126. **argument:** matter for discussion.
132. **naked frailties:** they were in their night clothes. 131. **manly readiness:** armor.

Shall keep us both the safer. Where we are,
There's daggers in men's smiles; the near in blood,
The nearer bloody.

Mal.   This murderous shaft that's shot
Hath not yet lighted, and our safest way
Is to avoid the aim. Therefore, to horse;
And let us not be dainty of leave-taking,   150
But shift away. There's warrant in that theft
Which steals itself, when there's no mercy left.   [*Exeunt.*

SCENE IV. *Outside Macbeth's castle.*

Enter Ross *and an* Old Man.

Old M. Threescore and ten I can remember well:
Within the volume of which time I have seen
Hours dreadful and things strange; but this sore night
Hath trifled former knowings.

Ross.   Ah, good father,
Thou seest, the heavens, as troubled with man's act,
Threaten his bloody stage. By the clock, 'tis day,
And yet dark night strangles the traveling lamp.
Is 't night's predominance, or the day's shame,
That darkness does the face of earth entomb,
When living light should kiss it?

Old M.   'Tis unnatural,   10
Even like the deed that's done. On Tuesday last,
A falcon, towering in her pride of place,
Was by a mousing owl hawked at and killed.

Ross. And Duncan's horses — a thing most strange and
      certain —
Beauteous and swift, the minions of their race,
Turned wild in nature, broke their stalls, flung out,
Contending 'gainst obedience, as they would make
War with mankind.

Old M.   'Tis said they eat each other.

Ross. They did so, to the amazement of mine eyes
That looked upon 't. Here comes the good Macduff.   20

---

148. **Hath not yet lighted:** i.e., more murder will follow. 151. **shift:** steal.
7. **traveling lamp:** the sun. 15. **minions:** favorites.

Enter Macduff.

How goes the world, sir, now?
  Macd.   Why, see you not?
  Ross. Is 't known who did this more than bloody deed?
  Macd. Those that Macbeth hath slain.
  Ross.   Alas, the day!
What good could they pretend?
  Macd.   They were suborned:
Malcolm and Donalbain, the king's two sons,
Are stolen away and fled; which puts upon them
Suspicion of the deed.
  Ross.   'Gainst nature still!
Thriftless ambition, that wilt ravin up
Thine own life's means!   Then 'tis most like
The sovereignty will fall upon Macbeth.   30
  Macd. He is already named, and gone to Scone
To be invested.
  Ross.   Where is Duncan's body?
  Macd. Carried to Colmekill,
The sacred storehouse of his predecessors,
And guardian of their bones.
  Ross.   Will you to Scone?
  Macd. No, cousin, I'll to Fife.
  Ross.   Well, I will thither.
  Macd. Well, may you see things well done there.   Adieu!
Lest our old robes sit easier than our new!
  Ross. Farewell, father.
  Old M. God's benison go with you; and with those   40
That would make good of bad, and friends of foes!   [*Exeunt.*

ACT III

Scene I. *Forres. The palace.*

Enter Banquo.

  Ban. Thou hast it now: king, Cawdor, Glamis, all,
As the weird women promised, and, I fear,
Thou play'dst most foully for 't; yet it was said

24. **suborned:** bribed. 28. **ravin up:** gobble up. 31. **Scone:** ancient home of the kings of Scotland. 36. **Fife:** Macduff's castle. 37. **thither:** i.e., to Scone.

It should not stand in thy posterity,
But that myself should be the root and father
Of many kings.   If there come truth from them —
As upon thee, Macbeth, their speeches shine —
Why, by the verities on thee made good,
May they not be my oracles as well,
And set me up in hope?   But hush! no more.   10

Sennet sounded.   Enter MACBETH, *as king,* LADY MACBETH,
   as Queen, LENNOX, ROSS, Lords, Ladies, *and* Attendants.

Macb.   Here's our chief guest.
Lady M.   If he had been forgotten,
It had been as a gap in our great feast,
And all-thing unbecoming.
Macb.   Tonight we hold a solemn supper, sir,
And I'll request your presence.
Ban.   Let your highness
Command upon me; to the which my duties
Are with a most indissoluble tie
For ever knit.
Macb.   Ride you this afternoon?
Ban.   Ay, my good lord.   20
Macb.   We should have else desired your good advice,
Which still hath been both grave and prosperous,
In this day's council; but we'll take tomorrow.
Is 't far you ride?
Ban.   As far, my lord, as will fill up the time
'Twixt this and supper.   Go not my horse the better,
I must become a borrower of the night
For a dark hour or twain.
Macb.   Fail not our feast.
Ban.   My lord, I will not.
Macb.   We hear, our bloody cousins are bestowed   30
In England and in Ireland, not confessing
Their cruel parricide, filling their hearers
With strange invention.   But of that tomorrow,
When therewithal we shall have cause of state
Craving us jointly.   Hie you to horse; adieu,
Till your return at night.   Goes Fleance with you?

4. **stand:** continue.   Stage direction: **Sennet:** sound of trumpets announc-
ing the entrance of persons of importance.   13. **all-thing:** altogether.
14. **solemn supper:** formal banquet.   33. **invention:** falsehoods.   34. **cause
of state, etc.:** affairs of state that concern us both.

Ban. Ay, my good lord. Our time does call upon 's.
Macb. I wish your horses swift and sure of foot;
And so I do commend you to their backs.
Farewell.   [*Exit Banquo.* 40
Let every man be master of his time
Till seven at night. To make society
The sweeter welcome, we will keep ourself
Till supper-time alone; while then, God be with you!
              [*Exeunt all but Macbeth, and an attendant.*
Sirrah, a word with you: attend those men
Our pleasure?
    Atten. They are, my lord, without the palace gate.
    Macb. Bring them before us.

                                          [*Exit Attendant.*
                        To be thus is nothing;
But to be safely thus. — Our fears in Banquo
Stick deep; and in his royalty of nature   50
Reigns that which would be feared. 'Tis much he dares;
And, to that dauntless temper of his mind,
He hath a wisdom that doth guide his valor
To act in safety. There is none but he
Whose being I do fear; and, under him,
My Genius is rebuked; as, it is said,
Mark Antony's was by Caesar. He chid the sisters
When first they put the name of king upon me,
And bade them speak to him; then prophet-like
They hailed him father to a line of kings.   60
Upon my head they placed a fruitless crown,
And put a barren scepter in my gripe,
Thence to be wrenched with an unlineal hand,
No son of mine succeeding. If 't be so,
For Banquo's issue have I filed my mind;
For them the gracious Duncan have I murdered;
Put rancors in the vessel of my peace
Only for them; and mine eternal jewel
Given to the common enemy of man,
To make them kings, the seed of Banquo kings!   70
Rather than so, come fate into the list,
And champion me to the utterance! Who's there?

44. **while:** until. 49. **But:** except. 50. **royalty:** nobility. 56. **Genius:** guardian spirit. 64. **son:** Macbeth had no children. Those referred to earlier by Lady Macbeth were hers by a previous marriage. 65. **filed:** defiled. 68. **jewel:** soul. 69. **common enemy:** devil.

Reënter Attendant, *with two* Murderers.

Now go to the door, and stay there till we call.

                                                          [Exit Attendant.

Was it not yesterday we spoke together?

    First Mur. It was, so please your highness.

    Macb.   Well then, now

Have you considered of my speeches? Know

That it was he in the times past which held you

So under fortune, which you thought had been

Our innocent self. This I made good to you

In our last conference, passed in probation with you,   80

How you were borne in hand, how crossed, the instruments,

Who wrought with them, and all things else that might

To half a soul and to a notion crazed

Say " Thus did Banquo."

    First Mur.   You made it known to us.

    Macb. I did so, and went further, which is now

Our point of second meeting. Do you find

Your patience so predominant in your nature

That you can let this go? Are you so gospeled

To pray for this good man and for his issue,

Whose heavy hand hath bowed you to the grave

And beggared yours for ever?

    First Mur.   We are men, my liege.   91

    Macb. Ay, in the catalogue ye go for men;

As hounds and greyhounds, mongrels, spaniels, curs,

Shoughs, water-rugs and demi-wolves are clept

All by the name of dogs; the valued file

Distinguishes the swift, the slow, the subtle,

The housekeeper, the hunter, every one

According to the gift which bounteous nature

Hath in him closed, whereby he does receive

Particular addition, from the bill   100

That writes them all alike; and so of men.

Now, if you have a station in the file,

Not i' the worst rank of manhood, say 't;

And I will put that business in your bosoms,

Whose execution takes your enemy off,

Grapples you to the heart and love of us,

---

80. **passed in probation:** proved in detail. 81. **borne in hand:** fooled.
88. **gospeled:** i.e., believers in the gospel of forgiveness. 95. **valued file:**
list of values. 100. **addition:** distinction. 100. **bill:** list.

Who wear our health but sickly in his life,
Which in his death were perfect.
   Sec. Mur.   I am one, my liege,
Whom the vile blows and buffets of the world
Have so incensed that I am reckless what   110
I do to spite the world.
   First Mur.   And I another
So weary with disasters, tugged with fortune,
That I would set my life on any chance,
To mend it, or be rid on 't.
   Macb.   Both of you
Know Banquo was your enemy.
   Both Mur.   True, my lord.
   Macb. So is he mine; and in such bloody distance,
That every minute of his being thrusts
Against my near'st of life; and though I could
With barefaced power sweep him from my sight
And bid my will avouch it, yet I must not,   120
For certain friends that are both his and mine,
Whose loves I may not drop, but wail his fall
Who I myself struck down; and thence it is,
That I to your assistance do make love,
Masking the business from the common eye
For sundry weighty reasons.
   Sec. Mur.   We shall, my lord,
Perform what you command us.
   First Mur.   Though our lives —
   Macb. Your spirits shine through you. Within this hour
      at most
I will advise you where to plant yourselves;
Acquaint you with the perfect spy o' the time,   130
The moment on 't; for 't must be done tonight,
And something from the palace; always thought
That I require a clearness: and with him —
To leave no rubs nor botches in the work —
Fleance his son, that keeps him company,
Whose absence is no less material to me
Than is his father's, must embrace the fate
Of that dark hour. Resolve yourselves apart;

---

112. **tugged with:** pulled hither and yon by. 120. **avouch:** account. 121.
For: because of. 122. **wail:** I must bewail. 130. **perfect spy, etc.:** the
exact time. 132. **always thought, etc.:** remember that I must remain clear
of this. 134. **leave no, etc.:** there must be no mistakes or bungling.

I'll come to you anon.
    Both Mur.   We are resolved, my lord.
    Macb. I'll call upon you straight: abide within.   140
                                    [*Exeunt Murderers.*
It is concluded. Banquo, thy soul's flight,
If it find heaven, must find it out tonight.   [*Exit.*

Scene II. *The palace.*

Enter Lady Macbeth *and a* Servant.

    Lady M. Is Banquo gone from court?
    Serv. Ay, madam, but returns again tonight.
    Lady M. Say to the king, I would attend his leisure
For a few words.
    Serv.   Madam, I will.   [*Exit.*
    Lady M.   Naught's had, all's spent,
Where our desire is got without content.
'Tis safer to be that which we destroy
Than by destruction dwell in doubtful joy.

Enter Macbeth.

How now, my lord! why do you keep alone,
Of sorriest fancies your companions making,
Using those thoughts which should indeed have died   10
With them they think on?   Things without all remedy
Should be without regard; what's done is done.
    Macb. We have scotched the snake, not killed it:
She'll close and be herself, whilst our poor malice
Remains in danger of her former tooth.
But let the frame of things disjoint, both the worlds suffer,
Ere we will eat our meal in fear and sleep
In the affliction of these terrible dreams
That shake us nightly.   Better be with the dead,
Whom we, to gain our peace, have sent to peace,   20
Than on the torture of the mind to lie
In restless ecstasy.   Duncan is in his grave;
After life's fitful fever he sleeps well;
Treason has done his worst: nor steel, nor poison,
Malice domestic, foreign levy, nothing,

---

    10. **Using:** constantly thinking.   13. **scotched:** cut.   16. **frame of things:** the universe.   21. **torture:** the rack.   22. **ecstasy:** mental torment.

Can touch him further.
  Lady M.   Come on;
Gentle my lord, sleek o'er your rugged looks;
Be bright and jovial among your guests tonight.
  Macb. So shall I, love; and so, I pray, be you.
Let your remembrance apply to Banquo;   30
Present him eminence, both with eye and tongue:
Unsafe the while, that we
Must lave our honors in these flattering streams,
And make our faces vizards to our hearts,
Disguising what they are.
  Lady M.   You must leave this.
  Macb. O, full of scorpions is my mind, dear wife!
Thou know'st that Banquo, and his Fleance, lives.
  Lady M. But in them nature's copy's not eterne.
  Macb. There's comfort yet; they are assailable;
Then be thou jocund; ere the bat hath flown
His cloistered flight, ere to black Hecate's summons   41
The shard-borne beetle with his drowsy hums
Hath rung night's yawning peal, there shall be done
A deed of dreadful note.
  Lady M.   What's to be done?
  Macb. Be innocent of the knowledge, dearest chuck,
Till thou applaud the deed. Come, seeling night,
Scarf up the tender eye of pitiful day;
And with thy bloody and invisible hand
Cancel and tear to pieces that great bond
Which keeps me pale! Light thickens, and the crow   50
Makes wing to the rooky wood;
Good things of day begin to droop and drowse;
Whiles night's black agents to their preys do rouse.
Thou marvel'st at my words: but hold thee still;
Things bad begun make strong themselves by ill.
So, prithee, go with me.   *[Exeunt.*

34. **vizards:** masks. 41. **cloistered flight:** irregular, as though in cloisters. 42. **shard-borne:** wings hard as pieces of pottery. 43. **yawning:** drowsy. 46. **seeling:** a term from falconry. The eyes of the falcon were covered (seeled) by a hood or scarf. 49. **bond:** Banquo's life, together with the promise of the witches. 51. **rooky:** fuil of rooks or crows.

Scene III.   *A park near the palace.*

Enter three Murderers.

First Mur.   But who did bid thee join with us?
Third Mur.   Macbeth.
Sec. Mur.   He needs not our mistrust, since he delivers
Our offices and what we have to do
To the direction just.
First Mur.   Then stand with us.
The west yet glimmers with some streaks of day;
Now spurs the lated traveler apace
To gain the timely inn; and near approaches
The subject of our watch.
Third Mur.   Hark! I hear horses.
Ban. [*Within*] Give us a light there, ho!
Sec. Mur.   Then 'tis he; the rest
That are within the note of expectation   10
Already are i' the court.
First Mur.   His horses go about.
Third Mur.   Almost a mile; but he does usually,
So all men do, from hence to the palace gate
Make it their walk.
Sec. Mur.   A light, a light!

Enter Banquo, *and* Fleance *with a torch.*

Third Mur.   'Tis he.
First Mur.   Stand to 't.
Ban.   It will be rain tonight.
First Mur.   Let it come down.
                                 [*They set upon Banquo.*
Ban.   O, treachery! Fly, good Fleance, fly, fly, fly!
Thou mayst revenge. O slave!   [*Dies. Fleance escapes.*
Third Mur.   Who did strike out the light?
First Mur.   Was 't not the way?
Third Mur.   There's but one down; the son is fled.
Sec. Mur.   We have lost   20
Best half of our affair.
First Mur.   Well, let's away, and say how much is done.
                                          [*Exeunt.*

2. **needs not:** we need not distrust the newcomer. 3. **offices:** duties.
10. **note of expectation:** invited guests. 11. **horses go about:** a Shakespearean device for avoiding the use of horses on the stage.

SCENE IV.   *The same.   Hall in the palace.*

A banquet prepared.   Enter MACBETH, LADY MACBETH, ROSS,
LENNOX, Lords, *and* Attendants.

Macb.   You know your own degrees; sit down.   At first
And last the hearty welcome.
   Lords.   Thanks to your majesty.
   Macb.   Ourself will mingle with society,
And play the humble host.
Our hostess keeps her state, but in best time
We will require her welcome.
   Lady M.   Pronounce it for me, sir, to all our friends;
For my heart speaks they are welcome.

First Murderer *appears at the door.*

   Macb.   See, they encounter thee with their hearts' thanks.
Both sides are even; here I'll sit i' the midst: 10
Be large in mirth; anon we'll drink a measure
The table round.   [*Approaching the door.*]   There's blood
    upon thy face.
   Mur.   'Tis Banquo's then.
   Macb.   'Tis better thee without than he within.
Is he dispatched?
   Mur.   My lord, his throat is cut; that I did for him.
   Macb.   Thou art the best o' the cutthroats: yet he's good
That did the like for Fleance.   If thou didst it,
Thou art the nonpareil.
   Mur.   Most royal sir,
Fleance is 'scaped.   20
   Macb.   Then comes my fit again.   I had else been perfect,
Whole as the marble, founded as the rock,
As broad and general as the casing air;
But now I am cabined, cribbed, confined, bound in
To saucy doubts and fears.   But Banquo's safe?
   Mur.   Ay, my good lord; safe in a ditch he bides,
With twenty trenchéd gashes on his head,
The least a death to nature.
   Macb.   Thanks for that;

1. **degrees:** rank.   8. **keeps her state:** remains on her chair of state.
15. " The blood is better outside thee than inside him."   19. **nonpareil:** without equal.   23. **casing:** enveloping.   25. **saucy:** insolent.

There the grown serpent lies; the worm that's fled
Hath nature that in time will venom breed,   30
No teeth for the present.   Get thee gone; tomorrow
We'll hear ourselves again.   [*Exit Murderer.*

    Lady M.   My royal lord,
You do not give the cheer.   The feast is sold
That is not often vouched, while 'tis a-making,
'Tis given with welcome.   To feed were best at home;
From thence the sauce to meat is ceremony;
Meeting were bare without it.

    Macb.   Sweet remembrancer!
Now, good digestion wait on appetite,
And health on both!

    Len.   May 't please your highness sit.

    [*The Ghost of Banquo enters, and sits in Macbeth's place.*

    Macb.   Here had we now our country's honor roofed,   40
Were the graced person of our Banquo present;
Who may I rather challenge for unkindness
Than pity for mischance!

    Ross.   His absence, sir,
Lays blame upon his promise.   Please 't your highness
To grace us with your royal company.

    Macb.   The table's full.

    Len.   Here is a place reserved, sir.

    Macb.   Where?

    Len.   Here, my good lord.   What is 't that moves your
      highness?

    Macb.   Which of you have done this?

    Lords.   What, my good lord?

    Macb.   Thou canst not say I did it; never shake   50
Thy gory locks at me.

    Ross.   Gentlemen, rise; his highness is not well.

    Lady M.   Sit, worthy friends; my lord is often thus,
And hath been from his youth.   Pray you, keep seat;
The fit is momentary; upon a thought
He will again be well.   If much you note him,
You shall offend him and extend his passion.
Feed, and regard him not.   Are you a man?

29. **worm:** a serpent's young.   32. **We'll hear, etc.:** i.e., talk the matter
over.   33. **feast is sold, etc.:** i.e., unless hospitality is openly shown to guests
one might as well dine at an inn; at home one merely eats, but away from
home he expects ceremony.

    Macb.   Ay, and a bold one, that dare look on that
Which might appall the devil.
    Lady M.   O proper stuff!   60
This is the very painting of your fear:
This is the air-drawn dagger which, you said,
Led you to Duncan.   O, these flaws and starts,
Impostors to true fear, would well become
A woman's story at a winter's fire,
Authorized by her grandam.   Shame itself!
Why do you make such faces!   When all's done,
You look but on a stool.
    Macb.   Prithee, see there! behold! look! lo! how say you?
Why, what care I?   If thou canst nod, speak too.   70
If charnel-houses and our graves must send
Those that we bury back, our monuments
Shall be the maws of kites.   [*Ghost vanishes.*
    Lady M.   What, quite unmanned in folly?
    Macb.   If I stand here, I saw him.
    Lady M.   Fie, for shame!
    Macb.   Blood hath been shed ere now, i' the olden time,
Ere humane statute purged the gentle weal;
Ay, and since too, murders have been performed
Too terrible for the ear.   The time has been,
That, when the brains were out, the man would die,
And there an end; but now they rise again,   80
With twenty mortal murders on their crowns,
And push us from our stools.   This is more strange
Than such a murder is.
    Lady M.   My worthy lord,
Your noble friends do lack you.
    Macb.   I do forget.
Do not muse at me, my most worthy friends;
I have a strange infirmity, which is nothing
To those that know me.   Come, love and health to all;
Then I'll sit down.   Give me some wine; fill full.
I drink to the general joy o' the whole table,
And to our dear friend Banquo, whom we miss;   90
Would he were here! to all, and him, we thirst;
And all to all.
    Lords.   Our duties, and the pledge.

63. **flaws:** emotional displays.   64. **Impostors:** imitations of.   73. **maws of kites:** i.e., instead of having monuments the dead shall be given to vultures to be devoured.   81. **murders:** wounds.

Reënter Ghost.

Macb. Avaunt! and quit my sight! let the earth hide thee!
Thy bones are marrowless, thy blood is cold;
Thou hast no speculation in those eyes
Which thou dost glare with!
    Lady M.   Think of this, good peers,
But as a thing of custom; 'tis no other;
Only it spoils the pleasure of the time.
    Macb. What man dare, I dare.   99
Approach thou like the rugged Russian bear,
The armed rhinoceros, or the Hyrcan tiger;
Take any shape but that, and my firm nerves
Shall never tremble; or be alive again,
And dare me to the desert with thy sword;
If trembling I inhabit then, protest me
The baby of a girl. Hence, horrible shadow!
Unreal mockery, hence!   *[Ghost vanishes.*
                    Why, so; being gone,
I am a man again. Pray you, sit still.
    Lady M. You have displaced the mirth, broke the good
        meeting,
With most admired disorder.
    Macb.   Can such things be,   110
And overcome us like a summer's cloud,
Without our special wonder? You make me strange
Even to the disposition that I owe,
When now I think you can behold such sights,
And keep the natural ruby of your cheeks,
When mine is blanched with fear.
    Ross.   What sights, my lord?
    Lady M. I pray you, speak not; he grows worse and worse;
Question enrages him. At once, good night.
Stand not upon the order of your going,
But go at once.
    Len.   Good night; and better health   120
Attend his majesty!
    Lady M.   A kind good night to all!
        [Exeunt all but Macbeth and Lady Macbeth.

95. **speculation:** i.e., the eyes are dead. 104. **desert:** open. 105. **inhabit:** confine. 105. **protest:** call me publicly. 110. **baby of a girl:** doll. 110. **admired:** wondered at. 112. **You make me, etc.:** I do not understand my own character.

Macb. It will have blood; they say, blood will have blood.
Stones have been known to move and trees to speak;
Augurs and understood relations have
By magot-pies and choughs and rooks brought forth
The secret'st man of blood. What is the night?
   Lady M. Almost at odds with morning, which is which.
   Macb. How say'st thou, that Macduff denies his person
At our great bidding?
   Lady M.   Did you send to him, sir?
   Macb. I hear it by the way; but I will send.   130
There's not a one of them but in his house
I keep a servant feed. I will tomorrow,
And betimes I will, to the weird sisters.
More shall they speak; for now I am bent to know,
By the worst means, the worst. For mine own good,
All causes shall give way. I am in blood
Stepped in so far that, should I wade no more,
Returning were as tedious as go o'er.
Strange things I have in head, that will to hand;
Which must be acted ere they may be scanned.
   Lady M. You lack the season of all natures, sleep.   141
   Macb. Come, we'll to sleep. My strange and self-abuse
Is the initiate fear that wants hard use:
We are yet but young in deed.   [*Exeunt.*

Scene V. *A Heath.*

Thunder. Enter the three Witches, *meeting* HECATE.

   First Witch. Why, how now, Hecate! you look angerly.
   Hec. Have I not reason, beldams as you are,
Saucy and overbold? How did you dare
To trade and traffic with Macbeth
In riddles and affairs of death;
And I, the mistress of your charms,
The close contriver of all harms,
Was never called to bear my part,
Or show the glory of our art?
And, which is worse, all you have done   10

---

124. **understood relations:** i.e., understood only by augurs. ˙ 125. **magot-pies and choughs:** magpies and jackdaws. 141. **season:** seasoning.
   7. **close:** secret.

Hath been but for a wayward son,
Spiteful and wrathful, who, as others do,
Loves for his own ends, not for you.
But make amends now; get you gone,
And at the pit of Acheron
Meet me i' the morning; thither he
Will come to know his destiny.
Your vessels and your spells provide,
Your charms and every thing beside.
I am for the air; this night I'll spend   20
Unto a dismal and a fatal end;
Great business must be wrought ere noon.
Upon the corner of the moon
There hangs a vaporous drop profound;
I'll catch it ere it come to ground;
And that distilled by magic sleights
Shall raise such artificial sprites
As by the strength of their illusion
Shall draw him on to his confusion.
He shall spurn fate, scorn death, and bear   30
His hopes 'bove wisdom, grace and fear;
And you all know, security
Is mortals' chiefest enemy.
    [*Music and a song within:* " Come away, come away," &c.
Hark! I am called; my little spirit, see,
Sits in a foggy cloud, and stays for me.   [*Exit.*
    First Witch. Come, let's make haste; she'll soon be back
        again.   [*Exeunt.*

SCENE VI.   *Forres.   The palace.*

Enter LENNOX *and another* Lord.

    Len. My former speeches have but hit your thoughts,
Which can interpret further; only, I say,
Things have been strangely borne.   The gracious Duncan
Was pitied of Macbeth; marry, he was dead:
And the right-valiant Banquo walked too late;
Whom, you may say, if 't please you, Fleance killed,

15. **Acheron:** one of the rivers of Hades, but here evidently some deep
local pit supposed to lead to Hades.
3. **borne:** carried on.

For Fleance fled; men must not walk too late.
Who cannot want the thought how monstrous
It was for Malcolm and for Donalbain
To kill their gracious father? Damnéd fact!   10
How it did grieve Macbeth! Did he not straight
In pious rage the two delinquents tear,
That were the slaves of drink and thralls of sleep?
Was not that nobly done? Ay, and wisely too;
For 'twould have angered any heart alive
To hear the men deny 't. So that, I say,
He has borne all things well; and I do think
That had he Duncan's sons under his key —
As, an 't please Heaven, he shall not — they should find
What 'twere to kill a father; so should Fleance.
But, peace! for from broad words and 'cause he failed   21
His presence at the tyrant's feast, I hear
Macduff lives in disgrace. Sir, can you tell
Where he bestows himself?
    Lord.   The son of Duncan,
From whom this tyrant holds the due of birth,
Lives in the English court, and is received
Of the most pious Edward with such grace
That the malevolence of fortune nothing
Takes from his high respect. Thither Macduff
Is gone to pray the holy king, upon his aid   30
To wake Northumberland and warlike Siward;
That by the help of these — with Him above
To ratify the work — we may again
Give to our tables meat, sleep to our nights,
Free from our feasts and banquets bloody knives,
Do faithful homage and receive free honors:
All which we pine for now: and this report
Hath so exasperated the king that he
Prepares for some attempt of war.
    Len.   Sent he to Macduff?
    Lord. He did: and with an absolute " Sir, not I,"   40
The cloudy messenger turns me his back,
And hums, as who should say, " You'll rue the time
That clogs me with this answer."
    Len.   And that well might

---

10. fact: deed.   21. **broad words:** plain speaking.   27. **pious Edward:**
Edward the Confessor (1004–1066).   36. **free:** unbribed.   41. **cloudy:** gloomy.

Advise him to a caution, to hold what distance
His wisdom can provide.   Some holy angel
Fly to the court of England and unfold
His message ere he come, that a swift blessing
May soon return to this our suffering country
Under a hand accursed!

    Lord.   I'll send my prayers with him.

                                     [*Exeunt.*

ACT IV

SCENE I.   *A cavern.   In the middle, a boiling caldron.*

Thunder.   Enter the three Witches.

First Witch.   Thrice the brinded cat hath mewed.
Sec. Witch.   Thrice and once the hedgepig whined.
Third Witch.   Harpier cries " 'Tis time, 'tis time."
First Witch.   Round about the caldron go;
In the poisoned entrails throw.
Toad, that under cold stone
Days and nights has thirty-one
Sweltered venom sleeping got,
Boil thou first i' the charméd pot.
    All.   Double, double toil and trouble;   10
Fire burn, and caldron bubble.
    Sec. Witch.   Fillet of a fenny snake,
In the caldron boil and bake;
Eye of newt and toe of frog,
Wool of bat and tongue of dog,
Adder's fork and blind-worm's sting,
Lizard's leg and howlet's wing,
For a charm of powerful trouble,
Like a hell-broth boil and bubble.
    All.   Double, double toil and trouble;   20
Fire burn, and caldron bubble.
    Third Witch.   Scale of dragon, tooth of wolf,
Witches' mummy, maw and gulf
Of the ravined salt-sea shark,

---

  1. **brinded:**   streaked.   3. **Harpier:**   probably coined from **harpy.**
8. **sweltered venom:**   poison sweated out from a toad.   23. **mummy:** In
Shakespeare's day a sticky fluid was actually concocted from mummies and
used as a medicine.   23. **gulf:** stomach.   24. **ravined:** full from overfeeding.

Root of hemlock digged i' the dark,
Liver of blaspheming Jew,
Gall of goat, and slips of yew
Slivered in the moon's eclipse,
Nose of Turk and Tartar's lips,
Finger of birth-strangled babe   30
Ditch-delivered by a drab,
Make the gruel thick and slab:
Add thereto a tiger's chaudron,
For the ingredients of our caldron.
    All.   Double, double toil and trouble;
Fire burn, and caldron bubble.
    Sec. Witch.   Cool it with a baboon's blood,
Then the charm is firm and good.

Enter HECATE *to the other three Witches.*

    Hec.   O, well done!   I commend your pains;
And every one shall share i' the gains: 40
And now about the caldron sing,
Like elves and fairies in a ring,
Enchanting all that you put in.
                    [Music and a song: " Black spirits," &c.
                                    [Hecate retires.
    Sec. Witch.   By the pricking of my thumbs,
Something wicked this way comes.
          Open, locks,
          Whoever knocks!

Enter MACBETH.

    Macb.   How now, you secret, black, and midnight hags!
What is 't you do?
    All.   A deed without a name.
    Macb.   I conjure you, by that which you profess,   50
Howe'er you come to know it, answer me:
Though you untie the winds and let them fight
Against the churches; though the yesty waves
Confound and swallow navigation up;
Though bladed corn be lodged and trees blown down;
Though castles topple on their warders' heads;
Though palaces and pyramids do slope

---

32. **slab:** slimy. 33 **chaudron:** entrails. 53. **yesty:** foamy. 55. **corn:** i.e., wheat, blown flat to the ground before it was ripe.

Their heads to their foundations; though the treasure
Of nature's germens tumble all together,
Even till destruction sicken; answer me   60
To what I ask you.
   First Witch. Speak.
   Sec. Witch.   Demand.
   Third Witch.   We'll answer.
   First Witch. Say, if thou'dst rather hear it from our
     mouths,
Or from our masters'?
   Macb.   Call 'em; let me see 'em.
   First Witch. Pour in sow's blood, that hath eaten
Her nine farrow; grease that's sweaten
From the murderer's gibbet throw
Into the flame.
   All.   Come, high or low;
Thyself and office deftly show!

    Thunder. First Apparition: *an armed Head.*

   Macb. Tell me, thou unknown power —
   First Witch.   He knows thy thought:
Hear his speech, but say thou naught.   70
   First App. Macbeth! Macbeth! Macbeth! beware Macduff;
Beware the thane of Fife. Dismiss me. Enough. [*Descends.*
   Macb. Whate'er thou art, for thy good caution, thanks;
Thou hast harped my fear aright: but one word more —
   First Witch. He will not be commanded: here's another,
More potent than the first.

    Thunder. Second Apparition: *a bloody Child.*

   Sec. App. Macbeth! Macbeth! Macbeth!
   Macb. Had I three ears, I 'ld hear thee.
   Sec. App. Be bloody, bold, and resolute; laugh to scorn
The power of man, for none of woman born   80
Shall harm Macbeth.   [*Descends.*
   Macb. Then live, Macduff: what need I fear of thee?
But yet I'll make assurance double sure,
And take a bond of fate. Thou shalt not live;

That I may tell pale-hearted fear it lies,
And sleep in spite of thunder.

*Thunder. Third Apparition: a Child crowned, with a tree
in his hand.*

          What is this
That rises like the issue of a king,
And wears upon his baby-brow the round
And top of sovereignty?
  All.   Listen, but speak not to 't.
  Third App. Be lion-mettled, proud; and take no care 90
Who chafes, who frets, or where conspirers are.
Macbeth shall never vanquished be until
Great Birnam wood to high Dunsinane hill
Shall come against him.   *[Descends.*
  Macb.   That will never be.
Who can impress the forest, bid the tree
Unfix his earth-bound root? Sweet bodements! good!
Rebellion's head, rise never till the wood
Of Birnam rise, and our high-placed Macbeth
Shall live the lease of nature, pay his breath
To time and mortal custom. Yet my heart   100
Throbs to know one thing: tell me, if your art
Can tell so much: shall Banquo's issue ever
Reign in this kingdom?
  All.   Seek to know no more.
  Macb. I will be satisfied: deny me this,
And an eternal curse fall on you! Let me know.
Why sinks that caldron? and what noise is this? *[Hautboys.*
  First Witch. Show!
  Sec. Witch. Show!
  Third Witch. Show!
  All. Show his eyes, and grieve his heart;
Come like shadows, so depart!   111

*A show of Eight Kings, the last with a glass in his hand;
Banquo's Ghost following.*

  Macb. Thou art too like the spirit of Banquo; down!
Thy crown doth sear mine eyeballs. And thy hair,
Thou other gold-bound brow, is like the first.

Stage direction: **Child crowned:** Malcolm. **Eight kings:** the Stuart kings
of Scotland.

A third is like the former. Filthy hags!
Why do you show me this? A fourth! Start, eyes!
What, will the line stretch out to the crack of doom?
Another yet! A seventh! I'll see no more.
And yet the eighth appears, who bears a glass
Which shows me many more; and some I see   120
That twofold balls and treble scepters carry.
Horrible sight! Now, I see, 'tis true;
For the blood-boltered Banquo smiles upon me,
And points at them for his. [*Apparitions vanish.*] What, is
    this so?
   First Witch. Ay, sir, all this is so: but why
Stands Macbeth thus amazedly?
Come, sisters, cheer we up his sprites,
And show the best of our delights.
I'll charm the air to give a sound,
While you perform your antic round;   130
That this great king may kindly say,
Our duties did his welcome pay.
   [*Music. The Witches dance, and then vanish, with Hecate.*
   Macb. Where are they? Gone! Let this pernicious hour
Stand aye accursed in the calendar!
Come in, without there!

Enter LENNOX.

   Len.   What's your grace's will?
   Macb. Saw you the weird sisters?
   Len.   No, my lord.
   Macb. Came they not by you?
   Len.   No, indeed, my lord.
   Macb. Infected be the air whereon they ride;
And damned all those that trust them! I did hear
The galloping of horse: who was 't came by?   140
   Len. 'Tis two or three, my lord, that bring you word
Macduff is fled to England.
   Macb.   Fled to England!
   Len. Ay, my good lord.
   Macb. Time, thou anticipatest my dread exploits:
The flighty purpose never is o'ertook

---

119. **glass:** magic mirror. 121. **twofold balls, etc.:** a reference to James
I, who united Scotland with England, and later Ireland. There was a tradition that he was descended from Banquo. 123. **blood-boltered:** hair wet with
blood. 127. **sprites:** spirits. 145. **flighty:** fleeting.

Unless the deed go with it.   From this moment
The very firstlings of my heart shall be
The firstlings of my hand.   And even now,
To crown my thoughts with acts, be it thought and done.
The castle of Macduff I will surprise;   150
Seize upon Fife; give to the edge o' the sword
His wife, his babes, and all unfortunate souls
That trace him in his line.   No boasting like a fool;
This deed I'll do before this purpose cool.
But no more sights! — Where are these gentlemen?
Come, bring me where they are.   [*Exeunt.*

Scene II.   *Fife.   Macduff's castle.*

Enter Lady Macduff, *her* Son, *and* Ross.

L. Macd.   What had he done, to make him fly the land?
Ross.   You must have patience, madam.
L. Macd.   He had none;
His flight was madness.   When our actions do not,
Our fears do make us traitors.
Ross.   You know not
Whether it was his wisdom or his fear.
L. Macd.   Wisdom! to leave his wife, to leave his babes,
His mansion and his titles in a place
From whence himself does fly?   He loves us not;
He wants the natural touch: for the poor wren,
The most diminutive of birds, will fight,   10
Her young ones in her nest, against the owl.
All is the fear and nothing is the love;
As little is the wisdom, where the flight
So runs against all reason.
Ross.   My dearest coz,
I pray you, school yourself; but for your husband,
He is noble, wise, judicious, and best knows
The fits o' the season.   I dare not speak much further;
But cruel are the times, when we are traitors
And do not know ourselves, when we hold rumor
From what we fear, yet know not what we fear,
But float upon a wild and violent sea   21

12. **All, etc.:** i.e., to Macduff fear is everything, love nothing.   17. **fits:** disorders.   19. **ourselves:** i.e., as traitors.

Each way and move. I take my leave of you;
Shall not be long but I'll be here again.
Things at the worst will cease, or else climb upward
To what they were before. My pretty cousin,
Blessing upon you!

> *L. Macd.* Fathered he is, and yet he's fatherless.

> *Ross.* I am so much a fool, should I stay longer,
It would be my disgrace and your discomfort.
I take my leave at once.   [*Exit.*

> *L. Macd.* Sirrah, your father's dead;   30
And what will you do now? How will you live?

> *Son.* As birds do, mother.

> *L. Macd.* What, with worms and flies?

> *Son.* With what I get, I mean; and so do they.

> *L. Macd.* Poor bird! thou 'ldst never fear the net nor lime,
The pitfall nor the gin.

> *Son.* Why should I, mother? Poor birds they are not set
> for.
My father is not dead, for all your saying.

> *L. Macd.* Yes, he is dead. How wilt thou do for a
> father?

> *Son.* Nay, how will you do for a husband?

> *L. Macd.* Why, I can buy me twenty at any market. 40

> *Son.* Then you'll buy 'em to sell again.

> *L. Macd.* Thou speak'st with all thy wit; and yet, i' faith,
With wit enough for thee.

> *Son.* Was my father a traitor, mother?

> *L. Macd.* Ay, that he was.

> *Son.* What is a traitor?

> *L. Macd.* Why, one that swears and lies.

> *Son.* And be all traitors that do so?

> *L. Macd.* Every one that does so is a traitor, and must be
hanged.   50

> *Son.* And must they all be hanged that swear and lie?

> *L. Macd.* Every one.

> *Son.* Who must hang them?

> *L. Macd.* Why, the honest men.

> *Son.* Then the liars and swearers are fools, for there are
liars and swearers enow to beat the honest men and hang up
them.

25. **My pretty cousin:** addressed to the boy. 29. **disgrace:** i.e., if I broke
down and wept. 34. **lime:** a sticky substance smeared on limbs of trees to
catch birds. 35. **gin:** trap.

L. Macd.   Now, God help thee, poor monkey!   But how
wilt thou do for a father?

Son.   If he were dead, you 'ld weep for him; if you would
not, it were a good sign that I should quickly have a new
father.

L. Macd.   Poor prattler, how thou talk'st!

Enter a Messenger.

Mess.   Bless you, fair dame!   I am not to you known,
Though in your state of honor I am perfect.
I doubt some danger does approach you nearly.
If you will take a homely man's advice,
Be not found here; hence, with your little ones.
To fright you thus, methinks, I am too savage:
To do worse to you were fell cruelty,   71
Which is too nigh your person.   Heaven preserve you!
I dare abide no longer.   [*Exit.*

    L. Macd.   Whither should I fly?
I have done no harm.   But I remember now
I am in this earthly world; where to do harm
Is often laudable, to do good sometime
Accounted dangerous folly.   Why then, alas,
Do I put up that womanly defence,
To say I have done no harm?

Enter Murderers.

                What are these faces?

First Mur.   Where is your husband?   80
L. Macd.   I hope, in no place so unsanctified
Where such as thou mayst find him.

    First Mur.   He's a traitor.

Son.   Thou liest, thou shag-haired villain!

First Mur.   What, you egg!   [*Stabbing him.*
Young fry of treachery!

    Son.   He has killed me, mother:
Run away, I pray you!   [*Dies.*

            [*Exit Lady Macduff, crying " Murder! "*
            [*Exeunt Murderers, following her.*

66. **perfect:** perfectly acquainted with.   68. **homely:** without rank.

Scene III. *England. Before the King's palace.*

Enter Malcolm *and* Macduff.

Mal. Let us seek out some desolate shade, and there
Weep our sad bosoms empty.
Macd.   Let us rather
Hold fast the mortal sword, and like good men
Bestride our downfall'n birthdom. Each new morn
New widows howl, new orphans cry, new sorrows
Strike heaven on the face, that it resounds
As if it felt with Scotland and yelled out
Like syllable of dolor.
Mal.   What I believe, I'll wail,
What know, believe, and what I can redress,
As I shall find the time to friend, I will.   10
What you have spoke, it may be so perchance.
This tyrant, whose sole name blisters our tongues,
Was once thought honest; you have loved him well;
He hath not touched you yet. I am young; but something
You may deserve of him through me, and wisdom
To offer up a weak poor innocent lamb
To appease an angry god.
Macd. I am not treacherous.
Mal.   But Macbeth is.
A good and virtuous nature may recoil
In an imperial charge. But I shall crave your pardon;   20
That which you are my thoughts cannot transpose.
Angels are bright still, though the brightest fell.
Though all things foul would wear the brows of grace,
Yet grace must still look so.
Macd.   I have lost my hopes.
Mal. Perchance even there where I did find my doubts.
Why in that rawness left you wife and child,
Those precious motives, those strong knots of love,
Without leave-taking? I pray you,
Let not my jealousies be your dishonors,
But mine own safeties. You may be rightly just,   30
Whatever I shall think.

10. **to friend:** suitable. 16. **offer up:** i.e., by betraying me to him you
will win favor. 19. **recoil:** revert to evil at the command of the king.
23. **foul:** ugly. 24. **so:** i.e., fair. 26. **rawness:** unseemly haste 29. **jealousies, etc.:** suspicions be insults to you. 29. **safeties:** precautions.

Macd.   Bleed, bleed, poor country!
Great tyranny! lay thou thy basis sure,
For goodness dare not check thee; wear thou thy wrongs;
The title is affeered!   Fare thee well, lord:
I would not be the villain that thou think'st
For the whole space that's in the tyrant's grasp,
And the rich East to boot.
    Mal.   Be not offended;
I speak not as in absolute fear of you.
I think our country sinks beneath the yoke;
It weeps, it bleeds; and each new day a gash   40
Is added to her wounds.   I think withal
There would be hands uplifted in my right;
And here from gracious England have I offer
Of goodly thousands.   But, for all this,
When I shall tread upon the tyrant's head,
Or wear it on my sword, yet my poor country
Shall have more vices than it had before,
More suffer and more sundry ways than ever,
By him that shall succeed.
    Macd.   What should he be?
    Mal.   It is myself I mean; in whom I know
All the particulars of vice so grafted   51
That, when they shall be opened, black Macbeth
Will seem as pure as snow, and the poor state
Esteem him as a lamb, being compared
With my confineless harms.
    Macd.   Not in the legions
Of horrid hell can come a devil more damned
In evils to top Macbeth.
    Mal.   I grant him bloody,
Luxurious, avaricious, false, deceitful,
Sudden, malicious, smacking of every sin
That has a name; but there's no bottom, none,
In my voluptuousness.   Your wives, your daughters,   61
Your matrons and your maids, could not fill up
The cistern of my lust, and my desire
All continent impediments would o'erbear
That did oppose my will.   Better Macbeth
Than such an one to reign.

---

34. **affeered:** confirmed, i.e., tyranny's title.   43. **England:** the king, Edward the Confessor.   64. **continent impediments:** restraining motives.

Macd.   Boundless intemperance
In nature is a tyranny; it hath been
The untimely emptying of the happy throne
And fall of many kings.   But fear not yet
To take upon you what is yours. You may   70
Convey your pleasures in a spacious plenty,
And yet seem cold, the time you may so hoodwink.
We have willing dames enough; there cannot be
That vulture in you, to devour so many
As will to greatness dedicate themselves,
Finding it so inclined.
Mal.   With this there grows
In my most ill-composed affection such
A stanchless avarice that, were I king,
I should cut off the nobles for their lands,
Desire his jewels and this other's house;   80
And my more-having would be as a sauce
To make me hunger more, that I should forge
Quarrels unjust against the good and loyal,
Destroying them for wealth.
Macd.   This avarice
Sticks deeper, grows with more pernicious root
Than summer-seeming lust, and it hath been
The sword of our slain kings. Yet do not fear;
Scotland hath foisons to fill up your will,
Of your mere own.   All these are portable,
With other graces weighed.   90
Mal. But I have none. The king-becoming graces,
As justice, verity, temperance, stableness,
Bounty, perseverance, mercy, lowliness
Devotion, patience, courage, fortitude,
I have no relish of them, but abound
In the division of each several crime,
Acting it many ways. Nay, had I power, I should
Pour the sweet milk of concord into hell,
Uproar the universal peace, confound
All unity on earth.
Macd.   O Scotland, Scotland!   100
Mal. If such a one be fit to govern, speak.
I am as I have spoken.

71. **convey:** have secretly. 77. **affection:** nature. 86. **summer-seeming:** youthful. 88. **foisons:** rich harvests. 89. **portable:** bearable.

Macd.   Fit to govern!
No, not to live.   O nation miserable,
With an untitled tyrant bloody-sceptered,
When shalt thou see thy wholesome days again,
Since that the truest issue of thy throne
By his own interdiction stands accursed,
And does blaspheme his breed?   Thy royal father
Was a most sainted king; the queen that bore thee,
Oftener upon her knees than on her feet,   110
Died every day she lived.   Fare thee well!
These evils thou repeat'st upon thyself
Have banished me from Scotland.   O my breast,
Thy hope ends here!
     Mal.   Macduff, this noble passion,
Child of integrity, hath from my soul
Wiped the black scruples, reconciled my thoughts
To thy good truth and honor.   Devilish Macbeth
By many of these trains hath sought to win me
Into his power, and modest wisdom plucks me
From overcredulous haste; but God above   120
Deal between thee and me! for even now
I put myself to thy direction, and
Unspeak mine own detraction, here abjure
The taints and blames I laid upon myself,
For strangers to my nature.   I am yet
Unknown to woman, never was forsworn,
Scarcely have coveted what was mine own,
At no time broke my faith, would not betray
The devil to his fellow, and delight
No less in truth than life; my first false speaking   130
Was this upon myself.   What I am truly,
Is thine and my poor country's to command;
Whither indeed, before thy here-approach,
Old Siward, with ten thousand warlike men,
Already at a point, was setting forth.
Now we'll together; and the chance of goodness
Be like our warranted quarrel!   Why are you silent?
     Macd.   Such welcome and unwelcome things at once
'Tis hard to reconcile.

---

107. **interdiction:** verdict.   118. **trains:** tricks.   135. **at a point:** prepared.
136. **goodness:** success.   137. **quarrel:** argument.   The sense of this passage is, "May our chance of success be as good to our cause as the outcome of
our quarrel was to us."

Enter a Doctor.

Mal. Well; more anon. — Comes the king forth, I pray
     you?   140
    Doct. Ay, sir; there are a crew of wretched souls
That stay his cure: their malady convinces
The great assay of art; but at his touch —
Such sanctity hath Heaven given his hand —
They presently amend.
    Mal. I thank you, Doctor.   [*Exit Doctor.*
    Macd. What's the disease he means?
    Mal.   'Tis called the evil:
A most miraculous work in this good king;
Which often, since my here-remain in England,
I have seen him do. How he solicits Heaven,
Himself best knows: but strangely visited people,   150
All swoln and ulcerous, pitiful to the eye,
The mere despair of surgery, he cures,
Hanging a golden stamp about their necks,
Put on with holy prayers; and 'tis spoken,
To the succeeding royalty he leaves
The healing benediction. With this strange virtue,
He hath a heavenly gift of prophecy,
And sundry blessings hang about his throne,
That speak him full of grace.

Enter Ross.

    Macd.   See, who comes here?
    Mal. My countryman; but yet I know him not.   160
    Macd. My ever-gentle cousin, welcome hither.
    Mal. I know him now. Good God, betimes remove
The means that makes us strangers!
    Ross.   Sir, amen.
    Macd. Stands Scotland where it did?
    Ross.   Alas, poor country!
Almost afraid to know itself. It cannot
Be called our mother, but our grave; where nothing,
But who knows nothing, is once seen to smile;
Where sighs and groans and shrieks that rend the air
Are made, not marked; where violent sorrow seems
A modern ecstasy. The dead man's knell   170

143. **assay:** effort; their maladies baffle the doctors. 146. **evil:** scrofula,
a skin disease. 152. **mere:** absolute. 153. **stamp:** coin. 162. **means:**
woes. 170. **modern ecstasy:** an everyday feeling.

Is there scarce asked for who; and good men's lives
Expire before the flowers in their caps,
Dying or ere they sicken.
   Macd.   O, relation
Too nice, and yet too true!
   Mal.   What's the newest grief?
   Ross.   That of an hour's age doth hiss the speaker;
Each minute teems a new one.
   Macd.   How does my wife?
   Ross.   Why, well.
   Macd.   And all my children?
   Ross.   Well too.
   Macd.   The tyrant has not battered at their peace?
   Ross.   No; they were well at peace when I did leave
'em.
   Macd.   Be not a niggard of your speech; how goes 't? 180
   Ross.   When I came hither to transport the tidings,
Which I have heavily borne, there ran a rumor
Of many worthy fellows that were out;
Which was to my belief witnessed the rather,
For that I saw the tyrant's power afoot.
Now is the time of help; your eye in Scotland
Would create soldiers, make our women fight,
To doff their dire distresses.
   Mal.   Be 't their comfort
We are coming thither.   Gracious England hath
Lent us good Siward and ten thousand men;
An older and a better soldier none   191
That Christendom gives out.
   Ross.   Would I could answer
This comfort with the like!   But I have words
That would be howled out in the desert air,
Where hearing should not latch them.
   Macd.   What concern they?
The general cause? or is it a fee-grief
Due to some single breast?
   Ross.   No mind that's honest
But in it shares some woe; though the main part
Pertains to you alone.

173. **relation:** account.   174. **nice:** exact.   175. **hiss:** i.e., because he tells
things that are out of date.   176. **teems:** brings forth.   183. **out:** up in
arms.   186. **your eye:** Macduff's.   195. **latch:** catch.   196. **fee-grief:** private grief.

Macd.   If it be mine,
Keep it not from me, quickly let me have it.   200
Ross.   Let not your ears despise my tongue forever,
Which shall possess them with the heaviest sound
That ever yet they heard.
Macd.   Hum! I guess at it.
Ross.   Your castle is surprised; your wife and babes
Savagely slaughtered: to relate the manner,
Were, on the quarry of these murdered deer,
To add the death of you.
Mal.   Merciful Heaven!
What, man! ne'er pull your hat upon your brows;
Give sorrow words.   The grief that does not speak
Whispers the o'erfraught heart and bids it break.   210
Macd.   My children too?
Ross.   Wife, children, servants, all
That could be found.
Macd.   And I must be from thence!
My wife killed too?
Ross.   I have said.
Mal.   Be comforted.
Let's make us medicines of our great revenge,
To cure this deadly grief.
Macd.   He has no children.   All my pretty ones?
Did you say all?   O hell-kite!   All?
What, all my pretty chickens and their dam
At one fell swoop?
Mal.   Dispute it like a man.
Macd.   I shall do so;   220
But I must also feel it as a man.
I cannot but remember such things were,
That were most precious to me.   Did Heaven look on,
And would not take their part?   Sinful Macduff,
They were all struck for thee! naught that I am,
Not for their own demerits, but for mine,
Fell slaughter on their souls.   Heaven rest them now!
Mal.   Be this the whetstone of your sword; let grief
Convert to anger; blunt not the heart, enrage it.
Macd.   O, I could play the woman with mine eyes   230
And braggart with my tongue!   But, gentle heavens,

206. **quarry:** dead bodies.   220. **Dispute:** fight with.   225. **Naught:**
worthless.

Cut short all intermission; front to front
Bring thou this fiend of Scotland and myself;
Within my sword's length set him; if he 'scape,
Heaven forgive him too!
　　Mal.　　　　　　　　This tune goes manly.
Come, go we to the king; our power is ready;
Our lack is nothing but our leave.　Macbeth
Is ripe for shaking, and the powers above
Put on their instruments.　Receive what cheer you may:
The night is long that never finds the day.　　*[Exeunt.*　240

237. **leave:** leave-taking.

ACT V

Scene I.　*Dunsinane.　Anteroom in the castle.*

Enter a Doctor of Physic *and a* Waiting-Gentlewoman.

Doct.　I have two nights watched with you, but can perceive no truth in your report.　When was it she last walked?

Gent.　Since his majesty went into the field, I have seen her rise from her bed, throw her nightgown upon her, unlock her closet, take forth paper, fold it, write upon 't, read it, afterwards seal it, and again return to bed; yet all this while in a most fast sleep.　　　　　　　　　　　　　　　　9

Doct.　A great perturbation in nature, to receive at once the benefit of sleep, and do the effects of watching!　In this slumbery agitation, besides her walking and other actual performances, what, at any time, have you heard her say?

Gent.　That, sir, which I will not report after her.

Doct.　You may to me: and 'tis most meet you should.

Gent.　Neither to you nor any one; having no witness to confirm my speech.　　　　　　　　　　　　　　　21

Enter Lady Macbeth, *with a taper.*

Lo you, here she comes!　This is her very guise; and, upon my life, fast asleep.　Observe her; stand close.

Doct.　How came she by that light?

Gent.　Why, it stood by her; she has light by her continually; 'tis her command.

11. **effects of watching:** actions done while awake.

Doct. You see, her eyes are open.

Gent. Ay, but their sense is shut.

Doct. What is it she does now?   Look, how she rubs her hands.   31

Gent. It is an accustomed action with her, to seem thus washing her hands.   I have known her continue in this a quarter of an hour.

Lady M. Yet here's a spot.

Doct. Hark! she speaks.   I will set down what comes from her, to satisfy my remembrance the more strongly.

Lady M. Out, damned spot! out, I say! — One: two: why, then 'tis time to do 't. — Hell is murky! — Fie, my lord, fie! a soldier, and afeard?   What need we fear who knows it, when none can call our power to account? — Yet who would have thought the old man to have had so much blood in him.

Doct. Do you mark that?

Lady M. The thane of Fife had a wife; where is she now? — What, will these hands ne'er be clean? — No more o' that, my lord, no more o' that; you mar all with this start-ing.   50

Doct. Go to, go to; you have known what you should not.

Gent. She has spoke what she should not, I am sure of that; Heaven knows what she has known.

Lady M. Here's the smell of the blood still; all the per-fumes of Arabia will not sweeten this little hand.   Oh, oh, oh!

Doct. What a sigh is there!   The heart is sorely charged.

Gent. I would not have such a heart in my bosom for the dignity of the whole body.

Doct. Well, well, well —

Gent. Pray God it be, sir.

Doct. This disease is beyond my practice; yet I have known those which have walked in their sleep who have died holily in their beds.

Lady M. Wash your hands, put on your nightgown; look not so pale. — I tell you yet again, Banquo's buried; he can-not come out on 's grave.   71

Doct. Even so?

Lady M. To bed, to bed!   There's knocking at the gate. Come, come, come, come, give me your hand.   What's done cannot be undone. — To bed, to bed, to bed!   [*Exit.*

Doct. Will she go now to bed?

Gent. Directly.

Doct. Foul whisperings are abroad; unnatural deeds
Do breed unnatural troubles; infected minds   80
To their deaf pillows will discharge their secrets.
More needs she the divine than the physician.
God, God forgive us all! Look after her;
Remove from her the means of all annoyance,
And still keep eyes upon her. So, good night:
My mind she has mated, and amazed my sight.
I think, but dare not speak.
  Gent.   Good night, good doctor. [*Exeunt.*

SCENE II. *The country near Dunsinane.*

Drum and colors. Enter MENTEITH, CAITHNESS, ANGUS, LEN-
NOX, *and* Soldiers.

Ment. The English power is near, led on by Malcolm,
His uncle Siward and the good Macduff.
Revenges burn in them; for their dear causes
Would to the bleeding and the grim alarm
Excite the mortified man.
  Ang.   Near Birnam wood
Shall we well meet them; that way are they coming.
  Caith. Who knows if Donalbain be with his brother?
  Len. For certain, sir, he is not; I have a file
Of all the gentry. There is Siward's son,
And many unrough youths that even now   10
Protest their first of manhood.
  Ment.   What does the tyrant?
  Caith. Great Dunsinane he strongly fortifies.
Some say he's mad; others that lesser hate him
Do call it valiant fury; but, for certain,
He cannot buckle his distempered cause
Within the belt of rule.
  Ang.   Now does he feel
His secret murders sticking on his hands;
Now minutely revolts upbraid his faith-breach;
Those he commands move only in command,

---

84. **annoyance:** doing herself violence. 86. **mated:** bewildered.
  4. **bleeding:** bloody deeds. 5. **mortified:** dead to feeling. 10. **unrough:**
beardless. 15. **buckle, etc.:** he is losing control of his affairs. 18. **minutely:**
every minute.

Nothing in love.   Now does he feel his title   20
Hang loose about him, like a giant's robe
Upon a dwarfish thief.
   Ment.   Who then shall blame
His pestered senses to recoil and start,
When all that is within him does condemn
Itself for being there?
   Caith.   Well, march we on,
To give obedience where 'tis truly owed.
Meet we the medicine of the sickly weal,
And with him pour we in our country's purge
Each drop of us.
   Len.   Or so much as it needs,
To dew the sovereign flower and drown the weeds.   30
Make we our march towards Birnam.   [*Exeunt, marching.*

Scene III.   *Dunsinane.   A room in the castle.*

Enter Macbeth, Doctor, *and* Attendants.

   Macb.   Bring me no more reports; let them fly all;
Till Birnam wood remove to Dunsinane,
I cannot taint with fear.   What's the boy Malcolm?
Was he not born of woman?   The spirits that know
All mortal consequences have pronounced me thus:
"Fear not, Macbeth; no man that's born of woman
Shall e'er have power upon thee."   Then fly, false thanes,
And mingle with the English epicures!
The mind I sway by and the heart I bear
Shall never sag with doubt nor shake with fear.

Enter a Servant.

The devil damn thee black, thou cream-faced loon!   11
Where got'st thou that goose look?
   Serv.   There is ten thousand —
   Macb.   Geese, villain?
   Serv.   Soldiers, sir.
   Macb.   Go, prick thy face, and over-red thy fear,
Thou lily-livered boy.   What soldiers, patch?

26. **owed:** i.e., to Malcolm.   27. **medicine:** Malcolm.
8. **epicures:** overinclined to luxury.   15. **patch:** fool.

Death of thy soul! those linen cheeks of thine
Are counselors to fear. What soldiers, whey-face?
  Serv. The English force, so please you.
  Macb. Take thy face hence.   [*Exit Servant.*
                Seyton! — I am sick at heart,
When I behold — Seyton, I say! — This push   20
Will cheer me ever, or disseat me now.
I have lived long enough. My way of life
Is fall'n into the sear, the yellow leaf;
And that which should accompany old age,
As honor, love, obedience, troops of friends,
I must not look to have; but, in their stead,
Curses, not loud but deep, mouth-honor, breath,
Which the poor heart would fain deny, and dare not.
Seyton!

Enter SEYTON.

  Sey. What is your gracious pleasure?
  Macb.   What news more? 30
  Sey. All is confirmed, my lord, which was reported.
  Macb. I'll fight till from my bones my flesh be hacked.
Give me my armor.
  Sey.   'Tis not needed yet.
  Macb. I'll put it on.
Send out moe horses; skirr the country round;
Hang those that talk of fear. Give me mine armor.
How does your patient, doctor?
  Doct.   Not so sick, my lord,
As she is troubled with thick-coming fancies,
That keep her from her rest.
  Macb.   Cure her of that.
Canst thou not minister to a mind diseased,   40
Pluck from the memory a rooted sorrow,
Raze out the written troubles of the brain
And with some sweet oblivious antidote
Cleanse the stuffed bosom of that perilous stuff
Which weighs upon the heart?
  Doct.   Therein the patient
Must minister to himself.
  Macb. Throw physic to the dogs; I'll none of it.
Come, put mine armor on; give me my staff.

20. **push:** attack. 35. **skirr:** scour. 43. **oblivious:** causing forgetfulness.
46. **physic:** medicine.

Seyton, send out.   Doctor, the thanes fly from me.
Come, sir, dispatch.   If thou couldst, doctor, cast   50
The water of my land, find her disease,
And purge it to a sound and pristine health,
I would applaud thee to the very echo,
That should applaud again. — Pull 't off, I say. —
What rhubarb, senna, or what purgative drug,
Would scour these English hence?   Hear'st thou of them?
     Doct.   Ay, my good lord; your royal preparation
Makes us hear something.
     Macb.   Bring it after me.
I will not be afraid of death and bane,
Till Birnam forest come to Dunsinane.   60
     Doct. [*Aside*] Were I from Dunsinane away and clear,
Profit again should hardly draw me here.   [*Exeunt.*

Scene IV.   *Country near Birnam wood.*

Drum and colors.   Enter Malcolm, *old* Siward *and his* Son,
     Macduff, Menteith, Caithness, Angus, Lennox,
     Ross, *and* Soldiers *marching.*

     Mal.   Cousins, I hope the days are near at hand
That chambers will be safe.
     Ment.   We doubt it nothing.
     Siw.   What wood is this before us?
     Ment.   The wood of Birnam.
     Mal.   Let every soldier hew him down a bough
And bear 't before him; thereby shall we shadow
The numbers of our host and make discovery,
Err in report of us.
     Soldiers.   It shall be done.
     Siw.   We learn no other but the confident tyrant
Keeps still in Dunsinane, and will endure
Our setting down before 't.
     Mal.   'Tis his main hope;   10
For where there is advantage to be given,
Both more or less have given him the revolt,

---

50. **cast:** examine.   52. **pristine:** former.   59. **bane:** ruin.
2. **chambers:** sleeping-rooms, referring to his father's murder.   10. **setting down:** laying siege.   11. **advantage:** opportunity.   12. **more or less:** higher and lower classes.

And none serve with him but constrainéd things
Whose hearts are absent too.
Macd.   Let our just censures
Attend the true event, and put we on
Industrious soldiership.
Siw.   The time approaches
That will with due decision make us know
What we shall say we have and what we owe.
Thoughts speculative their unsure hopes relate,
But certain issue strokes must arbitrate;   20
Towards which advance the war.   *[Exeunt, marching.*

Scene V. *Dunsinane. Within the castle.*

Enter Macbeth, Seyton, *and* Soldiers, *with drum and colors.*

Macb. Hang out our banners on the outward walls;
The cry is still " They come! " Our castle's strength
Will laugh a siege to scorn; here let them lie
Till famine and the ague eat them up.
Were they not forced with those that should be ours,
We might have met them dareful, beard to beard,
And beat them backward home.   *[A cry of women within.*
What is that noise?
Sey. It is the cry of women, my good lord.   *[Exit.*
Macb. I have almost forgot the taste of fears.
The time has been, my senses would have cooled   10
To hear a night-shriek; and my fell of hair
Would at a dismal treatise rouse and stir
As life were in 't. I have supped full with horrors;
Direness, familiar to my slaughterous thoughts,
Cannot once start me.

Reënter Seyton.

Wherefore was that cry?
Sey. The queen, my lord, is dead.
Macb. She should have died hereafter;

Sc. IV. 14-15. **just censures, etc.:** let our final judgment await the actual outcome, and meanwhile let's keep busy fighting. 19. **Thoughts speculative, etc.:** i.e., there's no use trying to figure things out beforehand; action alone will decide.
Sc. V. 5. **forced:** reinforced. 12. **treatise:** story. 17. **should:** i.e., would have died some day anyhow.

There would have been a time for such a word.
Tomorrow, and tomorrow, and tomorrow,
Creeps in this petty pace from day to day   20
To the last syllable of recorded time,
And all our yesterdays have lighted fools
The way to dusty death.   Out, out, brief candle!
Life's but a walking shadow, a poor player
That struts and frets his hour upon the stage
And then is heard no more.   It is a tale
Told by an idiot, full of sound and fury,
Signifying nothing.

Enter a Messenger.

Thou comest to use thy tongue; thy story quickly.
    Mess.   Gracious my lord,   30
I should report that which I say I saw,
But know not how to do it.
    Macb.   Well, say, sir.
    Mess.   As I did stand my watch upon the hill,
I looked toward Birnam, and anon, methought,
The wood began to move.
    Macb.   Liar and slave!
    Mess.   Let me endure your wrath, if 't be not so.
Within this three mile may you see it coming;
I say, a moving grove.
    Macb.   If thou speak'st false,
Upon the next tree shalt thou hang alive,
Till famine cling thee; if thy speech be sooth,
I care not if thou dost for me as much.   41
I pull in resolution, and begin
To doubt the equivocation of the fiend
That lies like truth: " Fear not, till Birnam wood
Do come to Dunsinane."   And now a wood
Comes toward Dunsinane.   Arm, arm, and out!
If this which he avouches does appear,
There is nor flying hence nor tarrying here.
I 'gin to be aweary of the sun,
And wish the estate o' the world were now undone.   50
Ring the alarum-bell!   Blow, wind! come, wrack!
At least we'll die with harness on our back.   [*Exeunt.*

    40. **cling:** shrivel up.   43. **equivocation:** deceit through double meaning.
50. **estate:** established order.

SCENE VI. *Dunsinane.   Before the castle.*

Drum and colors.   Enter MALCOLM, *old* SIWARD, MACDUFF,
and their Army, *with boughs.*

Mal. Now near enough; your leavy screens throw down,
And show like those you are.   You, worthy uncle,
Shall, with my cousin, your right-noble son,
Lead our first battle.   Worthy Macduff and we
Shall take upon 's what else remains to do,
According to our order.
Siw.   Fare you well.
Do we but find the tyrant's power tonight,
Let us be beaten, if we cannot fight.
   Macd. Make all our trumpets speak; give them all
      breath,   9
Those clamorous harbingers of blood and death.   [*Exeunt.*

SCENE VII. *Another part of the field.*

Alarums.   Enter MACBETH.

Macb. They have tied me to a stake; I cannot fly,
But, bearlike, I must fight the course.   What's he
That was not born of woman?   Such a one
Am I to fear, or none.

Enter young SIWARD.

Yo. Siw. What is thy name?
Macb.   Thou'lt be afraid to hear it.
Yo. Siw. No; though thou call'st thyself a hotter name
Than any is in hell.
Macb.   My name's Macbeth.
Yo. Siw. The devil himself could not pronounce a title
More hateful to mine ear.
Macb.   No, nor more fearful.
Yo. Siw. Thou liest, abhorréd tyrant; with my sword 10
I'll prove the lie thou speak'st.
      [*They fight and young Siward is slain.*

Sc. vi. 4. **battle:** division.   Sc. vii. 2. **course:** round.

Macb. Thou wast born of woman.
But swords I smile at, weapons laugh to scorn,
Brandished by man that's of a woman born. [*Exit.*

Alarums. Enter MACDUFF.

Macd. That way the noise is. Tyrant, show thy face!
If thou be'st slain and with no stroke of mine,
My wife and children's ghosts will haunt me still.
I cannot strike at wretched kerns, whose arms
Are hired to bear their staves; either thou, Macbeth,
Or else my sword with an unbattered edge
I sheathe again undeeded. There thou shouldst be; 20
By this great clatter, one of the greatest note
Seems bruited. Let me find him, fortune!
And more I beg not. [*Exit. Alarums.*

Enter MALCOLM *and old* SIWARD.

Siw. This way, my lord; the castle's gently rendered:
The tyrant's people on both sides do fight;
The noble thanes do bravely in the war;
The day almost itself professes yours,
And little is to do.
Mal. We have met with foes
That strike beside us.
Siw. Enter, sir, the castle. [*Exeunt. Alarums.*

SCENE VIII. *Another part of the field.*

Enter MACBETH.

Macb. Why should I play the Roman fool, and die
On mine own sword? Whiles I see lives, the gashes
Do better upon them.

Enter MACDUFF.

Macd. Turn, hell-hound, turn!
Macb. Of all men else I have avoided thee.
But get thee back; my soul is too much charged
With blood of thine already.

22. **bruited:** indicated. 24. **gently:** without resistance. 29. **strike be-side us:** i.e., as friends, so that they purposely miss us.
1. **Roman fool:** i.e., Romans who committed suicide, like Brutus and Cassius.

Macd.   I have no words;
My voice is in my sword, thou bloodier villain
Than terms can give thee out!   [*They fight.*
   Macb.   Thou losest labor:
As easy mayst thou the intrenchant air
With thy keen sword impress as make me bleed.   10
Let fall thy blade on vulnerable crests;
I bear a charmèd life, which must not yield
To one of woman born.
   Macd.   Despair thy charm;
And let the angel whom thou still hast served
Tell thee, Macduff was from his mother's womb
Untimely ripped.
   Macb. Accursèd be that tongue that tells me so,
For it hath cowed my better part of man!
And be these juggling fiends no more believed,
That palter with us in a double sense;   20
That keep the word of promise to our ear,
And break it to our hope. I'll not fight with thee.
   Macd. Then yield thee, coward,
And live to be the show and gaze o' the time.
We'll have thee, as our rarer monsters are,
Painted upon a pole, and underwrit,
" Here may you see the tyrant."
   Macb.   I will not yield,
To kiss the ground before young Malcolm's feet,
And to be baited with the rabble's curse.   29
Though Birnam wood be come to Dunsinane,
And thou opposed, being of no woman born,
Yet I will try the last. Before my body
I throw my warlike shield. Lay on, Macduff,
And damned be him that first cries " Hold, enough! "
            [*Exeunt, fighting. Alarums.*

Retreat. Flourish. Enter, with drum and colors, MALCOLM,
  old SIWARD, ROSS, *the other* Thanes, *and* Soldiers.

   Mal. I would the friends we miss were safe arrived.
   Siw. Some must go off; and yet, by these I see,
So great a day as this is cheaply bought.
   Mal. Macduff is missing, and your noble son.

8. **terms:** words. 9. **intrenchant:** that cannot be cut. 29. **baited:** pestered. 36. **go off:** die.

Ross. Your son, my lord, has paid a soldier's debt.
He only lived but till he was a man;   40
To which no sooner had his prowess confirmed
In the unshrinking station where he fought,
But like a man he died.
    Siw.   Then he is dead?
    Ross. Ay, and brought off the field. Your cause of sorrow
Must not be measured by his worth, for then
It hath no end.
    Siw.   Had he his hurts before?
    Ross. Ay, on the front.
    Siw.   Why then, God's soldier be he!
Had I as many sons as I have hairs,
I would not wish them to a fairer death.
And so, his knell is knolled.
    Mal.   He's worth more sorrow,   50
And that I'll spend for him.
    Siw.   He's worth no more.
They say he parted well, and paid his score;
And so, God be with him! Here comes newer comfort.

      Reënter MACDUFF, *with* MACBETH'S *head.*

    Macd. Hail, king! for so thou art. Behold, where stands
The usurper's cursèd head. The time is free.
I see thee compassed with thy kingdom's pearl,
That speak my salutation in their minds;
Whose voices I desire aloud with mine:
Hail, King of Scotland!
    All.   Hail, King of Scotland!   [*Flourish.*
    Mal. We shall not spend a large expense of time   60
Before we reckon with your several loves,
And make us even with you. My thanes and kinsmen,
Henceforth be earls, the first that ever Scotland
In such an honor named. What's more to do.
Which would be planted newly with the time,
As calling home our exiled friends abroad
That fled the snares of watchful tyranny;
Producing forth the cruel ministers
Of this dead butcher and his fiendlike queen,
Who, as 'tis thought, by self and violent hands   70

    52. **parted:** departed. 54. **stands:** i.e., on the end of a pike. 56. **pearl:** the nobility.

Took off her life; this, and what needful else
That calls upon us, by the grace of Grace,
We will perform in measure time and place:
So, thanks to all at once and to each one,
Whom we invite to see us crowned at Scone.

[*Flourish.   Exeunt.*

INTERPRETATIVE NOTE

Macbeth is one of Shakespeare's four greatest tragedies; many critics think it the greatest. As an acting play it outdistances them all because of its admirable construction and its many scenes that are theatrically powerful as well as inherently dramatic. It is also the shortest of Shakespeare's tragedies, with only 1993 lines as compared to the 3924 of *Hamlet*. It was written in 1606, and as far as is known the only source for the story is that found in Holinshed's *Chronicles,* a work frequently used by Shakespeare for his chronicle history plays.

The play opens in an atmosphere of evil. The barren storm-blown heath and the weird sisters, who are monstrosities, human perverts perhaps, with superhuman knowledge, constitute a dramatically effective introduction to the character of Macbeth, in whom are already germinating those seeds of evil which will eventually bring him to his doom. *Macbeth* resembles the ancient Greek plays in so far as the whole interest is centered on the two main characters. When the witches greet Macbeth as Thane of Cawdor, and when Lady Macbeth soliloquizes after she has read her husband's letter, the reader knows that their ambition is not something newly hatched. Their reactions clearly show that their hopes of achieving royalty had been previously discussed. But outwardly this middle-aged couple had led irreproachable lives, highly honored by the king, and respected by all. Throughout the first part of the play Macbeth is so keenly conscious of his own perfidy that he comes near letting opportunity slip. This at times wins him the reader's sympathies. But with Lady Macbeth it is far otherwise. She is bold, forward, aggressive, and likes to be so considered. One of the problems of the play is whether Lady Macbeth may have been the original instigator of her husband's ambition, but in any case she would forfeit all claims to human sympathy in these early scenes were it not for that one little touch where Shakespeare makes her say that but for Duncan's resemblance to her father as he slept she would have killed him herself.

The theme shows how an evil ambition brings about absolute disintegration of character. In the first half of the play Lady Macbeth triumphantly sweeps her husband to the throne. Her dominating forcefulness of character is in strong contrast to the vacillations of Macbeth. She consults no witches and she sees no ghosts. At all times she is herself. The trying scene at the banquet she carries off superbly. And then she is heard of no more until she appears walking in her sleep. What she says is proof sufficient that she is suffering the torments of remorse, but even so pitiable a plight wins barely a shred of sympathy. She has sinned heavily, and an avenging fate is exacting the penalty.

In the second half of the play it is Macbeth who becomes the dominating force. From the time of the banquet scene it is evident that for some reason he no longer shares his thoughts and plans with his wife. That may have been one of the causes of Lady Macbeth's mental decay. With no further incentive to outer action her mind turned upon itself. When Macbeth once got started in crime there was no stopping him. After his last visit to the weird sisters he became hardly less than a fiend, planning useless crimes for no apparent reason other than for satiating a lust for blood. It is obvious that the crown never brought him joy. The striking thing about Macbeth is that the deeper he wades in blood the stronger he seems to become, although it is strength based on crime. He no longer sees daggers before him, nor do the ghosts of his victims appear again except out of the witches' caldron. After that episode he is convinced that those uncouth creatures have deceived him, but he cannot retreat, nor has he anything else upon which to hang hopes. He deliberately chooses to believe in them, even after Birnam Wood began to come toward Dunsinane, leaving him only a gambler's last chance. What Macduff said finally undeceived him, but with the bravery born of despair he tells Macduff to "lay on," knowing that the fight will be his last.

In *Macbeth,* as in all of Shakespeare's tragedies, the exceptional calamity that befalls the main characters is to a large extent due to inherent weaknesses, and it is these that help to bring on the final catastrophe. In the other tragedies the reader invariably sympathizes with the unfortunates, but at the end of *Macbeth* one may seriously ask whether it is possible to do so in the case of both Macbeth and Lady Macbeth. In spite of Shakespeare's effective dramatic treatment of his theme, and in spite of the few redeeming bits here and there, the modern reader is left cold. That is one reason why *Macbeth* is played less often than *Hamlet,* for instance. Audiences want the thrills that *Macbeth* can give, but they also want more — an emotional sympathy, and that *Macbeth* cannot give.

QUESTIONS

I. i.

1. Contrast the opening of this play with others you have read.
2. Do you find it more dramatic than others? Explain.
3. Imagine how the witches looked, from this scene and later ones.
4. How did they talk, and how did they act?
5. Remember that in Shakespeare's day many people believed in witches.

I. ii.

1. What are your first impressions of Macbeth?
2. How was he regarded by his associates and his king? Why?
3. Why was Duncan not in the battle?
4. What information is given in this scene?

I. iii.

1. Pick out lines that indicate the witches to be evil-minded.
2. With the entrance of Macbeth the real action begins. Should this scene have been given first? Explain.
3. How is your picture of the witches made more definite? Give details.
4. Does Banquo have faith in witches as strongly as Macbeth?
5. Select passages suggesting that Macbeth's ambition to be king was not new.
6. Explain lines 134–41, noting especially what they tell of Macbeth's character.

7. Remember that originally Macbeth's claims to the throne had been as good as Duncan's.

I. iv.

1. Does Macbeth's pledge of loyalty ring true? Explain.
2. If Banquo has " no less deserved," why does he receive nothing but the king's embrace?
3. How do Banquo and Macbeth differ in personality?
4. What practical reasons may Duncan have had for heaping rewards upon Macbeth? See question 7, previous scene.
5. Whatever plans Macbeth may have had at this point, how were they complicated in this scene?
6. On the other hand, what fact seems to work directly into his hands?

I. v.

1. After reading the letter, Lady Macbeth at once comes to a decision. What is it?
2. How does she differ from her husband in this respect?
3. Write out the characteristics of Macbeth as given by his wife.
4. In general, do they fit in with your ideas of Macbeth so far?
5. From lines 39–52, what impressions do you get of Lady Macbeth?
6. Had they ever discussed the possibility of making away with Duncan?
7. Who takes the lead at this point, and why?
8. Have you any reason to believe that Macbeth's ambitions may in the first place have been due to his wife?

I. vi.

1. Contrast Lady Macbeth's speech of welcome with Macbeth's earlier pledge.
2. What traits in Duncan increase the horror of the impending tragedy?

I. vii.

1. If you have read *Hamlet,* compare the tone and trend of Macbeth's speech with the soliloquies of Hamlet.
2. Why was Macbeth not attending supper?
3. Name specifically the thoughts that hold him back from his purpose. Also those that urge him on.
4. How does Lady Macbeth restore his decision to go ahead?
5. Does " this enterprise " in line 48 refer to the letter, or to an earlier discussion?
6. At this point, sum up what you have so far learned about the plot.

II. i.

1. Visualize the setting as to time and place. Comment.
2. Do Banquo's " cursed thoughts " refer to himself or to Macbeth? Comment.
3. In his talk with Macbeth, what further development of this idea?
4. The " dagger " speech is a famous passage. For full effect, read it aloud.
5. State the reason for Macbeth's visions, as suggested by himself.
6. Is the dagger ever visible to the audience? Comment.
7. What brings him back to the business of the moment?

II. ii.

1. What has made Lady Macbeth bold (line 1)?
2. Why did she not commit the deed herself?
3. What do these two things indicate about her character?
4. How is Macbeth's tendency to have visions once more indicated?
5. Which unnerves him more, the picture of the crime or its possible consequences?
6. How does Lady Macbeth show her firmness? Is it real?
7. How does the "Knocking within" affect both?
8. Are the last two lines in harmony with Macbeth's character as so far indicated? Comment.

II. iii.

1. State briefly the dramatic importance of the porter episode.
2. After the discovery, does Macbeth keep up his part well, or not? Comment.
3. Why did he kill the grooms? Was it wise of him? Comment.
4. Did Lady Macbeth really faint? Explain.
5. Did she faint at an appropriate moment? Explain.
6. How does Banquo seal his own fate in this scene? Quote.
7. Were the suspicions of Malcolm and Donalbain correct?
8. Was their flight playing into Macbeth's hands, or not? Comment.

II. iv.

1. How does the first part fit in with the general atmosphere of the play?
2. What impression do you form of Macduff?
3. What necessary information is given in this scene?

III. i.

1. In your own words, Banquo's thoughts in lines 1–10.
2. Why does Macbeth fear Banquo?
3. What does Macbeth mean by line 71?
4. How does he secure the murderers?
5. What reasons does he give for not committing the deed himself?
6. Why does he include Fleance?
7. In planning this crime, is he as wavering as in the murder of Duncan?

III. ii.

1. What evidence do you find for changes in Lady Macbeth?
2. Does Macbeth still take his wife into his full confidence? Explain.
3. Discuss his state of mind as shown in this scene.
4. Is it conscience that worries him, or fear?

III. iii.

1. How does the third murderer win the confidence of the others?
2. Might he have been Macbeth himself?
3. How does the escape of Fleance complicate the story?

III. iv.

1. Picture the banquet scene. Why does Macbeth not sit down at once?

2. Does the escape of Fleance partially account for his state of mind?
3. Can you suggest an effective practical method of presenting the ghost?
4. Does Macbeth show any courage in his fear? Explain.
5. Is the second appearance of the ghost the more dramatic? Comment.
6. In this scene, who leads in planning, Macbeth or Lady Macbeth? Show by quoting passages.
7. What spy system had Macbeth instituted, and why?
8. Why was he going to the weird sisters once more? Did Lady Macbeth believe in them?
9. What " strange things " did he " have in head " ?
10. Connect the references to sleep with an earlier scene.

III. v.

1. How was Hecate related to the witches?
2. Why was she angry?

III. vi.

1. What necessary information is conveyed by this scene?
2. Were Macbeth's suspicions about Macduff evidently correct?
3. What hints do you find that justice is beginning to find herself?

IV. i.

1. Note carefully the ingredients of the hell-broth, and how the " charm " is made " firm and good."
2. What does Macbeth learn from the witches? Give all the details.
3. Does he learn all he wants to know? Explain.
4. Does he still believe in them? Note line 139, and then watch for more throughout the rest of the play.
5. Has his character deteriorated since he became king? Explain.
6. Has he become more forceful and more resolute? Explain.
7. Why should he continue to plan wholesale murder?

IV. ii.

1. What impression do you form of Lady Macduff?
2. Did she really believe that her husband did not love her?
3. What reasons may he have had for leaving abruptly?
4. Why did Elizabethans like this scene? (See Introduction.)
5. Would a modern audience enjoy it? Give specific reasons for your answer.

IV. iii.

1. Do you find the long opening conversation interesting?
2. What was Malcolm's reason for testing Macduff?
3. What plans are afoot for rescuing Scotland from Macbeth?
4. Why does Ross delay his real news?
5. How does Macduff receive it? Note all the details carefully.
6. By what bit of action does he show how deeply he is affected?
7. Defend the statement that this is the most dramatic moment in the play. Or the contrary.

V. i.

1. How is Lady Macbeth changed?
2. From earlier scenes, were you prepared for such a change? Comment.
3. In answering question 2, re-read the earlier passages and note how closely they parallel each other in details.
4. What line indicates that her suicide is feared?

V. ii.

1. Is there important information about Macbeth in this scene?
2. What is there dramatic in the "march towards Birnam"?

V. iii.

1. Does Macbeth still have confidence in the witches?
2. Does he feel what he says in lines 9 and 10, or is he bluffing?
3. How about the feeling expressed in lines 20–28, genuine or not?
4. Was his concern about Lady Macbeth due to his love for her, or because of the worry that her condition caused himself?
5. Answers to the two previous questions will go far in forming your final estimate of Macbeth. Think them over carefully.

V. iv.

1. Is the spirit of the invading army confident? Connect this idea with Scene ii.
2. Was Malcolm's reason for carrying branches good strategy?

V. v.

1. Fate is rapidly closing in on Macbeth. Does he realize it? Comment.
2. Comment on the way he receives the news of Lady Macbeth's death.
3. Lines 19–28 are the finest in the play. Memorize them.
4. Note especially how different is their spirit from that of the "dagger" speech.
5. How is his confidence in the witches further shaken?

V. vi.

1. Note how calmly the besieging forces set to work.
2. Contrast this with Macbeth's actions in the previous scene.

V. vii.

1. Does the episode of young Siward make good stage "business"? Comment.
2. Is Macbeth's confidence bolstered up for the moment? Explain.
3. Why is Macduff introduced in this scene?
4. What do we learn about Macbeth's forces?

V. viii.

1. The last of the prophecies is about to be tested. Is that one reason why Macbeth will not play the "Roman fool"?
2. Why does he not want to fight Macduff? Does it show real remorse?
3. What, in general, is your feeling about Macbeth in these final scenes? Give explicit reasons for your opinions.

4. How is your opinion affected by Macbeth's last spoken line?
5. Do you admire old Siward? Comment.
6. Are you enthusiastic over Malcolm? Explain.
7. Note how Shakespeare here, as in *Julius Caesar* and *Hamlet*, makes definite and adequate provision for a newer and better order in the state.

AS YOU LIKE IT

DRAMATIS PERSONAE

DUKE, living in banishment.
FREDERICK, his brother, and usurper of his dominions.
JAQUES } lords attending on the
AMIENS } banished duke.
LE BEAU, a courtier attending upon Frederick.
CHARLES, wrestler to Frederick.
OLIVER }
JAQUES } sons of Sir Rowland
ORLANDO } de Boys.
ADAM }
DENNIS } servants to Oliver.

TOUCHSTONE, a clown.
SIR OLIVER MARTEXT, a vicar.
CORIN }
SILVIUS } shepherds.
WILLIAM, a country fellow, in love with Audrey.
A person representing Hymen.
ROSALIND, daughter to the banished duke.
CELIA, daughter to Frederick.
PHEBE, a shepherdess.
AUDREY, a country wench.
Lords, pages, and attendants, &c.

SCENE: *Oliver's house; Duke Frederick's court; and the Forest of Arden.*

ACT I

SCENE I. *Orchard of* OLIVER'S *house.*

Enter ORLANDO *and* ADAM.

Orl. As I remember, Adam, it was upon this fashion: bequeathed me by will but poor a thousand crowns, and, as thou sayest, charged my brother, on his blessing, to breed me well; and there begins my sadness. My brother Jaques he keeps at school, and report speaks goldenly of his profit. For my part, he keeps me rustically at home, or, to speak more properly, stays me here at home unkept; for call you that keeping for a gentleman of my birth, that differs not from the stalling of an ox? His horses are bred better; for, besides that they are fair with their feeding, they are taught their manage, and to that end riders dearly hired; but I, his brother, gain nothing under him but growth; for the which his animals on his dung-hills are as much bound to him as I. Besides this nothing that he so plentifully gives me, the something that nature gave me his countenance seems to take from me. He lets me feed with his

---

4. **on his blessing:** the blessing depended on the carrying out of the father's instructions. 6. **Jaques:** note that there are two characters with this name. 8. **rustically:** like a rustic. 10. **countenance:** treatment.

hinds, bars me the place of a brother, and, as much as in him lies, mines my gentility with my education. This is it, Adam, that grieves me; and the spirit of my father, which I think is within me, begins to mutiny against this servitude. I will no longer endure it, though yet I know no wise remedy how to avoid it.

Adam. Yonder comes my master, your brother.

Orl. Go apart, Adam, and thou shalt hear how he will shake me up. 30

Enter OLIVER.

Oli. Now, sir! what make you here?

Orl. Nothing. I am not taught to make any thing.

Oli. What mar you then, sir?

Orl. Marry, sir, I am helping you to mar that which God made, a poor unworthy brother of yours, with idleness.

Oli. Marry, sir, be better employed, and be naught awhile. 39

Orl. Shall I keep your hogs and eat husks with them? What prodigal portion have I spent, that I should come to such penury?

Oli. Know you where you are, sir?

Orl. O, sir, very well; here in your orchard.

Oli. Know you before whom, sir?

Orl. Ay, better than him I am before knows me. I know you are my eldest brother; and, in the gentle condition of blood, you should so know me. The courtesy of nations allows you my better, in that you are the firstborn; but the same tradition takes not away my blood, were there twenty brothers betwixt us. I have as much of my father in me as you; albeit, I confess, your coming before me is nearer to his reverence.

Oli. What, boy!

Orl. Come, come, elder brother, you are too young in this.

Oli. Wilt thou lay hands on me, villain? 57

Orl. I am no villain; I am the youngest son of Sir Rowland de Boys; he was my father, and he is thrice a villain that says such a father begot villains. Wert thou not my brother, I would not take this hand from thy throat till this other had pulled out thy tongue for saying so. Thou hast railed on thyself.

21. **hinds:** common farm hands. 23. **mines:** undermines. 48. **gentle:** noble. 58. **villain:** Oliver means **rascal,** but Orlando, in the next line, purposely uses it as **peasant.**

Adam. Sweet masters, be patient; for your father's remembrance, be at accord.

Oli. Let me go, I say.

Orl. I will not, till I please. You shall hear me. My father charged you in his will to give me good education. You have trained me like a peasant, obscuring and hiding from me all gentlemanlike qualities. The spirit of my father grows strong in me, and I will no longer endure it; therefore allow me such exercises as may become a gentleman, or give me the poor allottery my father left me by testament; with that I will go buy my fortunes.   78

Oli. And what wilt thou do? Beg, when that is spent? Well, sir, get you in. I will not long be troubled with you; you shall have some part of your will. I pray you, leave me.

Orl. I will no further offend you than becomes me for my good.

Oli. Get you with him, you old dog.

Adam. Is " old dog " my reward? Most true, I have lost my teeth in your service. God be with my old master! He would not have spoke such a word.

                              [*Exeunt Orlando and Adam.*

Oli. Is it even so? Begin you to grow upon me? I will physic your rankness, and yet give no thousand crowns neither. Holla, Dennis.

Enter DENNIS.

Den. Calls your worship?

Oli. Was not Charles, the duke's wrestler, here to speak with me?

Den. So please you, he is here at the door and importunes access to you.

Oli. Call him in. [*Exit Dennis.*] 'Twill be a good way; and tomorrow the wrestling is.

Enter CHARLES.

Cha. Good morrow to your worship.   100

Oli. Good Monsieur Charles, what's the new news at the new court?

Cha. There's no news at the court, sir, but the old news: that is, the old duke is banished by his younger brother the new duke; and three or four loving lords have put themselves

90. **grow upon me:** too big to be controlled. 91. **physic your rankness:** cure you of this overgrowth.

into voluntary exile with him, whose lands and revenues en-
rich the new duke; therefore he gives them good leave to
wander.

Oli. Can you tell if Rosalind, the duke's daughter, be banished with her father?   111

Cha. O, no; for the duke's daughter, her cousin, so loves
her, being ever from their cradles bred together, that she would
have followed her exile, or have died to stay behind her. She
is at the court, and no less beloved of her uncle than his own
daughter; and never two ladies loved as they do.

Oli. Where will the old duke live?   119

Cha. They say he is already in the forest of Arden, and a
many merry men with him; and there they live like the old
Robin Hood of England. They say many young gentlemen
flock to him every day, and fleet the time carelessly, as they
did in the golden world.

Oli. What, you wrestle tomorrow before the new duke?

Cha. Marry, do I, sir; and I came to acquaint you with a
matter. I am given, sir, secretly to understand that your
younger brother Orlando hath a disposition to come in disguised against me to try a fall. Tomorrow, sir, I wrestle for
my credit; and he that escapes me without some broken limb
shall acquit him well. Your brother is but young and tender;
and, for your love, I would be loath to foil him, as I must, for
my own honor, if he come in; therefore, out of my love to you,
I came hither to acquaint you withal, that either you might
stay him from his intendment, or brook such disgrace well as
he shall run into, in that it is a thing of his own search and
altogether against my will.   141

Oli. Charles, I thank thee for thy love to me, which thou
shalt find I will most kindly requite. I had myself notice of
my brother's purpose herein and have by underhand means
labored to dissuade him from it, but he is resolute. I'll tell
thee, Charles, it is the stubbornest young fellow of France,
full of ambition, an envious emulator of every man's good
parts, a secret and villainous contriver against me his natural
brother; therefore use thy discretion; I had as lief thou didst
break his neck as his finger. And thou wert best look to 't;
for if thou dost him any slight disgrace or if he do not mightily grace himself on thee, he will practice against thee by
poison, entrap thee by some treacherous device and never

123. **fleet:** pass.

leave thee till he hath ta'en thy life by some indirect means or
other; for, I assure thee, and almost with tears I speak it, there
is not one so young and so villainous this day living. I speak
but brotherly of him; but should I anatomize him to thee as
he is, I must blush and weep and thou must look pale and
wonder.

Cha. I am heartily glad I came hither to you. If he come
tomorrow, I'll give him his payment. If ever he go alone
again, I'll never wrestle for prize more. And so God keep
your worship!   168

Oli. Farewell, good Charles. [*Exit Charles.*] Now will I
stir this gamester. I hope I shall see an end of him; for my
soul, yet I know not why, hates nothing more than he. Yet
he's gentle, never schooled and yet learned, full of noble device, of all sorts enchantingly beloved, and indeed so much in
the heart of the world, and especially of my own people, who
best know him, that I am altogether misprised. But it shall
not be so long; this wrestler shall clear all. Nothing remains
but that I kindle the boy thither; which now I'll go about.

[*Exit.*

166. **go alone:** without help, i.e., crippled.   172. **noble device:** high
ideals.   173. **of all sorts:** people of all classes.   175. **misprised:** undervalued.

SCENE II. *Lawn before the* DUKE'S *palace.*

Enter CELIA *and* ROSALIND.

Cel. I pray thee, Rosalind, sweet my coz, be merry.

Ros. Dear Celia, I show more mirth than I am mistress of;
and would you yet I were merrier? Unless you could teach
me to forget a banished father, you must not learn me how to
remember any extraordinary pleasure.

Cel. Herein I see thou lovest me not with the full weight
that I love thee. If my uncle, thy banished father, had banished thy uncle, the duke my father, so thou hadst been still
with me, I could have taught my love to take thy father for
mine; so wouldst thou, if the truth of thy love to me were so
righteously tempered as mine is to thee.

Ros. Well, I will forget the condition of my estate, to rejoice in yours.   17

Cel. You know my father hath no child but I, nor none is

1. **sweet my coz:** my sweet cousin.   4. **learn:** teach.

like to have: and, truly, when he dies, thou shalt be his heir, for what he hath taken away from thy father perforce, I will render thee again in affection; by mine honor, I will; and when I break that oath, let me turn monster. Therefore, my sweet Rose, my dear Rose, be merry.

Ros. From henceforth I will, coz, and devise sports. Let me see. What think you of falling in love?   27

Cel. Marry, I prithee, do, to make sport withal. But love no man in good earnest; nor no further in sport neither than with safety of a pure blush thou mayst in honor come off again.

Ros. What shall be our sport, then?

Cel. Let us sit and mock the good housewife Fortune from her wheel, that her gifts may henceforth be bestowed equally.

Ros. I would we could do so, for her benefits are mightily misplaced, and the bountiful blind woman doth most mistake in her gifts to women.   39

Cel. 'Tis true; for those that she makes fair she scarce makes honest, and those that she makes honest she makes very ill-favoredly.

Ros. Nay, now thou goest from Fortune's office to Nature's. Fortune reigns in gifts of the world, not in the lineaments of Nature.

Enter TOUCHSTONE.

Cel. No? When Nature hath made a fair creature, may she not by Fortune fall into the fire? Though Nature hath given us wit to flout at Fortune, hath not Fortune sent in this fool to cut off the argument?   50

Ros. Indeed, there is Fortune too hard for Nature, when Fortune makes Nature's natural the cutter-off of Nature's wit.

Cel. Peradventure this is not Fortune's work neither, but Nature's; who perceiveth our natural wits too dull to reason of such goddesses and hath sent this natural for our whetstone; for always the dullness of the fool is the whetstone of the wits. How now, wit! whither wander you?

Touch. Mistress, you must come away to your father.   61

Cel. Were you made the messenger?

Touch. No, by mine honor, but I was bid to come for you.

Ros. Where learned you that oath, fool?

Touch. Of a certain knight that swore by his honor they were good pancakes and swore by his honor the mustard was

38. **blind woman:** Fortune.   40. **honest:** virtuous.   50. **fool:** jester.   52. **Nature's natural:** idiot.

naught. Now I'll stand to it, the pancakes were naught and the mustard was good, and yet was not the knight forsworn.

Cel. How prove you that, in the great heap of your knowledge?

Ros. Ay, marry, now unmuzzle your wisdom.

Touch. Stand you both forth now. Stroke your chins, and swear by your beards that I am a knave.

Cel. By our beards, if we had them, thou art.   79

Touch. By my knavery, if I had it, then I were. But if you swear by that that is not, you are not forsworn. No more was this knight, swearing by his honor, for he never had any; or if he had, he had sworn it away before ever he saw those pancakes or that mustard.

Cel. Prithee, who is 't that thou meanest?

Touch. One that old Frederick, your father, loves.

Cel. My father's love is enough to honor him. Enough! speak no more of him. You'll be whipped for taxation one of these days.   91

Touch. The more pity, that fools may not speak wisely what wise men do foolishly.

Cel. By my troth, thou sayest true; for since the little wit that fools have was silenced, the little foolery that wise men have makes a great show. Here comes Monsieur Le Beau.

Ros. With his mouth full of news.

Cel. Which he will put on us, as pigeons feed their young.   100

Ros. Then shall we be news-crammed.

Cel. All the better; we shall be the more marketable.

Enter LE BEAU.

Bon jour, Monsieur Le Beau. What's the news?

Le Beau. Fair princess, you have lost much good sport.

Cel. Sport! Of what color?

Le Beau. What color, madam! How shall I answer you?

Ros. As wit and fortune will.   110

Touch. Or as the Destinies decree.

Cel. Well said. That was laid on with a trowel.

Touch. Nay, if I keep not my rank—

Ros. Thou losest thy old smell.

90. **for taxation:** for being too smart. 103. **Bon jour:** good day. 112. **laid, etc.:** i.e., laid on thick.

Le Beau. You amaze me, ladies. I would have told you of good wrestling, which you have lost the sight of.

Ros. Yet tell us the manner of the wrestling.

Le Beau. I will tell you the beginning; and, if it please your ladyships, you may see the end. For the best is yet to do; and here, where you are, they are coming to perform it.

Cel. Well, the beginning, that is dead and buried.

Le Beau. There comes an old man and his three sons—

Cel. I could match this beginning with an old tale.

Le Beau. Three proper young men, of excellent growth and presence.   130

Ros. With bills on their necks, " Be it known unto all men by these presents."

Le Beau. The eldest of the three wrestled with Charles, the duke's wrestler; which Charles in a moment threw him and broke three of his ribs, that there is little hope of life in him. So he served the second, and so the third. Yonder they lie; the poor old man, their father, making such pitiful dole over them that all the beholders take his part with weeping.   140

Ros. Alas!

Touch. But what is the sport, monsieur, that the ladies have lost?

Le Beau. Why, this that I speak of.

Touch. Thus men may grow wiser every day. It is the first time that ever I heard breaking of ribs was sport for ladies.

Cel. Or I, I promise thee.

Ros. But is there any else longs to see this broken music in his sides? Is there yet another dotes upon rib-breaking? Shall we see this wrestling, cousin?

Le Beau. You must, if you stay here; for here is the place appointed for the wrestling, and they are ready to perform it.

Cel. Yonder, sure, they are coming. Let us now stay and see it.

Flourish. Enter DUKE FREDERICK, Lords, ORLANDO,
CHARLES, *and* Attendants.

Duke F. Come on. Since the youth will not be entreated, his own peril on his forwardness.

Ros. Is yonder the man?   160

Le Beau. Even he, madam.

131. **bills:** legal document; also a forester's utensil.

Cel. Alas, he is too young! Yet he looks successfully.

Duke F. How now, daughter and cousin! are you crept hither to see the wrestling?

Ros. Ay, my liege, so please you give us leave.

Duke F. You will take little delight in it, I can tell you, there is such odds in the man. In pity of the challenger's youth I would fain dissuade him, but he will not be entreated. Speak to him, ladies; see if you can move him.

Cel. Call him hither, good Monsieur Le Beau.

Duke F. Do so; I'll not be by.

Le Beau. Monsieur the challenger, the princesses call for you.

Orl. I attend them with all respect and duty.

Ros. Young man, have you challenged Charles the wrestler?   179

Orl. No, fair princess; he is the general challenger. I come but in, as others do, to try with him the strength of my youth.

Cel. Young gentleman, your spirits are too bold for your years. You have seen cruel proof of this man's strength. If you saw yourself with your eyes or knew yourself with your judgment, the fear of your adventure would counsel you to a more equal enterprise. We pray you, for your own sake, to embrace your own safety and give over this attempt.   190

Ros. Do, young sir; your reputation shall not therefore be misprised. We will make it our suit to the duke that the wrestling might not go forward.

Orl. I beseech you, punish me not with your hard thoughts; wherein I confess me much guilty, to deny so fair and excellent ladies any thing. But let your fair eyes and gentle wishes go with me to my trial; wherein, if I be foiled, there is but one shamed that was never gracious; if killed, but one dead that is willing to be so. I shall do my friends no wrong, for I have none to lament me, the world no injury, for in it I have nothing. Only in the world I fill up a place, which may be better supplied when I have made it empty.

Ros. The little strength that I have, I would it were with you.

Cel. And mine, to eke out hers.

Ros. Fare you well! Pray heaven I be deceived in you!   210

---

162. **successfully:** as though he were going to succeed. 163. **cousin:** used for any relative.

Cel.   Your heart's desires be with you!

Cha.   Come, where is this young gallant that is so desirous to lie with his mother earth?

Orl.   Ready, sir; but his will hath in it a more modest working.

Duke F.   You shall try but one fall.

Cha.   No, I warrant your grace, you shall not entreat him to a second, that have so mightily persuaded him from a first.   219

Orl.   An you mean to mock me after, you should not have mocked me before.   But come your ways.

Ros.   Now Hercules be thy speed, young man!

Cel.   I would I were invisible, to catch the strong fellow by the leg.   [*They wrestle.*

Ros.   O excellent young man!

Cel.   If I had a thunderbolt in mine eye, I can tell who should down.   [*Shout. Charles is thrown.*

Duke F.   No more, no more.

Orl.   Yes, I beseech your grace.   I am not yet well breathed.   230

Duke F.   How dost thou, Charles?

Le Beau.   He cannot speak, my lord.

Duke F.   Bear him away.   What is thy name, young man?

Orl.   Orlando, my liege; the youngest son of Sir Rowland de Boys.

Duke F.   I would thou hadst been son to some man else.
The world esteemed thy father honorable,
But I did find him still mine enemy.
Thou shouldst have better pleased me with this deed,
Hadst thou descended from another house.   240
But fare thee well; thou art a gallant youth.
I would thou hadst told me of another father.

                  [*Exeunt Duke Frederick, train, and Le Beau.*

Cel.   Were I my father, coz, would I do this?

Orl.   I am more proud to be Sir Rowland's son,
His youngest son; and would not change that calling,
To be adopted heir to Frederick.

Ros.   My father loved Sir Rowland as his soul,
And all the world was of my father's mind.
Had I before known this young man his son,
I should have given him tears unto entreaties,   250

---

238. **still:** always.   244. Orlando is speaking to himself.

Ere he should thus have ventured.
   Cel.   Gentle cousin,
Let us go thank him and encourage him.
My father's rough and envious disposition
Sticks me at heart. Sir, you have well deserved.
If you do keep your promises in love
But justly, as you have exceeded all promise,
Your mistress shall be happy.
   Ros.   Gentleman,
               [Giving him a chain from her neck.
Wear this for me, one out of suits with fortune,
That could give more, but that her hand lacks means.
Shall we go, coz?
   Cel. Ay. Fare you well, fair gentleman.
   Orl. Can I not say, I thank you? My better parts   261
Are all thrown down, and that which here stands up
Is but a quintain, a mere lifeless block.
   Ros. He calls us back. My pride fell with my fortunes;
I'll ask him what he would. Did you call, sir?
Sir, you have wrestled well and overthrown
More than your enemies.
   Cel.   Will you go, coz?
   Ros. Have with you. Fare you well.
               [Exeunt Rosalind and Celia.
   Orl. What passion hangs these weights upon my tongue?
I cannot speak to her, yet she urged conference.
O poor Orlando, thou art overthrown!   271
Or Charles or something weaker masters thee.

Reënter Le Beau.

   Le Beau. Good sir, I do in friendship counsel you
To leave this place. Albeit you have deserved
High commendation, true applause and love,
Yet such is now the duke's condition
That he misconstrues all that you have done.
The duke is humorous: what he is indeed,
More suits you to conceive than I to speak of.
   Orl. I thank you, sir; and, pray you, tell me this: 280
Which of the two was daughter of the duke
That here was at the wrestling?

---

  263. **quintain:** wooden statue. 268. **have with you:** I'll be with you.
270. **urged conference:** invited conversation. 278. **humorous:** moody.

Le Beau. Neither his daughter, if we judge by manners;
But yet indeed the taller is his daughter.
The other is daughter to the banished duke,
And here detained by her usurping uncle,
To keep his daughter company; whose loves
Are dearer than the natural bond of sisters.
But I can tell you that of late this duke
Hath ta'en displeasure 'gainst his gentle niece,
Grounded upon no other argument   291
But that the people praise her for her virtues
And pity her for her good father's sake;
And, on my life, his malice 'gainst the lady
Will suddenly break forth. Sir, fare you well.
Hereafter, in a better world than this,
I shall desire more love and knowledge of you.
    Orl. I rest much bounden to you; fare you well.
                                              [*Exit Le Beau.*
Thus must I from the smoke into the smother;
From tyrant duke unto a tyrant brother.
But heavenly Rosalind!   300
                                                 [*Exit.*

Scene III. *A room in the palace.*

Enter CELIA *and* ROSALIND.

    Cel. Why, cousin! why, Rosalind! Cupid have mercy! not
a word?
    Ros. Not one to throw at a dog.
    Cel. No, thy words are too precious to be cast away upon
curs; throw some of them at me. Come, lame me with reasons.
    Ros. Then there were two cousins laid up; when the one
should be lamed with reasons and the other mad without any.
    Cel. But is all this for your father?   10
    Ros. No, some of it is for my child's father. O, how full
of briers is this working-day world!
    Cel. They are but burs, cousin, thrown upon thee in holi-
day foolery. If we walk not in the trodden paths, our very
petticoats will catch them.
    Ros. I could shake them off my coat. These burs are in
my heart.
    Cel. Hem them away.
    Ros. I would try, if I could cry " hem " and have him. 20

Cel. Come, come, wrestle with thy affections.

Ros. O, they take the part of a better wrestler than myself!

Cel. O, a good wish upon you! you will try in time, in despite of a fall. But, turning these jests out of service, let us talk in good earnest. Is it possible, on such a sudden, you should fall into so strong a liking with old Sir Rowland's youngest son?

Ros. The duke my father loved his father dearly.   31

Cel. Doth it therefore ensue that you should love his son dearly? By this kind of chase, I should hate him, for my father hated his father dearly; yet I hate not Orlando.

Ros. No, faith, hate him not, for my sake.

Cel. Why should I not? Doth he not deserve well?

Ros. Let me love him for that, and do you love him because I do. Look, here comes the duke.   41

Cel. With his eyes full of anger.

Enter Duke Frederick, *with* Lords.

Duke F. Mistress, dispatch you with your safest haste
And get you from our court.

Ros.   Me, uncle?

Duke F.   You, cousin.
Within these ten days if that thou be'st found
So near our public court as twenty miles,
Thou diest for it.

Ros.   I do beseech your grace,
Let me the knowledge of my fault bear with me.
If with myself I hold intelligence
Or have acquaintance with mine own desires,   50
If that I do not dream or be not frantic—
As I do trust I am not — then, dear uncle,
Never so much as in a thought unborn
Did I offend your highness.

Duke F.   Thus do all traitors.
If their purgation did consist in words,
They are as innocent as grace itself.
Let it suffice thee that I trust thee not.

Ros. Yet your mistrust cannot make me a traitor.
Tell me whereon the likelihood depends.

Duke F. Thou art thy father's daughter; there's enough. 60

59. **likelihood:** likeness.

Ros.   So was I when your highness took his dukedom;
So was I when your highness banished him.
Treason is not inherited, my lord;
Or, if we did derive it from our friends,
What's that to me?   My father was no traitor.
Then, good my liege, mistake me not so much
To think my poverty is treacherous.

Cel.   Dear sovereign, hear me speak.

Duke F.   Ay, Celia; we stayed her for your sake,
Else had she with her father ranged along.   70

Cel.   I did not then entreat to have her stay;
It was your pleasure and your own remorse.
I was too young that time to value her;
But now I know her.   If she be a traitor,
Why, so am I.   We still have slept together,
Rose at an instant, learned, played, eat together,
And wheresoe'er we went, like Juno's swans,
Still we went coupled and inseparable.

Duke F.   She is too subtle for thee; and her smoothness,
Her very silence and her patience   80
Speak to the people, and they pity her.
Thou art a fool.   She robs thee of thy name,
And thou wilt show more bright and seem more virtuous
When she is gone.   Then open not thy lips.
Firm and irrevocable is my doom
Which I have passed upon her; she is banished.

Cel.   Pronounce that sentence then on me, my liege;
I cannot live out of her company.

Duke F.   You are a fool.   You, niece, provide yourself.
If you outstay the time, upon mine honor,   90
And in the greatness of my word, you die.

                    [*Exeunt Duke Frederick and Lords.*

Cel.   O my poor Rosalind, whither wilt thou go?
Wilt thou change fathers?   I will give thee mine.
I charge thee, be not thou more grieved than I am.

Ros.   I have more cause.

Cel.   Thou hast not, cousin;
Prithee, be cheerful.   Know'st thou not, the duke
Hath banished me, his daughter?

Ros.   That he hath not.

Cel.   No, hath not?   Rosalind lacks then the love

---

77. **Juno's:** really Venus'.

Which teacheth thee that thou and I am one.
Shall we be sundered?   Shall we part, sweet girl?
No; let my father seek another heir.   101
Therefore devise with me how we may fly,
Whither to go and what to bear with us;
And do not seek to take your change upon you,
To bear your griefs yourself and leave me out;
For, by this heaven, now at our sorrows pale,
Say what thou canst, I'll go along with thee.
   Ros.   Why, whither shall we go?
   Cel.   To seek my uncle in the forest of Arden.
   Ros.   Alas, what danger will it be to us,   110
Maids as we are, to travel forth so far!
Beauty provoketh thieves sooner than gold.
   Cel.   I'll put myself in poor and mean attire
And with a kind of umber smirch my face;
The like do you.   So shall we pass along
And never stir assailants.
   Ros.   Were it not better,
Because that I am more than common tall,
That I did suit me all points like a man?
A gallant curtle-axe upon my thigh,   119
A boar-spear in my hand; and — in my heart
Lie there what hidden woman's fear there will —
We'll have a swashing and a martial outside,
As many other mannish cowards have
That do outface it with their semblances.
   Cel.   What shall I call thee when thou art a man?
   Ros.   I'll have no worse a name than Jove's own page;
And therefore look you call me Ganymede.
But what will you be called?
   Cel.   Something that hath a reference to my state;
No longer Celia, but Aliena.   130
   Ros.   But, cousin, what if we assayed to steal
The clownish fool out of your father's court?
Would he not be a comfort to our travel?
   Cel.   He'll go along o'er the wide world with me.
Leave me alone to woo him.   Let's away,
And get our jewels and our wealth together,
Devise the fittest time and safest way

117. **more than common tall:** see line 285, Sc. ii.   Shakespeare made a slip.
119. **curtle-axe:** short sword.   130. **Aliena:** i.e., stranger.

To hide us from pursuit that will be made
After my flight.   Now go we in content   139
To liberty and not to banishment.   [*Exeunt.*

ACT II

SCENE I. *The Forest of Arden.*

Enter DUKE senior, AMIENS, *and two or three* Lords,
like foresters.

Duke S.   Now, my co-mates and brothers in exile,
Hath not old custom made this life more sweet
Than that of painted pomp?   Are not these woods
More free from peril than the envious court?
Here feel we but the penalty of Adam,
The seasons' difference, as the icy fang
And churlish chiding of the winter's wind,
Which, when it bites and blows upon my body,
Even till I shrink with cold, I smile and say:
" This is no flattery: these are counselors   10
That feelingly persuade me what I am."
Sweet are the uses of adversity,
Which, like the toad, ugly and venomous,
Wears yet a precious jewel in his head;
And this our life exempt from public haunt
Finds tongues in trees, books in the running brooks,
Sermons in stones and good in every thing.
I would not change it.
     Ami.   Happy is your grace,
That can translate the stubbornness of fortune
Into so quiet and so sweet a style.   20
     Duke S.   Come, shall we go and kill us venison?
And yet it irks me the poor dappled fools,
Being native burghers of this desert city,
Should in their own confines with forkéd heads
Have their round haunches gored.
     First Lord.   Indeed, my lord,
The melancholy Jaques grieves at that,
And, in that kind, swears you do more usurp

5. **penalty:** i.e., exile.   11. **feelingly persuade:** make me feel.   27. **irks
me:** I hate the idea.   24. **forked heads:** arrows.   26. **Jaques:** two syllables,
the a long.

Than doth your brother that hath banished you.
Today my Lord of Amiens and myself
Did steal behind him as he lay along   30
Under an oak whose antique root peeps out
Upon the brook that brawls along this wood;
To the which place a poor sequestered stag,
That from the hunter's aim had ta'en a hurt,
Did come to languish; and indeed, my lord,
The wretched animal heaved forth such groans
That their discharge did stretch his leathern coat
Almost to bursting, and the big round tears
Coursed one another down his innocent nose
In piteous chase; and thus the hairy fool,   40
Much markéd of the melancholy Jaques,
Stood on the extremest verge of the swift brook,
Augmenting it with tears.
    Duke S.   But what said Jaques?
Did he not moralize this spectacle?
    First Lord. O, yes, into a thousand similes.
First, for his weeping into the needless stream:
" Poor deer," quoth he, " thou makest a testament
As worldlings do, giving thy sum of more
To that which had too much." Then, being there alone,
Left and abandoned of his velvet friends,   50
" 'Tis right," quoth he; " thus misery doth part
The flux of company." Anon a careless herd,
Full of the pasture, jumps along by him
And never stays to greet him. " Ay," quoth Jaques,
" Sweep on, you fat and greasy citizens.
'Tis just the fashion. Wherefore do you look
Upon that poor and broken bankrupt there? "
Thus most invectively he pierceth through
The body of the country, city, court,
Yea, and of this our life, swearing that we   60
Are mere usurpers, tyrants, and what's worse,
To fright the animals and to kill them up
In their assigned and native dwelling-place.
    Duke S.   And did you leave him in this contemplation?
    Sec. Lord.   We did, my lord, weeping and commenting
Upon the sobbing deer.

---

   29. **Amiens:** pronounce English style, the **a** long.   41. **marked:** observed.
58. **invectively:** bitterly.

Duke S.   Show me the place.
I love to cope him in these sullen fits,
For then he's full of matter.
    First Lord.   I'll bring him to you straight.   [*Exeunt.*

67. **cope:** meet.

Scene II. *A room in the palace.*

Enter Duke Frederick, *with* Lords.

Duke F.   Can it be possible that no man saw them?
It cannot be. Some villains of my court
Are of consent and sufferance in this.
    First Lord.   I cannot hear of any that did see her.
The ladies, her attendants of her chamber,
Saw her abed, and in the morning early
They found the bed untreasured of their mistress.
    Sec. Lord.   My lord, the roynish clown, at whom so oft
Your grace was wont to laugh, is also missing.
Hisperia, the princess' gentlewoman,   10
Confesses that she secretly o'erheard
Your daughter and her cousin much commend
The parts and graces of the wrestler
That did but lately foil the sinewy Charles;
And she believes, wherever they are gone,
That youth is surely in their company.
    Duke F.   Send to his brother. Fetch that gallant hither.
If he be absent, bring his brother to me;
I'll make him find him. Do this suddenly,
And let not search and inquisition quail   20
To bring again these foolish runaways.   [*Exeunt.*

3. **consent, etc.:** have assisted. 8. **roynish:** rough. 17. **that gallant:** Orlando. 19. **suddenly:** right away. 20. **quail:** cease.

Scene III. *Before* Oliver's *house.*

Enter Orlando *and* Adam, *meeting.*

Orl.   Who's there?
Adam.   What, my young master? O my gentle master!
O my sweet master! O you memory

Of old Sir Rowland! Why, what make you here?
Why are you virtuous? Why do people love you?
And wherefore are you gentle, strong and valiant?
Why would you be so fond to overcome
The bonny priser of the humorous duke?
Your praise is come too swiftly home before you.
Know you not, master, to some kind of men   10
Their graces serve them but as enemies?
No more do yours. Your virtues, gentle master,
Are sanctified and holy traitors to you.
O, what a world is this, when what is comely
Envenoms him that bears it!
   Orl. Why, what's the matter?
   Adam.   O unhappy youth!
Come not within these doors; within this roof
The enemy of all your graces lives.
Your brother — no, no brother; yet the son—
Yet not the son, I will not call him son   20
Of him I was about to call his father—
Hath heard your praises, and this night he means
To burn the lodging where you use to lie
And you within it. If he fail of that,
He will have other means to cut you off.
I overheard him and his practices.
This is no place; this house is but a butchery.
Abhor it, fear it, do not enter it.
   Orl. Why, whither, Adam, wouldst thou have me go?
   Adam. No matter whither, so you come not here.   30
   Orl. What, wouldst thou have me go and beg my food?
Or with a base and boisterous sword enforce
A thievish living on the common road?
This I must do, or know not what to do;
Yet this I will not do, do how I can.
I rather will subject me to the malice
Of a diverted blood and bloody brother.
   Adam. But do not so. I have five hundred crowns,
The thrifty hire I saved under your father,
Which I did store to be my foster-nurse   40
When service should in my old limbs lie lame
And unregarded age in corners thrown.

8. **bonny priser:** valiant fighter. 8. **humorous:** capricious. 26. **practices:** schemes. 37. **diverted:** unnatural.

Take that, and He that doth the ravens feed,
Yea, providently caters for the sparrow,
Be comfort to my age!   Here is the gold;
All this I give you.   Let me be your servant.
Though I look old, yet I am strong and lusty;
For in my youth I never did apply
Hot and rebellious liquors in my blood,
Nor did not with unbashful forehead woo   50
The means of weakness and debility;
Therefore my age is as a lusty winter,
Frosty, but kindly.   Let me go with you;
I'll do the service of a younger man
In all your business and necessities.
   Orl.   O good old man, how well in thee appears
The constant service of the antique world,
When service sweat for duty, not for meed!
Thou art not for the fashion of these times,
Where none will sweat but for promotion,   60
And having that, do choke their service up
Even with the having.   It is not so with thee,
But, poor old man, thou prunest a rotten tree,
That cannot so much as a blossom yield
In lieu of all thy pains and husbandry.
But come thy ways; we'll go along together,
And ere we have thy youthful wages spent,
We'll light upon some settled low content.
   Adam.   Master, go on, and I will follow thee,
To the last gasp, with truth and loyalty.   70
From seventeen years till now almost fourscore
Here lived I, but now live here no more.
At seventeen years many their fortunes seek;
But at fourscore it is too late a week:
Yet fortune cannot recompense me better
Than to die well and not my master's debtor.   [*Exeunt.*

68. **settled low content:** settle down in humble happiness.

Scene IV. *The forest of Arden.*

Enter Rosalind *for* Ganymede, Celia *for* Aliena, *and* Touchstone.

Ros. O Jupiter, how weary are my spirits!

Touch. I care not for my spirits, if my legs were not weary.

Ros. I could find in my heart to disgrace my man's apparel and to cry like a woman; but I must comfort the weaker vessel, as doublet and hose ought to show itself courageous to petticoat; therefore courage, good Aliena!

Cel. I pray you, bear with me; I cannot go no further.   10

Touch. For my part, I had rather bear with you than bear you; yet I should bear no cross if I did bear you, for I think you have no money in your purse.

Ros. Well, this is the forest of Arden.

Touch. Ay, now am I in Arden; the more fool I. When I was at home, I was in a better place; but travelers must be content.

Ros. Ay, be so, good Touchstone.

Enter Corin *and* Silvius.

Look you, who comes here; a young man and an old in solemn talk.   21

Cor. That is the way to make her scorn you still.

Sil. O Corin, that thou knew'st how I do love her!

Cor. I partly guess; for I have loved ere now.

Sil. No, Corin, being old, thou canst not guess,
Though in thy youth thou wast as true a lover
As ever sighed upon a midnight pillow.
But if thy love were ever like to mine —
As sure I think did never man love so —
How many actions most ridiculous   30
Hast thou been drawn to by thy fantasy?

Cor. Into a thousand that I have forgotten.

Sil. O, thou didst then ne'er love so heartily!
If thou remember'st not the slightest folly
That ever love did make thee run into,
Thou hast not loved;
Or if thou hast not sat as I do now,
Wearying thy hearer in thy mistress' praise,

---

12. **cross:** small coin stamped with a cross. 20. **solemn:** earnest.

Thou hast not loved:
Or if thou hast not broke from company   40
Abruptly, as my passion now makes me,
Thou hast not loved.
O Phebe, Phebe, Phebe!   [*Exit.*

    Ros. Alas, poor shepherd! searching of thy wound,
I have by hard adventure found mine own.
    Touch. And I mine. I remember, when I was in love I
broke my sword upon a stone and bid him take that for coming
a-night to Jane Smile; and I remember the kissing of her
batlet and the cow's dugs that her pretty chopt hands had
milked; and I remember the wooing of a peasecod instead of
her, from whom I took two cods and, giving her them again,
said with weeping tears, "Wear these for my sake." We that
are true lovers run into strange capers; but as all is mortal in
nature, so is all nature in love mortal in folly.
    Ros. Thou speakest wiser than thou art ware of.
    Touch. Nay, I shall ne'er be ware of mine own wit till I
break my shins against it.   60
    Ros. Jove, Jove! this shepherd's passion
        Is much upon my fashion.
    Touch. And mine; but it grows something stale with me.
    Cel. I pray you, one of you question yond man
If he for gold will give us any food.
I faint almost to death.
    Touch.   Holla, you clown!
    Ros. Peace, fool; he's not thy kinsman.
    Cor.   Who calls?
    Touch. Your betters, sir.
    Cor.   Else are they very wretched.
    Ros. Peace, I say. Good even to you, friend.
    Cor. And to you, gentle sir, and to you all.   70
    Ros. I prithee, shepherd, if that love or gold
Can in this desert place buy entertainment,
Bring us where we may rest ourselves and feed.
Here's a young maid with travel much oppressed
And faints for succor.
    Cor.   Fair sir, I pity her
And wish, for her sake more than for mine own,
My fortunes were more able to relieve her;

    49. **batlet:** in washing clothes a small bat was used for beating. 50. **pease-
cod:** pea pod.

But I am shepherd to another man
And do not shear the fleeces that I graze.
My master is of churlish disposition   80
And little recks to find the way to heaven
By doing deeds of hospitality.
Besides, his cote, his flocks and bounds of feed
Are now on sale, and at our sheepcote now,
By reason of his absence, there is nothing
That you will feed on; but what is, come see,
And in my voice most welcome shall you be.
 Ros. What is he that shall buy his flock and pasture?
 Cor. That young swain that you saw here but erewhile,
That little cares for buying any thing.   90
 Ros. I pray thee, if it stand with honesty,
Buy thou the cottage, pasture and the flock,
And thou shalt have to pay for it of us.
 Cel. And we will mend thy wages. I like this place,
And willingly could waste my time in it.
 Cor. Assuredly the thing is to be sold.
Go with me. If you like upon report
The soil, the profit and this kind of life,
I will your very faithful feeder be
And buy it with your gold right suddenly. *[Exeunt.*

83. **cote:** small cottage. 88. **What:** who. 95. **waste:** spend. 99. **feeder:** i.e., of sheep.

Scene V. *The forest.*

Enter Amiens, Jaques, *and others.*

Song

Ami.   Under the greenwood tree
     Who loves to lie with me,
     And turn his merry note
     Unto the sweet bird's throat,
  Come hither, come hither, come hither!
     Here shall he see
     No enemy
   But winter and rough weather.

Jaq. More, more, I prithee, more.
Ami. It will make you melancholy, Monsieur Jaques. 10
Jaq. I thank it. More, I prithee, more. I can suck

melancholy out of a song, as a weasel sucks eggs. More, I prithee, more.

Ami. My voice is ragged. I know I cannot please you.

Jaq. I do not desire you to please me; I do desire you to sing. Come, more; another stanzo. Call you 'em stanzos? 20

Ami. What you will, Monsieur Jaques.

Jaq. Nay, I care not for their names; they owe me nothing. Will you sing?

Ami. More at your request than to please myself.

Jaq. Well, then, if ever I thank any man, I'll thank you; but that they call compliment is like the encounter of two dog-apes, and when a man thanks me heartily, methinks I have given him a penny and he renders me the beggarly thanks. Come, sing; and you that will not, hold your tongues. 31

Ami. Well, I'll end the song. Sirs, cover the while; the duke will drink under this tree. He hath been all this day to look you.

Jaq. And I have been all this day to avoid him. He is too disputable for my company. I think of as many matters as he, but I give Heaven thanks and make no boast of them. Come, warble, come.

Song

Who doth ambition shun   [*All together here.*
And loves to live i' the sun,   41
Seeking the food he eats
And pleased with what he gets,
Come hither, come hither, come hither!
Here shall he see
No enemy
But winter and rough weather.

Jaq. I'll give you a verse to this note that I made yesterday in despite of my invention.

Ami. And I'll sing it. 50

Jaq. Thus it goes:

If it do come to pass
That any man turn ass,
Leaving his wealth and ease,
A stubborn will to please,

32. **cover:** set the table. 48. **note:** tune. 49. **despite of, etc.:** in spite of my poor imagination.

Ducdame, ducdame, ducdame!
Here shall he see
Gross fools as he,
An if he will come to me.

Ami. What's that " ducdame "?   60
Jaq. 'Tis a Greek invocation, to call fools into a circle.
I'll go sleep, if I can; if I cannot, I'll rail against all the first-
born of Egypt.
Ami. And I'll go seek the duke; his banquet is prepared.
[*Exeunt severally.*

SCENE VI.   *The forest.*

Enter ORLANDO *and* ADAM.

Adam. Dear master, I can go no further. O, I die for
food! Here lie I down, and measure out my grave. Farewell, kind master.
Orl. Why, how now, Adam! no greater heart in thee?
Live a little; comfort a little; cheer thyself a little. If this
uncouth forest yield any thing savage, I will either be food for
it or bring it for food to thee. Thy conceit is nearer death
than thy powers. For my sake be comfortable; hold death
awhile at the arm's end. I will here be with thee presently;
and if I bring thee not something to eat, I will give thee leave
to die; but if thou diest before I come, thou art a mocker of my
labor. Well said! thou lookest cheerly, and I'll be with thee
quickly. Yet thou liest in the bleak air. Come, I will bear
thee to some shelter; and thou shalt not die for lack of a
dinner, if there live any thing in this desert. Cheerly, good
Adam!   [*Exeunt.*

SCENE VII.   *The forest.*

A table set out.   Enter DUKE *senior,* AMIENS, *and* Lords *like*
outlaws.

Duke S. I think he be transformed into a beast,
For I can nowhere find him like a man.

Sc. v. 56. **ducdame:** a nonsensical term.
Sc. vi. 7. **conceit:** imagination. 8. **comfortable:** cheerful.

First Lord. My lord, he is but even now gone hence.
Here was he merry, hearing of a song.
Duke S. If he, compact of jars, grow musical,
We shall have shortly discord in the spheres.
Go, seek him; tell him I would speak with him.

Enter JAQUES.

First Lord. He saves my labor by his own approach.
Duke S. Why, how now, monsieur! what a life is this,
That your poor friends must woo your company?
What, you look merrily!   11
Jaq. A fool, a fool! I met a fool i' the forest,
A motley fool; a miserable world!
As I do live by food, I met a fool,
Who laid him down and basked him in the sun,
And railed on Lady Fortune in good terms,
In good set terms and yet a motley fool.
" Good morrow, fool," quoth I. " No, sir," quoth he,
" Call me not fool till Heaven hath sent me fortune."
And then he drew a dial from his poke,   20
And, looking on it with lackluster eye,
Says very wisely: " It is ten o'clock.
Thus we may see," quoth he, " how the world wags.
'Tis but an hour ago since it was nine,
And after one hour more 'twill be eleven;
And so, from hour to hour, we ripe and ripe,
And then, from hour to hour, we rot and rot;
And thereby hangs a tale." When I did hear
The motley fool thus moral on the time,
My lungs began to crow like chanticleer,   30
That fools should be so deep-contemplative,
And I did laugh sans intermission
An hour by his dial. O noble fool!
A worthy fool! Motley's the only wear.
Duke S. What fool is this?
Jaq. O worthy fool! One that hath been a courtier,
And says, if ladies be but young and fair,
They have the gift to know it; and in his brain,
Which is as dry as the remainder biscuit
After a voyage, he hath strange places crammed

---

5. **compact of jars:** full of discords. 20. **dial; poke:** watch; pocket.
32. **sans:** without.

With observation, the which he vents   41
In mangled forms. O that I were a fool!
I am ambitious for a motley coat.
 Duke S. Thou shalt have one.
 Jaq.   It is my only suit;
Provided that you weed your better judgments
Of all opinion that grows rank in them
That I am wise. I must have liberty
Withal, as large a charter as the wind,
To blow on whom I please; for so fools have;
And they that are most galléd with my folly,   50
They most must laugh. And why, sir, must they so?
The " why " is plain as way to parish church.
He that a fool doth very wisely hit
Doth very foolishly, although he smart,
Not to seem senseless of the bob; if not,
The wise man's folly is anatomized
Even by the squandering glances of the fool.
Invest me in my motley; give me leave
To speak my mind, and I will through and through
Cleanse the foul body of the infected world,   60
If they will patiently receive my medicine.
 Duke S. Fie on thee! I can tell what thou wouldst do.
 Jaq. What, for a counter, would I do but good?
 Duke S. Most mischievous foul sin, in chiding sin.
For thou thyself hast been a libertine,
As sensual as the brutish sting itself;
And all the embosséd sores and headed evils,
That thou with license of free foot hast caught,
Wouldst thou disgorge into the general world.
 Jaq. Why, who cries out on pride,   70
That can therein tax any private party?
Doth it not flow as hugely as the sea,
Till that the wearer's very means do ebb?
What woman in the city do I name,
When that I say the city woman bears
The cost of princes on unworthy shoulders?
Who can come in and say that I mean her,
When such a one as she such is her neighbor?
Or what is he of basest function

 55. **bob:** jest. 57. **squandering:** random. 63. **counter:** coin. 71. **tax:** blame. 79. **basest function:** lowest occupation.

That says his bravery is not on my cost,   80
Thinking that I mean him, but therein suits
His folly to the mettle of my speech?
There then; how then? what then? Let me see wherein
My tongue hath wronged him. If it do him right,
Then he hath wronged himself; if he be free,
Why, then my taxing like a wild-goose flies,
Unclaimed of any man. But who comes here?

Enter ORLANDO, *with his sword drawn.*

Orl. Forbear, and eat no more.
Jaq.   Why, I have eat none yet.
Orl. Nor shalt not, till necessity be served.
Jaq. Of what kind should this cock come of?   90
Duke S. Art thou thus boldened, man, by thy distress.
Or else a rude despiser of good manners,
That in civility thou seem'st so empty?
Orl. You touched my vein at first. The thorny point
Of bare distress hath ta'en from me the show
Of smooth civility. Yet am I inland bred
And know some nurture. But forbear, I say.
He dies that touches any of this fruit
Till I and my affairs are answered.
Jaq. An you will not be answered with reason, I must
die.   101
Duke S. What would you have? Your gentleness shall
       force
More than your force move us to gentleness.
Orl. I almost die for food; and let me have it.
Duke S. Sit down and feed, and welcome to our table.
Orl. Speak you so gently? Pardon me, I pray you.
I thought that all things had been savage here,
And therefore put I on the countenance
Of stern commandment. But whate'er you are
That in this desert inaccessible,   110
Under the shade of melancholy boughs,
Lose and neglect the creeping hours of time,
If ever you have looked on better days,
If ever been where bells have knolled to church,
If ever sat at any good man's feast,
If ever from your eyelids wiped a tear

80. **bravery:** finery. 96. **inland:** city. 97. **nurture:** culture.

And know what 'tis to pity and be pitied,
Let gentleness my strong enforcement be;
In the which hope I blush, and hide my sword.

    Duke S.   True is it that we have seen better days,   120
And have with holy bell been knolled to church,
And sat at good men's feasts and wiped our eyes
Of drops that sacred pity hath engendered;
And therefore sit you down in gentleness
And take upon command what help we have
That to your wanting may be ministered.

    Orl.   Then but forbear your food a little while,
Whiles, like a doe, I go to find my fawn
And give it food.   There is an old poor man,
Who after me hath many a weary step   130
Limped in pure love.   Till he be first sufficed,
Oppressed with two weak evils, age and hunger,
I will not touch a bit.

    Duke S.   Go find him out,
And we will nothing waste till you return.

    Orl.   I thank ye; and be blest for your good comfort! [*Exit.*

    Duke S.   Thou seest we are not all alone unhappy.
This wide and universal theater
Presents more woeful pageants than the scene
Wherein we play in.

    Jaq.   All the world's a stage,
And all the men and women merely players.   140
They have their exits and their entrances;
And one man in his time plays many parts,
His acts being seven ages.   At first the infant,
Mewling and puking in the nurse's arms.
And then the whining schoolboy, with his satchel
And shining morning face, creeping like snail
Unwillingly to school.   And then the lover,
Sighing like furnace, with a woeful ballad
Made to his mistress' eyebrow.   Then a soldier,
Full of strange oaths and bearded like the pard,   150
Jealous in honor, sudden and quick in quarrel,
Seeking the bubble reputation
Even in the cannon's mouth.   And then the justice,
In fair round belly with good capon lined,
With eyes severe and beard of formal cut,

150. **pard:** leopard.   151. **Jealous:** suspicious.

Full of wise saws and modern instances;
And so he plays his part.   The sixth age shifts
Into the lean and slippered pantaloon,
With spectacles on nose and pouch on side,
His youthful hose, well saved, a world too wide   160
For his shrunk shank; and his big manly voice,
Turning again toward childish treble, pipes
And whistles in his sound.   Last scene of all,
That ends this strange eventful history,
Is second childishness and mere oblivion,
Sans teeth, sans eyes, sans taste, sans every thing.]

Reënter ORLANDO, *with* ADAM.

Duke. Welcome.   Set down your venerable burden
And let him feed.
  Orl. I thank you most for him.
  Adam.   So had you need;
I scarce can speak to thank you for myself.   170
  Duke S. Welcome; fall to.   I will not trouble you
As yet, to question you about your fortunes.
Give us some music; and, good cousin, sing.

SONG

  Ami.   Blow, blow, thou winter wind,
          Thou art not so unkind
              As man's ingratitude;
          Thy tooth is not so keen,
          Because thou art not seen,
              Although thy breath be rude.   179
Heigh-ho! sing, heigh-ho! unto the green holly.
Most friendship is feigning, most loving mere folly.
          Then, heigh-ho, the holly!
          This life is most jolly.

          Freeze, freeze, thou bitter sky,
          That dost not bite so nigh
              As benefits forgot;
          Though thou the waters warp,
          Thy sting is not so sharp
              As friend remembered not.
Heigh-ho! sing, &c.   190

156. **saws:** proverbial sayings.   156. **modern instances:** commonplace examples.   158. **pantaloon:** a stock character type of the Italian stage, represented as a decrepit silly old man.

Duke S. If that you were the good Sir Rowland's son,
As you have whispered faithfully you were,
And as mine eye doth his effigies witness
Most truly limned and living in your face,
Be truly welcome hither. I am the duke
That loved your father. The residue of your fortune,
Go to my cave and tell me. Good old man,
Thou art right welcome as thy master is.
Support him by the arm. Give me your hand,
And let me all your fortunes understand.   200

                                                    [*Exeunt.*

ACT III

Scene I. *A room in the palace.*

Enter Duke Frederick, Lords, *and* Oliver.

Duke F. Not see him since? Sir, sir, that cannot be.
But were I not the better part made mercy,
I should not seek an absent argument
Of my revenge, thou present. But look to it.
Find out thy brother, wheresoe'er he is;
Seek him with candle; bring him dead or living
Within this twelvemonth, or turn thou no more
To seek a living in our territory.
Thy lands and all things that thou dost call thine
Worth seizure do we seize into our hands,   10
Till thou canst quit thee by thy brother's mouth
Of what we think against thee.

Oli. O that your highness knew my heart in this!
I never loved my brother in my life.

Duke F. More villain thou. Well, push him out of doors;
And let my officers of such a nature
Make an extent upon his house and lands.
Do this expediently and turn him going.   [*Exeunt.*

193. **effigies:** likeness. 194. **limned:** drawn.
7. **turn:** return. 11. **quit:** acquit. 16. **let my officers, etc.:** take the proper legal means to seize his property.

Scene II. *The forest.*

Enter Orlando, *with a paper.*

Orl. Hang there, my verse, in witness of my love;
  And thou, thrice-crownéd queen of night, survey
With thy chaste eye, from thy pale sphere above,
  Thy huntress' name that my full life doth sway.
O Rosalind! these trees shall be my books
  And in their barks my thoughts I'll character;
That every eye which in this forest looks
  Shall see thy virtue witnessed everywhere.
Run, run, Orlando; carve on every tree   9
The fair, the chaste and unexpressive she.   [*Exit.*

Enter Corin *and* Touchstone.

Cor. And how like you this shepherd's life, Master Touch-stone?

Touch. Truly, shepherd, in respect of itself, it is a good life; but in respect that it is a shepherd's life, it is naught. In respect that it is solitary, I like it very well; but in respect that it is private, it is a very vile life. Now, in respect it is in the fields, it pleaseth me well; but in respect it is not in the court, it is tedious. As it is a spare life, look you, it fits my humor well; but as there is no more plenty in it, it goes much against my stomach. Hast any philosophy in thee, shep-herd?

Cor. No more but that I know the more one sickens the worse at ease he is; and that he that wants money, means and content is without three good friends; that the property of rain is to wet and fire to burn; that good pasture makes fat sheep, and that a great cause of the night is lack of the sun; that he that hath learned no wit by nature nor art may com-plain of good breeding or comes of a very dull kindred.

Touch. Such a one is a natural philosopher. Wast ever in court, shepherd?

Cor. No, truly.

Touch. Then thou art damned.

Cor. Nay, I hope.

Touch. Truly, thou art damned, like an ill-roasted egg all on one side.   39

2. **queen:** Diana.   6. **character:** write.   10. **unexpressive:** inexpressible.

Cor. For not being at court? Your reason.

Touch. Why, if thou never wast at court, thou never sawest good manners; if thou never sawest good manners, then thy manners must be wicked; and wickedness is sin, and sin is damnation. Thou art in a parlous state, shepherd.

Cor. Not a whit, Touchstone. Those that are good manners at the court are as ridiculous in the country as the behavior of the country is most mockable at the court. You told me you salute not at the court, but you kiss your hands. That courtesy would be uncleanly, if courtiers were shepherds.

Touch. Instance, briefly; come, instance.

Cor. Why, we are still handling our ewes, and their fells, you know, are greasy.

Touch. Why, do not your courtier's hands sweat? And is not the grease of a mutton as wholesome as the sweat of a man? Shallow, shallow. A better instance, I say; come.

Cor. Besides, our hands are hard.   60

Touch. Your lips will feel them the sooner. Shallow again. A more sounder instance, come.

Cor. And they are often tarred over with the surgery of our sheep; and would you have us kiss tar? The courtier's hands are perfumed with civet.

Touch. Most shallow man! thou wormsmeat, in respect of a good piece of flesh indeed! Learn of the wise, and perpend. Civet is of a baser birth than tar, the very uncleanly flux of a cat. Mend the instance, shepherd.   71

Cor. You have too courtly a wit for me. I'll rest.

Touch. Wilt thou rest damned? God help thee, shallow man! God make incision in thee! Thou art raw.

Cor. Sir, I am a true laborer. I earn that I eat, get that I wear, owe no man hate, envy no man's happiness, glad of other men's good, content with my harm, and the greatest of my pride is to see my ewes graze and my lambs suck.

Touch. That is another simple sin in you, to bring the ewes and the rams together. If thou beest not damned for this, the devil himself will have no shepherds; I cannot see else how thou shouldst 'scape.   90

Cor. Here comes young Master Ganymede, my new mistress's brother.

---

52. **fells:** fleeces.   74. **God make, etc.:** may God cure you.   77. **harm:** misfortune.

Enter ROSALIND, *with a paper, reading.*

Ros.   From the east to western Ind,
    No jewel is like Rosalind.
    Her worth, being mounted on the wind,
    Through all the world bears Rosalind.
    All the pictures fairest lined
    Are but black to Rosalind.
    Let no fair be kept in mind
    But the fair of Rosalind.   100

Touch.   I'll rhyme you so eight years together, dinners and
suppers and sleeping-hours excepted: it is the right butter-
women's rank to market.

Ros.   Out, fool!

Touch.   For a taste:

    If a hart do lack a hind,
    Let him seek out Rosalind.
    If the cat will after kind,
    So be sure will Rosalind.   110
    Winter garments must be lined,
    So must slender Rosalind.
    They that reap must sheaf and bind;
    Then to cart with Rosalind.
    Sweetest nut hath sourest rind,
    Such a nut is Rosalind.
    He that sweetest rose will find
    Must find love's prick and Rosalind.

This is the very false gallop of verses. Why do you infect
yourself with them?   120

Ros.   Peace, you dull fool! I found them on a tree.

Touch.   Truly, the tree yields bad fruit.

Ros.   I'll graff it with you, and then I shall graff it with
a medlar. Then it will be the earliest fruit i' the country;
for you'll be rotten ere you be half ripe, and that's the right
virtue of the medlar.

Touch.   You have said; but whether wisely or no, let the
forest judge.   130

103. **butter-women's rank:** i.e., riding monotonously in a row.   124
medlar: fruit resembling a small pear.

Enter Celia, *with a writing.*

Ros. Peace!
Here comes my sister, reading; stand aside.
  Cel. [*Reads*]

    Why should this a desert be?
      For it is unpeopled? No;
    Tongues I'll hang on every tree,
      That shall civil sayings show:
    Some, how brief the life of man
      Runs his erring pilgrimage,
    That the stretching of a span
      Buckles in his sum of age;   140
    Some of violated vows
      'Twixt the souls of friend and friend;
    But upon the fairest boughs,
      Or at every sentence end,
    Will I Rosalinda write,
      Teaching all that read to know
    The quintessence of every sprite
      Heaven would in little show.
    Therefore Heaven Nature charged
      That one body should be filled   150
    With all graces wide-enlarged.
      Nature presently distilled
    Helen's cheek, but not her heart,
      Cleopatra's majesty,
    Atalanta's better part,
      Sad Lucretia's modesty.
    Thus Rosalind of many parts
      By heavenly synod was devised,
    Of many faces, eyes and hearts,
      To have the touches dearest prized.   160
  Heaven would that she these gifts should have,
  And I to live and die her slave.

  Ros. O most gentle pulpiter! what tedious homily of love
have you wearied your parishioners withal and never cried,
" Have patience, good people " !
  Cel. How now! Back, friends! Shepherd, go off a little.
Go with him, sirrah.

          136. **civil:** civilized.   163. **pulpiter:** preacher.

Touch.   Come, shepherd, let us make an honorable retreat; though not with bag and baggage, yet with scrip and scrippage.   [*Exeunt Corin and Touchstone.*

Cel.   Didst thou hear these verses?

Ros.   O, yes, I heard them all, and more too; for some of them had in them more feet than the verses would bear.

Cel.   That's no matter.   The feet might bear the verses.

Ros.   Ay, but the feet were lame and could not bear themselves without the verse and therefore stood lamely in the verse.   180

Cel.   But didst thou hear without wondering how thy name should be hanged and carved upon these trees?

Ros.   I was seven of the nine days out of the wonder before you came; for look here what I found on a palm-tree.   I was never so berhymed since Pythagoras' time, that I was an Irish rat, which I can hardly remember.

Cel.   Trow you who hath done this?

Ros.   Is it a man?   190

Cel.   And a chain, that you once wore, about his neck. Change you color?

Ros.   I prithee, who?

Cel.   O Lord, Lord! it is a hard matter for friends to meet; but mountains may be removed with earthquakes and so encounter.

Ros.   Nay, but who is it?

Cel.   Is it possible?

Ros.   Nay, I prithee now with most petitionary vehemence, tell me who it is.   200

Cel.   O wonderful, wonderful, and most wonderful wonderful! and yet again wonderful, and after that, out of all whooping!

Ros.   Good my complexion! dost thou think, though I am caparisoned like a man, I have a doublet and hose in my disposition?   One inch of delay more is a South Sea of discovery; I prithee, tell me who is it quickly, and speak apace. I would thou couldst stammer, that thou mightst pour this concealed man out of thy mouth, as wine comes out of a narrow-mouthed bottle, either too much at once, or none at all.   I prithee, take the cork out of thy mouth that I may

172. **scrip:** shepherd's pouch.   187. **Pythagoras:** he taught that souls could be embodied in animals.   189. **Trow:** know.

drink thy tidings. Is he of God's making? What manner of
man? Is his head worth a hat, or his chin worth a beard?

Cel. Nay, he hath but a little beard.   219

Ros. Why, God will send more, if the man will be thank-
ful. Let me stay the growth of his beard, if thou delay me
not the knowledge of his chin.

Cel. It is young Orlando, that tripped up the wrestler's
heels and your heart both in an instant.

Ros. Nay, but the devil take mocking: speak sad brow
and true maid.

Cel. I' faith, coz, 'tis he.

Ros. Orlando?

Cel. Orlando.   230

Ros. Alas the day! what shall I do with my doublet and
hose? What did he when thou sawest him? What said he?
How looked he? Wherein went he? What makes he here?
Did he ask for me? Where remains he? How parted he with
thee? And when shalt thou see him again? Answer me in
one word.

Cel. You must borrow me Gargantua's mouth first. 'Tis
a word too great for any mouth of this age's size. To say ay
and no to these particulars is more than to answer in a catechism.   241

Ros. But doth he know that I am in this forest and in
man's apparel? Looks he as freshly as he did the day he
wrestled?

Cel. It is as easy to count atomies as to resolve the prop-
ositions of a lover. But take a taste of my finding him, and
relish it with good observance. I found him under a tree,
like a dropped acorn.

Ros. It may well be called Jove's tree, when it drops forth
such fruit.   250

Cel. Give me audience, good madam.

Ros. Proceed.

Cel. There lay he, stretched along, like a wounded knight.

Ros. Though it be pity to see such a sight, it well becomes the ground.

Cel. Cry "holla" to thy tongue, I prithee; it curvets
unseasonably. He was furnished like a hunter.   259

---

221. **stay:** wait for.   238. **Gargantua:** a fabled giant who gobbled up five
persons at a mouthful.   249. **Jove's tree:** the oak.   258. **curvets:** frisks.

Ros. O, ominous! he comes to kill my heart.

Cel. I would sing my song without a burden. Thou bringest me out of tune.

Ros. Do you not know I am a woman? When I think, I must speak. Sweet, say on.

Cel. You bring me out. Soft! comes he not here?

 Enter ORLANDO *and* JAQUES.

Ros. 'Tis he. Slink by, and note him.

Jaq. I thank you for your company; but, good faith, I had as lief have been myself alone.   270

Orl. And so had I; but yet, for fashion sake, I thank you too for your society.

Jaq. God be wi' you; let's meet as little as we can.

Orl. I do desire we may be better strangers.

Jaq. I pray you, mar no more trees with writing love-songs in their barks.

Orl. I pray you, mar no moe of my verses with reading them ill-favoredly.

Jaq. Rosalind is your love's name?   280

Orl. Yes, just.

Jaq. I do not like her name.

Orl. There was no thought of pleasing you when she was christened.

Jaq. What stature is she of?

Orl. Just as high as my heart.

Jaq. You are full of pretty answers. Have you not been acquainted with goldsmiths' wives, and conned them out of rings?   289

Orl. Not so; but I answer you right painted cloth, from whence you have studied your questions.

Jac. You have a nimble wit. I think 'twas made of Atalanta's heels. Will you sit down with me? and we two will rail against our mistress the world and all our misery.

Orl. I will chide no breather in the world but myself, against whom I know most faults.

Jaq. The worst fault you have is to be in love.   300

Orl. 'Tis a fault I will not change for your best virtue. I am weary of you.

---

261. **burden:** accompaniment. 288. **conned, etc.:** learned them from mottoes in rings. 290. **painted cloths:** tapestries, which often contained figures and sayings.

Jaq. By my troth, I was seeking for a fool when I found you.

Orl. He is drowned in the brook. Look but in, and you shall see him.

Jaq. There I shall see mine own figure.

Orl. Which I take to be either a fool or a cipher.

Jaq. I'll tarry no longer with you. Farewell, good Signior Love.   310

Orl. I am glad of your departure. Adieu, good Monsieur Melancholy.   [*Exit Jaques.*

Ros. [*Aside to Celia*] I will speak to him like a saucy lackey and under that habit play the knave with him. Do you hear, forester?

Orl. Very well. What would you?

Ros. I pray you, what is 't o'clock?

Orl. You should ask me what time o' day. There's no clock in the forest.   319

Ros. Then there is no true lover in the forest; else sighing every minute and groaning every hour would detect the lazy foot of Time as well as a clock.

Orl. And why not the swift foot of Time? Had not that been as proper?

Ros. By no means, sir. Time travels in divers paces with divers persons. I'll tell you who Time ambles withal, who Time trots withal, who Time gallops withal and who he stands still withal.

Orl. I prithee, who doth he trot withal?   330

Ros. Marry, he trots hard with a young maid between the contract of her marriage and the day it is solemnized. If the interim be but a se'nnight, Time's pace is so hard that it seems the length of seven year.

Orl. Who ambles Time withal?

Ros. With a priest that lacks Latin and a rich man that hath not the gout, for the one sleeps easily because he cannot study and the other lives merrily because he feels no pain, the one lacking the burden of lean and wasteful learning, the other knowing no burden of heavy tedious penury; these Time ambles withal.

Orl. Who doth he gallop withal?

Ros. With a thief to the gallows, for though he go as softly as foot can fall, he thinks himself too soon there.

Orl. Who stays it still withal?

Ros. With lawyers in the vacation; for they sleep between term and term and then they perceive not how Time moves. 351

Orl. Where dwell you, pretty youth?

Ros. With this shepherdess, my sister; here in the skirts of the forest, like fringe upon a petticoat.

Orl. Are you native of this place?

Ros. As the cony that you see dwell where she is kindled.

Orl. Your accent is something finer than you could pur-chase in so removed a dwelling.

Ros. I have been told so of many; but indeed an old religious uncle of mine taught me to speak, who was in his youth an inland man; one that knew courtship too well, for there he fell in love. I have heard him read many lectures against it, and I thank God I am not a woman, to be touched with so many giddy offences as he hath generally taxed their whole sex withal.

Orl. Can you remember any of the principal evils that he laid to the charge of women? 370

Ros. There were none principal; they were all like one another as half-pence are, every one fault seeming monstrous till his fellow fault came to match it.

Orl. I prithee, recount some of them.

Ros. No, I will not cast away my physic but on those that are sick. There is a man haunts the forest, that abuses our young plants with carving " Rosalind " on their barks; hangs odes upon hawthorns and elegies on brambles, all, for-sooth, deifying the name of Rosalind. If I could meet that fancy-monger, I would give him some good counsel, for he seems to have the quotidian of love upon him.

Orl. I am he that is so love-shaked. I pray you, tell me your remedy.

Ros. There is none of my uncle's marks upon you. He taught me how to know a man in love; in which cage of rushes I am sure you are not prisoner. 390

Orl. What were his marks?

Ros. A lean cheek, which you have not, a blue eye and sunken, which you have not, an unquestionable spirit, which you have not, a beard neglected, which you have not; but I pardon you for that, for simply your having in beard is a

356. **cony:** rabbit. 382. **fancy-monger:** love-peddler. 383. **quotidian:** daily fever. 392. **blue eye:** with dark circles. 393. **unquestionable:** silent. 395. **having, etc.:** i.e., your beard is meager, like a younger son's income.

younger brother's revenue. Then your hose should be ungartered, your bonnet unbanded, your sleeve unbuttoned,
your shoe untied and every thing about you demonstrating a
careless desolation. But you are no such man; you are rather
point-device in your accouterments as loving yourself than
seeming the lover of any other.   403

Orl. Fair youth, I would I could make thee believe I
love.

Ros. Me believe it! You may as soon make her that you
love believe it; which, I warrant, she is apter to do than to
confess she does. That is one of the points in the which
women still give the lie to their consciences. But, in good
sooth, are you he that hangs the verses on the trees, wherein
Rosalind is so admired?

Orl. I swear to thee, youth, by the white hand of Rosalind, I am that he, that unfortunate he.

Ros. But are you so much in love as your rhymes speak?

Orl. Neither rhyme nor reason can express how much. 419

Ros. Love is merely a madness, and, I tell you, deserves
as well a dark house and a whip as madmen do; and the
reason why they are not so punished and cured is, that the
lunacy is so ordinary that the whippers are in love too. Yet
I profess curing it by counsel.

Orl. Did you ever cure any so?

Ros. Yes, one, and in this manner. He was to imagine
me his love, his mistress, and I set him every day to woo me;
at which time would I, being but a moonish youth, grieve, be
effeminate, changeable, longing and liking, proud, fantastical,
apish, shallow, inconstant, full of tears, full of smiles, for
every passion something and for no passion truly any thing,
as boys and women are for the most part cattle of this color;
would now like him, now loathe him; then entertain him, then
forswear him; now weep for him, then spit at him; that I
drave my suitor from his mad humor of love to a living humor
of madness; which was, to forswear the full stream of the
world and to live in a nook merely monastic. And thus I
cured him; and this way will I take upon me to wash your
liver as clean as a sound sheep's heart, that there shall not be
one spot of love in 't.   445

Orl. I would not be cured, youth.

402. **point-device:** everything as it should be.   444. **liver:** supposed to be
the seat of the affections.

Ros. I would cure you, if you would but call me Rosalind and come every day to my cote and woo me.

Orl. Now, by the faith of my love, I will. Tell me where it is.   450

Ros. Go with me to it and I'll show it you; and by the way you shall tell me where in the forest you live. Will you go?

Orl. With all my heart, good youth.

Ros. Nay, you must call me Rosalind. Come, sister, will you go?   [*Exeunt.*

Scene III. *The forest.*

Enter Touchstone *and* Audrey; Jaques *behind.*

Touch. Come apace, good Audrey. I will fetch up your goats, Audrey. And how, Audrey? am I the man yet? Doth my simple feature content you?

Aud. Your features! Lord warrant us! what features?

Touch. I am here with thee and thy goats as the most capricious poet, honest Ovid, was among the Goths.

Jaq. [*Aside*] O knowledge ill-inhabited, worse than Jove in a thatched house!   11

Touch. When a man's verses cannot be understood, nor a man's good wit seconded with the forward child Understanding, it strikes a man more dead than a great reckoning in a little room. Truly, I would the gods had made thee poetical.

Aud. I do not know what "poetical" is. Is it honest in deed and word? Is it a true thing?

Touch. No, truly; for the truest poetry is the most feigning; and lovers are given to poetry, and what they swear in poetry may be said as lovers they do feign.

Aud. Do you wish then that the gods had made me poetical?

Touch. I do, truly; for thou swearest to me thou art honest. Now, if thou wert a poet, I might have some hope thou didst feign.

Aud. Would you not have me honest?

Touch. No, truly, unless thou wert hard-favored; for honesty coupled to beauty is to have honey a sauce to sugar.   31

3. **feature:** figure.   6. **capricious:** a word derived from Latin **capra,** goat. Touchstone pronounced **Goths** like **goats.**   10. **ill-inhabited:** poorly housed.

Jaq. [*Aside*] A material fool!

Aud. Well, I am not fair; and therefore I pray the gods make me honest.

Touch. Truly, and to cast away honesty upon a foul slut were to put good meat into an unclean dish.

Aud. I am not a slut, though I thank the gods I am foul.

Touch. Well, praised be the gods for thy foulness! Sluttishness may come hereafter. But be it as it may be, I will marry thee, and to that end I have been with Sir Oliver Martext, the vicar of the next village, who hath promised to meet me in this place of the forest and to couple us.

Jaq. [*Aside*] I would fain see this meeting.

Aud. Well, the gods give us joy!   47

Touch. Amen. A man may, if he were of a fearful heart, stagger in this attempt; for here we have no temple but the wood, no assembly but horn-beasts. But what though? Courage! As horns are odious, they are necessary. It is said, "Many a man knows no end of his goods." Right; many a man has good horns, and knows no end of them. Well, that is the dowry of his wife; 'tis none of his own getting. Horns? Even so. Poor men alone? No, no; the noblest deer hath them as huge as the rascal. Is the single man therefore blessed? No: as a walled town is more worthier than a village, so is the forehead of a married man more honorable than the bare brow of a bachelor; and by how much defence is better than no skill, by so much is a horn more precious than to want. Here comes Sir Oliver.

Enter Sir Oliver Martext.

Sir Oliver Martext, you are well met. Will you dispatch us here under this tree, or shall we go with you to your chapel?

Sir Oli. Is there none here to give the woman?

Touch. I will not take her on gift of any man.

Sir Oli. Truly, she must be given, or the marriage is not lawful.   71

Jaq. [*Advancing*] Proceed, proceed. I'll give her.

Touch. Good even, good Master What-ye-call-'t; how do you, sir? You are very well met. God 'ild you for your last company. I am very glad to see you. Even a toy in hand here, sir. Nay, pray be covered.

32. **material:** full of matter or ideas. 35. **foul:** ugly. 43. **Sir Oliver:** the title **sir** was often given to the clergy. 74. **'ild:** yield or reward. 76. **covered:** put your hat on.

Jaq. Will you be married, motley?   79

Touch. As the ox hath his bow, sir, the horse his curb and the falcon her bells, so man hath his desires; and as pigeons bill, so wedlock would be nibbling.

Jaq. And will you, being a man of your breeding, be married under a bush like a beggar? Get you to church, and have a good priest that can tell you what marriage is. This fellow will but join you together as they join wainscot; then one of you will prove a shrunk panel and, like green timber, warp, warp.   90

Touch. [*Aside*] I am not in the mind but I were better to be married of him than of another; for he is not like to marry me well; and not being well married, it will be a good excuse for me hereafter to leave my wife.

Jaq. Go thou with me, and let me counsel thee.

Touch. Come, sweet Audrey;
We must be married, or we must live in bawdry.
Farewell, good Master Oliver: not —   100

O sweet Oliver,
O brave Oliver,
Leave me not behind thee;

but —

Wind away,
Begone, I say,
I will not to wedding with thee.

[*Exeunt Jaques, Touchstone and Audrey.*

Sir Oli. 'Tis no matter: ne'er a fantastical knave of them all shall flout me out of my calling.   [*Exit.*

SCENE IV. *The forest.*

Enter ROSALIND *and* CELIA.

Ros. Never talk to me; I will weep.

Cel. Do, I prithee; but yet have the grace to consider that tears do not become a man.

Ros. But have I not cause to weep?

Cel. As good cause as one would desire; therefore weep.

Ros. His very hair is of the dissembling color.

80. **bow:** yoke. 6. **dissembling color:** red-haired persons were supposed to be deceitful. Judas is always pictured as red-haired.

Cel. Something browner than Judas's. Marry, his kisses are Judas's own children.   10

Ros. I' faith, his hair is of a good color.

Cel. An excellent color. Your chestnut was ever the only color.

Ros. And his kissing is as full of sanctity as the touch of holy bread.

Cel. He hath bought a pair of cast lips of Diana. A nun of winter's sisterhood kisses not more religiously; the very ice of chastity is in them.

Ros. But why did he swear he would come this morning, and comes not?   21

Cel. Nay, certainly, there is no truth in him.

Ros. Do you think so?

Cel. Yes; I think he is not a pick-purse nor a horse-stealer, but for his verity in love I do think him as concave as a covered goblet or a worm-eaten nut.

Ros. Not true in love?

Cel. Yes, when he is in; but I think he is not in.   30

Ros. You have heard him swear downright he was.

Cel. "Was" is not "is." Besides, the oath of a lover is no stronger than the word of a tapster; they are both the confirmer of false reckonings. He attends here in the forest on the duke your father.

Ros. I met the duke yesterday and had much question with him. He asked me of what parentage I was; I told him, of as good as he; so he laughed and let me go. But what talk we of fathers, when there is such a man as Orlando? 42

Cel. O, that's a brave man! He writes brave verses, speaks brave words, swears brave oaths and breaks them bravely, quite traverse, athwart the heart of his lover; as a puisny tilter, that spurs his horse but on one side, breaks his staff like a noble goose. But all's brave that youth mounts and folly guides. Who comes here?

Enter CORIN.

Cor. Mistress and master, you have oft inquired   50
After the shepherd that complained of love,
Who you saw sitting by me on the turf,
Praising the proud disdainful shepherdess
That was his mistress.

16. **cast:** cast off.   46. **puisny:** puny.

Cel.   Well, and what of him?
Cor. If you will see a pageant truly played,
Between the pale complexion of true love
And the red glow of scorn and proud disdain,
Go hence a little and I shall conduct you,
If you will mark it.
Ros.   O, come, let us remove;
The sight of lovers feedeth those in love.   60
Bring us to this sight, and you shall say
I'll prove a busy actor in their play.   *[Exeunt.*

SCENE V. *Another part of the forest.*

Enter SILVIUS *and* PHEBE.

Sil. Sweet Phebe, do not scorn me; do not, Phebe;
Say that you love me not, but say not so
In bitterness. The common executioner,
Whose heart the accustomed sight of death makes hard,
Falls not the ax upon the humbled neck
But first begs pardon. Will you sterner be
Than he that dies and lives by bloody drops?

Enter ROSALIND, CELIA, *and* CORIN, *behind.*

Phe. I would not be thy executioner.
I fly thee, for I would not injure thee.
Thou tell'st me there is murder in mine eye: 10
'Tis pretty, sure, and very probable,
That eyes, that are the frail'st and softest things,
Who shut their coward gates on atomies,
Should be called tyrants, butchers, murderers!
Now I do frown on thee with all my heart;
And if mine eyes can wound, now let them kill thee.
Now counterfeit to swoon; why, now fall down;
Or if thou canst not, O, for shame, for shame,
Lie not, to say mine eyes are murderers!
Now show the wound mine eye hath made in thee.   20
Scratch thee but with a pin, and there remains
Some scar of it; lean but upon a rush,
The cicatrice and capable impressure

5. **falls not:** does not let fall. 23. **cicatrice:** mark. 23. **capable impressure:** impression that can be noticed.

Thy palm some moment keeps; but now mine eyes,
Which I have darted at thee, hurt thee not,
Nor, I am sure, there is no force in eyes
That can do hurt.
   Sil.   O dear Phebe,
If ever — as that ever may be near —
You meet in some fresh cheek the power of fancy,
Then shall you know the wounds invisible   30
That love's keen arrows make.
   Phe.   But till that time
Come not thou near me; and when that time comes,
Afflict me with thy mocks, pity me not;
As till that time I shall not pity thee.
   Ros. And why, I pray you? Who might be your mother,
That you insult, exult, and all at once,
Over the wretched? What though you have no beauty —
As, by my faith, I see no more in you
Than without candle may go dark to bed —
Must you be therefore proud and pitiless?   40
Why, what means this? Why do you look on me?
I see no more in you than in the ordinary
Of nature's sale-work. 'Od's my little life,
I think she means to tangle my eyes too!
No, faith, proud mistress, hope not after it.
'Tis not your inky brows, your black silk hair,
Your bugle eyeballs, nor your cheek of cream,
That can entame my spirits to your worship.
You foolish shepherd, wherefore do you follow her,
Like foggy south puffing with wind and rain?
You are a thousand times a properer man   51
Than she a woman. 'Tis such fools as you
That makes the world full of ill-favored children.
'Tis not her glass, but you, that flatter her;
And out of you she sees herself more proper
Than any of her lineaments can show her.
But, mistress, know yourself. Down on your knees,
And thank Heaven, fasting, for a good man's love;
For I must tell you friendly in your ear,   59
Sell when you can; you are not for all markets.
Cry the man mercy; love him; take his offer.

43. **sale-work:** ready-made. 51. **properer:** better looking. 61. **Cry the man mercy:** beg his pardon.

Foul is most foul, being foul to be a scoffer.
So take her to thee, shepherd. Fare you well.
    Phe. Sweet youth, I pray you, chide a year together.
I had rather hear you chide than this man woo.
    Ros. He's fallen in love with your foulness and she'll fall
in love with my anger. If it be so, as fast as she answers
thee with frowning looks, I'll sauce her with bitter words.
Why look you so upon me?   70
    Phe. For no ill will I bear you.
    Ros. I pray you, do not fall in love with me,
For I am falser than vows made in wine.
Besides, I like you not. If you will know my house,
'Tis at the tuft of olives here hard by.
Will you go, sister? Shepherd, ply her hard.
Come, sister. Shepherdess, look on him better,
And be not proud. Though all the world could see,
None could be so abused in sight as he.   79
Come, to our flock.   [*Exeunt Rosalind, Celia and Corin.*
    Phe. Dead shepherd, now I find thy saw of might,
"Who ever loved that loved not at first sight?"
    Sil. Sweet Phebe —
    Phe.   Ha, what say'st thou, Silvius?
    Sil. Sweet Phebe, pity me.
    Phe. Why, I am sorry for thee, gentle Silvius.
    Sil. Wherever sorrow is, relief would be.
If you do sorrow at my grief in love,
By giving love your sorrow and my grief
Were both extermined.
    Phe. Thou hast my love. Is not that neighborly?   90
    Sil. I would have you.
    Phe.   Why, that were covetousness.
Silvius, the time was that I hated thee,
And yet it is not that I bear thee love;
But since that thou canst talk of love so well,
Thy company, which erst was irksome to me,
I will endure, and I'll employ thee too.
But do not look for further recompense
Than thine own gladness that thou art employed.
    Sil. So holy and perfect is my love,
And I in such a poverty of grace,   100

62. **foul:** ugly. 81. **Dead shepherd:** Marlowe, from whose "Hero and Leander" the next line is quoted. 89. **extermined:** exterminated. 100. **grace:** favor.

That I shall think it a most plenteous crop
To glean the broken ears after the man
That the main harvest reaps. Loose now and then
A scattered smile, and that I'll live upon.
   Phe. Know'st thou the youth that spoke to me erewhile?
   Sil. Not very well, but I have met him oft;
And he hath bought the cottage and the bounds
That the old carlot once was master of.
   Phe. Think not I love him, though I ask for him;
'Tis but a peevish boy; yet he talks well;   110
But what care I for words? Yet words do well
When he that speaks them pleases those that hear.
It is a pretty youth; not very pretty;
But, sure, he's proud, and yet his pride becomes him.
He'll make a proper man. The best thing in him
Is his complexion; and faster than his tongue
Did make offence his eye did heal it up.
He is not very tall; yet for his years he's tall.
His leg is but so so; and yet 'tis well.
There was a pretty redness in his lip,   120
A little riper and more lusty red
Than that mixed in his cheek; 'twas just the difference
Betwixt the constant red and mingled damask.
There be some women, Silvius, had they marked him
In parcels as I did, would have gone near
To fall in love with him; but, for my part,
I love him not nor hate him not; and yet
I have more cause to hate him than to love him,
For what had he to do to chide at me?
He said mine eyes were black and my hair black;   130
And, now I am remembered, scorned at me.
I marvel why I answered not again.
But that's all one; omittance is no quittance.
I'll write to him a very taunting letter,
And thou shalt bear it; wilt thou, Silvius?
   Sil. Phebe, with all my heart.
   Phe.   I'll write it straight;
The matter's in my head and in my heart.
I will be bitter with him and passing short.
Go with me, Silvius.   *[Exeunt.*

108. **carlot:** peasant.   123. **damask:** a pink rose.

ACT IV

Scene I. *The forest.*

Enter Rosalind, Celia, *and* Jaques.

Jaq. I prithee, pretty youth, let me be better acquainted with thee.

Ros. They say you are a melancholy fellow.

Jaq. I am so; I do love it better than laughing.

Ros. Those that are in extremity of either are abominable fellows and betray themselves to every modern censure worse than drunkards.

Jaq. Why, 'tis good to be sad and say nothing.

Ros. Why then, 'tis good to be a post.   9

Jaq. I have neither the scholar's melancholy, which is emulation, nor the musician's, which is fantastical, nor the courtier's, which is proud, nor the soldier's, which is ambitious, nor the lawyer's, which is politic, nor the lady's, which is nice, nor the lover's, which is all these; but it is a melancholy of mine own, compounded of many simples, extracted from many objects, and indeed the sundry contemplation of my travels, in which my often rumination wraps me in a most humorous sadness.   20

Ros. A traveler! By my faith, you have great reason to be sad. I fear you have sold your own lands to see other men's; then, to have seen much and to have nothing, is to have rich eyes and poor hands.

Jaq. Yes, I have gained my experience.

Ros. And your experience makes you sad. I had rather have a fool to make me merry than experience to make me sad; and to travel for it too!

Enter Orlando.

Orl. Good day and happiness, dear Rosalind!   30

Jaq. Nay, then, God be wi' you, an you talk in blank verse.   [*Exit.*

Ros. Farewell, Monsieur Traveler: look you lisp and wear strange suits, disable all the benefits of your own country, be out of love with your nativity and almost chide God

5. **in extremity:** extremely given to.   6. **censure:** opinion.   17. **simples:** herbs.

for making you that countenance you are, or I will scarce
think you have swam in a gondola. Why, how now, Orlando!
Where have you been all this while? You a lover! An you
serve me such another trick, never come in my sight more. 41

Orl. My fair Rosalind, I come within an hour of my
promise.

Ros. Break an hour's promise in love! He that will
divide a minute into a thousand parts and break but a part
of the thousandth part of a minute in the affairs of love, it
may be said of him that Cupid hath clapped him o' the
shoulder, but I'll warrant him heart-whole.

Orl. Pardon me, dear Rosalind.   50

Ros. Nay, an you be so tardy, come no more in my sight.
I had as lief be wooed of a snail.

Orl. Of a snail?

Ros. Ay, of a snail; for though he comes slowly, he carries
his house on his head; a better jointure, I think, than you
make a woman. Besides, he brings his destiny with him.
And I am your Rosalind.

Cel. It pleases him to call you so; but he hath a Rosalind
of a better leer than you.

Ros. Come, woo me, woo me, for now I am in a holiday
humor and like enough to consent. What would you say to
me now, an I were your very very Rosalind?   71

Orl. I would kiss before I spoke.

Ros. Nay, you were better speak first, and when you were
graveled for lack of matter, you might take occasion to kiss.
Very good orators, when they are out, they will spit; and for
lovers lacking — God warn us! — matter, the cleanliest shift
is to kiss.

Orl. How if the kiss be denied?

Ros. Then she puts you to entreaty, and there begins new
matter.   81

Orl. Who could be out, being before his beloved mistress?

Ros. Marry, that should you, if I were your mistress, or
I should think my honesty ranker than my wit.

Orl. What, of my suit?

Ros. Not out of your apparel, and yet out of your suit.
Am not I your Rosalind?

Orl. I take some joy to say you are, because I would be
talking of her.   91

68. **leer:** appearance. 74. **graveled:** stuck. 75. **out:** at a loss.

Ros. Well, in her person I say I will not have you.

Orl. Then in mine own person I die.

Ros. No, faith, die by attorney. The poor world is almost six thousand years old, and in all this time there was not any man died in his own person, videlicet, in a love-cause. Troilus had his brains dashed out with a Grecian club; yet he did what he could to die before, and he is one of the patterns of love. Leander, he would have lived many a fair year, though Hero had turned nun, if it had not been for a hot midsummer night; for, good youth, he went but forth to wash him in the Hellespont and being taken with the cramp was drowned; and the foolish chroniclers of that age found it was " Hero of Sestos." But these are all lies. Men have died from time to time and worms have eaten them, but not for love.

Orl. I would not have my right Rosalind of this mind, for, I protest, her frown might kill me.   110

Ros. By this hand, it will not kill a fly. But come, now I will be your Rosalind in a more coming-on disposition, and ask me what you will, I will grant it.

Orl. Then love me, Rosalind.

Ros. Yes, faith, will I, Fridays and Saturdays and all.

Orl. And wilt thou have me?

Ros. Ay, and twenty such.

Orl. What sayest thou?   120

Ros. Are you not good?

Orl. I hope so.

Ros. Why then, can one desire too much of a good thing? Come, sister, you shall be the priest and marry us. Give me your hand, Orlando. What do you say, sister?

Orl. Pray thee, marry us.

Cel. I cannot say the words.

Ros. You must begin, " Will you, Orlando — "

Cel. Go to. Will you, Orlando, have to wife this Rosalind?   131

Orl. I will.

Ros. Ay, but when?

Orl. Why, now; as fast as she can marry us.

Ros. Then you must say, " I take thee, Rosalind, for wife."

Orl. I take thee, Rosalind, for wife.

---

94. **attorney:** proxy. 96. **videlicet:** namely. 97. **Troilus:** see cyclopedia for proper names in this passage.

Ros. I might ask you for your commission; but I do take thee, Orlando, for my husband. There's a girl goes before the priest; and certainly a woman's thought runs before her actions.   141

Orl. So do all thoughts; they are winged.

Ros. Now tell me how long you would have her after you have possessed her.

Orl. For ever and a day.

Ros. Say "a day," without the "ever." No, no, Orlando; men are April when they woo, December when they wed; maids are May when they are maids, but the sky changes when they are wives. I will be more jealous of thee than a Barbary cock-pigeon over his hen, more clamorous than a parrot against rain, more new-fangled than an ape, more giddy in my desires than a monkey. I will weep for nothing, like Diana in the fountain, and I will do that when you are disposed to be merry; I will laugh like a hyen, and that when thou art inclined to sleep.

Orl. But will my Rosalind do so?

Ros. By my life, she will do as I do.

Orl. O, but she is wise.   160

Ros. Or else she could not have the wit to do this. The wiser, the waywarder. Make the doors upon a woman's wit and it will out at the casement; shut that and 'twill out at the keyhole; stop that, 'twill fly with the smoke out at the chimney.

Orl. A man that had a wife with such a wit, he might say, "Wit, whither wilt?"

Ros. Nay, you might keep that check for it till you met your wife's wit going to your neighbor's bed.   171

Orl. And what wit could wit have to excuse that?

Ros. Marry, to say she came to seek you there. You shall never take her without her answer, unless you take her without her tongue. O, that woman that cannot make her fault her husband's occasion, let her never nurse her child herself, for she will breed it like a fool!

Orl. For these two hours, Rosalind, I will leave thee. 181

Ros. Alas, dear love, I cannot lack thee two hours!

Orl. I must attend the duke at dinner. By two o'clock I will be with thee again.

Ros. Ay, go your ways, go your ways; I knew what you would prove. My friends told me as much, and I thought no

138. **commission:** authority.

less. That flattering tongue of yours won me. 'Tis but one
cast away, and so, come, death! Two o'clock is your hour?

Orl. Ay, sweet Rosalind.   191

Ros. By my troth, and in good earnest, and so God mend
me, and by all pretty oaths that are not dangerous, if you
break one jot of your promise or come one minute behind your
hour, I will think you the most pathetical break-promise and
the most hollow lover and the most unworthy of her you call
Rosalind that may be chosen out of the gross band of the
unfaithful; therefore beware my censure and keep your
promise.   200

Orl. With no less religion than if thou wert indeed my
Rosalind; so adieu.

Ros. Well, Time is the old justice that examines all such
offenders, and let Time try. Adieu.   [*Exit Orlando.*

Cel. You have simply misused our sex in your love-prate.
We must have your doublet and hose plucked over your head,
and show the world what the bird hath done to her own nest.

Ros. O coz, coz, coz, my pretty little coz, that thou didst
know how many fathom deep I am in love! But it cannot
be sounded. My affection hath an unknown bottom, like the
bay of Portugal.   213

Cel. Or rather, bottomless, that as fast as you pour affection in, it runs out.

Ros. No, that same wicked bastard of Venus that was
begot of thought, conceived of spleen and born of madness,
that blind rascally boy that abuses every one's eyes because
his own are out, let him be judge how deep I am in love.
I'll tell thee, Aliena, I cannot be out of the sight of Orlando.
I'll go find a shadow and sigh till he come.

Cel. And I'll sleep.   [*Exeunt.*

205. **simply misused:** entirely abused.

Scene II. *The forest.*

Enter Jaques, Lords, *and* Foresters.

Jaq. Which is he that killed the deer?
A Lord. Sir, it was I.
Jaq. Let's present him to the duke, like a Roman con-

queror; and it would do well to set the deer's horns upon his head, for a branch of victory. Have you no song, forester, for this purpose?

For. Yes, sir.

Jaq. Sing it. 'Tis no matter how it be in tune, so it make noise enough.   10

Song

For.   What shall he have that killed the deer?
    His leather skin and horns to wear.
        Then sing him home;
                [The rest shall bear this burden.
    Take thou no scorn to wear the horn;
    It was a crest ere thou wast born
        Thy father's father wore it,
        And thy father bore it.
    The horn, the horn, the lusty horn
    Is not a thing to laugh to scorn.   *[Exeunt.*

Scene III.   *The forest.*

Enter Rosalind *and* Celia.

Ros. How say you now? Is it not past two o'clock? And here much Orlando!

Cel. I warrant you, with pure love and troubled brain, he hath ta'en his bow and arrows and is gone forth to sleep. Look, who comes here.

Enter Silvius.

Sil. My errand is to you, fair youth;
My gentle Phebe bid me give you this.
I know not the contents; but, as I guess
By the stern brow and waspish action
Which she did use as she was writing of it,   10
It bears an angry tenor. Pardon me;
I am but as a guiltless messenger.

Ros. Patience herself would startle at this letter
And play the swaggerer. Bear this, bear all.
She says I am not fair, that I lack manners;
She calls me proud, and that she could not love me,

11. **tenor:** meaning.

Were man as rare as phoenix. 'Od's my will!
Her love is not the hare that I do hunt.
Why writes she so to me? Well, shepherd, well,
This is a letter of your own device.   20
 Sil. No, I protest, I know not the contents. Phebe did
write it.
 Ros. Come, come, you are a fool
And turned into the extremity of love.
I saw her hand; she has a leathern hand,
A freestone-colored hand. I verily did think
That her old gloves were on, but 'twas her hands;
She has a huswife's hand; but that's no matter.
I say she never did invent this letter;
This is a man's invention and his hand.
 Sil. Sure, it is hers.   30
 Ros. Why, 'tis a boisterous and a cruel style,
A style for challengers; why, she defies me,
Like Turk to Christian. Women's gentle brain
Could not drop forth such giant-rude invention,
Such Ethiope words, blacker in their effect
Than in their countenance. Will you hear the letter?
 Sil. So please you, for I never heard it yet;
Yet heard too much of Phebe's cruelty.
 Ros. She Phebes me. Mark how the tyrant writes.
             [*Reads.*
  " Art thou god to shepherd turned,   40
    That a maiden's heart hath burned? "
Can a woman rail thus?
 Sil. Call you this railing?
 Ros. [*Reads*]
  " Why, thy godhead laid apart,
    Warr'st thou with a woman's heart? "
Did you ever hear such railing?
  " Whiles the eye of man did woo me,
    That could do no vengeance to me."
Meaning me a beast.
  " If the scorn of your bright eyne   50
    Have power to raise such love in mine,
    Alack, in me what strange effect
    Would they work in mild aspect!
    Whiles you chid me, I did love;

25. **freestone-colored:** dirty brown.

How then might your prayers move!
He that brings this love to thee
Little knows this love in me;
And by him seal up thy mind,
Whether that thy youth and kind
Will the faithful offer take   60
Of me and all that I can make;
Or else by him my love deny,
And then I'll study how to die."
  Sil. Call you this chiding?
  Cel. Alas, poor shepherd!
  Ros. Do you pity him? No, he deserves no pity. Wilt
thou love such a woman? What, to make thee an instrument
and play false strains upon thee! Not to be endured! Well,
go your way to her, for I see love hath made thee a tame
snake, and say this to her: that if she loves me, I charge her
to love thee; if she will not, I will never have her unless thou
entreat for her. If you be a true lover, hence, and not a
word; for here comes more company.   [*Exit Silvius.*

Enter OLIVER.

  Oli. Good morrow, fair ones. Pray you, if you know,
Where in the purlieus of this forest stands
A sheepcote fenced about with olive trees?
  Cel. West of this place, down in the neighbor bottom.
The rank of osiers by the murmuring stream   80
Left on your right hand brings you to the place.
But at this hour the house doth keep itself;
There's none within.
  Oli. If that an eye may profit by a tongue,
Then should I know you by description;
Such garments and such years. " The boy is fair,
Of female favor, and bestows himself
Like a ripe sister; the woman low
And browner than her brother." Are not you
The owner of the house I did inquire for?   90
  Cel. It is no boast, being asked, to say we are.
  Oli. Orlando doth commend him to you both,
And to that youth he calls his Rosalind
He sends this bloody napkin. Are you he?

77. **purlieus:** borders. 80. **rank of osiers:** row of willows. 94. **napkin:**
handkerchief.

Ros. I am. What must we understand by this?

Oli. Some of my shame, if you will know of me
What man I am, and how, and why, and where
This handkercher was stained.

Cel.   I pray you, tell it.

Oli. When last the young Orlando parted from you
He left a promise to return again   100
Within an hour, and pacing through the forest,
Chewing the food of sweet and bitter fancy,
Lo, what befell! He threw his eye aside,
And mark what object did present itself.
Under an oak, whose boughs were mossed with age
And high top bald with dry antiquity,
A wretched ragged man, o'ergrown with hair,
Lay sleeping on his back. About his neck
A green and gilded snake had wreathed itself,
Who with her head nimble in threats approached
The opening of his mouth; but suddenly,   111
Seeing Orlando, it unlinked itself,
And with indented glides did slip away
Into a bush; under which bush's shade
A lioness, with udders all drawn dry,
Lay crouching, head on ground, with catlike watch,
When that the sleeping man should stir; for 'tis
The royal disposition of that beast
To prey on nothing that doth seem as dead.
This seen, Orlando did approach the man   120
And found it was his brother, his elder brother.

Cel. O, I have heard him speak of that same brother;
And he did render him the most unnatural
That lived amongst men.

Oli.   And well he might so do,
For well I know he was unnatural.

Ros. But, to Orlando. Did he leave him there,
Food to the sucked and hungry lioness?

Oli. Twice did he turn his back and purposed so;
But kindness, nobler ever than revenge,
And nature, stronger than his just occasion,   130
Made him give battle to the lioness,
Who quickly fell before him; in which hurtling
From miserable slumber I awaked.

113. **indented:** zigzag.   117. **When:** until.

Cel. Are you his brother?
Ros.   Was 't you he rescued?
Cel. Was 't you that did so oft contrive to kill him?
Oli. 'Twas I; but 'tis not I.   I do not shame
To tell you what I was, since my conversion
So sweetly tastes, being the thing I am.
   Ros. But, for the bloody napkin?
   Oli.   By and by.
When from the first to last betwixt us two   140
Tears our recountments had most kindly bathed,
As how I came into that desert place —
In brief, he led me to the gentle duke,
Who gave me fresh array and entertainment,
Committing me unto my brother's love;
Who led me instantly unto his cave,
There stripped himself, and here upon his arm
The lioness had torn some flesh away,
Which all this while had bled; and now he fainted
And cried, in fainting, upon Rosalind.   150
Brief, I recovered him, bound up his wound;
And, after some small space, being strong at heart,
He sent me hither, stranger as I am,
To tell this story, that you might excuse
His broken promise, and to give this napkin
Dyed in his blood unto the shepherd youth
That he in sport doth call his Rosalind.   [*Rosalind swoons.*
   Cel. Why, how now, Ganymede! sweet Ganymede!
   Oli. Many will swoon when they do look on blood.
   Cel. There is more in it.   Cousin Ganymede!
   Oli. Look, he recovers.   161
   Ros. I would I were at home.
   Cel.   We'll lead you thither.
I pray you, will you take him by the arm?
   Oli. Be of good cheer, youth.   You a man!   You lack
a man's heart.
   Ros. I do so, I confess it.   Ah, sirrah, a body would
think this was well counterfeited!   I pray you, tell your
brother how well I counterfeited.   Heigh-ho!   169
   Oli. This was not counterfeit.   There is too great testi-
mony in your complexion that it was a passion of earnest.
   Ros. Counterfeit, I assure you.

141. **recountments:** stories.   171. **passion of earnest:** real feeling.

Oli. Well then, take a good heart and counterfeit to be a man.

Ros. So I do. But, i' faith, I should have been a woman by right.

Cel. Come, you look paler and paler. Pray you, draw homewards. Good sir, go with us.

Oli. That will I, for I must bear answer back
How you excuse my brother, Rosalind.

Ros. I shall devise something; but, I pray you, commend my counterfeiting to him. Will you go?   [*Exeunt.*

ACT V

Scene I. *The forest.*

Enter TOUCHSTONE *and* AUDREY.

Touch. We shall find a time, Audrey; patience, gentle Audrey.

Aud. Faith, the priest was good enough, for all the old gentleman's saying.

Touch. A most wicked Sir Oliver, Audrey, a most vile Martext. But, Audrey, there is a youth here in the forest lays claim to you.

Aud. Ay, I know who 'tis; he hath no interest in me in the world. Here comes the man you mean.   10

Touch. It is meat and drink to me to see a clown. By my troth, we that have good wits have much to answer for; we shall be flouting; we cannot hold.

Enter WILLIAM.

Will. Good even, Audrey.

Aud. God ye good even, William.

Will. And good even to you, sir.

Touch. Good even, gentle friend. Cover thy head, cover thy head; nay, prithee, be covered. How old are you, friend?   20

Will. Five and twenty, sir.

Touch. A ripe age. Is thy name William?

Will. William, sir.

Touch. A fair name. Wast born i' the forest here?

13. **flouting:** mocking.   13. **hold:** restrain ourselves.

Will. Ay, sir, I thank God.

Touch. " Thank God " — a good answer. Art rich?

Will. Faith, sir, so so.

Touch. " So so " is good, very good, very excellent good; and yet it is not; it is but so so. Art thou wise?   31

Will. Ay, sir, I have a pretty wit.

Touch. Why, thou sayest well. I do now remember a saying, " The fool doth think he is wise, but the wise man knows himself to be a fool." The heathen philosopher, when he had a desire to eat a grape, would open his lips when he put it into his mouth; meaning thereby that grapes were made to eat and lips to open. You do love this maid?   40

Will. I do, sir.

Touch. Give me your hand. Art thou learned?

Will. No, sir.

Touch. Then learn this of me; to have, is to have; for it is a figure in rhetoric that drink, being poured out of a cup into a glass, by filling the one doth empty the other. For all your writers do consent that *ipse* is he: now, you are not *ipse*, for I am he.

Will. Which he, sir?   50

Touch. He, sir, that must marry this woman. Therefore, you clown, abandon — which is in the vulgar leave — the society — which in the boorish is company — of this female — which in the common is woman; which together is, abandon the society of this female, or, clown, thou perishest; or, to thy better understanding, diest; or, to wit, I kill thee, make thee away, translate thy life into death, thy liberty into bondage. I will deal in poison with thee, or in bastinado, or in steel; I will bandy with thee in faction; I will o'errun thee with policy; I will kill thee a hundred and fifty ways: therefore tremble, and depart.

Aud. Do, good William.

Will. God rest you merry, sir.   [*Exit*.

Enter Corin.

Cor. Our master and mistress seeks you. Come, away, away!

Touch. Trip, Audrey! trip, Audrey! I attend, I attend.
[*Exeunt*.

48. **ipse:** he. 59. **bandy, etc.:** conspire against you.

SCENE II. *The forest.*

Enter ORLANDO *and* OLIVER.

Orl. Is 't possible that on so little acquaintance you should like her? that but seeing you should love her? and loving woo? and, wooing, she should grant? And will you persever to enjoy her?

Oli. Neither call the giddiness of it in question, the poverty of her, the small acquaintance, my sudden wooing, nor her sudden consenting; but say with me, I love Aliena; say with her that she loves me; consent with both that we may enjoy each other. It shall be to your good; for my father's house and all the revenue that was old Sir Rowland's will I estate upon you, and here live and die a shepherd.

Orl. You have my consent. Let your wedding be to-morrow; thither will I invite the duke and all 's contented followers. Go you and prepare Aliena; for look you, here comes my Rosalind.

Enter ROSALIND.

Ros. God save you, brother.   20

Oli. And you, fair sister.   [*Exit.*

Ros. O, my dear Orlando, how it grieves me to see thee wear thy heart in a scarf!

Orl. It is my arm.

Ros. I thought thy heart had been wounded with the claws of a lion.

Orl. Wounded it is, but with the eyes of a lady.

Ros. Did your brother tell you how I counterfeited to swoon when he showed me your handkercher?   30

Orl. Ay, and greater wonders than that.

Ros. O, I know where you are. Nay, 'tis true. There was never any thing so sudden but the fight of two rams and Caesar's thrasonical brag of " I came, saw, and overcame." For your brother and my sister no sooner met but they looked, no sooner looked but they loved, no sooner loved but they sighed, no sooner sighed but they asked one another the reason, no sooner knew the reason but they sought the remedy; and in these degrees have they made a pair of stairs to mar-

---

34. **thrasonical:** boastful.   39. **degrees:** formerly meant **steps.**

riage which they will climb incontinent, or else be incontinent
before marriage. They are in the very wrath of love and
they will together; clubs cannot part them.

Orl. They shall be married tomorrow, and I will bid the
duke to the nuptial. But, O, how bitter a thing it is to look
into happiness through another man's eyes! By so much the
more shall I tomorrow be at the height of heart-heaviness, by
how much I shall think my brother happy in having what he
wishes for.

Ros. Why, then, tomorrow I cannot serve your turn for
Rosalind?

Orl. I can live no longer by thinking.   55

Ros. I will weary you then no longer with idle talking.
Know of me then, for now I speak to some purpose, that I
know you are a gentleman of good conceit. I speak not this
that you should bear a good opinion of my knowledge, inso-
much I say I know you are; neither do I labor for a greater
esteem than may in some little measure draw a belief from
you, to do yourself good and not to grace me. Believe then,
if you please, that I can do strange things. I have, since I
was three year old, conversed with a magician, most profound
in his art and yet not damnable. If you do love Rosalind so
near the heart as your gesture cries it out, when your brother
marries Aliena, shall you marry her. I know into what straits
of fortune she is driven; and it is not impossible to me, if it
appear not inconvenient to you, to set her before your eyes
tomorrow, human as she is, and without any danger.

Orl. Speakest thou in sober meanings?

Ros. By my life, I do; which I tender dearly, though I
say I am a magician. Therefore, put you in your best array;
bid your friends; for if you will be married tomorrow, you
shall, and to Rosalind, if you will.   81

Enter Silvius *and* Phebe.

Look, here comes a lover of mine and a lover of hers.

Phe. Youth, you have done me much ungentleness,
To show the letter that I writ to you.

Ros. I care not if I have. It is my study
To seem despiteful and ungentle to you.
You are there followed by a faithful shepherd;

40. **incontinent:** at once.   58. **conceit:** understanding.   65. **damnable:**
not damned by law because he did not practice black magic.

Look upon him, love him. He worships you.

Phe. Good shepherd, tell this youth what 'tis to love.

Sil. It is to be all made of sighs and tears;
And so am I for Phebe.   91

Phe. And I for Ganymede.

Orl. And I for Rosalind.

Ros. And I for no woman.

Sil. It is to be all made of faith and service;
And so am I for Phebe.

Phe. And I for Ganymede.

Orl. And I for Rosalind.

Ros. And I for no woman.

Sil. It is to be all made of fantasy,   100
All made of passion and all made of wishes,
All adoration, duty, and observance,
All humbleness, all patience and impatience,
All purity, all trial, all observance;
And so am I for Phebe.

Phe. And so am I for Ganymede.

Orl. And so am I for Rosalind.

Ros. And so am I for no woman.

Phe. If this be so, why blame you me to love you?   110

Sil. If this be so, why blame you me to love you?

Orl. If this be so, why blame you me to love you?

Ros. Who do you speak to, " Why blame you me to love you? "

Orl. To her that is not here, nor doth not hear.

Ros. Pray you, no more of this; 'tis like the howling of Irish wolves against the moon. [*To Sil.*] I will help you, if I can. [*To Phe.*] I would love you, if I could. Tomorrow meet me all together. [*To Phe.*] I will marry you, if ever I marry woman, and I'll be married tomorrow. [*To Orl.*] I will satisfy you, if ever I satisfied man, and you shall be married tomorrow. [*To Sil.*] I will content you, if what pleases you contents you, and you shall be married tomorrow. [*To Orl.*] As you love Rosalind, meet. [*To Sil.*] As you love Phebe, meet. And as I love no woman, I'll meet. So fare you well. I have left you commands.   131

Sil. I'll not fail, if I live.

Phe. Nor I.

Orl. Nor I.

                              [*Exeunt.*

Scene III. *The forest.*

Enter Touchstone *and* Audrey.

Touch. Tomorrow is the joyful day, Audrey; tomorrow will we be married.

Aud. I do desire it with all my heart; and I hope it is no dishonest desire to desire to be a woman of the world. Here come two of the banished duke's pages.

Enter two Pages.

First Page. Well met, honest gentleman.

Touch. By my troth, well met. Come, sit, sit, and a song.

Sec. Page. We are for you. Sit i' the middle.   10

First Page. Shall we clap into 't roundly, without hawking or spitting or saying we are hoarse, which are the only pro- logues to a bad voice?

Sec. Page. I' faith, i' faith; and both in a tune, like two gipsies on a horse.

Song

It was a lover and his lass,
　　With a hey, and a ho, and a hey nonino,
That o'er the green cornfield did pass
　　In the springtime, the only pretty ring time,
When birds do sing, hey ding a ding, ding;   21
　　Sweet lovers love the spring.

Between the acres of the rye,
　　With a hey, and a ho, and a hey nonino,
These pretty country folks would lie,
　　In springtime, &c.

This carol they began that hour,
　　With a hey, and a ho, and a hey nonino,
How that a life was but a flower
　　In springtime, &c.   30

And therefore take the present time,
　　With a hey, and a ho, and a hey nonino;
For love is crownéd with the prime
　　In springtime, &c.

11. **clap into it roundly:** begin at once.

Touch. Truly, young gentlemen, though there was no great matter in the ditty, yet the note was very untunable.

First Page. You are deceived, sir. We kept time, we lost not our time.   39

Touch. By my troth, yes; I count it but time lost to hear such a foolish song. God be wi' you; and God mend your voices! Come, Audrey.   [*Exeunt.*

SCENE IV. *The forest.*

Enter DUKE *senior,* AMIENS, JAQUES, ORLANDO, OLIVER, *and* CELIA.

Duke S. Dost thou believe, Orlando, that the boy
Can do all this that he hath promised?

Orl. I sometimes do believe, and sometimes do not;
As those that fear they hope, and know they fear.

Enter ROSALIND, SILVIUS, *and* PHEBE.

Ros. Patience once more, whiles our compact is urged.
You say, if I bring in your Rosalind,
You will bestow her on Orlando here?

Duke S. That would I, had I kingdoms to give with her.

Ros. And you say, you will have her, when I bring her?

Orl. That would I, were I of all kingdoms king.   10

Ros. You say, you'll marry me, if I be willing?

Phe. That will I, should I die the hour after.

Ros. But if you do refuse to marry me,
You'll give yourself to this most faithful shepherd?

Phe. So is the bargain.

Ros. You say, that you'll have Phebe, if she will?

Sil. Though to have her and death were both one thing.

Ros. I have promised to make all this matter even.
Keep you your word, O duke, to give your daughter;
You yours, Orlando, to receive his daughter;   20
Keep your word, Phebe, that you'll marry me,
Or else refusing me, to wed this shepherd;
Keep your word, Silvius, that you'll marry her,
If she refuse me; and from hence I go,
To make these doubts all even. [*Exeunt Rosalind and Celia.*

Duke S. I do remember in this shepherd boy
Some lively touches of my daughter's favor.

Orl. My lord, the first time that I ever saw him
Methought he was a brother to your daughter:
But, my good lord, this boy is forest-born,   30
And hath been tutored in the rudiments
Of many desperate studies by his uncle,
Whom he reports to be a great magician,
Obscuréd in the circle of this forest.

Enter Touchstone *and* Audrey.

Jaq. There is, sure, another flood toward, and these couples
are coming to the ark. Here comes a pair of very strange
beasts, which in all tongues are called fools.

Touch. Salutation and greeting to you all!   39

Jaq. Good my lord, bid him welcome: this is the motley-
minded gentleman that I have so often met in the forest.
He hath been a courtier, he swears.

Touch. If any man doubt that, let him put me to my
purgation. I have trod a measure; I have flattered a lady;
I have been politic with my friend, smooth with mine enemy;
I have undone three tailors; I have had four quarrels, and
like to have fought one.

Jaq. And how was that ta'en up?   50

Touch. Faith, we met, and found the quarrel was upon
the seventh cause.

Jaq. How seventh cause? Good my lord, like this fellow.

Duke S. I like him very well.

Touch. God 'ild you, sir; I desire you of the like. I
press in here, sir, amongst the rest of the country copulatives,
to swear and to forswear; according as marriage binds and
blood breaks. A poor virgin, sir, an ill-favored thing, sir, but
mine own. A poor humor of mine, sir, to take that that no
man else will. Rich honesty dwells like a miser, sir, in a
poorhouse, as your pearl in your foul oyster.

Duke S. By my faith, he is very swift and sententious.

Touch. According to the fool's bolt, sir, and such dulcet
diseases.

Jaq. But, for the seventh cause; how did you find the
quarrel on the seventh cause?   70

Touch. Upon a lie seven times removed — bear your body
more seeming, Audrey — as thus, sir. I did dislike the cut

---

32. **desperate:** forbidden. 44. **my purgation:** chance to make good.
56. **copulatives:** those about to be married.

of a certain courtier's beard. He sent me word, if I said his
beard was not cut well, he was in the mind it was: this is
called the Retort Courteous. If I sent him word again " it
was not well cut," he would send me word, he cut it to
please himself: this is called the Quip Modest. If again " it
was not well cut," he disabled my judgment: this is called the
Reply Churlish. If again " it was not well cut," he would
answer, I spake not true: this is called the Reproof Valiant.
If again " it was not well cut," he would say, I lied: this is
called the Countercheck Quarrelsome: and so to the Lie Circumstantial and the Lie Direct.

Jaq. And how oft did you say his beard was not well cut?

Touch. I durst go no further than the Lie Circumstantial,
nor he durst not give me the Lie Direct; and so we measured
swords and parted.   91

Jaq. Can you nominate in order now the degrees of the lie?

Touch. O sir, we quarrel in print, by the book, as you
have books for good manners. I will name you the degrees.
The first, the Retort Courteous; the second, the Quip Modest;
the third, the Reply Churlish; the fourth, the Reproof Valiant;
the fifth, the Countercheck Quarrelsome; the sixth, the Lie
with Circumstance; the seventh, the Lie Direct. All these
you may avoid but the Lie Direct; and you may avoid that
too, with an If. I knew when seven justices could not take
up a quarrel, but when the parties were met themselves, one of
them thought but of an If, as, " If you said so, then I said
so "; and they shook hands and swore brothers. Your If is
the only peacemaker; much virtue in If.

Jaq. Is not this a rare fellow, my lord? He's as good at
any thing and yet a fool.   110

Duke S. He uses his folly like a stalking-horse and under
the presentation of that he shoots his wit.

Enter Hymen, Rosalind, *and* Celia.

Still Music

Hym.   Then is there mirth in heaven,
          When earthly things made even
               Atone together.
          Good duke, receive thy daughter.

93. **by the book:** a satirical reference to books of etiquette. 111. **stalk-ing-horse:** one used as a blind in hunting.

>   Hymen from heaven brought her,
>   Yea, brought her hither,
>   That thou mightst join her hand with his
>   Whose heart within his bosom is.   121

Ros. [*To duke*] To you I give myself, for I am yours.
[*To Orl.*] To you I give myself, for I am yours.
   Duke S. If there be truth in sight, you are my daughter.
   Orl. If there be truth in sight, you are my Rosalind.
   Phe. If sight and shape be true,
Why then, my love, adieu!
   Ros. I'll have no father, if you be not he;
I'll have no husband, if you be not he;
Nor ne'er wed woman, if you be not she.   130
   Hym. Peace, ho! I bar confusion:
      'Tis I must make conclusion
        Of these most strange events.
      Here's eight that must take hands
      To join in Hymen's bands,
        If truth holds true contents.
      You and you no cross shall part;
      You and you are heart in heart;
      You to his love must accord,
      Or have a woman to your lord;   140
      You and you are sure together,
      As the winter to foul weather,
      Whiles a wedlock-hymn we sing,
      Feed yourselves with questioning;
      That reason wonder may diminish,
      How thus we met, and these things finish.

Song

>   Wedding is great Juno's crown:
>   O blessed bond of board and bed!
>   'Tis Hymen peoples every town;
>   High wedlock then be honoréd.   150
>   Honor, high honor and renown,
>   To Hymen, god of every town!

   Duke S. O my dear niece, welcome thou art to me!
Even daughter, welcome, in no less degree.

118. **Hymen:** god of marriage.

Phe. I will not eat my word, now thou art mine;
Thy faith my fancy to thee doth combine.

Enter JAQUES DE BOYS.

Jaq. de B. Let me have audience for a word or two.
I am the second son of old Sir Rowland,
That bring these tidings to this fair assembly.
Duke Frederick, hearing how that every day
Men of great worth resorted to this forest,   161
Addressed a mighty power, which were on foot,
In his own conduct, purposely to take
His brother here and put him to the sword;
And to the skirts of this wild wood he came,
Where meeting with an old religious man,
After some question with him, was converted
Both from his enterprise and from the world,
His crown bequeathing to his banished brother,
And all their lands restored to them again   170
That were with him exiled. This to be true,
I do engage my life.
   Duke S.   Welcome, young man;
Thou offer'st fairly to thy brothers' wedding:
To one his lands withheld, and to the other
A land itself at large, a potent dukedom.
First, in this forest let us do those ends
That here were well begun and well begot;
And after, every of this happy number
That have endured shrewd days and nights with us
Shall share the good of our returnéd fortune,
According to the measure of their states.   181
Meantime, forget this new-fall'n dignity
And fall into our rustic revelry.
Play, music! And you, brides and bridegrooms all,
With measure heaped in joy, to the measures fall.
   Jaq. Sir, by your patience. If I heard you rightly,
The duke hath put on a religious life
And thrown into neglect the pompous court?
   Jaq. de B. He hath.   189
   Jaq. To him will I. Out of these convertites
There is much matter to be heard and learned.

---

162. **addressed:** gathered.   173. **offer'st fairly:** make a desirable present.
181. **states:** estates and former rank.

[*To duke*] You to your former honor I bequeath;
Your patience and your virtue well deserves it;
[*To Orl.*] You to a love that your true faith doth merit;
[*To Oli.*] You to your land and love and great allies;
[*To Sil.*] You to a long and well-deservéd bed;
[*To Touch.*] And you to wrangling; for thy loving voyage
Is but for two months victualed. So, to your pleasures;
I am for other than for dancing measures.
     Duke S.   Stay, Jaques, stay.   200
     Jaq.   To see no pastime I. What you would have
I'll stay to know at your abandoned cave.   [*Exit.*
     Duke S.   Proceed, proceed. We will begin these rites,
As we do trust they'll end, in true delights. [*A dance. Exeunt.*

EPILOGUE

Ros. It is not the fashion to see the lady the epilogue,
but it is no more unhandsome than to see the lord the prologue. If it be true that good wine needs no bush, 'tis true
that a good play needs no epilogue; yet to good wine they do
use good bushes, and good plays prove the better by the help
of good epilogues. What a case am I in then, that am neither
a good epilogue nor cannot insinuate with you in the behalf
of a good play! I am not furnished like a beggar, therefore
to beg will not become me. My way is to conjure you; and
I'll begin with the women. I charge you, O women, for the
love you bear to men, to like as much of this play as please
you; and I charge you, O men, for the love you bear to
women — as I perceive by your simpering, none of you hates
them — that between you and the women the play may please.
If I were a woman I would kiss as many of you as had beards
that pleased me, complexions that liked me, and breaths that
I defied not; and, I am sure, as many as have good beards or
good faces or sweet breaths will, for my kind offer, when I
make curtsy, bid me farewell.   [*Exit.*

15. **If I were a woman:** the boy who played Rosalind speaks here in his
own person.

INTERPRETATIVE NOTE

Of all the comedies of Shakespeare, none is more romantically joyous than *As You Like It*. The scene is laid in some mythical dukedom, but all that matters is the Forest of Arden, the details of which Shakespeare drew from the forests surrounding his native Stratford. The story is not unlike some that tell of Robin Hood and his Merry Men in Sherwood Forest. It is possible that Shakespeare wrote his play to compete with several Robin Hood plays that were being given by other companies. The idea for the play and much of its material he drew from a contemporary novel, Lodge's *Rosalynde*. Here, as always, Shakespeare transmuted base metal into pure gold. When this play was written in 1599, Shakespeare was approaching the full maturity of his dramatic genius. In only one other later comedy, *Twelfth Night* (1600), do we find the type of romance that characterizes *As You Like It*. Beginning with the year 1601 he entered upon the period of the great tragedies, and when he returned to comedy toward the end of his career the type was different.

There is hardly any plot to *As You Like It*; the story consists mainly of a series of episodes that tell of young loves that run smooth. There is not a really discordant note in the whole play, as the reader feels from the first. There is no need to worry about the situation between Orlando and his nasty brother; we know at once that the hero is able to take care of himself. Likewise, we know enough about banished dukes to feel indifferent over their fate. They always come back. With the entrance of Rosalind, her part of the story is given away at once; she can fall in love only with Orlando.

It is interesting to note how differently from many other authors Shakespeare manages his love stories. When Rosalind's position at the ducal court is made plain to the reader, he might expect Orlando to play the rôle of rescuing hero who afterward marries the fair lady. In medieval romances he would have done that, but not so in Shakespeare. A glance, a word, and the wooing is over, and it is Rosalind who has been the aggressor, for the tongue-tied Orlando can say never a syllable. All that is necessary now is to get everybody out into the Land of Romance. The stage is set for that, and the real story begins.

In this play Shakespeare uses all the stock devices of romantic comedy that were current in his day, such as the heroine disguised as a boy, and the wanderings in a forest. The audiences were used to that sort of thing and liked it, even though they knew that everything would turn out happily. They wanted to see interesting characters doing interesting things. Of that they got plenty in *As You Like It*. There is no struggle. The heroine is won before she is wooed, and every other love is at first sight, with the pleasant variation of one in which a foolish country girl falls in love with the handsome young city chap, who turns out to be a woman. That particular trick was not uncommon, and had been most effectively used by Greene in his *James IV*. The best variation from the normal in this play is the Touchstone-Audrey episode. It is a safe assumption that Shakespeare's audiences found it as funny as we do today. So the plan of the play is merely to get all these couples safely married, with the monotony relieved by the Duke Senior scenes, the highly theatrical story of Orlando's brother Oliver, with whom Celia proceeds at once to fall in love, and the sudden reform of the usurping Frederick. In the Forest of Arden everybody must be happy — and is.

But how about the melancholy Jaques? Was he happy at the end of the play? About him, as about all the characters in the play, there is no mystery. His melancholy is entirely intellectual, and nobody takes him seriously, not even himself. He is simply a disillusioned man of the world who takes a morbid pride in railing against what he can no longer enjoy. He has the gift of pungent speech, and he probably likes to hear himself talk as much as the Duke and his followers like listening to him. He is not far removed from the professional jesters so common in Shakespeare. At the end, when he mockingly refuses to return to court, we can rest assured that he is as happy as he ever can be. He is going to do exactly what he pleases: surely an element of happiness.

QUESTIONS

I. i.

1. State definitely what you learn about Orlando.
2. Does Orlando have the courage of his convictions? Explain.
3. Compare this opening scene with that of *Julius Caesar*.
4. What impression do you form of Adam?
5. Note all the information about the court.
6. Who is the greater rascal, Oliver or Charles?

I. ii.

1. Form definite pictures of Rosalind and Celia.
2. Which of the two is the more romantic? Explain.
3. How does Le Beau's idea of sport differ from that of Touchstone?
4. How does Orlando win the romantic interest of the two girls?
5. At what point do Rosalind and Orlando fall in love?
6. In this scene, visualize the action, more especially the grouping of the characters, throughout.

I. iii.

1. Form a definite impression of Frederick, giving possible reasons for his crustiness.
2. Who is the more practical, Celia or Rosalind? Comment.
3. Where are they going? Why?
4. What plot elements have so far been introduced?

II. i.

1. Visualize the stage setting for the Forest of Arden.
2. Of what your imagination pictures, how much was there on the stage in Shakespeare's day?
3. Duke Senior's opening speech is a good one to memorize.
4. Is he sincere in saying that he would not change this life for the court?
5. From this scene, what was there "melancholy" about Jaques?

II. ii.

1. What dramatic value in this short scene?
2. What hint about Orlando?

II. iii.

1. How old was Orlando? Adam?
2. What connection does this scene have with the action of the play?
3. Does the scene afford opportunity for good acting? Comment.
4. What does this scene prepare for?

II. iv.

1. Picture the entrance of the three wanderers. Do you think it comic?
2. What subordinate story introduced?
3. How were the characters grouped at first?
4. Since they were in the Forest of Arden, why did they not ask for the Duke Senior?
5. What practical detail is settled for the wanderers?

II. v.

1. This scene belongs to the melancholy Jaques. Give him your attention.
2. Why were the Duke and his followers fond of him?
3. On the Elizabethan stage, where was the banquet prepared?

II. vi.

1. What does an audience like about this scene?
2. Why does Orlando not leave Adam on the stage?

II. vii.

1. How do you account for Jaques' enthusiasm for Touchstone?
2. Why does Jaques say that " motley's your only wear " ?
3. How does Duke Senior puncture the philosophy of Jaques?
4. Why does Orlando enter the way he does?
5. What makes him change his tune?
6. The " All the world's a stage " speech is a famous passage. Learn it.
7. The main characters are now in the Forest of Arden. What do you expect next?

III. i.

1. What new character is set wandering? Why?
2. What dramatic value in this short scene?

III. ii.

1. What is brought out in the dialogue between Touchstone and Corin?
2. From now on, what do you think will be the most important factor in the plot? Comment.
3. Had Rosalind known about Orlando's love prior to this scene?
4. Why does Jaques suggest to Orlando that they " rail " against the world?
5. How does Orlando respond? Why?
6. Does Orlando recognize Rosalind?
7. What saves this long conversation between the lovers from being tedious?

III. iii.

1. Describe Audrey.
2. Why should Jaques enjoy Touchstone and Audrey?
3. Why is the marriage put off?

III. iv.

1. Does Rosalind show a true lover's impatience? Was it real?
2. Do you think Celia romantic? Comment.

III. v.

1. As a lover, what mistake did Silvius make?
2. Why does Phebe fall in love with Rosalind?
3. How does this help in keeping the story from sagging in this act?

IV. i.

1. What reasons does Jaques give for his melancholy?
2. Is Rosalind's scorn justifiable? Comment.
3. Is the love story of Orlando and Rosalind advanced by their eloquent fooling? Comment.
4. Could this have gone on without the presence of Celia?
5. How does Celia show her attitude toward this artificial situation?

IV. ii.

1. Does this scene advance the plot?
2. Is it of any interest in itself? Comment.

IV. iii.

1. Do Rosalind's remarks have any effect on Silvius?
2. How does Celia feel toward him?
3. What do you think of Oliver's sudden transformation?
4. Why does Rosalind faint? Or doesn't she?
5. Does Oliver suspect the truth about Rosalind? Comment.
6. At this point gather up the threads of the plot to see how matters stand with all the characters.

V. i.

1. Describe William.
2. Would he have been suited better for Audrey than Touchstone? Comment.
3. Why did he depart so meekly?
4. Why did Audrey prefer Touchstone? Or didn't she?

V. ii.

1. How do you account for Celia's love for Oliver? Does it change your opinion of her?
2. Does Oliver win your sympathy? Explain.
3. Does Rosalind's scheme seem artificial?
4. Why does Orlando fall in with it?
5. Rosalind and Orlando are together alone for the first time. Does she talk in her usual vein?
6. Do you agree with Silvius' idea of love?

V. iii.

1. Compare this scene with previous similar ones as to dramatic purpose.
2. Picture the action of Audrey during this hilarity.

V. iv.

1. Do Orlando and Duke Senior have more than an inkling of the truth about Rosalind? Comment.
2. Do you see any stage necessity for the Touchstone part of this scene?
3. Is it good in itself? Comment.
4. Picture the characters and the grouping for the final scene.
5. Do you like the ending? Comment.
6. What becomes of Jaques? Why?
7. What news brought by Jaques de Boys?
8. In the second act Duke Senior says that he would not give up this idyllic simple life. What becomes of that theory? Why?
9. Would a modern audience care for the Epilogue? Comment.

HAMLET

PRINCE OF DENMARK

DRAMATIS PERSONAE

CLAUDIUS, king of Denmark.
HAMLET, son to the late, and nephew to the present king.
POLONIUS, lord chamberlain.
HORATIO, friend to Hamlet.
LAERTES, son to Polonius.
VOLTIMAND ⎤
CORNELIUS ⎟
ROSENCRANTZ ⎬ courtiers.
GUILDENSTERN ⎟
OSRIC ⎟
A Gentleman ⎦
A Priest.
MARCELLUS ⎤ officers.
BERNARDO ⎦

FRANCISCO, a soldier.
REYNALDO, servant to Polonius.
Players.
Two Clowns, grave-diggers.
FORTINBRAS, prince of Norway.
A Captain.
English Ambassadors.
GERTRUDE, queen of Denmark, and mother to Hamlet.
OPHELIA, daughter to Polonius.
Lords, Ladies, Officers, Soldiers, Sailors, Messengers, and other Attendants. Ghost of Hamlet's Father.

SCENE: *Denmark.*

ACT I

SCENE I. *Elsinore. A platform before the castle.*

FRANCISCO *at his post. Enter to him* BERNARDO.

Ber. Who's there?
Fran. Nay, answer me: stand, and unfold yourself.
Ber. Long live the king!
Fran. Bernardo?
Ber. He.
Fran. You come most carefully upon your hour.
Ber. 'Tis now struck twelve; get thee to bed, Francisco.
Fran. For this relief much thanks: 'tis bitter cold,
And I am sick at heart.
Ber. Have you had quiet guard?
Fran.   Not a mouse stirring. 10

Elsinore: English name for Helsingör, a Danish seaport on the island of Zealand.   1. **Who's there?:** the guard Francisco should have challenged, but Bernardo is excited.   2. **me:** the emphasis on **me** corrects Bernardo, and in the next line he gives the password.   8. **sick at heart:** compare with the opening line of "The Merchant of Venice."

Ber. Well, good night.
If you do meet Horatio and Marcellus,
The rivals of my watch, bid them make haste.
    Fran. I think I hear them. Stand, ho! Who's there?

Enter HORATIO *and* MARCELLUS.

    Hor. Friends to this ground.
    Mar.   And liegemen to the Dane.
    Fran. Give you good night.
    Mar.   O, farewell, honest soldier:
Who hath relieved you?
    Fran.   Bernardo has my place.
Give you good night.   [*Exit.*
    Mar.   Holla! Bernardo!
    Ber.   Say,
What, is Horatio there?
    Hor.   A piece of him.
    Ber. Welcome, Horatio; welcome, good Marcellus.   20
    Mar. What, has this thing appeared again tonight?
    Ber. I have seen nothing.
    Mar. Horatio says 'tis but our fantasy,
And will not let belief take hold of him
Touching this dreaded sight, twice seen of us;
Therefore I have entreated him along
With us to watch the minutes of this night,
That if again this apparition come,
He may approve our eyes and speak to it.
    Hor. Tush, tush, 'twill not appear.
    Ber.   Sit down awhile;   30
And let us once again assail your ears,
That are so fortified against our story,
What we have two nights seen.
    Hor.   Well, sit we down,
And let us hear Bernardo speak of this.
    Ber. Last night of all,
When yond same star that's westward from the pole
Had made his course to illume that part of heaven
Where now it burns, Marcellus and myself,
The bell then beating one —

13. **rivals:** sharers.   21. **this thing:** a vague reference to previous experiences of the soldiers.   23. **fantasy:** imagination.   29. **approve:** confirm.

Enter Ghost.

Mar.   Peace, break thee off; look, where it comes again! 40
Ber.   In the same figure, like the king that's dead.
Mar.   Thou art a scholar; speak to it, Horatio.
Ber.   Looks it not like the king?   Mark it, Horatio.
Hor.   Most like: it harrows me with fear and wonder.
Ber.   It would be spoke to.
Mar.   Question it, Horatio.
Hor.   What art thou that usurp'st this time of night,
Together with that fair and warlike form
In which the majesty of buried Denmark
Did sometimes march? by heaven I charge thee, speak!
Mar.   It is offended.
Ber.   See, it stalks away!   50
Hor.   Stay! speak, speak!   I charge thee, speak!

                                        [*Exit Ghost.*

Mar.   'Tis gone, and will not answer.
Ber.   How now, Horatio! you tremble and look pale:
Is not this something more than fantasy?
What think you on 't?
Hor.   Before my God, I might not this believe
Without the sensible and true avouch
Of mine own eyes.
Mar.   Is it not like the king?
Hor.   As thou art to thyself:
Such was the very armor he had on   60
When he the ambitious Norway combated;
So frowned he once, when, in an angry parle,
He smote the sledded Polacks on the ice.
'Tis strange.
Mar.   Thus twice before, and jump at this dead hour,
With martial stalk hath he gone by our watch.
Hor.   In what particular thought to work I know not;
But in the gross and scope of my opinion,
This bodes some strange eruption to our state.
Mar.   Good now, sit down, and tell me, he that knows, 70
Why this same strict and most observant watch
So nightly toils the subject of the land,

42. **scholar:** the belief was that a ghost could speak only if spoken to.
Horatio, the scholar, was best fitted.   45. **question:** speak to.   46. **usurp'st:**
use wrongly.   48. **Denmark:** the king.   63. **sledded:** using sleds.   58.
gross, etc.: in general, my opinion is.

And why such daily cast of brazen cannon,
And foreign mart for implements of war;
Why such impress of shipwrights, whose sore task
Does not divide the Sunday from the week;
What might be toward, that this sweaty haste
Doth make the night joint-laborer with the day:
Who is 't that can inform me?
    Hor.   That can I;
At least, the whisper goes so. Our last king,   80
Whose image even but now appeared to us,
Was, as you know, by Fortinbras of Norway,
Thereto pricked on by a most emulate pride,
Dared to the combat; in which our valiant Hamlet —
For so this side of our known world esteemed him —
Did slay this Fortinbras; who, by a sealed compact,
Well ratified by law and heraldry,
Did forfeit, with his life, all those his lands
Which he stood seized of, to the conqueror.
Against the which, a moiety competent   90
Was gaged by our king, which had returned
To the inheritance of Fortinbras,
Had he been vanquisher; as, by the same covenant,
And carriage of the article designed,
His fell to Hamlet. Now, sir, young Fortinbras,
Of unimprovéd mettle hot and full,
Hath in the skirts of Norway here and there
Sharked up a list of lawless resolutes,
For food and diet, to some enterprise
That hath a stomach in 't; which is no other —
As it doth well appear unto our state —   101
But to recover of us, by strong hand
And terms compulsatory, those foresaid lands
So by his father lost. And this, I take it,
Is the main motive of our preparations,
The source of this our watch and the chief head
Of this posthaste and romage in the land.
    Ber. I think it be no other but e'en so.
Well may it sort that this portentous figure

74. **foreign mart:** i.e., for purchasing. 83. **emulate:** emulous. 84. **Hamlet:** the father, not the hero of the play. 89. **seized of:** possessed of. 90 **moiety competent:** equal part. 96. **unimproved:** untried. 98. **sharked up:** gobbled up any old way, as a shark eats. 100. **stomach:** requiring courage. 107. **romage:** bustle. 109. **portentous:** ominous.

Comes arméd through our watch, so like the king   110
That was and is the question of these wars.
   Hor.   A mote it is to trouble the mind's eye.
In the most high and palmy state of Rome,
A little ere the mightiest Julius fell,
The graves stood tenantless and the sheeted dead
Did squeak and gibber in the Roman streets.
As stars with trains of fire and dews of blood,
Disasters in the sun; and the moist star
Upon whose influence Neptune's empire stands
Was sick almost to doomsday with eclipse.   120
And even the like precurse of fierce events,
As harbingers preceding still the fates
And prologue to the omen coming on,
Have heaven and earth together demonstrated
Unto our climatures and countrymen. —
But soft, behold!   Lo, where it comes again!

              Reënter Ghost.

I'll cross it, though it blast me.   Stay, illusion!
If thou hast any sound, or use of voice,
Speak to me;
If there be any good thing to be done,   130
That may to thee do ease and grace to me,
Speak to me;   [*Cock crows.*
If thou art privy to thy country's fate,
Which, happily, foreknowing may avoid,
O, speak!
Or if thou hast uphoarded in thy life
Extorted treasure in the womb of earth,
For which, they say, you spirits oft walk in death,
Speak of it; stay, and speak!   Stop it, Marcellus.
   Mar.   Shall I strike at it with my partisan?   140
   Hor.   Do, if it will not stand.
   Ber.   'Tis here!
   Hor.   'Tis here!
   Mar.   'Tis gone!   [*Exit Ghost.*
We do it wrong, being so majestical,

114. **Julius:** Shakespeare wrote "Julius Caesar" about a year before
"Hamlet." See I. iii. of the earlier play.   117. A line seems missing.   118
moist star: the moon, which causes the tides.   127. **cross it:** to " cross " a
ghost was to pass over the spot where it has been, thereby putting yourself
under its influence.   140. **partisan:** long spear.

To offer it the show of violence;
For it is, as the air, invulnerable,
And our vain blows malicious mockery.
   Ber. It was about to speak, when the cock crew.
   Hor. And then it started like a guilty thing
Upon a fearful summons. I have heard,
The cock, that is the trumpet to the morn,   150
Doth with his lofty and shrill-sounding throat
Awake the god of day; and, at his warning,
Whether in sea or fire, in earth or air,
The extravagant and erring spirit hies
To his confine: and of the truth herein
This present object made probation.
   Mar. It faded on the crowing of the cock.
Some say that ever 'gainst that season comes
Wherein our Savior's birth is celebrated,
The bird of dawning singeth all night long;   160
And then, they say, no spirit dare stir abroad;
The nights are wholesome; then no planets strike,
No fairy takes, nor witch hath power to charm,
So hallowed and so gracious is the time.
   Hor. So have I heard and do in part believe it.
But, look, the morn, in russet mantle clad,
Walks o'er the dew of yon high eastward hill.
Break we our watch up; and by my advice,
Let us impart what we have seen tonight
Unto young Hamlet; for, upon my life,   170
This spirit, dumb to us, will speak to him.
Do you consent we shall acquaint him with it,
As needful in our loves, fitting our duty?
   Mar. Let's do 't, I pray; and I this morning know
Where we shall find him most conveniently.   *[Exeunt.*

SCENE II. *A room of state in the castle.*

Enter the KING, QUEEN, HAMLET, POLONIUS, LAERTES, VOLTI-
MAND, CORNELIUS, Lords, *and* Attendants.

   King. Though yet of Hamlet our dear brother's death
The memory be green, and that it us befitted

---

154. **extravagant:** out of his bounds. 154. **erring:** wandering. 156. **probation:** proof. 162. **wholesome:** in Shakespeare's day night air was
thought unhealthy. 162–63. **strike; takes:** do damage, according to astrology.

To bear our hearts in grief and our whole kingdom
To be contracted in one brow of woe,
Yet so far hath discretion fought with nature
That we with wisest sorrow think on him,
Together with remembrance of ourselves.
Therefore our sometime sister, now our queen,
The imperial jointress to this warlike state,
Have we, as 'twere with a defeated joy, —   10
With an auspicious and a dropping eye,
With mirth in funeral and with dirge in marriage,
In equal scale weighing delight and dole, —
Taken to wife; nor have we herein barred
Your better wisdoms, which have freely gone
With this affair along. For all, our thanks.
Now follows that you know, young Fortinbras,
Holding a weak supposal of our worth,
Or thinking by our late dear brother's death
Our state to be disjoint and out of frame,   20
Colleaguéd with the dream of his advantage,
He hath not failed to pester us with message,
Importing the surrender of those lands
Lost by his father, with all bonds of law,
To our most valiant brother. So much for him.
Now for ourself and for this time of meeting.
Thus much the business is: we have here writ
To Norway, uncle of young Fortinbras, —
Who, impotent and bed-rid, scarcely hears
Of this his nephew's purpose, — to suppress   30
His further gait herein, in that the levies,
The lists and full proportions, are all made
Out of his subject; and we here dispatch
You, good Cornelius, and you, Voltimand,
For bearers of this greeting to old Norway;
Giving to you no further personal power
To business with the king, more than the scope
Of these delated articles allow.
Farewell, and let your haste commend your duty.

Cor.⎫
Vol.⎭ In that and all things will we show our duty. 40

8. **sister:** sister-in-law. 10. **defeated:** disfigured. 11. **auspicious, etc.:**
laugh with one eye, weep with the other. 18. **weak supposal:** poor opinion.
32. **proportions:** number of soldiers. 38. **delated:** set forth in detail.

King. We doubt it nothing; heartily farewell.
>   [*Exeunt Voltimand and Cornelius.*

And now, Laertes, what's the news with you?
You told us of some suit; what is 't, Laertes?
You cannot speak of reason to the Dane,
And lose your voice. What wouldst thou beg, Laertes,
That shall not be my offer, not thy asking?
The head is not more native to the heart,
The hand more instrumental to the mouth,
Than is the throne of Denmark to thy father.
What wouldst thou have, Laertes?

Laer.   My dread lord,   50
Your leave and favor to return to France;
From whence though willingly I came to Denmark,
To show my duty in your coronation,
Yet now, I must confess, that duty done,
My thoughts and wishes bend again toward France
And bow them to your gracious leave and pardon.

King. Have you your father's leave? What says Polonius?

Pol. He hath, my lord, wrung from me my slow leave
By laborsome petition, and at last
Upon his will I sealed my hard consent.   60
I do beseech you, give him leave to go.

King. Take thy fair hour, Laertes. Time be thine,
And thy best graces spend it at thy will!
But now, my cousin Hamlet, and my son —

Ham. [*Aside*] A little more than kin, and less than kind.

King. How is it that the clouds still hang on you?

Ham. Not so, my lord; I am too much i' the sun.

Queen. Good Hamlet, cast thy nighted color off,
And let thine eye look like a friend on Denmark.
Do not for ever with thy vailéd lids   70
Seek for thy noble father in the dust:
Thou know'st 'tis common; all that lives must die,
Passing through nature to eternity.

Ham. Ay, madam, it is common.

Queen.   If it be,
Why seems it so particular with thee?

Ham. Seems, madam! nay, it is; I know not " seems."

---

56. **pardon:** permission. 64. **cousin:** kinsman. 65. **more than kin, etc.:**
too much related. 68. **nighted color:** refers to his black clothes. 70. **vailed:**
lowered.

'Tis not alone my inky cloak, good mother,
Nor customary suits of solemn black,
Nor windy suspiration of forced breath,
No, nor the fruitful river in the eye,   80
Nor the dejected 'havior of the visage,
Together with all forms, moods, shows of grief,
That can denote me truly.   These indeed seem,
For they are actions that a man might play;
But I have that within which passeth show,
These but the trappings and the suits of woe.
    King.   'Tis sweet and commendable in your nature, Hamlet,
To give these mourning duties to your father:
But, you must know, your father lost a father;
That father lost, lost his, and the survivor bound
In filial obligation for some term   91
To do obsequious sorrow.   But to persever
In obstinate condolement is a course
Of impious stubbornness; 'tis unmanly grief;
It shows a will most incorrect to heaven,
A heart unfortified, a mind impatient,
An understanding simple and unschooled;
For what we know must be and is as common
As any the most vulgar thing to sense,
Why should we in our peevish opposition   100
Take it to heart?   Fie! 'tis a fault to heaven,
A fault against the dead, a fault to nature,
To reason most absurd, whose common theme
Is death of fathers, and who still hath cried,
From the first corse till he that died today,
" This must be so."   We pray you, throw to earth
This unprevailing woe, and think of us
As of a father, for let the world take note,
You are the most immediate to our throne;
And with no less nobility of love   110
Than that which dearest father bears his son,
Do I impart toward you.   For your intent
In going back to school in Wittenberg,
It is most retrograde to our desire;

  79. **windy suspiration, etc.:** deep sighing.   92. **obsequious:** dutiful.   95.
incorrect: not submissive.   97. **simple:** foolish.   99. **vulgar, etc.:** usual experience.   107. **unprevailing:** unavailing.   109. **most immediate:** the throne
of Denmark was elective, but royal blood was preferred.   113. **Wittenberg:** a
German university.   114. **retrograde:** contrary.

And we beseech you, bend you to remain
Here, in the cheer and comfort of our eye,
Our chiefest courtier, cousin, and our son.

   Queen. Let not thy mother lose her prayers, Hamlet.
I pray thee, stay with us; go not to Wittenberg.

     Ham. I shall in all my best obey you, madam.   120

     King. Why, 'tis a loving and a fair reply.
Be as ourself in Denmark. Madam, come;
This gentle and unforced accord of Hamlet
Sits smiling to my heart: in grace whereof,
No jocund health that Denmark drinks today,
But the great cannon to the clouds shall tell,
And the king's rouse the heavens shall bruit again,
Re-speaking earthly thunder. Come away.

                        [Exeunt all but Hamlet.

   Ham. O, that this too too solid flesh would melt,
Thaw and resolve itself into a dew!   130
Or that the Everlasting had not fixed
His canon 'gainst self-slaughter! O God! God!
How weary, stale, flat and unprofitable,
Seem to me all the uses of this world!
Fie on 't! ah fie! 'Tis an unweeded garden,
That grows to seed; things rank and gross in nature
Possess it merely. That it should come to this!
But two months dead; nay, not so much, not two.
So excellent a king; that was, to this,   139
Hyperion to a satyr; so loving to my mother
That he might not beteem the winds of heaven
Visit her face too roughly. Heaven and earth!
Must I remember? Why, she would hang on him,
As if increase of appetite had grown
By what it fed on: and yet, within a month —
Let me not think on 't — Frailty, thy name is woman! —
A little month, or ere those shoes were old
With which she followed my poor father's body,
Like Niobe, all tears: — why, she, even she —
O God! a beast, that wants discourse of reason,
Would have mourned longer — married with my uncle,   151
My father's brother, but no more like my father

   120. **in all my best:** do my best.   127. **rouse:** drinking to a toast.   130.
resolve: dissolve.   137. **merely:** entirely.   140. **Hyperion, satyr:** the first
is a type of manly beauty, the other of ugliness.   141. **beteem:** allow.   149.
Niobe: see cyclopedia.   150. **discourse of reason:** reasoning power.

Than I to Hercules; within a month,
Ere yet the salt of most unrighteous tears
Had left the flushing in her galléd eyes,
She married. O, most wicked speed, to post
With such dexterity to incestuous sheets!
It is not nor it cannot come to good:
But break, my heart; for I must hold my tongue.

Enter Horatio, Marcellus, *and* Bernardo.

Hor. Hail to your lordship!
Ham.   I am glad to see you well. 160
Horatio — or I do forget myself.
Hor. The same, my lord, and your poor servant ever.
Ham. Sir, my good friend; I'll change that name with you.
And what make you from Wittenberg, Horatio?
Marcellus?
Mar. My good lord —
Ham. I am very glad to see you. [*To* Ber.] Good even, sir.
But what, in faith, make you from Wittenberg?
Hor. A truant disposition, good my lord.
Ham. I would not hear your enemy say so,
Nor shall you do mine ear that violence,   171
To make it truster of your own report
Against yourself. I know you are no truant.
But what is your affair in Elsinore?
We'll teach you to drink deep ere you depart.
Hor. My lord, I came to see your father's funeral.
Ham. I pray thee, do not mock me, fellow-student;
I think it was to see my mother's wedding.
Hor. Indeed, my lord, it followed hard upon.
Ham. Thrift, thrift, Horatio! the funeral baked meats 180
Did coldly furnish forth the marriage tables.
Would I had met my dearest foe in heaven
Or ever I had seen that day, Horatio!
My father! — methinks I see my father.
Hor. Where, my lord?
Ham.   In my mind's eye, Horatio.
Hor. I saw him once; he was a goodly king.
Ham. He was a man, take him for all in all,

155. **flushing:** redness from weeping. 155. **galled:** sore from weeping.
169. **truant disposition:** desire to shirk. 180. **baked meats:** feasts at
funerals were the custom. 182. **dearest:** bitterest.

I shall not look upon his like again.
    Hor. My lord, I think I saw him yesternight.
    Ham. Saw? Who?   190
    Hor. My lord, the king your father.
    Ham.   The king my father!
    Hor. Season your admiration for a while
With an attent ear, till I may deliver,
Upon the witness of these gentlemen,
This marvel to you.
    Ham.   For God's love, let me hear.
    Hor. Two nights together had these gentlemen,
Marcellus and Bernardo, on their watch,
In the dead vast and middle of the night,
Been thus encountered. A figure like your father,
Armed at point exactly, cap-a-pe,   200
Appears before them, and with solemn march
Goes slow and stately by them. Thrice he walked
By their oppressed and fear-surprisèd eyes,
Within his truncheon's length; whilst they, distilled
Almost to jelly with the act of fear,
Stand dumb and speak not to him. This to me
In dreadful secrecy impart they did;
And I with them the third night kept the watch:
Where, as they had delivered, both in time,
Form of the thing, each word made true and good,   210
The apparition comes. I knew your father;
These hands are not more like.
    Ham.   But where was this?
    Mar. My lord, upon the platform where we watched.
    Ham. Did you not speak to it?
    Hor.   My lord, I did;
But answer made it none. Yet once methought
It lifted up its head and did address
Itself to motion, like as it would speak;
But even then the morning cock crew loud,
And at the sound it shrunk in haste away,
And vanished from our sight.
    Ham.   'Tis very strange.   220
    Hor. As I do live, my honored lord, 'tis true;

---

192. **season:** restrain. 192. **admiration:** wonder. 200. **cap-a-pe:** from head to foot. 204. **truncheon:** staff of office.

And we did think it writ down in our duty
To let you know of it.
    Ham. Indeed, indeed, sirs; but this troubles me.
Hold you the watch tonight?
    Mar.⎱
    Ber.⎰   We do, my lord.
    Ham. Armed, say you?
    Mar.⎱
    Ber.⎰ Armed, my lord.
    Ham. From top to toe?
    Mar.⎱
    Ber.⎰   My lord, from head to foot.
    Ham. Then saw you not his face?
    Hor. O, yes, my lord; he wore his beaver up.
    Ham. What, looked he frowningly?   231
    Hor. A countenance more in sorrow than in anger.
    Ham. Pale or red?
    Hor. Nay, very pale.
    Ham.   And fixed his eyes upon you?
    Hor. Most constantly.
    Ham.   I would I had been there.
    Hor. It would have much amazed you.
    Ham. Very like, very like. Stayed it long?
    Hor. While one with moderate haste might tell a hundred.
    Mar.⎱
    Ber.⎰ Longer, longer.
    Hor. Not when I saw 't.
    Ham. His beard was grizzled — no?   240
    Hor. It was, as I have seen it in his life,
A sable silvered.
    Ham.   I will watch tonight;
Perchance 'twill walk again.
    Hor.   I warrant you it will.
    Ham. If it assume my noble father's person,
I'll speak to it, though hell itself should gape
And bid me hold my peace. I pray you all,
If you have hitherto concealed this sight,
Let it be tenable in your silence still;
And whatsoever else shall hap tonight,
Give it an understanding, but no tongue.   250
I will requite your loves. So, fare you well.

Upon the platform, 'twixt eleven and twelve,
I'll visit you.
    All.   Our duty to your honor.
    Ham. Your loves, as mine to you; farewell.
                            [Exeunt all but Hamlet.
My father's spirit in arms! All is not well;
I doubt some foul play. Would the night were come!
Till then sit still, my soul. Foul deeds will rise,
Though all the earth o'erwhelm them, to men's eyes.   *[Exit.*

SCENE III.   *A room in Polonius' house.*

Enter LAERTES *and* OPHELIA.

    Laer. My necessaries are embarked. Farewell; .
And, sister, as the winds give benefit
And convoy is assistant, do not sleep,
But let me hear from you.
    Oph.   Do you doubt that?
    Laer. For Hamlet and the trifling of his favor,
Hold it a fashion and a toy in blood,
A violet in the youth of primy nature,
Forward, not permanent, sweet, not lasting,
The perfume and suppliance of a minute;
No more.
    Oph. No more but so?
    Laer.   Think it no more: 10
For nature, crescent, does not grow alone
In thews and bulk, but, as this temple waxes,
The inward service of the mind and soul
Grows wide withal. Perhaps he loves you now,
And now no soil nor cautel doth besmirch
The virtue of his will; but you must fear,
His greatness weighed, his will is not his own;
For he himself is subject to his birth.
He may not, as unvalued persons do,
Carve for himself; for on his choice depends   20
The safety and health of this whole state;
And therefore must his choice be circumscribed
Unto the voice and yielding of that body
Whereof he is the head. Then if he says he loves you,

2-3. **winds give, etc.:** Write whenever you have a chance. 6. **toy in blood:** idle fancy. 7. **primy:** like spring. 12. **temple:** body. 15. **cautel:** falseness. 19. **unvalued:** of no account.

It fits your wisdom so far to believe it
As he in his particular act and place
May give his saying deed; which is no further
Than the main voice of Denmark goes withal.
Then weigh what loss your honor may sustain,
If with too credent ear you list his songs,   30
Or lose your heart, or your chaste treasure open
To his unmastered importunity.
Fear it, Ophelia, fear it, my dear sister,
And keep you in the rear of your affection,
Out of the shot and danger of desire.
The chariest maid is prodigal enough,
If she unmask her beauty to the moon.
Virtue itself 'scapes not calumnious strokes.
The canker galls the infants of the spring,
Too oft before their buttons be disclosed,   40
And in the morn and liquid dew of youth
Contagious blastments are most imminent.
Be wary then; best safety lies in fear;
Youth to itself rebels, though none else near.
  Oph. I shall the effect of this good lesson keep,
As watchman to my heart.   But, good my brother,
Do not, as some ungracious pastors do,
Show me the steep and thorny way to heaven,
Whiles, like a puffed and reckless libertine,
Himself the primrose path of dalliance treads,
And recks not his own rede.
  Laer.   O, fear me not.   51
I stay too long: but here my father comes.

                          Enter POLONIUS.

A double blessing is a double grace;
Occasion smiles upon a second leave.
  Pol. Yet here, Laertes! aboard, aboard, for shame!
The wind sits in the shoulder of your sail,
And you are stayed for.   There; my blessing with thee!
And these few precepts in thy memory
See thou character.   Give thy thoughts no tongue,
Nor any unproportioned thought his act.   60

  40. **buttons:** buds.   51. **rede:** advice.   59. **character:** inscribe. Accent
on second syllable.   60. **unproportioned:** unsuitable.

Be thou familiar, but by no means vulgar.
Those friends thou hast, and their adoption tried,
Grapple them to thy soul with hoops of steel;
But do not dull thy palm with entertainment
Of each new-hatched, unfledged comrade. Beware
Of entrance to a quarrel, but being in,
Bear 't that the opposed may beware of thee.
Give every man thy ear, but few thy voice;
Take each man's censure, but reserve thy judgment.
Costly thy habit as thy purse can buy, 70
But not expressed in fancy; rich, not gaudy;
For the apparel oft proclaims the man,
And they in France of the best rank and station
Are of a most select and generous chief in that.
Neither a borrower nor a lender be;
For loan oft loses both itself and friend,
And borrowing dulls the edge of husbandry.
This above all: to thine own self be true,
And it must follow, as the night the day,
Thou canst not then be false to any man. 80
Farewell; my blessing season this in thee!
    Laer. Most humbly do I take my leave, my lord.
    Pol. The time invites you; go; your servants tend.
    Laer. Farewell, Ophelia; and remember well
What I have said to you.
    Oph.   'Tis in my memory locked,
And you yourself shall keep the key of it.
    Laer. Farewell.   [*Exit.*
    Pol. What is 't, Ophelia, he hath said to you?
    Oph. So please you, something touching the Lord Ham-
let.
    Pol. Marry, well bethought. 90
'Tis told me, he hath very oft of late
Given private time to you; and you yourself
Have of your audience been most free and bounteous.
If it be so, as so 'tis put on me,
And that in way of caution, I must tell you,
You do not understand yourself so clearly
As it behoves my daughter and your honor.
What is between you? Give me up the truth.

61. **vulgar:** cheap. 64. **dull:** i.e., by shaking hands too freely. 69. **censure:** opinion. 81. **season:** make it bear fruit. 83. **tend:** wait for you.
90. **marry:** by Mary, a mild oath common in Shakespeare.

Oph. He hath, my lord, of late made many tenders
Of his affection to me.   100
  Pol. Affection! pooh! You speak like a green girl,
Unsifted in such perilous circumstance.
Do you believe his tenders, as you call them?
  Oph. I do not know, my lord, what I should think.
  Pol. Marry, I'll teach you: think yourself a baby,
That you have ta'en these tenders for true pay,
Which are not sterling. Tender yourself more dearly;
Or — not to crack the wind of the poor phrase,
Running it thus — you'll tender me a fool.
  Oph. My lord, he hath importuned me with love   110
In honorable fashion.
  Pol. Ah, fashion you may call it. Go to, go to.
  Oph. And hath given countenance to his speech, my lord,
With almost all the holy vows of heaven.
  Pol. Ay, springes to catch woodcocks. I do know,
When the blood burns, how prodigal the soul
Lends the tongue vows. These blazes, daughter,
Giving more light than heat, extinct in both,
Even in their promise, as it is a-making,   119
You must not take for fire. From this time
Be somewhat scanter of your maiden presence;
Set your entreatments at a higher rate
Than a command to parley. For Lord Hamlet,
Believe so much in him, that he is young,
And with a larger tether may he walk
Than may be given you. In few, Ophelia,
Do not believe his vows; for they are brokers,
Not of that dye which their investments show,
But mere implorators of unholy suits,
Breathing like sanctified and pious bawds,   130
The better to beguile. This is for all:
I would not, in plain terms, from this time forth,
Have you so slander any moment leisure,
As to give words or talk with the Lord Hamlet.
Look to 't, I charge you: come your ways.
  Oph. I shall obey, my lord.   [*Exeunt.*

  99. **tenders:** offers. 101. **green:** inexperienced. 102. **unsifted:** untried.
109. **tender,** etc.: make a [fool out of me. 112. **go to:** expression of impatience, common in Shakespeare. 115. **springes:** snares. 122. **entreatments:** interviews. 127. **brokers:** go-betweens. 133. **moment leisure:**
leisure moment.

SCENE IV. *The platform.*

Enter HAMLET, HORATIO, *and* MARCELLUS.

Ham.　The air bites shrewdly; it is very cold.
Hor.　It is a nipping and an eager air.
Ham.　What hour now?
Hor.　　　　　　　　I think it lacks of twelve.
Mar.　No, it is struck.
Hor.　Indeed? I heard it not. Then it draws near the
　　　season
Wherein the spirit held his wont to walk.
　　　　[*A flourish of trumpets, and ordnance shot off, within.*
What does this mean, my lord?
Ham.　The king doth wake tonight and takes his rouse,
Keeps wassail, and the swaggering up-spring reels;
And, as he drains his draughts of Rhenish down,
The kettledrum and trumpet thus bray out　　　　　　11
The triumph of his pledge.
Hor.　　　　　　　Is it a custom?
Ham.　Ay, marry, is 't;
But to my mind, though I am native here
And to the manner born, it is a custom
More honored in the breach than the observance.
This heavy-headed revel east and west
Makes us traduced and taxed of other nations.
They clepe us drunkards, and with swinish phrase
Soil our addition; and indeed it takes　　　　　　　20
From our achievements, though performed at height,
The pith and marrow of our attribute.
So, oft it chances in particular men,
That for some vicious mole of nature in them,
As, in their birth — wherein they are not guilty,
Since nature cannot choose his origin —
By the o'ergrowth of some complexion,
Oft breaking down the pales and forts of reason,
Or by some habit that too much o'er-leavens
The form of plausive manners, that these men,

---

1. **shrewdly:** sharply.　2. **eager:** biting.　8. **wake:** hold revel.　9. **wassail:** drinking-party.　9. **swaggering, etc.:** indulges in wild dancing.　18. **traduced and taxed:** gives us a bad reputation.　19. **clepe:** call.　20. **soil our addition:** soil our fair name.　22. **attribute:** reputation.　24. **mole:** natural blemish.　30. **plausive:** pleasing.

Carrying, I say, the stamp of one defect,   31
Being nature's livery, or fortune's star, —
Their virtues else — be they as pure as grace,
As infinite as man may undergo —
Shall in the general censure take corruption
From that particular fault. The dram of eale
Doth all the noble substance of a doubt
To his own scandal.
    Hor.   Look, my lord, it comes!

Enter Ghost.

    Ham. Angels and ministers of grace defend us!
Be thou a spirit of health or goblin damned,   40
Bring with thee airs from heaven or blasts from hell,
Be thy intents wicked or charitable,
Thou comest in such a questionable shape
That I will speak to thee. I'll call thee Hamlet,
King, father, royal Dane. O, answer me!
Let me not burst in ignorance, but tell
Why thy canonized bones, hearséd in death,
Have burst their cerements; why the sepulcher,
Wherein we saw thee quietly inurned,
Hath oped his ponderous and marble jaws,   50
To cast thee up again. What may this mean,
That thou, dead corse, again in complete steel
Revisit'st thus the glimpses of the moon,
Making night hideous; and we fools of nature
So horridly to shake our disposition
With thoughts beyond the reaches of our souls?
Say, why is this? wherefore? what should we do?
                       [Ghost beckons Hamlet.
    Hor. It beckons you to go away with it,
As if it some impartment did desire
To you alone.
    Mar.   Look, with what courteous action   60
It waves you to a more removéd ground.
But do not go with it.
    Hor.   No, by no means.
    Ham. It will not speak; then I will follow it.
    Hor. Do not, my lord.

---

   36. **eale:** probably means **evil.** This whole passage is difficult because of
corrupt text. 40. **health:** saved. 43. **questionable:** inviting talk. 47
canonized: buried with full rites of the church.

Ham.   Why, what should be the fear?
I do not set my life at a pin's fee;
And for my soul, what can it do to that,
Being a thing immortal as itself?
It waves me forth again. I'll follow it.
   Hor. What if it tempt you toward the flood, my lord,
Or to the dreadful summit of the cliff   70
That beetles o'er his base into the sea,
And there assume some other horrible form,
Which might deprive your sovereignty of reason
And draw you into madness? Think of it.
The very place puts toys of desperation,
Without more motive, into every brain
That looks so many fathoms to the sea
And hears it roar beneath.
   Ham.   It waves me still.
Go on; I'll follow thee.
   Mar. You shall not go, my lord.
   Ham.   Hold off your hands.   80
   Hor. Be ruled; you shall not go.
   Ham.   My fate cries out,
And makes each petty artery in this body
As hardy as the Nemean lion's nerve.
Still am I called. Unhand me, gentlemen.
By heaven, I'll make a ghost of him that lets me!
I say, away! Go on; I'll follow thee.
                         [Exeunt Ghost and Hamlet.
   Hor. He waxes desperate with imagination.
   Mar. Let's follow; 'tis not fit thus to obey him.
   Hor. Have after. To what issue will this come?
   Mar. Something is rotten in the state of Denmark.   90
   Hor. Heaven will direct it.
   Mar.   Nay, let's follow him. *[Exeunt.*

SCENE V. *Another part of the platform.*

Enter GHOST *and* HAMLET.

   Ham. Where wilt thou lead me? Speak. I'll go no
     further.
   Ghost. Mark me.

---

83. **Nemean lion:** the first of the labors of Hercules was to overcome this
beast. 85. **lets:** hinders.

Ham.   I will.
Ghost.   My hour is almost come,
When I to sulphurous and tormenting flames
Must render up myself.
    Ham.   Alas, poor ghost!
    Ghost. Pity me not, but lend thy serious hearing
To what I shall unfold.
    Ham.   Speak; I am bound to hear.
    Ghost. So art thou to revenge, when thou shalt hear.
    Ham. What?
    Ghost. I am thy father's spirit,
Doomed for a certain term to walk the night,   10
And for the day confined to fast in fires,
Till the foul crimes done in my days of nature
Are burnt and purged away. But that I am forbid
To tell the secrets of my prison-house,
I could a tale unfold whose lightest word
Would harrow up thy soul, freeze thy young blood,
Make thy two eyes, like stars, start from their spheres,
Thy knotted and combinéd locks to part
And each particular hair to stand on end,
Like quills upon the fretful porpentine.   20
But this eternal blazon must not be
To ears of flesh and blood. List, list, O, list!
If thou didst ever thy dear father love —
    Ham. O God!
    Ghost. Revenge his foul and most unnatural murder.
    Ham. Murder!
    Ghost. Murder most foul, as in the best it is;
But this most foul, strange and unnatural.
    Ham. Haste me to know 't, that I, with wings as swift
As meditation or the thoughts of love,   30
May sweep to my revenge.
    Ghost.   I find thee apt;
And duller shouldst thou be than the fat weed
That roots itself in ease on Lethe wharf,
Wouldst thou not stir in this. Now, Hamlet, hear:
'Tis given out that, sleeping in my orchard,
A serpent stung me; so the whole ear of Denmark
Is by a forgéd process of my death

---

20. **porpentine:** porcupine. 21. **blazon: revelation.** 33. **Lethe:** a stream
in Hades whose waters brought forgetfulness. 37. **process:** report.

Rankly abused; but know, thou noble youth,
The serpent that did sting thy father's life
Now wears his crown.
   Ham.   O my prophetic soul!   40
My uncle!
   Ghost.   Ay, that incestuous, that adulterate beast,
With witchcraft of his wit, with traitorous gifts, —
O wicked wit and gifts, that have the power
So to seduce! — won to his shameful lust
The will of my most seeming-virtuous queen:
O Hamlet, what a falling-off was there!
From me, whose love was of that dignity
That it went hand in hand even with the vow
I made to her in marriage, and to decline   50
Upon a wretch whose natural gifts were poor
To those of mine!
But virtue, as it never will be moved,
Though lewdness court it in a shape of heaven,
So lust, though to a radiant angel linked,
Will sate itself in a celestial bed,
And prey on garbage.
But, soft! methinks I scent the morning air;
Brief let me be. Sleeping within my orchard,
My custom always in the afternoon,   60
Upon my secure hour thy uncle stole,
With juice of cursed hebenon in a vial,
And in the porches of my ears did pour
The leperous distilment; whose effect
Holds such an enmity with blood of man
That swift as quicksilver it courses through
The natural gates and alleys of the body,
And with a sudden vigor it doth posset
And curd, like eager droppings into milk,
The thin and wholesome blood. So did it mine;   70
And a most instant tetter barked about,
Most lazar-like, with vile and loathsome crust,
All my smooth body.
Thus was I, sleeping, by a brother's hand
Of life, of crown, of queen, at once dispatched.
Cut off even in the blossoms of my sin,

---

   62. **hebenon:** strong poison. 68. **posset:** curdle. 71. **tetter:** skin disease. 72. **lazar-like:** like a leper.

Unhouseled, disappointed, unaneled,
No reckoning made, but sent to my account
With all my imperfections on my head.
O, horrible! O, horrible! most horrible!   80
If thou hast nature in thee, bear it not;
Let not the royal bed of Denmark be
A couch for luxury and damnéd incest.
But, howsoever thou pursuest this act,
Taint not thy mind, nor let thy soul contrive
Against thy mother aught. Leave her to Heaven
And to those thorns that in her bosom lodge,
To prick and sting her. Fare thee well at once!
The glow-worm shows the matin to be near,
And 'gins to pale his uneffectual fire.   90
Adieu, adieu! Hamlet, remember me.   [*Exit.*

    Ham. O all you host of heaven! O earth! what else?
And shall I couple hell? O, fie! Hold, hold, my heart;
And you, my sinews, grow not instant old,
But bear me stiffly up. Remember thee!
Ay, thou poor ghost, while memory holds a seat
In this distracted globe. Remember thee!
Yea, from the table of my memory
I'll wipe away all trivial fond records,
All saws of books, all forms, all pressures past,
That youth and observation copied there;   101
And thy commandment all alone shall live
Within the book and volume of my brain,
Unmixed with baser matter. Yes, by heaven!
O most pernicious woman!
O villain, villain, smiling, damnéd villain!
My tables — meet it is I set it down,
That one may smile, and smile, and be a villain;
At least I'm sure it may be so in Denmark: [*Writing.*
So, uncle, there you are. Now to my word;
It is " Adieu, adieu! remember me."   111
I have sworn 't.

    Mar. ⎫ [*Within*] My lord, my lord, —
    Hor. ⎭
    Mar.   [*Within*] Lord Hamlet, —
    Hor.   [*Within*] Heaven secure him!

77. **Unhouseled, etc.:** without the death rites of the church. 97. **globe:**
head. 98. **table:** tablet. 100. **pressures:** impressions.

Ham. So be it!

Hor. [*Within*] Hillo, ho, ho, my lord!

Ham. Hillo, ho, ho, boy! Come, bird, come.

Enter HORATIO and MARCELLUS.

Mar. How is 't, my noble lord?

Hor.   What news, my lord?

Ham. O, wonderful!

Hor.   Good my lord, tell it.

Ham. No; you'll reveal it.

Hor. Not I, my lord, by heaven.

Mar.   Nor I, my lord.   120

Ham. How say you, then, would heart of man once think it?
But you'll be secret?

Hor. }
Mar. }   Ay, by heaven, my lord.

Ham. There's ne'er a villain dwelling in all Denmark
But he's an arrant knave.

Hor. There needs no ghost, my lord, come from the
grave
To tell us this.

Ham.   Why, right; you are i' the right;
And so, without more circumstance at all,
I hold it fit that we shake hands and part:
You, as your business and desire shall point you;
For every man has business and desire,   130
Such as it is; and for mine own poor part,
Look you, I'll go pray.

Hor. These are but wild and whirling words, my lord.

Ham. I am sorry they offend you, heartily;
Yes, faith, heartily.

Hor.   There's no offence, my lord.

Ham. Yes, by Saint Patrick, but there is, Horatio,
And much offence too. Touching this vision here,
It is an honest ghost, that let me tell you.
For your desire to know what is between us,
O'ermaster 't as you may. And now, good friends,   140
As you are friends, scholars, and soldiers,
Give me one poor request.

Hor. What is 't, my lord? We will.

Ham. Never make known what you have seen tonight.

115. **Hillo, etc.:** a falconer's cry to his bird. 121. **once:** even. 138. **honest:** real, not an evil spirit.

Hor. \
Mar. / My lord, we will not.

Ham.   Nay, but swear 't.

Hor.   In faith,
My lord, not I.

Mar.   Nor I, my lord, in faith.

Ham.   Upon my sword.

Mar.   We have sworn, my lord, already.

Ham.   Indeed, upon my sword, indeed.

Ghost.   [*Beneath*] Swear.

Ham.   Ah, ha, boy! say'st thou so?   Art thou there, true-
          penny?   150
Come on — you hear this fellow in the cellarage —
Consent to swear.

Hor.   Propose the oath, my lord.

Ham.   Never to speak of this that you have seen,
Swear by my sword.

Ghost.   [*Beneath*] Swear.

Ham.   *Hic et ubique?*   Then we'll shift our ground.
Come hither, gentlemen,
And lay your hands again upon my sword:
Never to speak of this that you have heard,
Swear by my sword.   160

Ghost.   [*Beneath*] Swear.

Ham.   Well said, old mole!   Canst work i' the earth so
          fast?
A worthy pioner!   Once more remove, good friends.

Hor.   O day and night, but this is wondrous strange!

Ham.   And therefore as a stranger give it welcome.
There are more things in heaven and earth, Horatio,
Than are dreamt of in your philosophy.
But come;
Here, as before, never, so help you mercy,
How strange or odd soe'er I bear myself,   170
As I perchance hereafter shall think meet
To put an antic disposition on,
That you, at such times seeing me, never shall,
With arms encumbered thus, or this headshake,
Or by pronouncing of some doubtful phrase,

145. **Not I:** i.e., I'll not tell 147. **sword:** an old custom, the hilt of
the sword being considered a cross. 150. **truepenny:** good old chap. 156.
Hic et ubique: here and everywhere. 163. **pioner:** a soldier digging trenches.
172. **antic:** fantastic. 174. **encumbered:** folded.

As " Well, well, we know," or " We could, an if we would,"
Or " If we list to speak," or " There be, an if they might,"
Or such ambiguous giving out, to note
That you know aught of me: this not to do,
So grace and mercy at your most need help you,   180
Swear.
    Ghost. [*Beneath*] Swear.
    Ham.   Rest, rest, perturbéd spirit!   [*They swear.*]   So,
        gentlemen,
With all my love I do commend me to you:
And what so poor a man as Hamlet is
May do, to express his love and friending to you,
God willing, shall not lack.   Let us go in together;
And still your fingers on your lips, I pray.
The time is out of joint: O cursed spite,
That ever I was born to set it right!   190
Nay, come, let's go together.   [*Exeunt.*

ACT II

SCENE I.   *A room in Polonius' house.*

Enter POLONIUS *and* REYNALDO.

    Pol.   Give him this money and these notes, Reynaldo.
    Rey.   I will, my lord.
    Pol.   You shall do marvelous wisely, good Reynaldo,
Before you visit him, to make inquiry
Of his behavior.
    Rey.   My lord, I did intend it.
    Pol.   Marry, well said; very well said.   Look you, sir,
Inquire me first what Danskers are in Paris;
And how, and who, what means, and where they keep,
What company, at what expense; and finding
By this encompassment and drift of question   10
That they do know my son, come you more nearer
Than your particular demands will touch it.
Take you, as 'twere, some distant knowledge of him;
As thus, " I know his father and his friends,
And in part him."   Do you mark this, Reynaldo?
    Rey.   Ay, very well, my lord.

    10. **encompassment, etc.:** roundabout way.

Pol. " And in part him; but," you may say, " not well.
But, if 't be he I mean, he's very wild;
Addicted so and so ": and there put on him
What forgeries you please; marry, none so rank　20
As may dishonor him; take heed of that;
But, sir, such wanton, wild and usual slips
As are companions noted and most known
To youth and liberty.
　　Rey. 　　　　As gaming, my lord.
　　Pol. Ay, or drinking, fencing, swearing, quarreling:
You may go so far.
　　Rey. My lord, that would dishonor him.
　　Pol. Faith, no; as you may season it in the charge.
You must not put another scandal on him,
That he is open to incontinency;　30
That's not my meaning; but breathe his faults so quaintly
That they may seem the taints of liberty,
The flash and outbreak of a fiery mind,
A savageness in unreclaiméd blood,
Of general assault.
　　Rey. 　　　　But, my good lord, —
　　Pol. Wherefore should you do this?
　　Rey. 　　　　　　　Ay, my lord,
I would know that.
　　Pol. 　　　　Marry, sir, here's my drift;
And, I believe, it is a fetch of warrant:
You laying these slight sullies on my son,
As 'twere a thing a little soiled i' the working,
Mark you,　41
Your party in converse, him you would sound,
Having ever seen in the prenominate crimes
The youth you breathe of guilty, be assured
He closes with you in this consequence;
" Good sir," or so, or " friend," or " gentleman,"
According to the phrase or the addition
Of man and country.
　　Rey. 　　　　Very good, my lord.
　　Pol. And then, sir, does he this — he does — what was I
about to say? By the mass, I was about to say something.
Where did I leave?　51

31. **quaintly:** cleverly.　35. **general assault:** common to all men.　38.
fetch of warrant: justifiable trick.

Rey. At " closes in the consequence," at " friend or so,"
and " gentleman."

Pol. At " closes in the consequence," ay, marry;
He closes thus: " I know the gentleman;
I saw him yesterday, or t' other day,
Or then, or then; with such, or such; and, as you say,
There was a' gaming; there o'ertook in 's rouse;
There falling out at tennis "; or perchance,
" I saw him enter such a house of sale,"   60
Videlicet, a brothel, or so forth.
See you now;
Your bait of falsehood takes this carp of truth:
And thus do we of wisdom and of reach,
With windlasses and with assays of bias,
By indirections find directions out.
So by my former lecture and advice,
Shall you my son. You have me, have you not?
      Rey. My lord, I have.
      Pol.   God be wi' you; fare you well.
      Rey. Good my lord!   70
      Pol. Observe his inclination in yourself.
      Rey. I shall, my lord.
      Pol. And let him ply his music.
      Rey.   Well, my lord.
      Pol. Farewell!   [*Exit Reynaldo.*

Enter OPHELIA.

                  How now, Ophelia! what's the matter?
      Oph. O, my lord, my lord, I have been so affrighted!
      Pol. With what, i' the name of God?
      Oph. My lord, as I was sewing in my closet,
Lord Hamlet, with his doublet all unbraced;
No hat upon his head; his stockings fouled,
Ungartered, and down-gyvéd to his ankle;   80
Pale as his shirt; his knees knocking each other;
And with a look so piteous in purport
As if he had been loosed out of hell
To speak of horrors — he comes before me.
      Pol. Mad for thy love?

---

61. **videlicet:** namely.   64. **we of, etc.:** we wise and farsighted people.
65. " With roundabout and indirect ways." 71. **in yourself:** for yourself.
73. **ply his music:** follow his own way. 80. **down-gyvéd:** resembling fetters.

Oph.   My lord, I do not know;
But truly, I do fear it.
    Pol.   What said he?
    Oph. He took me by the wrist and held me hard;
Then goes he to the length of all his arm;
And, with his other hand thus o'er his brow,
He falls to such perusal of my face   90
As he would draw it. Long stayed he so;
At last, a little shaking of mine arm
And thrice his head thus waving up and down,
He raised a sigh so piteous and profound
As it did seem to shatter all his bulk
And end his being: that done, he lets me go;
And, with his head over his shoulder turned,
He seemed to find his way without his eyes;
For out o' doors he went without their helps,
And, to the last, bended their light on me.   100
    Pol. Come, go with me: I will go seek the king.
This is the very ecstasy of love,
Whose violent property fordoes itself
And leads the will to desperate undertakings
As oft as any passion under heaven
That does afflict our natures. I am sorry.
What, have you given him any hard words of late?
    Oph. No, my good lord, but, as you did command,
I did repel his letters and denied
His access to me.
    Pol.   That hath made him mad.   110
I am sorry that with better heed and judgment
I had not quoted him. I feared he did but trifle,
And meant to wreck thee; but, beshrew my jealousy!
By heaven, it is as proper to our age
To cast beyond ourselves in our opinions
As it is common for the younger sort
To lack discretion. Come, go we to the king:
This must be known; which, being kept close, might move
More grief to hide than hate to utter love.   [*Exeunt.*

  102. **ecstasy:** frenzy. 112. **quoted:** observed. 115. **cast beyond:** over-shoot.

Scene II. *A room in the castle.*

Enter King, Queen, Rosencrantz, Guildenstern, *and* Attendants.

King. Welcome, dear Rosencrantz and Guildenstern!
Moreover that we much did long to see you,
The need we have to use you did provoke
Our hasty sending. Something have you heard
Of Hamlet's transformation; so call it,
Sith nor the exterior nor the inward man
Resembles that it was. What it should be,
More than his father's death, that thus hath put him
So much from the understanding of himself,
I cannot dream of. I entreat you both,   10
That, being of so young days brought up with him,
And sith so neighbored to his youth and havior,
That you vouchsafe your rest here in our court
Some little time; so by your companies
To draw him on to pleasures, and to gather,
So much as from occasion you may glean,
Whether aught, to us unknown, afflicts him thus,
That, opened, lies within our remedy.
Queen. Good gentlemen, he hath much talked of you;
And sure I am two men there are not living   20
To whom he more adheres. If it will please you
To show us so much gentry and good will
As to expend your time with us awhile,
For the supply and profit of our hope,
Your visitation shall receive such thanks
As fits a king's remembrance.
Ros.   Both your majesties
Might, by the sovereign power you have of us,
Put your dread pleasures more into command
Than to entreaty.
Guil.   But we both obey,
And here give up ourselves, in the full bent   30
To lay our service freely at your feet,
To be commanded.
King. Thanks, Rosencrantz and gentle Guildenstern.
Queen. Thanks, Guildenstern and gentle Rosencrantz:

2. **moreover that:** besides that. 22. **gentry:** courtesy.

And I beseech you instantly to visit
My too much changéd son. Go, some of you,
And bring these gentlemen where Hamlet is.
   Guil. Heavens make our presence and our practices
Pleasant and helpful to him!
   Queen.   Ay, amen!
   [*Exeunt Rosencrantz, Guildenstern, and some Attendants.*

Enter POLONIUS.

   Pol. The ambassadors from Norway, my good lord,   40
Are joyfully returned.
   King. Thou still hast been the father of good news.
   Pol. Have I, my lord? I assure you, my good liege,
I hold my duty, as I hold my soul,
Both to my God and to my gracious king.
And I do think, or else this brain of mine
Hunts not the trail of policy so sure
As it hath used to do, that I have found
The very cause of Hamlet's lunacy.
   King. O, speak of that; that do I long to hear.   50
   Pol. Give first admittance to the ambassadors;
My news shall be the fruit to that great feast.
   King. Thyself do grace to them, and bring them in.
                          [*Exit Polonius.*
He tells me, my dear Gertrude, he hath found
The head and source of all your son's distemper.
   Queen. I doubt it is no other but the main,
His father's death, and our o'erhasty marriage.
   King. Well, we shall sift him.

   Reënter POLONIUS, *with* VOLTIMAND *and* CORNELIUS.

                    Welcome, my good friends!
Say, Voltimand, what from our brother Norway?
   Volt. Most fair return of greetings and desires.   60
Upon our first, he sent out to suppress
His nephew's levies; which to him appeared
To be a preparation 'gainst the Polack;
But, better looked into, he truly found
It was against your highness: whereat grieved,
That so his sickness, age and impotence
Was falsely borne in hand, sends out arrests

   42. **still:** always. 47. **policy:** public affairs. 67. **arrests:** measures to
stop him.

On Fortinbras; which he, in brief, obeys;
Receives rebuke from Norway, and in fine
Makes vow before his uncle never more   70
To give the assay of arms against your majesty.
Whereon old Norway, overcome with joy,
Gives him three thousand crowns in annual fee,
And his commission to employ those soldiers,
So levied as before, against the Polack:
With an entreaty, herein further shown,   [*Giving a paper.*
That it might please you to give quiet pass
Through your dominions for this enterprise,
On such regards of safety and allowance
As therein are set down.
      King.   It likes us well;   80
And at our more considered time we'll read,
Answer, and think upon this business.
Meantime we thank you for your well-took labor:
Go to your rest; at night we'll feast together.
Most welcome home!   [*Exeunt Voltimand and Cornelius.*
      Pol.   This business is well ended.
My liege, and madam, to expostulate
What majesty should be, what duty is,
Why day is day, night night, and time is time,
Were nothing but to waste night, day and time.
Therefore, since brevity is the soul of wit,   90
And tediousness the limbs and outward flourishes,
I will be brief. Your noble son is mad.
Mad call I it; for, to define true madness,
What is 't but to be nothing else but mad?
But let that go.
      Queen.   More matter, with less art.
      Pol.   Madam, I swear I use no art at all.
That he is mad, 'tis true: 'tis true 'tis pity;
And pity 'tis 'tis true. A foolish figure;
But farewell it, for I will use no art.
Mad let us grant him, then; and now remains
That we find out the cause of this effect,   101
Or rather say, the cause of this defect,
For this effect defective comes by cause.
Thus it remains, and the remainder thus.

71. **assay:** trial. 81. **considered time:** fitter time to consider. 86. **ex-postulate:** discuss. 90. **wit:** wisdom.

Perpend.
I have a daughter — have while she is mine —
Who, in her duty and obedience, mark,
Hath given me this. Now gather, and surmise.   [*Reads.*
" To the celestial and my soul's idol, the most beautified
Ophelia," —   110
That's an ill phrase, a vile phrase; " beautified " is a vile
phrase. But you shall hear. Thus: [*Reads.*
" In her excellent white bosom, these, &c."
    Queen.   Came this from Hamlet to her?
    Pol.   Good madam, stay awhile; I will be faithful. [*Reads.*
            " Doubt thou the stars are fire;
                Doubt that the sun doth move;
                Doubt truth to be a liar;
                    But never doubt I love.   119
" O dear Ophelia, I am ill at these numbers; I have not art
to reckon my groans: but that I love thee best, O most best,
believe it. Adieu.
    " Thine evermore, most dear lady, whilst this machine is to
him,   Hamlet."
This, in obedience, hath my daughter shown me,
And more above, hath his solicitings,
As they fell out by time, by means and place,
All given to mine ear.
    King.   But how hath she
Received his love?
    Pol.   What do you think of me?
    King.   As of a man faithful and honorable.
    Pol.   I would fain prove so. But what might you think, 131
When I had seen this hot love on the wing —
As I perceived it, I must tell you that,
Before my daughter told me — what might you,
Or my dear majesty your queen here, think,
If I had played the desk or table-book,
Or given my heart a winking, mute and dumb,
Or looked upon this love with idle sight;
What might you think? No, I went round to work,
And my young mistress thus I did bespeak:
" Lord Hamlet is a prince, out of thy star;   141
This must not be." And then I prescripts gave her,

---

105. **Perpend:** consider. 126. **more above:** besides. 136. **desk or table-book:** kept it secret. 141. **out of thy star:** of higher rank.

That she should lock herself from his resort,
Admit no messengers, receive no tokens.
Which done, she took the fruits of my advice;
And he, repulsed — a short tale to make —
Fell into a sadness, then into a fast,
Thence to a watch, thence into a weakness,
Thence to a lightness, and, by this declension,
Into the madness wherein now he raves,   150
And all we mourn for.
   King.   Do you think 'tis this?
   Queen. It may be, very likely.
   Pol. Hath there been such a time — I'd fain know that —
That I have positive said " 'Tis so,"
When it proved otherwise?
   King.   Not that I know.
   Pol. [*Pointing to his head and shoulders*] Take this from
      this, if this be otherwise:
If circumstances lead me, I will find
Where truth is hid, though it were hid indeed
Within the center.
   King.   How may we try it further?
   Pol. You know, sometimes he walks four hours together
Here in the lobby.
   Queen.   So he does indeed.   161
   Pol. At such a time I'll loose my daughter to him:
Be you and I behind an arras then;
Mark the encounter: if he love her not
And be not from his reason fall'n thereon,
Let me be no assistant for a state,
But keep a farm and carters.
   King.   We will try it.
   Queen. But, look, where sadly the poor wretch comes read-
      ing.
   Pol. Away, I do beseech you, both away.
I'll board him presently.

              [*Exeunt King, Queen, and Attendants.*

        Enter Hamlet, *reading.*

                O, give me leave: 170
How does my good Lord Hamlet?
   Ham. Well, God-a-mercy.
   Pol. Do you know me, my lord?

        148. **watch:** sleeplessness.

Ham.   Excellent well; you are a fishmonger.

Pol.   Not I, my lord.

Ham.   Then I would you were so honest a man.

Pol.   Honest, my lord!

Ham.   Ay, sir; to be honest, as this world goes, is to be one man picked out of ten thousand.

Pol.   That's very true, my lord.   180

Ham.   For if the sun breed maggots in a dead dog, being a god kissing carrion — Have you a daughter?

Pol.   I have, my lord.

Ham.   Let her not walk i' the sun. Conception is a blessing: but not as your daughter may conceive. Friend, look to 't.

Pol.   [*Aside*] How say you by that? Still harping on my daughter. Yet he knew me not at first; he said I was a fishmonger. He is far gone, far gone; and truly in my youth I suffered much extremity for love; very near this. I'll speak to him again. What do you read, my lord?

Ham.   Words, words, words.

Pol.   What is the matter, my lord?

Ham.   Between who?

Pol.   I mean, the matter that you read, my lord.

Ham.   Slanders, sir; for the satirical rogue says here that old men have gray beards, that their faces are wrinkled, their eyes purging thick amber and plum-tree gum and that they have a plentiful lack of wit, together with most weak hams: all which, sir, though I most powerfully and potently believe, yet I hold it not honesty to have it thus set down, for yourself, sir, should be old as I am, if like a crab you could go backward.

Pol.   [*Aside*] Though this be madness, yet there is method in 't. Will you walk out of the air, my lord?

Ham.   Into my grave.   210

Pol.   Indeed, that is out o' the air. [*Aside*] How pregnant sometimes his replies are! a happiness that often madness hits on, which reason and sanity could not so prosperously be delivered of. I will leave him, and suddenly contrive the means of meeting between him and my daughter. — My honorable lord, I will most humbly take my leave of you.

Ham.   You cannot, sir, take from me any thing that I will more willingly part withal: except my life, except my life, except my life.

---

182. **god:** sometimes amended to **good.** 201. **honesty:** decency.

Pol.   Fare you well, my lord.

Ham.   These tedious old fools!

Enter ROSENCRANTZ *and* GUILDENSTERN.

Pol.   You go to seek the Lord Hamlet; there he is.

Ros.   [*To Polonius*] God save you, sir!   [*Exit Polonius.*

Guil.   My honored lord!

Ros.   My most dear lord!

Ham.   My excellent good friends!   How dost thou, Guildenstern?   Ah, Rosencrantz!   Good lads, how do ye both? 230

Ros.   As the indifferent children of the earth.

Guil.   Happy, in that we are not overhappy;
On fortune's cap we are not the very button.

Ham.   Nor the soles of her shoe?

Ros.   Neither, my lord.

Ham.   Then you live about her waist, or in the middle of her favors?   What's the news?

Ros.   None, my lord, but that the world's grown honest.

Ham.   Then is doomsday near: but your news is not true. Let me question more in particular: what have you, my good friends, deserved at the hands of fortune, that she sends you to prison thither?

Guil.   Prison, my lord!

Ham.   Denmark's a prison.

Ros.   Then is the world one.   250

Ham.   A goodly one; in which there are many confines, wards and dungeons, Denmark being one o' the worst.

Ros.   We think not so, my lord.

Ham.   Why, then, 'tis none to you; for there is nothing either good or bad, but thinking makes it so.   To me it is a prison.

Ros.   Why then, your ambition makes it one; 'tis too narrow for your mind.   259

Ham.   O God, I could be bounded in a nutshell and count myself a king of infinite space, were it not that I have bad dreams.

Guil.   Which dreams indeed are ambition, for the very substance of the ambition is merely the shadow of a dream.

Ham.   A dream itself is but a shadow.

Ros.   Truly, and I hold ambition of so airy and light a quality that it is but a shadow's shadow.

Ham.   Then are our beggars bodies, and our monarchs and

outstretched heroes the beggars' shadows. Shall we to the
court? for, by my fay, I cannot reason.

Ros. ⎫
Guil. ⎭ We'll wait upon you.

Ham. No such matter: I will not sort you with the rest of
my servants, for, to speak to you like an honest man, I am
most dreadfully attended. But, in the beaten way of friendship, what make you at Elsinore?

Ros. To visit you, my lord; no other occasion.   279

Ham. Beggar that I am, I am even poor in thanks; but I
thank you; and sure, dear friends, my thanks are too dear a
halfpenny. Were you not sent for? Is it your own inclining?
Is it a free visitation? Come, deal justly with me. Come,
come; nay, speak.

Guil. What should we say, my lord?

Ham. Why, any thing, but to the purpose. You were sent
for; and there is a kind of confession in your looks which your
modesties have not craft enough to color. I know the good
king and queen have sent for you.   291

Ros. To what end, my lord?

Ham. That you must teach me. But let me conjure you,
by the rights of our fellowship, by the consonancy of our youth,
by the obligation of our ever-preserved love, and by what more
dear a better proposer could charge you withal, be even and
direct with me, whether you were sent for, or no?

Ros. [*Aside to Guil.*] What say you?   300

Ham. [*Aside*] Nay, then, I have an eye of you. — If you
love me, hold not off.

Guil. My lord, we were sent for.

Ham. I will tell you why; so shall my anticipation prevent
your discovery, and your secrecy to the king and queen molt
no feather. I have of late — but wherefore I know not — lost
all my mirth, forgone all custom of exercises; and indeed it goes
so heavily with my disposition that this goodly frame, the
earth, seems to me a sterile promontory, this most excellent
canopy, the air, look you, this brave o'erhanging firmament,
this majestical roof fretted with golden fire, why, it appears no
other thing to me than a foul and pestilent congregation of
vapors. What a piece of work is a man! how noble in reason!
how infinite in faculty! in form and moving how express and
admirable! in action how like an angel! in apprehension how

296. **proposer:** speaker. 301. **eye of you:** i.e., I'm " on " to you.

like a god! the beauty of the world! the paragon of animals!
And yet, to me, what is this quintessence of dust? Man delights not me; no, nor woman neither, though by your smiling
you seem to say so.   323

Ros. My lord, there was no such stuff in my thoughts.

Ham. Why did you laugh then, when I said " man delights not me " ?

Ros. To think, my lord, if you delight not in man, what
lenten entertainment the players shall receive from you. We
coted them on the way; and hither are they coming, to offer
you service.

Ham. He that plays the king shall be welcome; his majesty shall have tribute of me; the adventurous knight shall use
his foil and target; the lover shall not sigh gratis; the humorous man shall end his part in peace; the clown shall make
those laugh whose lungs are tickle o' the sere; and the lady
shall say her mind freely, or the blank verse shall halt for 't.
What players are they?   340

Ros. Even those you were wont to take delight in, the
tragedians of the city.

Ham. How chances it they travel? Their residence, both in
reputation and profit, was better both ways.

Ros. I think their inhibition comes by the means of the late
innovation.

Ham. Do they hold the same estimation they did when I
was in the city? Are they so followed?   350

Ros. No, indeed, are they not.

Ham. How comes it? Do they grow rusty?

Ros. Nay, their endeavor keeps in the wonted pace; but
there is, sir, an aery of children, little eyases, that cry out on
the top of question, and are most tyrannically clapped for 't:
these are now the fashion, and so berattle the common stages
— so they call them — that many wearing rapiers are afraid
of goose-quills and dare scarce come thither.   360

Ham. What, are they children? Who maintains 'em?
How are they escoted? Will they pursue the quality no longer

---

328. **lenten:** meager. 329. **coted:** passed. 336. **humorous:** not the
" funny " man, but the eccentric one. 338. **tickle o' the sere:** easily moved
to laughter. 345. **inhibition:** because of the " late innovation," i.e., the
children's companies, the regular players were out of favor. 354. **aery;
eyases:** comparing the child actors to young hawks in a nest, crying out their
lines " on the top of the question," i.e., shrilly. 360. **goose-quills:** theatergoers are afraid of being satirized if they do not attend the children's
performances. 362. **escoted:** supported. 362. **quality:** profession.

than they can sing? Will they not say afterwards, if they should grow themselves to common players — as it is most like, if their means are no better — their writers do them wrong, to make them exclaim against their own succession?

Ros. Faith, there has been much to do on both sides; and the nation holds it no sin to tarre them to controversy. There was, for a while, no money bid for argument, unless the poet and the player went to cuffs in the question.

Ham. Is 't possible?

Guil. O, there has been much throwing about of brains.

Ham. Do the boys carry it away?

Ros. Ay, that they do, my lord; Hercules and his load too.   379

Ham. It is not very strange; for mine uncle is king of Denmark, and those that would make mows at him while my father lived, give twenty, forty, fifty, an hundred ducats apiece for his picture in little. 'Sblood, there is something in this more than natural, if philosophy could find it out.

[*Flourish of trumpets within.*

Guil. There are the players.

Ham. Gentlemen, you are welcome to Elsinore. Your hands, come then. The appurtenance of welcome is fashion and ceremony. Let me comply with you in this garb, lest my extent to the players, which, I tell you, must show fairly outward, should more appear like entertainment than yours. You are welcome: but my uncle-father and aunt-mother are deceived.

Guil. In what, my dear lord?

Ham. I am but mad north-northwest: when the wind is southerly I know a hawk from a handsaw.

Reënter POLONIUS.

Pol. Well be with you, gentlemen!

Ham. Hark you, Guildenstern; and you too: at each ear a hearer: that great baby you see there is not yet out of his swaddling-clouts.   401

---

363. **sing:** the child actors were choir boys. 368. **tarre:** set on. 369. **argument:** plot, i.e., no play was accepted unless the " cuffs in the question " were introduced. 377. **carry it away:** win out. 378. **Hercules:** Hercules carrying the globe was the sign of the Globe Theater. 383. **in this:** i.e., in this fickleness of the public. 388. **comply with:** i.e., I'll show you the customary courtesy. 389. **extent:** behavior. 397. **handsaw:** a corruption of the word **heronshaw,** heron. The idea of the passage is taken from falconry.

Ros. Happily he's the second time come to them; for they say an old man is twice a child.

Ham. I will prophesy he comes to tell me of the players; mark it. You say right, sir: o' Monday morning; 'twas so indeed.

Pol. My lord, I have news to tell you.

Ham. My lord, I have news to tell you. When Roscius was an actor in Rome —   410

Pol. The actors, are come hither, my lord.

Ham. Buzz, buzz!

Pol. Upon mine honor —

Ham. Then came each actor on his ass —

Pol. The best actors in the world, either for tragedy, comedy, history, pastoral, pastoral-comical, historical-pastoral, tragical-historical, tragical-comical-historical-pastoral, scene individable, or poem unlimited: Seneca cannot be too heavy, nor Plautus too light. For the law of writ and the liberty, these are the only men.   421

Ham. O Jephthah, judge of Israel, what a treasure hadst thou!

Pol. What a treasure had he, my lord?

Ham. Why,
        "One fair daughter, and no more,
            The which he lovéd passing well."

Pol. [*Aside*] Still on my daughter.

Ham. Am I not i' the right, old Jephthah?

Pol. If you call me Jephthah, my lord, I have a daughter that I love passing well.   431

Ham. Nay, that follows not.

Pol. What follows, then, my lord?

Ham. Why,
        "As by lot, God wot,"
and then, you know,
        "It came to pass, as most like it was — "
The first row of the pious chanson will show you more; for look, where my abridgment comes.   439

412. **Buzz, buzz:** equivalent to "old stuff." 418–19. **Seneca, Plautus:** the one a Roman writer of tragedy; the other a Roman writer of comedy. Both greatly influenced the Elizabethan drama. 420. **For the law, etc.:** for repeating the text accurately and for making additions of their own. 422. **Jephthah:** an Old Testament story popular in ballads. 439. **abridgment:** something that interrupts. The word was also used to mean **play.**

Enter four or five Players.

You are welcome, masters; welcome all. I am glad to see
thee well. Welcome, good friends. O, my old friend! thy
face is valanced since I saw thee last: comest thou to beard
me in Denmark? What, my young lady and mistress! By 'r
lady, your ladyship is nearer to heaven than when I saw you
last, by the altitude of a chopine. Pray God, your voice, like
a piece of uncurrent gold, be not cracked within the ring.
Masters, you are all welcome. We'll e'en to 't like French fal-
coners, fly at any thing we see; we'll have a speech straight.
Come, give us a taste of your quality; come, a passionate
speech.   451

First Play. What speech, my lord?

Ham. I heard thee speak me a speech once, but it was
never acted; or, if it was, not above once; for the play, I remember, pleased not the million; 'twas caviare to the general;
but it was — as I received it, and others, whose judgments in
such matters cried in the top of mine — an excellent play, well
digested in the scenes, set down with as much modesty as cunning. I remember, one said there were no sallets in the lines
to make the matter savory, nor no matter in the phrase that
might indict the author of affectation; but called it an honest
method, as wholesome as sweet, and by very much more handsome than fine. One speech in it I chiefly loved: 'twas
Aeneas' tale to Dido; and thereabout of it especially, where he
speaks of Priam's slaughter. If it live in your memory, begin
at this line: let me see, let me see —   471
   " The rugged Pyrrhus, like the Hyrcanian beast — "
it is not so — it begins with Pyrrhus:
   " The rugged Pyrrhus, he whose sable arms,
     Black as his purpose, did the night resemble
     When he lay couched in the ominous horse,
     Hath now this dread and black complexion smeared
     With heraldry more dismal; head to foot
     Now is he total gules; horridly tricked
     With blood of fathers, mothers, daughters, sons,   480

---

442. **Valanced:** bearded. 443. **my young lady:** pleasantly spoken to the boy
who played feminine rôles. 445. **chopine:** high-heeled shoe, much in style.
455. **caviare:** too good for the common public. 457. **in the top of:** superior.
459. **no sallets:** nothing spicy, in an indecent sense. 463. **Aeneas' tale:** see
cyclopedia. 472. **Pyrrhus:** the son of Achilles and one of the Greeks in the
" ominous horse," i.e., the wooden horse in the story of the fall of Troy.
472. **Hyrcanian beast:** tiger. 479. **total gules:** red from head to foot.

      Baked and impasted with the parching streets,
      That lend a tyrannous and damnéd light
      To their lord's murder. Roasted in wrath and fire,
      And thus o'er-sized with coagulate gore,
      With eyes like carbuncles, the hellish Pyrrhus
      Old grandsire Priam seeks."
So, proceed you.

   Pol. 'Fore God, my lord, well spoken, with good accent and
good discretion.

   First Play.   " Anon he finds him   490
      Striking too short at Greeks; his antique sword,
      Rebellious to his arm, lies where it falls,
      Repugnant to command. Unequal matched,
      Pyrrhus at Priam drives; in rage strikes wide;
      But with the whiff and wind of his fell sword
      The unnervéd father falls. Then senseless Ilium,
      Seeming to feel this blow, with flaming top
      Stoops to his base, and with a hideous crash
      Takes prisoner Pyrrhus' ear; for, lo! his sword,
      Which was declining on the milky head   500
      Of reverend Priam, seemed i' the air to stick.
      So, as a painted tyrant, Pyrrhus stood,
      And like a neutral to his will and matter,
      Did nothing.
      But, as we often see, against some storm,
      A silence in the heavens, the rack stand still,
      The bold winds speechless and the orb below
      As hush as death, anon the dreadful thunder
      Doth rend the region, so, after Pyrrhus' pause,
      Aroused vengeance sets him new a-work;   510
      And never did the Cyclops' hammers fall
      On Mars's armor forged for proof eterne
      With less remorse than Pyrrhus' bleeding sword
      Now falls on Priam.
      Out, out, thou strumpet, Fortune! All you gods,
      In general synod, take away her power;
      Break all the spokes and fellies from her wheel,
      And bowl the round nave down the hill of heaven,
      As low as to the fiends! "

482. **tyrannous:** savage.   484. **o'er-sized:** besmeared.   496. **senseless:**
without feeling.   502. **painted:** stationary, as in a picture.   503. **neutral:**
undecided.   505. **against:** before.   506. **rack:** clouds.   517. **fellies:** rim of
a wheel.

Pol.   This is too long.   520
Ham.   It shall to the barber's, with your beard.   Prithee,
say on; he's for a jig or a tale of bawdry, or he sleeps.   Say
on; come to Hecuba.
First Play.   " But who, O, who had seen the mobled
queen — "
Ham.   " The mobled queen " ?
Pol.   That's good; " mobled queen " is good.
First Play.   " Run barefoot up and down threatening the
          flames
   With bisson rheum; a clout upon that head
   Where late the diadem stood, and for a robe,   530
   About her lank and all o'er-teeméd loins,
   A blanket, in the alarm of fear caught up;
   Who this had seen, with tongue in venom steeped,
   'Gainst Fortune's state would treason have pronounced.
   But if the gods themselves did see her then
   When she saw Pyrrhus make malicious sport
   In mincing with his sword her husband's limbs,
   The instant burst of clamor that she made,
   Unless things mortal move them not at all,
   Would have made milch the burning eyes of heaven,   540
   And passion in the gods."
Pol.   Look, whether he has not turned his color and has
tears in 's eyes.   Pray you, no more.
Ham.   'Tis well; I'll have thee speak out the rest soon.
Good my lord, will you see the players well bestowed?   Do you
hear, let them be well used; for they are the abstract and brief
chronicles of the time; after your death you were better have a
bad epitaph than their ill report while you live.
Pol.   My lord, I will use them according to their desert.
Ham.   God's bodykins, man, much better.   Use every man
after his desert, and who should 'scape whipping?   Use them
after your own honor and dignity.   The less they deserve, the
more merit is in your bounty.   Take them in.
Pol.   Come, sirs.   559
Ham.   Follow him, friends: we'll hear a play tomorrow.
[*Exit Polonius with all the Players but the First.*]   Dost thou
hear me, old friend?   Can you play the Murder of Gonzago?
First Play.   Ay, my lord.

524. **mobled:** with head covered.   529. **bisson rheum:** blinding tears.
529. **clout:** cloth.   540. **milch:** moist.   541. **passion:** sympathy.

Ham. We'll ha 't tomorrow night. You could, for a need, study a speech of some dozen or sixteen lines, which I would set down and insert in 't, could you not?

First Play. Ay, my lord. 569

Ham. Very well. Follow that lord; and look you mock him not. [*Exit First Player.*] My good friends, I'll leave you till night. You are welcome to Elsinore.

Ros. Good my lord!

Ham. Ay, so, God be wi' ye. [*Exeunt Rosencrantz and Guildenstern.*] Now I am alone.

O, what a rogue and peasant slave am I!
Is it not monstrous that this player here,
But in a fiction, in a dream of passion,
Could force his soul so to his own conceit
That from her working all his visage wanned,
Tears in his eyes, distraction in 's aspect, 581
A broken voice, and his whole function suiting
With forms to his conceit? And all for nothing!
For Hecuba!
What's Hecuba to him, or he to Hecuba,
That he should weep for her? What would he do,
Had he the motive and the cue for passion
That I have? He would drown the stage with tears
And cleave the general ear with horrid speech,
Make mad the guilty and appall the free, 590
Confound the ignorant, and amaze indeed
The very faculties of eyes and ears.
Yet I,
A dull and muddy-mettled rascal, peak,
Like John-a-dreams, unpregnant of my cause,
And can say nothing; no, not for a king,
Upon whose property and most dear life
A damned defeat was made. Am I a coward?
Who calls me villain? breaks my pate across?
Plucks off my beard, and blows it in my face?
Tweaks me by the nose? gives me the lie i' the throat, 601
As deep as to the lungs? who does me this?

566. **study:** learn by heart. 576. **peasant slave:** one bound to the land; a serf. 579. **conceit:** his conception of the part he was playing. 580. **her:** the soul's. 582. **function, etc.:** acting as fitted the part. 590. **free:** innocent. 594. **muddy-mettled:** irresolute. 594. **peak:** mope. 595. **John-a-dreams:** John the dreamer. 595. **unpregnant of:** indifferent to. 597. **property:** kingly rights

Ha!
'Swounds, I should take it; for it cannot be
But I am pigeon-livered and lack gall
To make oppression bitter, or ere this
I should have fatted all the region kites
With this slave's offal: bloody, bawdy villain!
Remorseless, treacherous, lecherous, kindless villain!
O, vengeance!   610
Why, what an ass am I!   This is most brave,
That I, the son of a dear father murdered,
Prompted to my revenge by heaven and hell,
Must, like a wench, unpack my heart with words,
And fall a-cursing, like a very drab,
A scullion!
Fie upon 't! foh!   About, my brain!   I have heard
That guilty creatures sitting at a play
Have by the very cunning of the scene
Been struck so to the soul that presently   620
They have proclaimed their malefactions;
For murder, though it have no tongue, will speak
With most miraculous organ.   I'll have these players
Play something like the murder of my father
Before mine uncle.   I'll observe his looks;
I'll tent him to the quick.   If he but blench,
I know my course.   The spirit that I have seen
May be the devil; and the devil hath power
To assume a pleasing shape; yea, and perhaps
Out of my weakness and my melancholy,   630
As he is very potent with such spirits,
Abuses me to damn me.   I'll have grounds
More relative than this.   The play's the thing
Wherein I'll catch the conscience of the king.   [*Exit.*

604. **'Swounds:** God's wounds, a common oath. 605. **pigeon-livered:**
gentle, not necessarily cowardly. 605. **gall:** spirit. The lack of gall was
supposed to make pigeons gentle. 607. **region kites:** kites (vultures) of the
air. 609. **kindless:** unnatural. 617. **about:** i.e., act instead of talk. 626.
tent: probe. 633. **this:** i.e., the ghost's revelation.

ACT III

Scene I. *A room in the castle.*

Enter King, Queen, Polonius, Ophelia, Rosencrantz, *and* Guildenstern.

King. And can you, by no drift of circumstance,
Get from him why he puts on this confusion,
Grating so harshly all his days of quiet
With turbulent and dangerous lunacy?
Ros. He does confess he feels himself distracted;
But from what cause he will by no means speak.
Guil. Nor do we find him forward to be sounded,
But, with a crafty madness, keeps aloof,
When we would bring him on to some confession
Of his true state.
Queen. Did he receive you well? 10
Ros. Most like a gentleman.
Guil. But with much forcing of his disposition.
Ros. Niggard of question; but, of our demands,
Most free in his reply.
Queen. Did you assay him
To any pastime?
Ros. Madam, it so fell out, that certain players
We o'er-raught on the way; of these we told him;
And there did seem in him a kind of joy
To hear of it. They are about the court,
And, as I think, they have already order 20
This night to play before him.
Pol. 'Tis most true.
And he beseeched me to entreat your majesties
To hear and see the matter.
King. With all my heart; and it doth much content me
To hear him so inclined.
Good gentlemen, give him a further edge,
And drive his purpose on to these delights.
Ros. We shall, my lord.
[*Exeunt Rosencrantz and Guildenstern.*
King. Sweet Gertrude, leave us too;
For we have closely sent for Hamlet hither,

1. **drift of circumstance:** roundabout way. 7. **forward:** inclined.

That he, as 'twere by accident, may here   30
Affront Ophelia.
Her father and myself, lawful espials,
Will so bestow ourselves that, seeing, unseen,
We may of their encounter frankly judge,
And gather by him, as he is behaved,
If 't be the affliction of his love or no
That thus he suffers for.
   Queen.   I shall obey you.
And for your part, Ophelia, I do wish
That your good beauties be the happy cause
Of Hamlet's wildness. So shall I hope your virtues   40
Will bring him to his wonted way again,
To both your honors.
   Oph.   Madam, I wish it may.   [*Exit Queen.*
   Pol. Ophelia, walk you here. Gracious, so please you,
We will bestow ourselves. [*To Ophelia*] Read on this book;
That show of such an exercise may color
Your loneliness. We are oft to blame in this —
'Tis too much proved — that with devotion's visage
And pious action we do sugar o'er
The devil himself.
   King. [*Aside*] O, 'tis too true!
How smart a lash that speech doth give my conscience!   50
The harlot's cheek, beautied with plastering art,
Is not more ugly to the thing that helps it
Than is my deed to my most painted word.
O heavy burthen!
   Pol. I hear him coming: let's withdraw, my lord.
                    [*Exeunt King and Polonius.*

               Enter Hamlet.

   Ham. To be, or not to be: that is the question.
Whether 'tis nobler in the mind to suffer
The slings and arrows of outrageous fortune,
Or to take arms against a sea of troubles,
And by opposing end them? To die: to sleep;
No more; and by a sleep to say we end   61
The heartache and the thousand natural shocks
That flesh is heir to, 'tis a consummation

        31. **affront:** confront. 56. **To be:** to live.

Devoutly to be wished. To die, to sleep;
To sleep: perchance to dream. Ay, there's the rub;
For in that sleep of death what dreams may come
When we have shuffled off this mortal coil,
Must give us pause. There's the respect
That makes calamity of so long life;
For who would bear the whips and scorns of time,   70
The oppressor's wrong, the proud man's contumely,
The pangs of despised love, the law's delay,
The insolence of office and the spurns
That patient merit of the unworthy takes,
When he himself might his quietus make
With a bare bodkin? Who would fardels bear,
To grunt and sweat under a weary life,
But that the dread of something after death,
The undiscovered country from whose bourn
No traveler returns, puzzles the will   80
And makes us rather bear those ills we have
Than fly to others that we know not of?
Thus conscience does make cowards of us all;
And thus the native hue of resolution
Is sicklied o'er with the pale cast of thought,
And enterprises of great pith and moment
With this regard their currents turn awry,
And lose the name of action. — Soft you now!
The fair Ophelia! Nymph, in thy orisons
Be all my sins remembered.

Oph.   Good my lord,   90
How does your honor for this many a day?

Ham. I humbly thank you; well, well, well.

Oph. My lord, I have remembrances of yours,
That I have longed long to re-deliver;
I pray you, now receive them.

Ham.   No, not I;
I never gave you aught.

Oph. My honored lord, you know right well you did;
And, with them, words of so sweet breath composed
As made the things more rich. Their perfume lost,
Take these again; for to the noble mind   100

---

65. **rub:** difficulty. 68. **respect:** matter for thought. 75. **quietus:** final
settlement, a legal term. 76. **bare bodkin:** mere dagger. 76. **fardels:**
burdens. 79. **bourn:** boundary. 83. **conscience:** consciousness or thought.
87. **this regard:** i.e., the thought of " something after death."

Rich gifts wax poor when givers prove unkind.
There, my lord.

Ham. Ha, ha! are you honest?

Oph. My lord?

Ham. Are you fair?

Oph. What means your lordship?

Ham. That if you be honest and fair, your honesty should
admit no discourse to your beauty.

Oph. Could beauty, my lord, have better commerce than
with honesty?   110

Ham. Ay, truly; for the power of beauty will sooner trans-
form honesty from what it is to a bawd than the force of honesty can translate beauty into his likeness: this was sometime
a paradox, but now the time gives it proof. I did love you once.

Oph. Indeed, my lord, you made me believe so.

Ham. You should not have believed me; for virtue cannot
so inoculate our old stock but we shall relish of it. I loved you
not.   120

Oph. I was the more deceived.

Ham. Get thee to a nunnery; why wouldst thou be a
breeder of sinners? I am myself indifferent honest; but yet I
could accuse me of such things that it were better my mother
had not borne me. I am very proud, revengeful, ambitious,
with more offences at my beck than I have thoughts to put
them in, imagination to give them shape, or time to act them
in. What should such fellows as I do crawling between earth
and heaven? We are arrant knaves, all; believe none of us.
Go thy ways to a nunnery. Where's your father?   133

Oph. At home, my lord.

Ham. Let the doors be shut upon him, that he may play
the fool nowhere but in 's own house. Farewell.

Oph. O, help him, you sweet heavens!

Ham. If thou dost marry, I'll give thee this plague for thy
dowry: be thou as chaste as ice, as pure as snow, thou shalt not
escape calumny. Get thee to a nunnery, go. Farewell. Or,
if thou wilt needs marry, marry a fool; for wise men know
well enough what monsters you make of them. To a nunnery,
go, and quickly too. Farewell.

Oph. O heavenly powers, restore him!   147

Ham. I have heard of your paintings too, well enough;
God has given you one face, and you make yourselves another.

103. **Ha, ha:** Hamlet hears a rustle in the arras and suspects the truth.

You jig, you amble, and you lisp, and nick-name God's creatures, and make your wantonness your ignorance. Go to, I'll
no more on 't; it hath made me mad. I say, we will have no
more marriages: those that are married already, all but one,
shall live; the rest shall keep as they are. To a nunnery, go.
                                                    [*Exit.*

  Oph. O, what a noble mind is here o'erthrown!
The courtier's, soldier's, scholar's, eye, tongue, sword;
The expectancy and rose of the fair state,   160
The glass of fashion and the mold of form,
The observed of all observers, quite, quite down!
And I, of ladies most deject and wretched,
That sucked the honey of his music vows,
Now see that noble and most sovereign reason,
Like sweet bells jangled, out of tune and harsh;
That unmatched form and feature of blown youth
Blasted with ecstasy. O, woe is me,
To have seen what I have seen, see what I see!

                Reënter KING *and* POLONIUS.

  King. Love! His affections do not that way tend;   170
Nor what he spake, though it lacked form a little,
Was not like madness. There's something in his soul
O'er which his melancholy sits on brood,
And I do doubt the hatch and the disclose
Will be some danger; which for to prevent,
I have in quick determination
Thus set it down: he shall with speed to England,
For the demand of our neglected tribute.
Haply the seas and country different
With variable objects shall expel   180
This something-settled matter in his heart,
Whereon his brains still beating puts him thus
From fashion of himself. What think you on 't?
  Pol. It shall do well; but yet do I believe
The origin and commencement of his grief
Sprung from neglected love. How now, Ophelia!
You need not tell us what Lord Hamlet said;
We heard it all. My lord, do as you please;
But, if you hold it fit, after the play

---

150. **nick-name:** give affected names. 151. **ignorance:** i.e., you excuse your
shortcomings by pretending ignorance. 161. **mold of form:** model gentleman.

Let his queen mother all alone entreat him　　　　　　190
To show his grief.　Let her be round with him;
And I'll be placed, so please you, in the ear
Of all their conference.　If she find him not,
To England send him, or confine him where
Your wisdom best shall think.

　　King.　　　　　　　　　It shall be so:
Madness in great ones must not unwatched go.　　　　[*Exeunt*.

Scene II.　*A hall in the castle*.

Enter Hamlet *and* Players.

　Ham.　Speak the speech, I pray you, as I pronounced it to
you, trippingly on the tongue; but if you mouth it, as many of
your players do, I had as lief the town-crier spoke my lines.
Nor do not saw the air too much with your hand, thus, but use
all gently; for in the very torrent, tempest, and, as I may say,
the whirlwind of passion, you must acquire and beget a temperance that may give it smoothness.　O, it offends me to the
soul to hear a robustious periwig-pated fellow tear a passion
to tatters, to very rags, to split the ears of the groundlings, who
for the most part are capable of nothing but inexplicable dumb-
shows and noise.　I would have such a fellow whipped for o'er-
doing Termagant.　It out-herods Herod.　Pray you, avoid it.

　First Play.　I warrant your honor.　　　　　　　　　17

　Ham.　Be not too tame neither, but let your own discretion
be your tutor.　Suit the action to the word, the word to the action; with this special observance, that you o'erstep not the
modesty of nature: for any thing so overdone is from the purpose of playing, whose end, both at the first and now, was and
is to hold, as 'twere, the mirror up to nature; to show virtue
her own feature, scorn her own image, and the very age and
body of the time his form and pressure.　Now this overdone,
or come tardy off, though it make the unskilful laugh, cannot
but make the judicious grieve; the censure of the which one
must in your allowance o'erweigh a whole theater of others.　O,
there be players that I have seen play, and heard others praise,
and that highly, not to speak it profanely, that, neither having
the accent of Christians nor the gait of Christian, pagan, nor

　　2. **trippingly:** clearly.　13. **groundlings:** the pit audience, or "gallery
gods."　16. **Termagant: Herod:** boisterous characters familiar to the audience from the Miracle plays.　21. **modesty:** moderation.

man, have so strutted and bellowed that I have thought some
of nature's journeymen had made men and not made them well,
they imitated humanity so abominably.

First Play. I hope we have reformed that indifferently with
us, sir. 41

Ham. O, reform it altogether. And let those that play your
clowns speak no more than is set down for them; for there be
of them that will themselves laugh, to set on some quantity
of barren spectators to laugh too; though, in the mean time,
some necessary question of the play be then to be considered.
That's villainous, and shows a most pitiful ambition in the
fool that uses it. Go, make you ready. [*Exeunt Players.*

Enter POLONIUS, ROSENCRANTZ, *and* GUILDENSTERN.

How now, my lord! Will the king hear this piece of work?

Pol. And the queen too, and that presently.

Ham. Bid the players make haste. [*Exit Polonius.*] Will
you two help to hasten them?

Ros. ⎫
Guil. ⎬ We will, my lord.

[*Exeunt Rosencrantz and Guildenstern.*
Ham. What ho! Horatio!

Enter HORATIO.

Hor. Here, sweet lord, at your service.

Ham. Horatio, thou art e'en as just a man
As e'er my conversation coped withal. 60

Hor. O, my dear lord —

Ham. Nay, do not think I flatter;
For what advancement may I hope from thee
That no revenue hast but thy good spirits,
To feed and clothe thee? Why should the poor be flattered?
No, let the candied tongue lick absurd pomp,
And crook the pregnant hinges of the knee
Where thrift may follow fawning. Dost thou hear?
Since my dear soul was mistress of her choice
And could of men distinguish, her election
Hath sealed thee for herself; for thou hast been
As one, in suffering all, that suffers nothing, 71
A man that fortune's buffets and rewards

40. **indifferently:** to some extent. 60. **coped withal:** met with.

Hast ta'en with equal thanks; and blest are those
Whose blood and judgment are so well commingled,
That they are not a pipe for fortune's finger
To sound what stop she please. Give me that man
That is not passion's slave, and I will wear him
In my heart's core, ay, in my heart of heart,
As I do thee. — Something too much of this. —
There is a play tonight before the king;   80
One scene of it comes near the circumstance
Which I have told thee of my father's death.
I prithee, when thou seest that act afoot,
Even with the very comment of thy soul
Observe mine uncle. If his occulted guilt
Do not itself unkennel in one speech,
It is a damnéd ghost that we have seen,
And my imaginations are as foul
As Vulcan's stithy. Give him heedful note;
For I mine eyes will rivet to his face,   90
And after we will both our judgments join
To censure of his seeming.
   Hor.   Well, my lord.
If he steal aught the whilst this play is playing,
And 'scape detecting, I will pay the theft.
   Ham.   They are coming to the play; I must be idle.
Get you a place.

Danish march. A flourish. Enter KING, QUEEN, POLONIUS,
   OPHELIA, ROSENCRANTZ, GUILDENSTERN, *and others*.

   King.   How fares our cousin Hamlet?
   Ham.   Excellent, i' faith; of the chameleon's dish. I eat
the air, promise-crammed. You cannot feed capons so.   100
   King.   I have nothing with this answer, Hamlet; these
words are not mine.
   Ham.   No, nor mine now. [*To Polonius*] My lord, you
played once i' the university, you say?
   Pol.   That did I, my lord; and was accounted a good actor.
   Ham.   What did you enact?
   Pol.   I did enact Julius Caesar. I was killed i' the Capitol;
Brutus killed me.

84. **comment of thy soul:** with all your faculties alert. 85. **occulted:**
hidden. 89. **stithy:** forge. 92. **To censure:** reach a conclusion. 95. **idle:**
seem indifferent. 98. **chameleon's dish:** air. 101. **have nothing with:** make
nothing of.

Ham. It was a brute part of him to kill so capital a calf
there. Be the players ready?

Ros. Ay, my lord; they stay upon your patience.

Queen. Come hither, my dear Hamlet, sit by me.

Ham. No, good mother, here's metal more attractive.

Pol. [*To the King*] Oho! Do you mark that?

Ham. Lady, shall I lie in your lap?

                         [*Lying down at Ophelia's feet.*

Oph. No, my lord.   120

Ham. I mean, my head upon your lap?

Oph. Ay, my lord.

Ham. Do you think I meant country matters?

Oph. I think nothing, my lord.

Ham. That's a fair thought.

Oph. What is, my lord?

Ham. Nothing.

Oph. You are merry, my lord.

Ham. Who, I?   130

Oph. Ay, my lord.

Ham. O God, your only jig-maker. What should a man
do but be merry? For, look you, how cheerfully my mother
looks, and my father died within these two hours.

Oph. Nay, 'tis twice two months, my lord.

Ham. So long? Nay then, let the devil wear black, for
I'll have a suit of sables. O heavens! die two months ago, and
not forgotten yet! Then there's hope a great man's memory
may outlive his life half a year; but, by 'r lady, he must build
churches, then; or else shall he suffer not thinking on, with the
hobby-horse, whose epitaph is " For, O, for O, the hobby-
horse is forgot."   145

Hautboys play. The dumb-show enters.

Enter a King *and a* Queen *very lovingly; the* Queen *embracing
him, and he her. She kneels, and makes show of protesta-
tion unto him. He takes her up, and declines his head
upon her neck; lays him down upon a bank of flowers.
She, seeing him asleep, leaves him. Anon comes in a fellow, takes off his crown, kisses it, and pours poison in the*
King's *ears, and exit. The* Queen *returns; finds the* King
dead, and makes passionate action. The Poisoner, *with*

115. **stay, etc.:** wait for your permission.   123. **country matters:** impro-
prieties.   145. **hobby-horse:** a figure in the morris dances.

some two or three Mutes, *comes in again, seeming to
lament with her. The dead body is carried away. The*
Poisoner *woos the* Queen *with gifts: she seems loath and
unwilling awhile, but in the end accepts his love.* [*Exeunt.*

Oph. What means this, my lord?
Ham. Marry, this is miching mallecho; it means mischief.
Oph. Belike this show imports the argument of the
play.   150
               Enter Prologue.

Ham. We shall know by this fellow. The players cannot
keep counsel; they'il tell all.
Oph. Will he tell us what this show meant?
Ham. Ay, or any show that you'll show him. Be not you
ashamed to show, he'll not shame to tell you what it means.
Oph. You are naught, you are naught. I'll mark the play.
Pro. For us, and for our tragedy,
       Here stooping to your clemency,   160
       We beg your hearing patiently.   [*Exit.*
Ham. Is this a prologue, or the posy of a ring?
Oph. 'Tis brief, my lord.
Ham. As woman's love.

          Enter two Players, King *and* Queen.

P. King. Full thirty times hath Phoebus' cart gone round
Neptune's salt wash and Tellus' orbéd ground,
And thirty dozen moons with borrowed sheen
About the world have times twelve thirties been,
Since love our hearts and Hymen did our hands
Unite commutual in most sacred bands.   170
P. Queen. So many journeys may the sun and moon
Make us again count o'er ere love be done!
But, woe is me, you are so sick of late,
So far from cheer and from your former state,
That I distrust you. Yet, though I distrust,
Discomfort you, my lord, it nothing must;
For women's fear and love holds quantity;
In neither aught, or in extremity.

148. **miching mallecho:** secret mischief. 162. **posy:** motto. 165. **Phoebus' cart:** the sun. 166. **Neptune's salt wash:** the sea. 166. **Tellus' orbéd
ground:** the earth. 175. **distrust:** am worried. 178. The lines following
explain.

Now, what my love is, proof hath made you know;
And as my love is sized, my fear is so.   180
Where love is great, the littlest doubts are fear;
Where little fears grow great, great love grows there.
   P. King.   Faith, I must leave thee, love, and shortly too;
My operant powers their functions leave to do;
And thou shalt live in this fair world behind,
Honored, beloved; and haply one as kind
For husband shalt thou —
   P. Queen.   O, confound the rest!
Such love must needs be treason in my breast.
In second husband let me be accurst!   189
None wed the second but who killed the first.
   Ham.   [*Aside*] Wormwood, wormwood.
   P. Queen.   The instances that second marriage move
Are base respects of thrift, but none of love.
A second time I kill my husband dead,
When second husband kisses me in bed.
   P. King.   I do believe you think what now you speak;
But what we do determine oft we break.
Purpose is but the slave to memory,
Of violent birth, but poor validity;
Which now, like fruit unripe, sticks on the tree;   200
But fall, unshaken, when they mellow be.
Most necessary 'tis that we forget
To pay ourselves what to ourselves is debt.
What to ourselves in passion we propose,
The passion ending, doth the purpose lose.
The violence of either grief or joy
Their own enactures with themselves destroy.
Where joy most revels, grief doth most lament;
Grief joys, joy grieves, on slender accident.
This world is not for aye, nor 'tis not strange
That even our loves should with our fortunes change;   211
For 'tis a question left us yet to prove,
Whether love lead fortune, or else fortune love.
The great man down, you mark his favorite flies;
The poor advanced makes friends of enemies,
And hitherto doth love on fortune tend;
For who not needs shall never lack a friend,

184. **operant powers:** active powers.   187. **confound:** i.e., do not finish
what you started to say.   191. **wormwood:** a symbol of remorse.   192.
instances: motives.   193. **respects of thrift:** considerations of gain.

And who in want a hollow friend doth try,
Directly seasons him his enemy.
But, orderly to end where I begun,   220
Our wills and fates do so contrary run
That our devices still are overthrown;
Our thoughts are ours, their ends none of our own.
So think thou wilt no second husband wed;
But die thy thoughts when thy first lord is dead.
    P. Queen. Nor earth to me give food, nor heaven light!
Sport and repose lock from me day and night!
To desperation turn my trust and hope!
An anchor's cheer in prison be my scope!
Each opposite that blanks the face of joy   230
Meet what I would have well and it destroy!
Both here and hence pursue me lasting strife,
If, once a widow, ever I be wife!
    Ham. If she should break it now!
    P. King. 'Tis deeply sworn. Sweet, leave me here awhile;
My spirits grow dull, and fain I would beguile
The tedious day with sleep.   [*Sleeps.*
    P. Queen.   Sleep rock thy brain;
And never come mischance between us twain!   [*Exit.*
    Ham. Madam, how like you this play?
    Queen. The lady doth protest too much, methinks.   240
    Ham. O, but she'll keep her word.
    King. Have you heard the argument? Is there no offence
in 't?
    Ham. No, no, they do but jest, poison in jest; no offence
i' the world.
    King. What do you call the play?
    Ham. The Mouse-trap. Marry, how? Tropically. This
play is the image of a murder done in Vienna. Gonzago is the
duke's name; his wife, Baptista; you shall see anon; 'tis a
knavish piece of work. But what o' that? Your majesty and
we that have free souls, it touches us not. Let the galled jade
wince, our withers are unwrung.

---

219. **seasons:** turns him into.   229. **anchor:** an anchorite or hermit.
230. **opposite:** obstacle.   230. **blanks:** blanches.   247. **tropically:** figura-
tively.   251. **let the galled jade, etc.:** what matter how sore a horse is from
the saddle as long as our bodies are unhurt!

Enter LUCIANUS.

This is one Lucianus, nephew to the king.

Oph.   You are as good as a chorus, my lord.

Ham.   I could interpret between you and your love, if I could see the puppets dallying.

Oph.   You are keen, my lord, you are keen.

Ham.   It would cost you a groaning to take off my edge. 260

Oph.   Still better, and worse.

Ham.   So you mistake your husbands. Begin, murderer; pox, leave thy damnable faces, and begin. Come: "the croaking raven doth bellow for revenge."

Luc.   Thoughts black, hands apt, drugs fit, and time agree-
          ing;
Confederate season, else no creature seeing;
Thou mixture rank, of midnight weeds collected,
With Hecate's ban thrice blasted, thrice infected,
Thy natural magic and dire property,   270
On wholesome life usurp immediately.

                    [*Pours the poison into the sleeper's ears.*

Ham.   He poisons him i' the garden for 's estate. His name's Gonzago; the story is extant, and writ in choice Italian. You shall see anon how the murderer gets the love of Gonzago's wife.

Oph.   The king rises.

Ham.   What, frighted with false fire!

Queen.   How fares my lord?

Pol.   Give o'er the play.

King.   Give some light. Away!   280

All.   Lights, lights, lights!

                    [*Exeunt all but Hamlet and Horatio.*

Ham.   Why, let the stricken deer go weep,
              The hart ungallèd play;
          For some must watch, while some must sleep:
              So runs the world away.

Would not this, sir, and a forest of feathers — if the rest of my fortunes turn Turk with me — with two Provincial roses on my razed shoes, get me a fellowship in a cry of players, sir?

255. **chorus:** a device in old plays to explain the action. 257. **puppets:** puppet show, in which the action is explained by a speaker. 269. **ban:** curse. 270. **dire property:** deadly quality. 273. **story is extant:** it may have been, but the whole play within the play is Shakespeare's. 276. **The king rises:** an important crisis in the action, Hamlet having now learned what he wanted to know. 287. **turn Turk:** go to the bad. 288. **cry:** company.

Hor. Half a share.   290
Ham. A whole one, I.
          For thou dost know, O Damon dear,
              This realm dismantled was
          Of Jove himself; and now reigns here
              A very, very — pajock.
Hor. You might have rhymed.
Ham. O good Horatio, I'll take the ghost's word for a thou-
sand pound. Didst perceive?
Hor. Very well, my lord.
Ham. Upon the talk of the poisoning?   300
Hor. I did very well note him.
Ham. Aha! Come, some music! Come, the recorders!
      For if the king like not the comedy,
          Why, then, belike, he likes it not, perdy.
Come, some music!

Reënter Rosencrantz *and* Guildenstern.

Guil. Good my lord, vouchsafe me a word with you.
Ham. Sir, a whole history.
Guil. The king, sir —   310
Ham. Ay, sir, what of him?
Guil. Is in his retirement marvelous distempered.
Ham. With drink, sir?
Guil. No, my lord, rather with choler.
Ham. Your wisdom should show itself more richer to sig-
nify this to his doctor; for, for me to put him to his purgation
would perhaps plunge him into far more choler.   319
Guil. Good my lord, put your discourse into some frame
and start not so wildly from my affair.
Ham. I am tame, sir: pronounce.
Guil. The queen, your mother, in most great affliction of
spirit, hath sent me to you.
Ham. You are welcome.
Guil. Nay, good my lord, this courtesy is not of the right
breed. If it shall please you to make me a wholesome answer,
I will do your mother's commandment; if not, your pardon
and my return shall be the end of my business.
Ham. Sir, I cannot.   331

290. **Half a share:** i.e., in a company of players. 295. **pajock:** peacock.
302. **recorders:** a variety of flute played in the manner of a clarinet. 312. **distempered:** upset.

Guil. What, my lord?

Ham. Make you a wholesome answer; my wit's diseased; but, sir, such answer as I can make, you shall command; or, rather, as you say, my mother. Therefore no more, but to the matter: my mother, you say —

Ros. Then thus she says: your behavior hath struck her into amazement and admiration.   339

Ham. O wonderful son, that can so astonish a mother! But is there no sequel at the heels of this mother's admiration? Impart.

Ros. She desires to speak with you in her closet, ere you go to bed.

Ham. We shall obey, were she ten times our mother. Have you any further trade with us?

Ros. My lord, you once did love me.

Ham. So I do still, by these pickers and stealers.   349

Ros. Good my lord, what is your cause of distemper? You do, surely, bar the door upon your own liberty, if you deny your griefs to your friend.

Ham. Sir, I lack advancement.

Ros. How can that be, when you have the voice of the king himself for your succession in Denmark?

Ham. Ay, sir, but "While the grass grows —" The proverb is something musty.   359

Reënter Players *with recorders.*

O, the recorders! let me see one. To withdraw with you: — why do you go about to recover the wind of me, as if you would drive me into a toil?

Guil. O, my lord, if my duty be too bold, my love is too unmannerly.

Ham. I do not well understand that. Will you play upon this pipe?

Guil. My lord, I cannot.

Ham. I pray you.

Guil. Believe me, I cannot.

Ham. I do beseech you.   370

Guil. I know no touch of it, my lord.

Ham. 'Tis as easy as lying. Govern these ventages with your fingers and thumb, give it breath with your mouth, and it

330. **admiration:** wonder. 343. **closet:** private room. 349. **pickers and stealers:** hands, from a phrase in the English catechism. 372. **ventages:** holes in the recorder.

will discourse most eloquent music.   Look you, these are the
stops.

Guil.   But these cannot I command to any utterance of
harmony; I have not the skill.

Ham.   Why, look you now, how unworthy a thing you make
of me!   You would play upon me; you would seem to know
my stops; you would pluck out the heart of my mystery; you
would sound me from my lowest note to the top of my compass; and there is much music, excellent voice, in this little
organ; yet cannot you make it speak.   'Sblood, do you think
I am easier to be played on than a pipe?   Call me what instrument you will, though you can fret me, yet you cannot play
upon me.

Enter POLONIUS.

God bless you, sir!   390
Pol.   My lord, the queen would speak with you, and presently.

Ham.   Do you see yonder cloud that's almost in shape of
a camel?

Pol.   By the mass, and 'tis like a camel, indeed.

Ham.   Methinks it is like a weasel.

Pol.   It is backed like a weasel.

Ham.   Or like a whale?

Pol.   Very like a whale.   399
Ham.   Then I will come to my mother by and by.   They
fool me to the top of my bent.   I will come by and by.

Pol.   I will say so.

Ham.   By and by is easily said.   [*Exit Polonius.*]   Leave
me, friends.   [*Exeunt all but Hamlet.*
'Tis now the very witching time of night,
When churchyards yawn and hell itself breathes out
Contagion to this world: now could I drink hot blood,
And do such bitter business as the day
Would quake to look on.   Soft! now to my mother.   410
O heart, lose not thy nature; let not ever
The soul of Nero enter this firm bosom;
Let me be cruel, not unnatural;
I will speak daggers to her, but use none;
My tongue and soul in this be hypocrites;

---

388. **fret:** Hamlet uses the word in a double sense, to annoy and to finger
the instrument.   412. **Nero:** Roman emperor who killed his mother.

How in my words soever she be shent,
To give them seals never, my soul, consent!   [*Exit.*

SCENE III.   *A room in the castle.*

Enter KING, ROSENCRANTZ, *and* GUILDENSTERN.

King. I like him not, nor stands it safe with us
To let his madness range.   Therefore prepare you;
I your commission will forthwith dispatch,
And he to England shall along with you.
The terms of our estate may not endure
Hazard so dangerous as doth hourly grow
Out of his lunacies.
Guil.   We will ourselves provide.
Most holy and religious fear it is
To keep those many many bodies safe
That live and feed upon your majesty.   10
Ros.   The single and peculiar life is bound,
With all the strength and armor of the mind,
To keep itself from noyance; but much more
That spirit upon whose weal depend and rest
The lives of many.   The cease of majesty
Dies not alone; but, like a gulf, doth draw
What's near it with it; it is a massy wheel,
Fixed on the summit of the highest mount,
To whose huge spokes ten thousand lesser things
Are mortised and adjoined: which, when it falls,   20
Each small annexment, petty consequence,
Attends the boisterous ruin.   Never alone
Did the king sigh, but with a general groan.
King.   Arm you, I pray you, to this speedy voyage;
For we will fetters put upon this fear,
Which now goes too free-footed.
Ros. ⎱
Guil. ⎰   We will haste us.

          [*Exeunt Rosencrantz and Guildenstern.*

416. **shent:** shamed.   417. **give them seals:** put into execution.
  1. **like him not:** i.e., I do not like the situation he has brought about.
16. **gulf:** whirlpool.   20. **mortised, etc.:** building terms.   24. **Arm:** prepare.

Enter Polonius.

Pol. My lord, he's going to his mother's closet.
Behind the arras I'll convey myself,
To hear the process; I'll warrant she'll tax him home;
And, as you said, and wisely was it said,   30
'Tis meet that some more audience than a mother,
Since nature makes them partial, should o'erhear
The speech, of vantage. Fare you well, my liege.
I'll call upon you ere you go to bed,
And tell you what I know.

    King.   Thanks, dear my lord. [*Exit Polonius.*
O, my offence is rank, it smells to heaven;
It hath the primal eldest curse upon 't,
A brother's murder. Pray can I not,
Though inclination be as sharp as will:
My stronger guilt defeats my strong intent;   40
And, like a man to double business bound,
I stand in pause where I shall first begin,
And both neglect. What if this cursèd hand
Were thicker than itself with brother's blood,
Is there not rain enough in the sweet heavens
To wash it white as snow? Whereto serves mercy
But to confront the visage of offence?
And what's in prayer but this twofold force,
To be forestallèd ere we come to fall,   49
Or pardoned being down? Then I'll look up;
My fault is past. But, O, what form of prayer
Can serve my term? " Forgive me my foul murder " ?
That cannot be; since I am still possessed
Of those effects for which I did the murder,
My crown, mine own ambition and my queen.
May one be pardoned and retain the offence?
In the corrupted currents of this world
Offence's gilded hand may shove by justice,
And oft 'tis seen the wicked prize itself
Buys out the law. But 'tis not so above;   60
There is no shuffling, there the action lies
In his true nature; and we ourselves compelled,
Even to the teeth and forehead of our faults,

    33. **of vantage:** from an advantageous place. 37. **eldest curse:** that of
Cain. 49. **forestalled:** prevented. 56. **offence:** i.e., the benefits derived
from it. 58. **gilded hand:** bribery.

To give in evidence. What then? What rests?
Try what repentance can. What can it not?
Yet what can it when one can not repent?
O wretched state! O bosom black as death!
O liméd soul, that, struggling to be free,
Art more engaged! Help, angels! Make assay!
Bow, stubborn knees; and, heart with strings of steel,   70
Be soft as sinews of the newborn babe!
All may be well.   [*Retires and kneels.*

Enter HAMLET.

Ham. Now might I do it pat, now he is praying;
And now I'll do 't. And so he goes to heaven;
And so am I revenged. That would be scanned.
A villain kills my father; and for that,
I, his sole son, do this same villain send
To heaven.
O, this is hire and salary, not revenge.
He took my father grossly, full of bread;   80
With all his crimes broad blown, as flush as May;
And how his audit stands who knows save Heaven?
But in our circumstance and course of thought,
'Tis heavy with him. And am I then revenged,
To take him in the purging of his soul,
When he is fit and seasoned for his passage?
No!
Up, sword; and know thou a more horrid hent:
When he is drunk asleep, or in his rage,
Or in the incestuous pleasure of his bed;   90
At gaming, swearing, or about some act
That has no relish of salvation in 't;
Then trip him, that his heels may kick at heaven,
And that his soul may be as damned and black
As hell, whereto it goes. My mother stays:
This physic but prolongs thy sickly days.   [*Exit.*
    King. [*Rising*] My words fly up, my thoughts remain be-
        low:
Words without thoughts never to heaven go.   [*Exit.*

68. **liméd:** stuck fast. 69. **engaged:** entangled. 69. **assay:** attempt.
73. **pat:** readily. 88. **hent:** grip. 96. **physic:** delay.

SCENE IV. *The Queen's closet.*

Enter QUEEN *and* POLONIUS.

Pol. He will come straight. Look you lay home to him;
Tell him his pranks have been too broad to bear with,
And that your grace hath screened and stood between
Much heat and him. I'll sconce me even here.
Pray you, be round with him.
    Ham. [*Within*] Mother, mother, mother!
    Queen.   I'll warrant you,
Fear me not: withdraw, I hear him coming.
                 [*Polonius hides behind the arras.*

Enter HAMLET.

    Ham. Now, mother, what's the matter?
    Queen. Hamlet, thou hast thy father much offended.
    Ham. Mother, you have my father much offended.   10
    Queen. Come, come, you answer with an idle tongue.
    Ham. Go, go, you question with a wicked tongue.
    Queen. Why, how now, Hamlet!
    Ham.   What's the matter now?
    Queen. Have you forgot me?
    Ham.   No, by the rood, not so:
You are the queen, your husband's brother's wife;
And — would it were not so! — you are my mother.
    Queen. Nay, then, I'll set those to you that can speak.
    Ham. Come, come, and sit you down; you shall not budge;
You go not till I set you up a glass
Where you may see the inmost part of you.   20
    Queen. What wilt thou do? Thou wilt not murder me?
Help, help, ho!
    Pol. [*Behind*] What, ho! help, help, help!
    Ham. [*Drawing*] How now! A rat? Dead, for a ducat,
      dead!   [*Makes a pass through the arras.*
    Pol. [*Behind*] O, I am slain!   [*Falls and dies.*
    Queen. O me, what hast thou done?
    Ham.   Nay, I know not.
Is it the king?
    Queen. O, what a rash and bloody deed is this!
    Ham. A bloody deed! almost as bad, good mother,
As kill a king, and marry with his brother.

Queen.   As kill a king!
Ham.   Ay, lady, 'twas my word.   30
                    [*Lifts up the arras and discovers Polonius.*
Thou wretched, rash, intruding fool, farewell!
I took thee for thy better.   Take thy fortune;
Thou find'st to be too busy is some danger.
Leave wringing of your hands.   Peace!   Sit you down,
And let me wring your heart; for so I shall,
If it be made of penetrable stuff,
If damnéd custom have not brassed it so
That it be proof and bulwark against sense.
Queen.   What have I done, that thou darest wag thy tongue
In noise so rude against me?
Ham.   Such an act   40
That blurs the grace and blush of modesty,
Calls virtue hypocrite, takes off the rose
From the fair forehead of an innocent love
And sets a blister there, makes marriage vows
As false as dicers' oaths; O, such a deed
As from the body of contraction plucks
The very soul, and sweet religion makes
A rhapsody of words.   Heaven's face doth glow;
Yea, this solidity and compound mass,
With tristful visage, as against the doom,   50
Is thought-sick at the act.
Queen.   Ay me, what act,
That roars so loud, and thunders in the index?
Ham.   Look here, upon this picture, and on this,
The counterfeit presentment of two brothers.
See, what a grace was seated on this brow;
Hyperion's curls; the front of Jove himself;
An eye like Mars, to threaten and command;
A station like the herald Mercury
New-lighted on a heaven-kissing hill;
A combination and a form indeed,   60
Where every god did seem to set his seal,
To give the world assurance of a man:
This was your husband.   Look you now, what follows:
Here is your husband; like a mildewed ear,
Blasting his wholesome brother.   Have you eyes?
Could you on this fair mountain leave to feed,

46. **contraction:**   marriage contract. 48. **glow:**   blush with shame.
49. **solidity, etc.:** earth.   50. **as against, etc.:** as if the day of doom were at
hand.   52. **index:** prelude.   54. **counterfeit:** portrayed.   58. **station:** posture.

And batten on this moor?   Ha! have you eyes?
You cannot call it love; for at your age
The heyday in the blood is tame, it's humble,
And waits upon the judgment; and what judgment   70
Would step from this to this?   Sense, sure, you have,
Else could you not have motion; but sure, that sense
Is apoplexed; for madness would not err,
Nor sense to ecstasy was ne'er so thralled
But it reserved some quantity of choice,
To serve in such a difference.   What devil was 't
That thus hath cozened you at hoodman-blind?
Eyes without feeling, feeling without sight,
Ears without hands or eyes, smelling sans all,
Or but a sickly part of one true sense   80
Could not so mope.
O shame! where is thy blush?   Rebellious hell,
If thou canst mutine in a matron's bones,
To flaming youth let virtue be as wax,
And melt in her own fire.   Proclaim no shame
When the compulsive ardor gives the charge.
Since frost itself as actively doth burn
And reason panders will.
    Queen.   O Hamlet, speak no more:
Thou turn'st mine eyes into my very soul;
And there I see such black and grainéd spots   90
As will not leave their tinct,
    Ham.   Nay, but to live
In the rank sweat of an enseaméd bed,
Stewed in corruption, honeying and making love
Over the nasty sty —
    Queen.   O, speak to me no more;
These words, like daggers, enter in mine ears;
No more, sweet Hamlet!
    Ham.   A murderer and a villain;
A slave that is not twentieth part the tithe
Of your precedent lord; a vice of kings;
A cutpurse of the empire and the rule,
That from a shelf the precious diadem stole,   100
And put it in his pocket!
    Queen.   No more!
    Ham.   A king of shreds and patches —

67. **batten:** fatten.   79. **sans:** without.   81. **mope:** act so stupidly.
91. **leave their tinct:** give up their color.   98. **vice:** buffoon.   99. **cutpurse:**
sneak thief.

Enter Ghost.

Save me, and hover o'er me with your wings,
You heavenly guards!   What would your gracious figure?
   Queen.   Alas, he's mad!
   Ham.   Do you not come your tardy son to chide,
That, lapsed in time and passion, lets go by
The important acting of your dread command?
O, say!
   Ghost.   Do not forget: this visitation   110
Is but to whet thy almost blunted purpose.
But, look, amazement on thy mother sits.
O, step between her and her fighting soul.
Conceit in weakest bodies strongest works.
Speak to her, Hamlet.
   Ham.   How is it with you, lady?
   Queen.   Alas, how is 't with you,
That you do bend your eye on vacancy
And with the incorporal air do hold discourse?
Forth at your eyes your spirits wildly peep;
And, as the sleeping soldiers in the alarm,   120
Your bedded hair, like life in excrements,
Start up, and stand on end.   O gentle son,
Upon the heat and flame of thy distemper
Sprinkle cool patience.   Whereon do you look?
   Ham.   On him, on him!   Look you, how pale he glares!
His form and cause conjoined, preaching to stones,
Would make them capable.   Do not look upon me;
Lest with this piteous action you convert
My stern effects; then what I have to do
Will want true color; tears perchance for blood.   130
   Queen.   To whom do you speak this?
   Ham.   Do you see nothing there?
   Queen.   Nothing at all; yet all that is I see.
   Ham.   Nor did you nothing hear?
   Queen.   No, nothing but ourselves.
   Ham.   Why, look you there!   Look, how it steals away!
My father, in his habit as he lived!
Look, where he goes, even now, out at the portal! [*Exit Ghost.*
   Queen.   This is the very coinage of your brain.

---

114. **conceit:** fancy.   121. **bedded:** lying flat, as in a bed.   121. **excrements:** everything growing on the body, here the hair.   128–29. **convert,** etc.: change my purpose.

This bodiless creation ecstasy
Is very cunning in.
   Ham.   Ecstasy!
My pulse, as yours, doth temperately keep time   140
And makes as healthful music. It is not madness
That I have uttered. Bring me to the test,
And I the matter will re-word; which madness
Would gambol from. Mother, for love of grace,
Lay not that flattering unction to your soul,
That not your trespass, but my madness speaks.
It will but skin and film the ulcerous place,
Whiles rank corruption, mining all within,
Infects unseen. Confess yourself to heaven;
Repent what's past; avoid what is to come;   150
And do not spread the compost on the weeds,
To make them ranker. Forgive me this my virtue;
For in the fatness of these pursy times
Virtue itself of vice must pardon beg,
Yea, curb and woo for leave to do him good.
   Queen. O Hamlet, thou hast cleft my heart in twain.
   Ham. O, throw away the worser part of it,
And live the purer with the other half.
Good night; but go not to mine uncle's bed;
Assume a virtue, if you have it not.   160
That monster, custom, who all sense doth eat,
Of habits devil, is angel yet in this,
That to the use of actions fair and good
He likewise gives a frock or livery,
That aptly is put on. Refrain tonight,
And that shall lend a kind of easiness
To the next abstinence; the next more easy;
For use almost can change the stamp of nature,
And either master the devil, or throw him out
With wondrous potency. Once more, good night;   170
And when you are desirous to be blessed,
I'll blessing beg of you. For this same lord,
                        [Pointing to Polonius.
I do repent; but Heaven hath pleased it so,
To punish me with this and this with me,
That I must be their scourge and minister.
I will bestow him, and will answer well
The death I gave him. So, again, good night.

I must be cruel, only to be kind.
Thus bad begins and worse remains behind.
One word more, good lady.
    Queen.   What shall I do?   180
    Ham.   Not this, by no means, that I bid you do:
Let the bloat king tempt you again to bed,
Pinch wanton on your cheek, call you his mouse;
And let him, for a pair of reechy kisses,
Or paddling in your neck with his damned fingers,
Make you to ravel all this matter out,
That I essentially am not in madness,
But mad in craft. 'Twere good you let him know;
For who, that's but a queen, fair, sober, wise,
Would from a paddock, from a bat, a gib,   190
Such dear concernings hide? Who would do so?
No, in despite of sense and secrecy,
Unpeg the basket on the house's top,
Let the birds fly, and, like the famous ape,
To try conclusions, in the basket creep,
And break your own neck down.
    Queen.   Be thou assured, if words be made of breath,
And breath of life, I have no life to breathe
What thou hast said to me.
    Ham.   I must to England; you know that?
    Queen.   Alack,   200
I had forgot. 'Tis so concluded on.
    Ham.   There's letters sealed; and my two schoolfellows,
Whom I will trust as I will adders fanged,
They bear the mandate; they must sweep my way,
And marshal me to knavery. Let it work;
For 'tis the sport to have the enginer
Hoist with his own petar; and 't shall go hard
But I will delve one yard below their mines,
And blow them at the moon. O, 'tis most sweet,
When in one line two crafts directly meet.   210
This man shall set me packing.
I'll lug the guts into the neighbor room.
Mother, good night. Indeed this counselor
Is now most still, most secret and most grave,
Who was in life a foolish prating knave.

---

   190. **paddock:** toad.   190. **gib:** tom cat.   205. **petar:** " an engine
wherewith strong gates are blown open.''

Come, sir, to draw toward an end with you.
Good night, mother.
        [Exeunt severally; Hamlet dragging in Polonius.

ACT IV

Scene I. *A room in the castle.*

Enter King, Queen, Rosencrantz, *and* Guildenstern.

King.   There's matter in these sighs, these profound heaves:
You must translate; 'tis fit we understand them.
Where is your son?
    Queen.   Bestow this place on us a little while.
                [Exeunt Rosencrantz and Guildenstern.
Ah, mine own lord, what have I seen tonight!
    King.   What, Gertrude? How does Hamlet?
    Queen.   Mad as the sea and wind, when both contend
Which is the mightier. In his lawless fit,
Behind the arras hearing something stir,
Whips out his rapier, cries, " A rat, a rat! "   10
And, in his brainish apprehension, kills
The unseen good old man.
    King.   O heavy deed!
It had been so with us, had we been there.
His liberty is full of threats to all;
To you yourself, to us, to every one.
Alas, how shall this bloody deed be answered?
It will be laid to us, whose providence
Should have kept short, restrained and out of haunt,
This mad young man; but so much was our love,
We would not understand what was most fit;
But, like the owner of a foul disease,   21
To keep it from divulging, let it feed
Even on the pith of life. Where is he gone?
    Queen.   To draw apart the body he hath killed;
O'er whom his very madness, like some ore
Among a mineral of metals base,
Shows itself pure; he weeps for what is done.
    King.   O Gertrude, come away!

11. **brainish:** brainsick. 25. **ore:** gold. 26. **mineral:** mine.

The sun no sooner shall the mountains touch,
But we will ship him hence; and this vile deed   30
We must, with all our majesty and skill,
Both countenance and excuse. Ho, Guildenstern!

Reënter ROSENCRANTZ *and* GUILDENSTERN.

Friends both, go join you with some further aid.
Hamlet in madness hath Polonius slain,
And from his mother's closet hath he dragged him.
Go seek him out; speak fair, and bring the body
Into the chapel. I pray you, haste in this.
                    [*Exeunt Rosencrantz and Guildenstern.*
Come, Gertrude, we'll call up our wisest friends;
And let them know, both what we mean to do,
And what's untimely done; so, haply, slander,   40
Whose whisper o'er the world's diameter,
As level as the cannon to his blank,
Transports his poisoned shot, may miss our name,
And hit the woundless air. O, come away!
My soul is full of discord and dismay.   [*Exeunt.*

SCENE II. *Another room in the castle.*

Enter HAMLET.

Ham. Safely stowed.
Ros.
Guil. } [*Within*] Hamlet! Lord Hamlet!
Ham. But soft, what noise? Who calls on Hamlet? O,
here they come.

Enter ROSENCRANTZ *and* GUILDENSTERN.

Ros. What have you done, my lord, with the dead body?
Ham. Compounded it with dust, whereto 'tis kin.
Ros. Tell us where 'tis, that we may take it thence
And bear it to the chapel.
Ham. Do not believe it.
Ros. Believe what?   10
Ham. That I can keep your counsel and not mine own.

32. **countenance:** assume responsibility for. 42. **blank:** white spot in a
target.

Besides, to be demanded of a sponge!   What replication should
be made by the son of a king?

Ros.   Take you me for a sponge, my lord?

Ham.   Ay, sir, that soaks up the king's countenance, his
rewards, his authorities.   But such officers do the king best
service in the end.   He keeps them, like an ape, in the corner
of his jaw; first mouthed, to be last swallowed.   When he needs
what you have gleaned, it is but squeezing you, and, sponge,
you shall be dry again.

Ros.   I understand you not, my lord.

Ham.   I am glad of it: a knavish speech sleeps in a foolish
ear.

Ros.   My lord, you must tell us where the body is, and go
with us to the king.

Ham.   The body is with the king, but the king is not with
the body.   The king is a thing —

Guil.   A thing, my lord!   31

Ham.   Of nothing: bring me to him.   Hide fox, and all
after.   [*Exeunt.*

SCENE III.   *Another room in the castle.*

Enter KING *attended.*

King.   I have sent to seek him, and to find the body.
How dangerous is it that this man goes loose!
Yet must not we put the strong law on him.
He's loved of the distracted multitude,
Who like not in their judgment, but their eyes;
And where 'tis so, the offender's scourge is weighed,
But never the offence.   To bear all smooth and even,
This sudden sending him away must seem
Deliberate pause.   Diseases desperate grown
By desperate appliance are relieved,   10
Or not at all.

Enter ROSENCRANTZ.

How now!   What hath befall'n?

Ros.   Where the dead body is bestowed, my lord,
We cannot get from him.

Sc. ii.   12. **demanded of:** questioned by.   12. **replication:** answer.   15.
countenance: favor.

Sc. iii.   4. **distracted:** brainless.   6. **scourge:** punishment.   9. **pause:**
reflection.

King.   But where is he?

Ros.   Without, my lord; guarded, to know your pleasure.

King.   Bring him before us.

Ros.   Ho, Guildenstern! bring in my lord.

Enter Hamlet *and* Guildenstern.

King.   Now, Hamlet, where's Polonius?

Ham.   At supper.

King.   At supper! Where?   19

Ham.   Not where he eats, but where he is eaten. A certain
convocation of politic worms are e'en at him. Your worm is
your only emperor for diet. We fat all creatures else to fat us,
and we fat ourselves for maggots. Your fat king and your
lean beggar is but variable service, two dishes, but to one table:
that's the end.

King.   Alas, alas!

Ham.   A man may fish with the worm that hath eat of a
king, and eat of the fish that hath fed of that worm.   30

King.   What does thou mean by this?

Ham.   Nothing but to show you how a king may go a progress through the guts of a beggar.

King.   Where is Polonius?

Ham.   In heaven; send thither to see. If your messenger
find him not there, seek him i' the other place yourself. But
indeed, if you find him not within this month, you shall nose
him as you go up the stairs into the lobby.   39

King.   Go seek him there.   [*To some Attendants.*

Ham.   He will stay till you come.   [*Exeunt Attendants.*

King.   Hamlet, this deed, for thine especial safety, —

Which we do tender, as we dearly grieve

For that which thou hast done, — must send thee hence

With fiery quickness; therefore prepare thyself;

The bark is ready, and the wind at help,

The associates tend, and every thing is bent

For England.

Ham.   For England!

King.   Ay, Hamlet.

Ham.   Good.

King.   So is it, if thou knew'st our purposes.   49

33. **progress:** royal journey of state.   43. **tender:** regard.   47. **tend:** wait
for.

Ham. I see a cherub that sees them. But, come; for England! Farewell, dear mother.

King. Thy loving father, Hamlet.

Ham. My mother: father and mother is man and wife;
man and wife is one flesh; and so, my mother. Come, for
England!   [*Exit.*

King. Follow him at foot; tempt him with speed aboard;
Delay it not; I'll have him hence tonight.
Away! for every thing is sealed and done
That else leans on the affair: pray you, make haste.

                  [*Exeunt Rosencrantz and Guildenstern.*

And, England, if my love thou hold'st at aught —   60
As my great power thereof may give thee sense,
Since yet thy cicatrice looks raw and red
After the Danish sword, and thy free awe
Pays homage to us — thou mayst not coldly set
Our sovereign process; which imports at full,
By letters congruing to that effect,
The present death of Hamlet. Do it, England;
For like the hectic in my blood he rages,
And thou must cure me: till I know 'tis done,
Howe'er my haps, my joys were ne'er begun.   [*Exit.*

SCENE IV. *A plain in Denmark.*

Enter FORTINBRAS, *a* Captain, *and* Soldiers, *marching.*

For. Go, captain, from me greet the Danish king;
Tell him that, by his license, Fortinbras
Craves the conveyance of a promised march
Over his kingdom. You know the rendezvous.
If that his majesty would aught with us,
We shall express our duty in his eye;
And let him know so.

Cap.   I will do 't, my lord.

For. Go softly on.   [*Exeunt Fortinbras and Soldiers.*

Enter HAMLET, ROSENCRANTZ, GUILDENSTERN, *and others.*

Ham. Good sir, whose powers are these?

Cap. They are of Norway, sir.   10

62. **cicatrice:** scar. 64. **coldly set:** regard indifferently. 66. **congruing:** agreeing.
   8. **softly:** slowly.

Ham. How purposed, sir, I pray you?
Cap. Against some part of Poland.
Ham. Who commands them, sir?
Cap. The nephew to old Norway, Fortinbras.
Ham. Goes it against the main of Poland, sir,
Or some frontier?
Cap. Truly to speak, and with no addition,
We go to gain a little patch of ground
That hath in it no profit but the name.
To pay five ducats, five, I would not farm it; 20
Nor will it yield to Norway or the Pole
A ranker rate, should it be sold in fee.
Ham. Why, then the Polack never will defend it.
Cap. Yes, it is already garrisoned.
Ham. Two thousand souls and twenty thousand ducats
Will not debate the question of this straw;
This is the imposthume of much wealth and peace,
That inward breaks, and shows no cause without
Why the man dies. I humbly thank you, sir.
Cap. God be wi' you, sir.   [*Exit.*
Ros.   Will 't please you go, my lord? 30
Ham. I'll be with you straight. Go a little before.
              [*Exeunt all except Hamlet.*
How all occasions do inform against me,
And spur my dull revenge! What is a man,
If his chief good and market of his time
Be but to sleep and feed? a beast, no more.
Sure, He that made us with such large discourse,
Looking before and after, gave us not
That capability and god-like reason
To fust in us unused. Now, whether it be
Bestial oblivion, or some craven scruple 40
Of thinking too precisely on the event,
A thought which, quartered, hath but one part wisdom
And ever three parts coward, I do not know
Why yet I live to say " This thing's to do,"
Sith I have cause and will and strength and means
To do 't. Examples gross as earth exhort me.
Witness this army of such mass and charge
Led by a delicate and tender prince,

22. **ranker:** greater. 22. **in fee:** for legal ownership. 26. **debate:** be enough to fight it out. 27. **imposthume:** abscess. 34. **market:** value. 36. **discourse:** power of thought. 39. **fust:** grow moldy.

Whose spirit with divine ambition puffed
Makes mouths at the invisible event,   50
Exposing what is mortal and unsure
To all that fortune, death and danger dare,
Even for an eggshell.   Rightly to be great
Is not to stir without great argument,
But greatly to find quarrel in a straw
When honor's at the stake.   How stand I then,
That have a father killed, a mother stained,
Excitements of my reason and my blood,
And let all sleep? while, to my shame, I see
The imminent death of twenty thousand men,
That, for a fantasy and trick of fame,   61
Go to their graves like beds, fight for a plot
Whereon the numbers cannot try the cause,
Which is not tomb enough and continent
To hide the slain?   O, from this time forth,
My thoughts be bloody, or be nothing worth!   [*Exit.*

SCENE V. *Elsinore. A room in the castle.*

Enter QUEEN, HORATIO, *and a* Gentleman.

Queen. I will not speak with her.
Gent. She is importunate, indeed distract.
Her mood will needs be pitied.
Queen.   What would she have?
Gent. She speaks much of her father; says she hears
There's tricks i' the world; and hems, and beats her heart;
Spurns enviously at straws; speaks things in doubt,
That carry but half sense. Her speech is nothing,
Yet the unshaped use of it doth move
The hearers to collection; they aim at it,
And botch the words up fit to their own thoughts;   10
Which, as her winks, and nods, and gestures yield them,
Indeed would make one think there might be thought,
Though nothing sure, yet much unhappily.
Hor. 'Twere good she were spoken with: for she may strew
Dangerous conjectures in ill-breeding minds.
Queen. Let her come in.   [*Exit Horatio.*

6. **spurns enviously:** kicks angrily. 9. **collection:** endeavor to gather a
meaning.

To my sick soul, as sin's true nature is,
Each toy seems prologue to some great amiss:
So full of artless jealousy is guilt,
It spills itself in fearing to be spilt.   20

Reënter HORATIO, *with* OPHELIA.

Oph.   Where is the beauteous majesty of Denmark?
Queen.   How now, Ophelia!
Oph.   [*Sings*] " How should I your true love know
        From another one?
    By his cockle hat and staff,
        And his sandal shoon."
Queen.   Alas, sweet lady, what imports this song?
Oph.   Say you? Nay, pray you, mark.
[*Sings*]   " He is dead and gone, lady,
            He is dead and gone;   30
        At his head a grass-green turf,
            At his heels a stone."
Queen.   Nay, but, Ophelia, —
Oph.   Pray you, mark.
[*Sings*]   " White his shroud as the mountain snow — "

Enter KING.

Queen.   Alas, look here, my lord.
Oph.   [*Sings*]   " Larded with sweet flowers;
    Which bewept to the grave did go
        With true-love showers."
King.   How do you, pretty lady?   40
Oph.   Well, God 'ild you! They say the owl was a baker's
daughter. Lord, we know what we are, but know not what we
may be. God be at your table!
King.   Conceit upon her father.
Oph.   Pray you, let's have no words of this; but when they
ask you what it means, say you this:
[*Sings*]   " Tomorrow is Saint Valentine's day,
            All in the morning betime,
            And I a maid at your window,   50
            To be your Valentine."
King.   Pretty Ophelia!
Oph.   Indeed, la, without an oath, I'll make an end on 't:

19. **jealousy:** suspicion. 41. **'ild:** yield, i.e., reward. 45. **conceit:**
fancies.

King. How long hath she been thus?

Oph. I hope all will be well. We must be patient: but I
cannot choose but weep, to think they should lay him i' the
cold ground. My brother shall know of it: and so I thank you
for your good counsel. Come, my coach! Good night, ladies;
good night, sweet ladies; good night, good night.   [*Exit.*

King. Follow her close; give her good watch, I pray you.
[*Exit Horatio.*

O, this is the poison of deep grief; it springs
All from her father's death. O Gertrude, Gertrude,
When sorrows come, they come not single spies,
But in battalions. First, her father slain;
Next, your son gone; and he most violent author   80
Of his own just remove; the people muddied,
Thick and unwholesome in their thoughts and whispers,
For good Polonius' death; and we have done but greenly,
In hugger-mugger to inter him; poor Ophelia
Divided from herself and her fair judgment,
Without the which we are pictures, or mere beasts;
Last, and as much containing as all these,
Her brother is in secret come from France;
Feeds on his wonder, keeps himself in clouds,
And wants not buzzers to infect his ear   90
With pestilent speeches of his father's death;
Wherein necessity, of matter beggared,
Will nothing stick our person to arraign
In ear and ear. O my dear Gertrude, this,
Like to a murdering-piece, in many places
Gives me superfluous death.   [*A noise within.*

Queen.   Alack, what noise is this?

King. Where are my Switzers? Let them guard the door.

Enter another Gentleman.

What is the matter?

Gent.   Save yourself, my lord.
The ocean, overpeering of his list,
Eats not the flats with more impetuous haste
Than young Laertes, in a riotous head,   101
O'erbears your officers. The rabble call him lord;
And, as the world were now but to begin,

81. **muddied:** stirred up. 84. **hugger-mugger:** secret haste. 97. **Switzers:** Swiss guards. 99. **overpeering:** overflowing its boundaries.

Antiquity forgot, custom not known,
The ratifiers and props of every word,
They cry, " Choose we: Laertes shall be king."
Caps, hands, and tongues, applaud it to the clouds:
" Laertes shall be king, Laertes king! "
  Queen.   How cheerfully on the false trail they cry!
O, this is counter, you false Danish dogs!   110
  King.   The doors are broke.   *[Noise within.*

      Enter Laertes, *armed;* Danes *following.*

  Laer.   Where is this king?   Sirs, stand you all without.
  Danes.   No, let's come in.
  Laer.   I pray you, give me leave.
  Danes.   We will, we will.   *[They retire without the door.*
  Laer.   I thank you; keep the door.   O thou vile king,
Give me my father!
  Queen.   Calmly, good Laertes.
  Laer.   That drop of blood that's calm proclaims me bastard,
Cries cuckold to my father, brands the harlot
Even here, between the chaste unsmirchéd brow
Of my true mother.
  King.   What is the cause, Laertes,   120
That thy rebellion looks so giant-like?
Let him go, Gertrude; do not fear our person.
There's such divinity doth hedge a king,
That treason can but peep to what it would,
Acts little of his will.   Tell us, Laertes,
Why thou art thus incensed.   Let him go, Gertrude.
Speak, man.
  Laer.   Where is my father?
  King.   Dead.
  Queen.   But not by him.
  King.   Let him demand his fill.
  Laer.   How came he dead?   I'll not be juggled with.   130
To hell, allegiance!   Vows, to the blackest devil!
Conscience and grace, to the profoundest pit!
I dare damnation.   To this point I stand,
That both the worlds I give to negligence,
Let come what comes; only I'll be revenged
Most throughly for my father.
  King.   Who shall stay you?

    110. **counter:** going in the wrong direction.

Laer.   My will, not all the world.
And for my means, I'll husband them so well,
They shall go far with little.
   King.   Good Laertes,
If you desire to know the certainty   140
Of your dear father's death, is 't writ in your revenge,
That, swoopstake, you will draw both friend and foe,
Winner and loser?
   Laer.   None but his enemies.
   King.   Will you know them then?
   Laer.   To his good friends thus wide I'll ope my arms;
And like the kind life-rendering pelican,
Repast them with my blood.
   King.   Why, now you speak
Like a good child and a true gentleman.
That I am guiltless of your father's death,
And am most sensibly in grief for it,   150
It shall as level to your judgment pierce
As day does to your eye.
   Danes.   [*Within*]   Let her come in.
   Laer.   How now!   What noise is that?

Reënter OPHELIA.

O heat, dry up my brains!   Tears seven times salt,
Burn out the sense and virtue of mine eye!
By heaven, thy madness shall be paid with weight,
Till our scale turn the beam.   O rose of May!
Dear maid, kind sister, sweet Ophelia!
O heavens! is 't possible, a young maid's wits
Should be as mortal as an old man's life?   160
Nature is fine in love, and where 'tis fine,
It sends some precious instance of itself
After the thing it loves.
   Oph.   [*Sings*]
     " They bore him barefaced on the bier;
       Hey non nonny, nonny, hey nonny;
       And in his grave rained many a tear: — "
Fare you well, my dove!
   Laer.   Hadst thou thy wits, and didst persuade revenge,
It could not move thus.

142. **swoopstake:** indiscriminately.

Oph. [*Sings*] " You must sing a-down a-down,
    An you call him a-down-a."   171
O, how the wheel becomes it! It is the false steward, that
stole his master's daughter.

Laer. This nothing's more than matter.

Oph. There's rosemary, that's for remembrance; pray, love,
remember. And there is pansies, that's for thoughts.

Laer. A document in madness, thoughts and remembrance
fitted.   179

Oph. There's fennel for you, and columbines; there's rue
for you; and here's some for me; we may call it herb-grace o'
Sundays. O, you must wear your rue with a difference.
There's a daisy; I would give you some violets, but they withered all when my father died. They say he made a good
end —

[*Sings*] " For bonny sweet Robin is all my joy."

Laer. Thought and affliction, passion, hell itself,
She turns to favor and to prettiness.

Oph. [*Sings*] " And will he not come again?   190
           And will he not come again?
              No, no, he is dead:
              Go to thy death-bed:
           He never will come again.

           His beard was as white as snow,
           All flaxen was his poll:
              He is gone, he is gone,
              And we cast away moan:
           God ha' mercy on his soul! "

And of all Christian souls, I pray God. God be wi' ye. [*Exit.*

Laer. Do you see this, O God?   201

King. Laertes, I must commune with your grief,
Or you deny me right. Go but apart,
Make choice of whom your wisest friends you will,
And they shall hear and judge 'twixt you and me.
If by direct or by collateral hand
They find us touched, we will our kingdom give,
Our crown, our life, and all that we call ours,
To you in satisfaction; but if not,
Be you content to lend your patience to us,   210
And we shall jointly labor with your soul
To give it due content.

178. **document:** instruction.

Laer.   Let this be so;
His means of death, his obscure funeral —
No trophy, sword, nor hatchment o'er his bones,
No noble rite nor formal ostentation —
Cry to be heard, as 'twere from heaven to earth,
That I must call 't in question.
  King.   So you shall;
And where the offence is let the great ax fall.
I pray you, go with me.   [*Exeunt.*

SCENE VI. *Another room in the castle.*

Enter HORATIO *and a* Servant.

Hor. What are they that would speak with me?
Serv. Sailors, sir. They say they have letters for you.
Hor. Let them come in.   [*Exit Servant.*
I do not know from what part of the world
I should be greeted, if not from Lord Hamlet.

Enter Sailors.

First Sail. God bless you, sir.
Hor. Let him bless thee too.
First Sail. He shall, sir, an 't please him. There's a letter
for you, sir; it comes from the ambassador that was bound for
England; if your name be Horatio, as I am let to know it is.
Hor. [*Reads*] " Horatio, when thou shalt have overlooked
this, give these fellows some means to the king: they have
letters for him. Ere we were two days old at sea, a pirate of
very warlike appointment gave us chase. Finding ourselves too
slow of sail, we put on a compelled valor, and in the grapple I
boarded them. On the instant they got clear of our ship; so
I alone became their prisoner. They have dealt with me like
thieves of mercy; but they knew what they did; I am to do a
good turn for them. Let the king have the letters I have sent;
and repair thou to me with as much speed as thou wouldst fly
death. I have words to speak in thine ear will make thee
dumb; yet are they much too light for the bore of the matter.
These good fellows will bring thee where I am. Rosencrantz
and Guildenstern hold their course for England; of them I
have much to tell thee. Farewell.
                  " He that thou knowest thine, HAMLET."
          214. **hatchment:** coat of arms.

Come, I will make you way for these your letters;
And do 't the speedier, that you may direct me
To him from whom you brought them.　　　　　[*Exeunt.*

SCENE VII.　*Another room in the castle.*

Enter KING *and* LAERTES.

King.　Now must your conscience my acquittance seal,
And you must put me in your heart for friend,
Sith you have heard, and with a knowing ear,
That he which hath your noble father slain
Pursued my life.
　　Laer.　　　　　It well appears.　But tell me
Why you proceeded not against these feats,
So crimeful and so capital in nature,
As by your safety, wisdom, all things else,
You mainly were stirred up.
　　King.　　　　　　　O, for two special reasons;
Which may to you, perhaps, seem much unsinewed,　　　10
But yet to me they are strong.　The queen his mother
Lives almost by his looks; and for myself —
My virtue or my plague, be it either which —
She's so conjunctive to my life and soul,
That, as the star moves not but in his sphere,
I could not but by her.　The other motive,
Why to a public count I might not go,
Is the great love the general gender bear him;
Who, dipping all his faults in their affection,
Would, like the spring that turneth wood to stone,　　20
Convert his gyves to graces; so that my arrows,
Too slightly timbered for so loud a wind,
Would have reverted to my bow again,
And not where I had aimed them.
　　Laer.　And so have I a noble father lost;
A sister driven into desperate terms,
Whose worth, if praises may go back again,
Stood challenger on mount of all the age
For her perfections.　But my revenge will come.

　1. **conscience**: consciousness.　1. **acquittance**: innocence.　10. **unsinewed:**
weak.　21. **gyves**: fetters.

King. Break not your sleeps for that. You must not
        think   30
That we are made of stuff so flat and dull
That we can let our beard be shook with danger
And think it pastime. You shortly shall hear more.
I loved your father, and we love ourself;
And that, I hope, will teach you to imagine —

                Enter a Messenger.

How now! What news?
    Mess.   Letters, my lord, from Hamlet:
This to your majesty; this to the queen.
    King. From Hamlet! Who brought them?
    Mess. Sailors, my lord, they say; I saw them not:
They were given me by Claudio; he received them   40
Of him that brought them.
    King.   Laertes, you shall hear them.
Leave us.   [*Exit Messenger.*
[*Reads*] " High and mighty, You shall know I am set naked
on your kingdom. Tomorrow shall I beg leave to see your
kingly eyes: when I shall, first asking your pardon thereunto,
recount the occasion of my sudden and more strange return.
                              " HAMLET."

What should this mean? Are all the rest come back?   50
Or is it some abuse and no such thing?
    Laer. Know you the hand?
    King. 'Tis Hamlet's character. " Naked! "
And in a postscript here, he says " alone."
Can you advise me?
    Laer. I'm lost in it, my lord. But let him come;
It warms the very sickness in my heart,
That I shall live and tell him to his teeth,
" Thus didest thou."
    King.   If it be so, Laertes —
As how should it be so? How otherwise? —
Will you be ruled by me?
    Laer.   Ay, my lord;   60
So you will not o'errule me to a peace.
    King. To thine own peace. If he be now returned,
As checking at his voyage, and that he means
No more to undertake it, I will work him

---

51. **abuse:** deception. 63. **checking at:** giving it up for something else.

To an exploit, now ripe in my device,
Under the which he shall not choose but fall:
And for his death no wind of blame shall breathe,
But even his mother shall uncharge the practice
And call it accident.

  Laer.   My lord, I will be ruled;
The rather, if you could devise it so   70
That I might be the organ.

  King.   It falls right.
You have been talked of since your travel much,
And that in Hamlet's hearing, for a quality
Wherein, they say, you shine. Your sum of parts
Did not together pluck such envy from him
As did that one, and that, in my regard,
Of the unworthiest siege.

  Laer.   What part is that, my lord?

  King. A very riband in the cap of youth,
Yet needful too; for youth no less becomes
The light and careless livery that it wears   80
Than settled age his sables and his weeds,
Importing health and graveness. Two months since,
Here was a gentleman of Normandy.
I've seen myself, and served against, the French,
And they can well on horseback; but this gallant
Had witchcraft in 't; he grew unto his seat;
And to such wondrous doing brought his horse,
As had he been incorpsed and demi-natured
With the brave beast. So far he topped my thought,
That I, in forgery of shapes and tricks,   90
Come short of what he did.

  Laer.   A Norman, was 't?

  King. A Norman.

  Laer. Upon my life, Lamond.

  King.   The very same.

  Laer. I know him well. He is the brooch indeed
And gem of all the nation.

  King. He made confession of you,
And gave you such a masterly report
For art and exercise in your defence
And for your rapier most especial,

---

68. **uncharge:** make no accusation. 77. **siege:** rank. 88. **incorpsed,
etc.:** made one in body and spirit.

That he cried out, 'twould be a sight indeed,
If one could match you. The scrimers of their nation,   101
He swore, had neither motion, guard, nor eye,
If you opposed them. Sir, this report of his
Did Hamlet so envenom with his envy
That he could nothing do but wish and beg
Your sudden coming o'er, to play with him.
Now, out of this —
    Laer.   What out of this, my lord?
    King. Laertes, was your father dear to you?
Or are you like the painting of a sorrow,
A face without a heart?
    Laer.   Why ask you this?   110
    King. Not that I think you did not love your father;
But that I know love is begun by time;
And that I see, in passages of proof,
Time qualifies the spark and fire of it.
There lives within the very flame of love
A kind of wick or snuff that will abate it;
And nothing is at a like goodness still;
For goodness, growing to a pleurisy,
Dies in his own too much. That we would do,
We should do when we would; for this " would " changes   120
And hath abatements and delays as many
As there are tongues, are hands, are accidents;
And then this " should " is like a spendthrift sigh,
That hurts by easing. But, to the quick o' the ulcer:
Hamlet comes back. What would you undertake,
To show yourself your father's son in deed
More than in words?
    Laer.   To cut his throat i' the church.
    King. No place, indeed, should murder sanctuarize;
Revenge should have no bounds. But, good Laertes,
Will you do this, keep close within your chamber?   130
Hamlet returned shall know you are come home.
We'll put on those shall praise your excellence
And set a double varnish on the fame
The Frenchman gave you, bring you in fine together
And wager on your heads. He, being remiss,

---

101. **scrimers:** fencers. 113. **passages of proof:** proved cases. 117. **pleurisy:** excess. 128. **sanctuarize:** give sanctuary or protection. 135. **remiss:** careless.

Most generous and free from all contriving,
Will not peruse the foils; so that, with ease,
Or with a little shuffling, you may choose
A sword unbated, and in a pass of practice
Requite him for your father.
    Laer.   I will do 't;   140
And, for that purpose, I'll anoint my sword.
I bought an unction of a mountebank,
So mortal that, but dip a knife in it,
Where it draws blood no cataplasm so rare,
Collected from all simples that have virtue
Under the moon, can save the thing from death
That is but scratched withal. I'll touch my point
With this contagion, that, if I gall him slightly,
It may be death.
    King.   Let's further think of this;
Weigh what convenience both of time and means   150
May fit us to our shape. If this should fail,
And that our drift look through our bad performance,
'Twere better not assayed; therefore this project
Should have a back or second, that might hold,
If this should blast in proof. Soft! Let me see:
We'll make a solemn wager on your cunnings —
I ha 't:
When in your motion you are hot and dry —
And make your bouts more violent to that end —
And that he calls for drink, I'll have prepared him   160
A chalice for the nonce, whereon but sipping,
If he by chance escape your venomed stuck,
Our purpose may hold there.

Enter QUEEN.

                  How now, sweet queen!
    Queen. One woe doth tread upon another's heel,
So fast they follow: your sister's drowned, Laertes.
    Laer. Drowned! O, where?
    Queen. There is a willow grows aslant a brook,
That shows his hoar leaves in the glassy stream;
There with fantastic garlands did she come

137. **peruse the foils:** examine the fencing swords. 139. **unbated:** not blunted by the button. 139. **pass of practice:** treacherous thrust. 144. **cataplasm:** ointment. 155. **blast in proof:** miscarry.

Of crow-flowers, nettles, daisies, and long purples   170
That liberal shepherds give a grosser name,
But our cold maids do dead men's fingers call them;
There, on the pendent boughs her coronet weeds
Clambering to hang, an envious sliver broke;
When down her weedy trophies and herself
Fell in the weeping brook. Her clothes spread wide,
And, mermaid-like, awhile they bore her up;
Which time she chanted snatches of old tunes,
As one incapable of her own distress,
Or like a creature native and indued   180
Unto that element. But long it could not be
Till that her garments, heavy with their drink,
Pulled the poor wretch from her melodious lay
To muddy death.
   Laer.   Alas, then, she is drowned?
   Queen.   Drowned, drowned.
   Laer.   Too much of water hast thou, poor Ophelia,
And therefore I forbid my tears. But yet
It is our trick. Nature her custom holds,
Let shame say what it will; when these are gone,
The woman will be out. Adieu, my lord: 190
I have a speech of fire, that fain would blaze,
But that this folly douts it.   *[Exit.*
   King.   Let's follow, Gertrude:
How much I had to do to calm his rage!
Now fear I this will give it start again;
Therefore let's follow.   *[Exeunt.*

ACT V

Scene I. *A churchyard.*

Enter two Clowns, *with spades, &c.*

   First Clo.   Is she to be buried in Christian burial that wil-
fully seeks her own salvation?
   Sec. Clo.   I tell thee she is; and therefore make her grave
straight. The crowner hath sat on her, and finds it Christian
burial.

179. **incapable:** not sensible.   192. **douts:** extinguishes.
4. **straight:** right away.   4. **crowner hath sat:** coroner has decided.

First Clo. How can that be, unless she drowned herself in her own defence?

Sec. Clo. Why, 'tis found so.

First Clo. It must be *"se offendendo"*; it cannot be else. For here lies the point: if I drown myself wittingly, it argues an act, and an act hath three branches; it is, to act, to do, and to perform: argal, she drowned herself wittingly.

Sec. Clo. Nay, but hear you, goodman delver —

First Clo. Give me leave. Here lies the water; good. Here stands the man; good. If the man go to this water, and drown himself, it is, will he, nill he, he goes — mark you that; but if the water come to him and drown him, he drowns not himself. Argal, he that is not guilty of his own death shortens not his own life.   22

Sec. Clo. But is this law?

First Clo. Ay, marry, is 't; crowner's quest law.

Sec. Clo. Will you ha' the truth on 't? If this had not been a gentlewoman, she should have been buried out o' Christian burial.

First Clo. Why, there thou say'st. And the more pity that great folk should have countenance in this world to drown or hang themselves, more than their even Christian. Come, my spade. There is no ancient gentlemen but gardeners, ditchers, and grave-makers; they hold up Adam's profession.

Sec. Clo. Was he a gentleman?

First Clo. A' was the first that ever bore arms.

Sec. Clo. Why, he had none.   39

First Clo. What, art a heathen? How dost thou understand the Scripture? The Scripture says "Adam digged." Could he dig without arms? I'll put another question to thee; if thou answerest me not to the purpose, confess thyself —

Sec. Clo. Go to.

First Clo. What is he that builds stronger than either the mason, the shipwright, or the carpenter?

Sec. Clo. The gallows-maker; for that frame outlives a thousand tenants.   50

First Clo. I like thy wit well, in good faith. The gallows does well; but how does it well? It does well to those that do ill. Now thou dost ill to say the gallows is built stronger than the church; argal, the gallows may do well to thee. To 't again, come.

9. **se offendendo:** i.e., **se defendendo,** in self-defense.   12. **argal:** therefore.   24. **quest:** inquest.   30. **even Christian:** fellow Christian.

Sec. Clo. "Who builds stronger than a mason, a shipwright, or a carpenter? "

First Clo. Ay, tell me that, and unyoke.

Sec. Clo. Marry, now I can tell.   60

First Clo. To 't.

Sec. Clo. Mass, I cannot tell.

Enter HAMLET *and* HORATIO, *at a distance.*

First Clo. Cudgel thy brains no more about it, for your dull ass will not mend his pace with beating; and, when you are asked this question next, say " A grave-maker ": the houses that he makes last till doomsday. Go, get thee to Yaughan: fetch me a stoup of liquor.   [*Exit Sec. Clown.*
[*He digs, and sings.*

> " In youth, when I did love, did love,
> > Methought it was very sweet,   70
> > To contract, O, the time, for, ah, my behove,
> > O, methought, there was nothing meet."

Ham. Has this fellow no feeling of his business, that he sings at grave-making?

Hor. Custom hath made it in him a property of easiness.

Ham. 'Tis e'en so: the hand of little employment hath the daintier sense.

First Clo. [*Sings*]

> " But age, with his stealing steps,
> > Hath clawed me in his clutch,   80
> > And hath shipped me intil the land,
> > As if I had never been such."

[*Throws up a skull.*

Ham. That skull had a tongue in it, and could sing once: how the knave jowls it to the ground, as if it were Cain's jawbone, that did the first murder! It might be the pate of a politician, which this ass now o'erreaches; one that would circumvent God, might it not?

Hor. It might, my lord.   89

Ham. Or of a courtier; which could say: " Good morrow, sweet lord! How dost thou, good lord? " This might be my lord such-a-one, that praised my lord such-a-one's horse, when he meant to beg it; might it not?

Hor. Ay, my lord.

59. **unyoke:** stop work.   71. " O " and " ah " are grunts as he shovels.
81. **intil:** into.   87. **politician:** a schemer.

Ham. Why, e'en so; and now my Lady Worm's; chapless, and knocked about the mazzard with a sexton's spade. Here's fine revolution, an we had the trick to see 't. Did these bones cost no more the breeding, but to play at loggats with 'em? Mine ache to think on 't.   101

First Clo.   [*Sings*]
>"A pickax, and a spade, a spade,
>   For and a shrouding sheet:
>O, a pit of clay for to be made
>   For such a guest is meet."
>   [*Throws up another skull.*

Ham. There's another. Why may not that be the skull of a lawyer? Where be his quiddities now, his quillets, his cases, his tenures, and his tricks? Why does he suffer this rude knave now to knock him about the sconce with a dirty shovel, and will not tell him of his action of battery? Hum! This fellow might be in 's time a great buyer of land, with his statutes, his recognizances, his fines, his double vouchers, his recoveries. Is this the fine of his fines, and the recovery of his recoveries, to have his fine pate full of fine dirt? Will his vouchers vouch him no more of his purchases, and double ones too, than the length and breadth of a pair of indentures? The very conveyances of his lands will hardly lie in this box; and must the inheritor himself have no more, ha?   121

Hor. Not a jot more, my lord.

Ham. Is not parchment made of sheepskins?

Hor. Ay, my lord, and of calf-skins too.

Ham. They are sheep and calves which seek out assurance in that. I will speak to this fellow. Whose grave's this, sirrah?

First Clo. Mine, sir.

[*Sings*]   "O, a pit of clay for to be made
>   For such a guest is meet."   130

Ham. I think it be thine, indeed; for thou liest in 't.

First Clo. You lie out on 't, sir, and therefore it is not yours. For my part, I do not lie in 't, and yet it is mine.

Ham. Thou dost lie in 't, to be in 't and say it is thine. 'Tis for the dead, not for the quick; therefore thou liest.

First Clo. 'Tis a quick lie, sir; 'twill away again, from me to you.   140

95. **chapless:** jawless.   96. **mazzard:** Elizabethan slang for head.   100. **loggats:** a game like bowls.   107. **lawyer:** what follow are terms in law. 109. **sconce:** another slang word for head.

Ham.   What man dost thou dig it for?

First Clo.   For no man, sir.

Ham.   What woman, then?

First Clo.   For none, neither.

Ham.   Who is to be buried in 't?

First Clo.   One that was a woman, sir; but, rest her soul, she's dead.   147

Ham.   How absolute the knave is! We must speak by the card, or equivocation will undo us. By the Lord, Horatio, these three years I have taken note of it; the age is grown so picked that the toe of the peasant comes so near the heel of the courtier, he galls his kibe. How long hast thou been a grave-digger?

First Clo.   Of all the days i' the year, I came to 't that day that our last king Hamlet overcame Fortinbras.

Ham.   How long is that since?   158

First Clo.   Cannot you tell that? Every fool can tell that. It was the very day that young Hamlet was born; he that is mad, and sent into England.

Ham.   Ay, marry, why was he sent into England?

First Clo.   Why, because he was mad. He shall recover his wits there; or, if he do not, it's no great matter there.

Ham.   Why?

First Clo.   'Twill not be seen in him there; there the men are as mad as he.   170

Ham.   How came he mad?

First Clo.   Very strangely, they say.

Ham.   How strangely?

First Clo.   Faith, e'en with losing his wits.

Ham.   Upon what ground?

First Clo.   Why, here in Denmark. I have been sexton here, man and boy, thirty years.

Ham.   How long will a man lie i' the earth ere he rot?   179

First Clo.   I' faith, if he be not rotten before he die — as we have many pocky corses nowadays, that will scarce hold the laying in — he will last you some eight year or nine year. A tanner will last you nine year.

Ham.   Why he more than another?

First Clo.   Why, sir, his hide is so tanned with his trade, that he will keep out water a great while; and your water is a

---

151. **picked:** smart.   152. **galls his kibe:** i.e., wears the heel sore.   178. **thirty years:** note Hamlet's age.

sore decayer of your whoreson dead body. Here's a skull now;
this skull has lain in the earth three and twenty years.   191

Ham.   Whose was it?

First Clo.   A whoreson mad fellow's it was. Whose do you
think it was?

Ham.   Nay, I know not.

First Clo.   A pestilence on him for a mad rogue! A' poured
a flagon of Rhenish on my head once. This same skull, sir,
was Yorick's skull, the king's jester.

Ham.   This?   200

First Clo.   E'en that.

Ham.   Let me see. [*Takes the skull.*] Alas, poor Yorick!
I knew him, Horatio: a fellow of infinite jest, of most excellent
fancy: he hath borne me on his back a thousand times; and
now, how abhorred in my imagination it is! My gorge rises
at it. Here hung those lips that I have kissed I know not how
oft. Where be your gibes now? your gambols? your songs?
your flashes of merriment, that were wont to set the table on a
roar? Not one now, to mock your own grinning? quite chap-
fallen? Now get you to my lady's chamber, and tell her, let
her paint an inch thick, to this favor she must come; make her
laugh at that. Prithee, Horatio, tell me one thing.

Hor.   What's that, my lord?

Ham.   Dost thou think Alexander looked o' this fashion i'
the earth?

Hor.   E'en so.   220

Ham.   And smelt so? Pah!   [*Puts down the skull.*

Hor.   E'en so, my lord.

Ham.   To what base uses we may return, Horatio! Why
may not imagination trace the noble dust of Alexander, till he
find it stopping a bung-hole?

Hor.   'Twere to consider too curiously, to consider so.

Ham.   No, faith, not a jot; but to follow him thither with
modesty enough, and likelihood to lead it; as thus: Alexander
died, Alexander was buried, Alexander returneth into dust;
the dust is earth; of earth we make loam; and why of that
loam, whereto he was converted, might they not stop a beer-
barrel?

> Imperious Caesar, dead and turned to clay,
> Might stop a hole to keep the wind away:
> O, that that earth, which kept the world in awe,
> Should patch a wall to expel the winter's flaw!

But soft! but soft! Aside: here comes the king,

Enter Priests, *etc., in procession; the Corpse of* Ophelia,
    Laertes *and* Mourners *following;* King, Queen, *their*
    trains, etc.

The queen, the courtiers. Who is this they follow?   241
And with such maiméd rites? This doth betoken
The corse they follow did with desperate hand
Fordo its own life. 'Twas of some estate.
Couch we a while, and mark.   *[Retiring with Horatio.*
    Laer. What ceremony else?
    Ham.   That is Laertes,
A very noble youth. Mark.
    Laer. What ceremony else?
    First Priest. Her obsequies have been as far enlarged
As we have warranty. Her death was doubtful;
And, but that great command o'ersways the order,   251
She should in ground unsanctified have lodged
Till the last trumpet; for charitable prayers,
Shards, flints and pebbles should be thrown on her.
Yet here she is allowed her virgin crants,
Her maiden strewments and the bringing home
Of bell and burial.
    Laer. Must there no more be done?
    First Priest.   No more be done.
We should profane the service of the dead
To sing a requiem and such rest to her   260
As to peace-parted souls.
    Laer.   Lay her i' the earth,
And from her fair and unpolluted flesh
May violets spring! I tell thee, churlish priest,
A ministering angel shall my sister be,
When thou liest howling.
    Ham.   What, the fair Ophelia!
    Queen. Sweets to the sweet: farewell! *[Scattering flowers.*
I hoped thou shouldst have been my Hamlet's wife;
I thought thy bride-bed to have decked, sweet maid,
And not have strewed thy grave.
    Laer.   O, treble woe
Fall ten times treble on that curséd head,   270
Whose wicked deed thy most ingenious sense

242. **maimed:** curtailed. 255. **crants:** garlands. 256. **strewments:** wreaths.
257. **bell and burial:** part of the burial ceremony. 271. **ingenious sense:**
fair intelligence.

Deprived thee of! Hold off the earth awhile,
Till I have caught her once more in mine arms:
                    [*Leaps into the grave.*
Now pile your dust upon the quick and dead,
Till of this flat a mountain you have made,
To o'ertop old Pelion, or the skyish head
Of blue Olympus.
    Ham. [*Advancing*] What is he whose grief
Bears such an emphasis? whose phrase of sorrow
Conjures the wandering stars, and makes them stand
Like wonder-wounded hearers? This is I,   280
Hamlet the Dane.   [*Leaps into the grave.*
    Laer.   The devil take thy soul! [*Grappling with him.*
    Ham. Thou pray'st not well.
I prithee, take thy fingers from my throat;
For, though I am not splenitive and rash,
Yet have I something in me dangerous,
Which let thy wiseness fear. Hold off thy hand.
    King. Pluck them asunder.
    Queen.   Hamlet, Hamlet!
    All. Gentlemen —
    Hor.   Good my lord, be quiet.
              [*The Attendants part them, and they
come out of the grave.*
    Ham. Why, I will fight with him upon this theme
Until my eyelids will no longer wag.   290
    Queen. O my son, what theme?
    Ham. I loved Ophelia. Forty thousand brothers
Could not, with all their quantity of love,
Make up my sum. What wilt thou do for her?
    King. O, he is mad, Laertes.
    Queen. For love of God, forbear him.
    Ham. 'Swounds, show me what thou 'lt do:
Woo 't weep? woo 't fight? woo 't fast? woo 't tear thyself?
Woo 't drink up eisel? eat a crocodile?
I'll do 't. Dost thou come here to whine?   300
To outface me with leaping in her grave?
Be buried quick with her, and so will I;
And, if thou prate of mountains, let them throw
Millions of acres on us, till our ground,
Singeing his pate against the burning zone,

284. **splenitive**: full of spleen, i.e., hot-headed. 299. **eisel**: vinegar.

Make Ossa like a wart!   Nay, an thou'lt mouth,
I'll rant as well as thou.
    Queen.   This is mere madness,
And thus awhile the fit will work on him;
Anon, as patient as the female dove,
When that her golden couplets are disclosed,
His silence will sit drooping.
    Ham.   Hear you, sir;   311
What is the reason that you use me thus?
I loved you ever.   But it is no matter;
Let Hercules himself do what he may,
The cat will mew and dog will have his day.   *[Exit*.
    King.   I pray you, good Horatio, wait upon him.
                           [Exit Horatio.
[To Laertes] Strengthen your patience in our last night's
    speech;
We'll put the matter to the present push.
Good Gertrude, set some watch over your son.
This grave shall have a living monument.   320
An hour of quiet shortly shall we see;
Till then, in patience our proceeding be.   *[Exeunt*.

310. **golden couplets:** two newly hatched nestlings.   318. **push:** test.
320. **living:** probably a reference to the plot against Hamlet.

SCENE II. *A hall in the castle.*

Enter HAMLET *and* HORATIO.

    Ham.   So much for this, sir: now shall you see the other;
You do remember all the circumstance?
    Hor.   Remember it, my lord!
    Ham.   Sir, in my heart there was a kind of fighting,
That would not let me sleep.   Methought I lay
Worse than the mutines in the bilboes.   Rashly,
And praised be rashness for it; let us know,
Our indiscretion sometimes serves us well,
When our deep plots do pall; and that should teach us
There's a divinity that shapes our ends,   10
Roughhew them how we will —
    Hor.   That is most certain.
    Ham.   Up from my cabin,
My sea-gown scarfed about me, in the dark
      6. **mutines in the bilboes:** mutineers in shackles.

Groped I to find out them; had my desire,
Fingered their packet, and in fine withdrew
To mine own room again; making so bold,
My fears forgetting manners, to unseal
Their grand commission; where I found, Horatio —
O royal knavery! — an exact command,
Larded with many several sorts of reasons   20
Importing Denmark's health and England's too,
With, ho! such bugs and goblins in my life,
That, on the supervise, no leisure bated,
No, not to stay the grinding of the ax,
My head should be struck off.
    Hor.   Is 't possible?
    Ham.   Here's the commission; read it at more leisure.
But wilt thou hear me how I did proceed?
    Hor.   I beseech you.
    Ham.   Being thus be-netted round with villainies —
Ere I could make a prologue to my brains,   30
They had begun the play — I sat me down,
Devised a new commission, wrote it fair.
I once did hold it, as our statists do,
A baseness to write fair and labored much
How to forget that learning, but, sir, now
It did me yeoman's service. Wilt thou know
The effect of what I wrote?
    Hor.   Ay, good my lord.
    Ham.   An earnest conjuration from the king,
As England was his faithful tributary,
As love between them like the palm might flourish,   40
As peace should still her wheaten garland wear
And stand a comma 'tween their amities,
And many such-like *as*'s of great charge,
That, on the view and knowing of these contents,
Without debatement further, more or less,
He should the bearers put to sudden death,
Not shriving-time allowed.
    Hor.   How was this sealed?
    Ham.   Why, even in that was Heaven ordinant.
I had my father's signet in my purse,
Which was the model of that Danish seal;   50

15. **fingered:** stole. 23. **supervise; bated:** first hurried reading. 33.
statists: statesmen. 42. **comma:** link.

Folded the writ up in form of the other,
Subscribed it, gave 't the impression, placed it safely,
The changeling never known. Now, the next day
Was our sea-fight; and what to this was sequent
Thou know'st already.
   Hor. So Guildenstern and Rosencrantz go to 't.
   Ham. Why, man, they did make love to this employment;
They are not near my conscience; their defeat
Does by their own insinuation grow.
'Tis dangerous when the baser nature comes   60
Between the pass and fell incensèd points
Of mighty opposites.
   Hor.   Why, what a king is this!
   Ham. Does it not, think'st thee, stand me now upon —
He that hath killed my king and wed my mother,
Popped in between the election and my hopes,
Thrown out his angle for my proper life,
And with such cozenage — is 't not perfect conscience,
To quit him with this arm? and is 't not to be damned,
To let this canker of our nature come
In further evil?   70
   Hor. It must be shortly known to him from England
What is the issue of the business there.
   Ham. It will be short; the interim is mine;
And a man's life's no more than to say " One."
But I am very sorry, good Horatio,
That to Laertes I forgot myself;
For, by the image of my cause, I see
The portraiture of his. I'll court his favors.
But, sure, the bravery of his grief did put me
Into a towering passion.
   Hor.   Peace! who comes here?   80

Enter Osric.

   Osr. Your lordship is right welcome back to Denmark.
   Ham. I humbly thank you, sir. Dost know this water-fly?
   Hor. No, my good lord.
   Ham. Thy state is the more gracious; for 'tis a vice to
know him. He hath much land, and fertile; let a beast be
lord of beasts, and his crib shall stand at the king's mess.

---

  70. **In:** into. 82. **water-fly:** a skipper, engaged in trifling matters

'Tis a chough; but, as I say, spacious in the possession of
dirt.   90

Osr. Sweet lord, if your lordship were at leisure, I should
impart a thing to you from his majesty.

Ham. I will receive it, sir, with all diligence of spirit. Put
your bonnet to his right use; 'tis for the head.

Osr. I thank your lordship, it is very hot.

Ham. No, believe me, 'tis very cold; the wind is north-
erly.   99

Osr. It is indifferent cold, my lord, indeed.

Ham. But yet methinks it is very sultry and hot for my
complexion.

Osr. Exceedingly, my lord; it is very sultry — as 'twere,
— I cannot tell how. But, my lord, his majesty bade me signify to you that he has laid a great wager on your head. Sir,
this is the matter —

Ham. I beseech you, remember —

> [*Hamlet moves him to put on his hat.*

Osr. Nay, good my lord; for mine ease, in good faith. Sir,
here is newly come to court Laertes; believe me, an absolute
gentleman, full of most excellent differences, of very soft society and great showing; indeed, to speak feelingly of him, he
is the card or calendar of gentry, for you shall find in him the
continent of what part a gentleman would see.   116

Ham. Sir, his definement suffers no perdition in you;
though, I know, to divide him inventorially would dizzy the
arithmetic of memory, and yet but yaw neither, in respect of
his quick sail. But, in the verity of extolment, I take him to
be a soul of great article; and his infusion of such dearth and
rareness, as, to make true direction of him, his semblable is his
mirror; and who else would trace him, his umbrage, nothing
more.

Osr. Your lordship speaks most infallibly of him.

Ham. The concernancy, sir? Why do we wrap the gentleman in our more rawer breath?

Osr. Sir?   130

Hor. Is 't not possible to understand in another tongue?
You will do 't, sir, really.

Ham. What imports the nomination of this gentleman?

Osr. Of Laertes?

89. **chough:** a countryman, much like our word " rube." 117. In this
speech Hamlet mocks Osric by imitation. 128. **concernancy:** meaning.
133. **nomination:** naming.

Hor. His purse is empty already; all 's golden words are spent.

Ham. Of him, sir.

Osr. I know you are not ignorant —   139

Ham. I would you did, sir; yet, in faith, if you did, it would not much approve me. Well, sir?

Osr. You are not ignorant of what excellence Laertes is —

Ham. I dare not confess that, lest I should compare with him in excellence; but, to know a man well, were to know himself.

Osr. I mean, sir, for his weapon; but in the imputation laid on him by them, in his meed he's unfellowed.   150

Ham. What's his weapon?

Osr. Rapier and dagger.

Ham. That's two of his weapons; but, well.

Osr. The king, sir, hath wagered with him six Barbary horses, against the which he has imponed, as I take it, six French rapiers and poniards, with their assigns, as girdle, hangers, and so. Three of the carriages, in faith, are very dear to fancy, very responsive to the hilts, most delicate carriages, and of very liberal conceit.   160

Ham. What call you the carriages?

Hor. I knew you must be edified by the margent ere you had done.

Osr. The carriages, sir, are the hangers.

Ham. The phrase would be more german to the matter, if we could carry cannon by our sides; I would it might be hangers till then. But, on: six Barbary horses against six French swords, their assigns, and three liberal-conceited carriages; that's the French bet against the Danish. Why is this " imponed," as you call it?

Osr. The king, sir, hath laid, that in a dozen passes between yourself and him, he shall not exceed you three hits: he hath laid on twelve for nine; and it would come to immediate trial, if your lordship would vouchsafe the answer.

Ham. How if I answer " no " ?

Osr. I mean, my lord, the opposition of your person in trial.   179

Ham. Sir, I will walk here in the hall; if it please his majesty, 'tis the breathing time of day with me; let the foils be

---

150. **unfellowed:** unequaled.   155. **imponed:** wagered.   157. **hangers:** straps.   162. **edified, etc.:** instructed by explanation.   165. **german:** related.

brought, the gentleman willing, and the king hold his purpose,
I will win for him an I can; if not, I will gain nothing but my
shame and the odd hits.

Osr. Shall I re-deliver you e'en so?

Ham. To this effect, sir; after what flourish your nature
will.

Osr. I commend my duty to your lordship.

Ham. Yours, yours. [*Exit Osric.*] He does well to commend it himself; there are no tongues else for 's turn.   191

Hor. This lapwing runs away with the shell on his head.

Ham. He did comply with his dug, before he sucked it.
Thus has he — and many more of the same breed that I know
the drossy age dotes on — only got the tune of the time and
outward habit of encounter; a kind of yesty collection, which
carries them through and through the most fond and win-
nowed opinions; and do but blow them to their trial, the
bubbles are out.

Enter a Lord.

Lord. My lord, his majesty commended him to you by
young Osric, who brings back to him, that you attend him in
the hall: he sends to know if your pleasure hold to play with
Laertes, or that you will take longer time.

Ham. I am constant to my purposes; they follow the king's
pleasure. If his fitness speaks, mine is ready; now or whenso-
ever, provided I be so able as now.   211

Lord. The king and queen and all are coming down.

Ham. In happy time.

Lord. The queen desires you to use some gentle entertainment to Laertes before you fall to play.

Ham. She well instructs me.   [*Exit Lord.*

Hor. You will lose this wager, my lord.

Ham. I do not think so; since he went into France, I have
been in continual practice; I shall win at the odds. But thou
wouldst not think how ill all's here about my heart. But it is
no matter.

Hor. Nay, good my lord —

Ham. It is but foolery; but it is such a kind of gain-giving,
as would perhaps trouble a woman.

Hor. If your mind dislike any thing, obey it. I will fore-
stall their repair hither, and say you are not fit.   229

195. **drossy:** slang akin to our word "rotten." 196. **yesty:** frothy.
215. **gentle entertainment:** courteous behavior. 229. **repair:** coming.

Ham.   Not a whit, we defy augury.   There's a special providence in the fall of a sparrow.   If it be now, 'tis not to come;
if it be not to come, it will be now; if it be not now, yet it will
come: the readiness is all.   Since no man has aught of what he
leaves, what is 't to leave betimes?   Let be.

Enter KING, QUEEN, LAERTES, Lords, OSRIC, *and* Attendants
with foils, etc.

King.   Come, Hamlet, come, and take this hand from me.
                    [*The King puts Laertes' hand into Hamlet's.*
Ham.   Give me your pardon, sir.   I've done you wrong;
But pardon 't, as you are a gentleman.
This presence knows,
And you must needs have heard, how I am punished   240
With sore distraction.   What I have done,
That might your nature, honor and exception
Roughly awake, I here proclaim was madness.
Was 't Hamlet wrong'd Laertes?   Never Hamlet:
If Hamlet from himself be ta'en away,
And when he's not himself does wrong Laertes,
Then Hamlet does it not, Hamlet denies it.
Who does it, then?   His madness.   If 't be so,
Hamlet is of the faction that is wronged;
His madness is poor Hamlet's enemy.   250
Sir, in this audience,
Let my disclaiming from a purposed evil
Free me so far in your most generous thoughts,
That I have shot mine arrow o'er the house,
And hurt my brother.
Laer.   I am satisfied in nature,
Whose motive, in this case, should stir me most
To my revenge; but in my terms of honor
I stand aloof, and will no reconcilement,
Till by some elder masters, of known honor,
I have a voice and precedent of peace,   260
To keep my name ungored.   But till that time,
I do receive your offered love like love,
And will not wrong it.
Ham.   I embrace it freely;
And will this brother's wager frankly play.
Give us the foils.   Come on.
Laer.   Come, one for me.

Ham. I'll be your foil, Laertes; in mine ignorance
Your skill shall, like a star i' the darkest night,
Stick fiery off indeed.

Laer.   You mock me, sir.

Ham. No, by this hand.

King. Give them the foils, young Osric. Cousin Ham-
    let,   270
You know the wager?

Ham.   Very well, my lord;
Your grace hath laid the odds o' the weaker side.

King. I do not fear it; I have seen you both;
But since he is bettered, we have therefore odds.

Laer. This is too heavy, let me see another.

Ham. This likes me well. These foils have all a length?
                              [*They prepare to play.*

Osr. Ay, my good lord.

King. Set me the stoups of wine upon that table.
If Hamlet give the first or second hit,
Or quit in answer of the third exchange,   280
Let all the battlements their ordnance fire;
The king shall drink to Hamlet's better breath;
And in the cup an union shall he throw,
Richer than that which four successive kings
In Denmark's crown have worn. Give me the cups;
And let the kettle to the trumpet speak,
The trumpet to the cannoneer without,
The cannons to the heavens, the heavens to earth,
" Now the king drinks to Hamlet." Come, begin;
And you, the judges, bear a wary eye.   290

Ham. Come on, sir.

Laer.   Come, my lord.   [*They play.*

Ham.   One.

Laer.   No.

Ham.   Judgment.

Osr. A hit, a very palpable hit.

Laer.   Well; again.

King. Stay; give me drink. Hamlet, this pearl is thine;
Here's to thy health.
              [*Trumpets sound, and cannon shot off within.*
              Give him the cup.

268. **stick fiery off**: be brilliant. 283. **union**: valuable pearl. 286. **kettle**: kettledrum.

Ham. I'll play this bout first; set it by awhile.
Come. [*They play.*]   Another hit; what say you?
  Laer. A touch, a touch, I do confess.
  King. Our son shall win.
  Queen.   He's fat, and scant of breath.
Here, Hamlet, take my napkin, rub thy brows:
The queen carouses to thy fortune, Hamlet.   300
  Ham. Good madam!
  King.   Gertrude, do not drink.
  Queen. I will, my lord; I pray you, pardon me.
  King. [*Aside*] It is the poisoned cup; it is too late.
  Ham. I dare not drink yet, madam; by and by.
  Queen. Come, let me wipe thy face.
  Laer. My lord, I'll hit him now.
  King.   I do not think 't.
  Laer. [*Aside*] And yet 'tis almost 'gainst my conscience.
  Ham. Come, for the third, Laertes; you but dally;
I pray you, pass with our best violence;
I am afeard you make a wanton of me.   310
  Laer. Say you so? Come on.   [*They play.*
  Osr. Nothing, neither way.
  Laer. Have at you now!
  [*Laertes wounds Hamlet; then, in scuffling, they change
      rapiers, and Hamlet wounds Laertes.*
  King. Part them; they are incensed.
  Ham. Nay, come, again.   [*The Queen falls.*
  Osr.   Look to the queen there, ho!
  Hor. They bleed on both sides. How is it, my lord?
  Osr. How is 't, Laertes?
  Laer. Why, as a woodcock to mine own springe, Osric;
I am justly killed with mine own treachery.
  Ham. How does the queen?
  King.   She swounds to see them bleed.
  Queen. No, no, the drink, the drink — O my dear Ham-
      let —   320
The drink, the drink! I am poisoned.   [*Dies.*
  Ham. O villainy! Ho! let the door be locked:
Treachery! Seek it out.
  Laer. It is here, Hamlet. Hamlet, thou art slain;
No medicine in the world can do thee good;
In thee there is not half an hour of life;

300. **carouses**: drinks.

The treacherous instrument is in thy hand,
Unbated and envenomed. The foul practice
Hath turned itself on me; lo, here I lie,   329
Never to rise again. Thy mother's poisoned.
I can no more. The king, the king's to blame.
    Ham. The point envenomed too!
Then, venom, to thy work.   [*Stabs the King.*
    All. Treason! treason!
    King. O, yet defend me, friends; I am but hurt.
    Ham. Here, thou incestuous, murderous, damnéd Dane,
Drink off this potion. Is thy union here?
Follow my mother.   [*King dies.*
    Laer.   He is justly served;
It is a poison tempered by himself.
Exchange forgiveness with me, noble Hamlet.
Mine and my father's death come not upon thee,   341
Nor thine on me!   [*Dies.*
    Ham. Heaven make thee free of it! I follow thee.
I am dead, Horatio. Wretched queen, adieu!
You that look pale and tremble at this chance,
That are but mutes or audience to this act,
Had I but time — as this fell sergeant, death,
Is strict in his arrest — O, I could tell you —
But let it be. Horatio, I am dead;
Thou livest; report me and my cause aright
To the unsatisfied.
    Hor.   Never believe it: 351
I am more an antique Roman than a Dane:
Here's yet some liquor left.
    Ham.   As thou 'rt a man,
Give me the cup. Let go! By heaven, I'll have 't.
O good Horatio, what a wounded name,
Things standing thus unknown, shall live behind me!
If thou didst ever hold me in thy heart,
Absent thee from felicity awhile,
And in this harsh world draw thy breath in pain,
To tell my story.   [*March afar off, and shot within.*
          What warlike noise is this?   360
    Osr. Young Fortinbras, with conquest come from Poland,
To the ambassadors of England gives
This warlike volley.

328. **practice:** plot.

Ham.   O, I die, Horatio;
The potent poison quite o'er-crows my spirit:
I cannot live to hear the news from England;
But I do prophesy the election lights
On Fortinbras; he has my dying voice;
So tell him, with the occurrents, more and less,
Which have solicited.   The rest is silence.   [*Dies.*
    Hor.   Now cracks a noble heart.   Good night, sweet
            prince;   370
And flights of angels sing thee to thy rest!
Why does the drum come hither?   [*March within.*

    Enter Fortinbras, *the* English Ambassadors, *and others.*

    Fort.   Where is this sight?
    Hor.   What is it ye would see?
If aught of woe or wonder, cease your search.
    Fort.   This quarry cries on havoc.   O proud death,
What feast is toward in thine eternal cell,
That thou so many princes at a shot
So bloodily hast struck?
    First Amb.   The sight is dismal;
And our affairs from England come too late.
The ears are senseless that should give us hearing,   380
To tell him his commandment is fulfilled,
That Rosencrantz and Guildenstern are dead.
Where should we have our thanks?
    Hor.   Not from his mouth,
Had it the ability of life to thank you.
He never gave commandment for their death.
But since, so jump upon this bloody question,
You from the Polack wars, and you from England,
Are here arrived, give order that these bodies
High on a stage be placéd to the view;   389
And let me speak to the yet unknowing world
How these things came about.   So shall you hear
Of carnal, bloody, and unnatural acts,
Of accidental judgments, casual slaughters,
Of deaths put on by cunning and forcéd cause,
And, in this upshot, purposes mistook
Fall'n on the inventors' heads: all this can I
Truly deliver.

    364. **o'er-crows:** triumphs.   369. **cracks:** breaks.   375. **cries:** proclaims.

Fort.   Let us haste to hear it,
And call the noblest to the audience.
For me, with sorrow I embrace my fortune.
I have some rights of memory in this kingdom,
Which now to claim my vantage doth invite me.   401
    Hor.   Of that I shall have also cause to speak,
And from his mouth whose voice will draw on more.
But let this same be presently performed,
Even while men's minds are wild; lest more mischance,
On plots and errors, happen.
    Fort.   Let four captains
Bear Hamlet, like a soldier, to the stage;
For he was likely, had he been put on,
To have proved most royally; and, for his passage,
The soldiers' music and the rites of war   410
Speak loudly for him.
Take up the bodies. Such a sight as this
Becomes the field, but here shows much amiss.
Go, bid the soldiers shoot.
      [*A dead march. Exeunt, bearing off the dead bodies;
        after which a peal of ordnance is shot off.*

     400. rights of memory: rights which I now remember.

INTERPRETATIVE NOTE

Hamlet is one of the world's literary masterpieces. This fact need not discourage students from undertaking a study of the play, for a great work of art is not necessarily difficult to appreciate. Quite the contrary, indeed, is often true. Without going into the question of what constitutes literary excellence, we may say that a truthful presentation of life and human nature is one of its essentials. To this ideal *Hamlet* conforms.

In *Hamlet,* as in all of his plays, Shakespeare was not giving the audience of the Globe Theater anything new and strange. For a number of years prior to 1602, when *Hamlet* was given its final form, tragedies of blood had been the fashion, and they remained popular many years thereafter. The particular type of blood-tragedy to which *Hamlet* belongs was originated by Thomas Kyd, whose *Spanish Tragedy* was produced by Henslowe in 1585. This play dealt with revenge, and its tremendous popularity led other dramatists, including Shakespeare, to write similar plays. Not only that; it is more than likely that Shakespeare's play is in part a rewriting of an earlier *Hamlet* by Kyd himself. However that may be, in *Hamlet* Shakespeare did not use a single device which had not already been employed by Kyd in *The Spanish Tragedy.* Here, as always, Shakespeare did what other writers were doing, only he did it vastly better. If any one is troubled with doubts about the superiority of Shakespeare's genius, he can do nothing more illuminating than to read *The Spanish Tragedy* in conjunction with *Hamlet.*

The formula for a revenge play was ordinary enough. Some one was murdered and some one else sought revenge, the preference seeming to be a father killed and the revenge carried out by a son. In *The Spanish Tragedy* it was the reverse, a father revenging the death of his son. In all of these plays the revenge was supervised by a ghost. Other common motives were hesitation on the part of the revenger, madness real or assumed, much soliloquizing, a minor revenge motive, exhibition of dead bodies, and a final orgy of death. In *The Spanish Tragedy* there were ten deaths, with five of the bodies strewn about the stage at the end. In *Hamlet* there were five deaths and four bodies left for the soldiers of Fortinbras to carry off. In Kyd's play the revenge was consummated in a play within a play; in Shakespeare's, the play within the play determined the guilt of the king. It must be remembered that in these plays the idea of revenge was considered a virtue, practically a moral obligation for the injured party, following the doctrine of the Old Testament of an eye for an eye rather than that of the New Testament, in which turning the other cheek is advocated.

The plot of *Hamlet* is simple. With Hamlet given the facts of his father's death by the ghost, and pledged to revenge, the story resolves itself into a struggle between Hamlet and the king, with the Polonius family providing the outer entanglements which lead to the ultimate developments and the final outcome. But the greatness of the play and its intrinsic interest do not lie in the plot merely as such. It is the analysis of character and the study of human motives under the stress of peculiarly sinister conditions that arrest the attention of the reader.

Hesitation on the part of the hero to carry out his revenge is the main motive of *Hamlet*. Why did he postpone a task that he knew would have to be done? The answer, of course, lies in Hamlet's character. At the time of the action of the play Hamlet was a man thirty years old; he had a university education; prior to the death of his father he had been the heir apparent to the Danish throne; he was what a young man in his position was expected to be, and more. Instead of spending his time in gay frivolities, as he might have done without reproof, he devoted it to study and thought; and he was not prone to physical activity. At the university he probably gave much time to philosophy, a study that tends to make one reflect seriously on life and its problems. In Hamlet this tendency had turned into introspection, that is, thought about his own life and his own problems.

All this would not have led to anything tragic had not something happened to intensify this trait of introspection in Hamlet — his father's unexpected and mysterious death. From that shock Hamlet would have recovered in spite of the love he had for his father; but other events occurred to color his sorrow with a bitter and hopeless pessimism. His uncle Claudius, brother to his father, not only was elected king but married the recently widowed queen, Hamlet's mother. How this affected Hamlet is told in the first of the famous soliloquies. In the main, he felt sorrowful disgust — nothing that called for action. But when he learned from the ghost how the disgusting situation had become possible, there was an immediate impulse to action. Had Claudius been on the spot Hamlet would no doubt have killed him instantly. Even as it was, he wanted to speed to his revenge. But at the end of the first act the clue to Hamlet's character is given when he laments that he was born to set right a time that was " out of joint."

The more he brooded over the facts, the more he hesitated to carry out the injunction of the ghost. The thought of suicide as the easiest way out he more than once rejected. He tried to convince himself that the ghost might have been an evil spirit and not really that of his father; he persuaded himself into thinking that he must wait for a suitable opportunity to kill the king — and after all, that did require thought. Hamlet would have been in an uncomfortable position should he have had to explain the murder by telling the ghost's story. To involve Hamlet still more, complications arose in his love affair with Ophelia. Suspicion had made the king wary, but even after Claudius plainly showed his guilt, and later unknowingly put himself into Hamlet's hands (in the prayer scene), Hamlet put off the evil moment.

In short, Hamlet, constituted as he was mentally, did not want to kill, and it took the exceptional circumstances of the duel to bring on the final act, which was quick and decisive.

In studying *Hamlet* the character of the hero should be analyzed at much greater length than is possible here. Many phases of his situation have not been touched upon, especially those which will also help to bring out the other characters in the play. The king, the queen, Ophelia, Laertes, and Horatio deserve serious study in themselves as well as in their relations with Hamlet. Even the doddering Polonius is not without personal interest. When you have read the play through, ask yourself what Hamlet's problem was. Your ability to answer that question is what matters most in a study of this play.

QUESTIONS

I. i.

1. From the first part of this scene, select words that prepare for mystery.
2. What necessary information is given?
3. How does Horatio differ from his companions?
4. What is the first reference to the hero of the play?
5. How do you think the part of the ghost should be played?
6. Compare the opening scene with those of other plays in this book.

I. ii.

1. What general impression do you form of the king?
2. What facts do you learn from the first part of his speech?
3. Condense Polonius' first speech into two words.
4. Note carefully Hamlet's appearance and manner of speaking.
5. How old was Hamlet? his mother?
6. How does the queen speak, forcefully or flatly?
7. Why does Hamlet wish to go to Wittenberg? Had he been there recently?
8. Why does the king oppose his going? Does Hamlet obey him?
9. From the first of Hamlet's soliloquies, what important facts do you learn?
10. What do you make of Hamlet's state of mind? Remember that in England it was illegal for a man to marry his brother's widow.
11. Does the soliloquy give dramatic preparation for Horatio's news?
12. Had Hamlet and Horatio known each other long? Had they seen each other recently?
13. Did Hamlet have suspicions of " foul play " before he heard of the ghost?
14. What elements of suspense in this scene?

I. iii.

1. How is this scene indirectly about Hamlet?
2. What does Laertes' speech suggest in this connection?
3. The speech of Polonius to his son is one of the famous passages in the play. Does it ring true, or as something learned and repeated?
4. How does Ophelia react to her advice-giving family?
5. Had Polonius really heard gossip about his daughter?
6. Why should both he and Laertes have objected to Hamlet?
7. What definite command does Polonius finally give her?
8. From her bringing up, is she likely to obey? Keep this in mind for reference later.
9. What was Polonius' position at court? Was he capable?
10. The three members of this family form the connecting link in the struggle between Hamlet and the king. Form definite views of them.

I. iv.

1. Considering the purpose of the watch, is the trivial opening conversation natural?
2. What custom of the king's does Hamlet censure? Comment.
3. Comment on Hamlet's tendency to philosophize.

   4. Does this give a definite clue to his character?   Explain.
   5. What sort of thing urges him to action?

I. v.

   1. Was it necessary for the ghost to go into detail about his torments?
   2. Note carefully all the important facts imparted to Hamlet.
   3. Had Hamlet suspected murder prior to the ghost's statement?
   4. What was Hamlet's immediate thought about revenge?
   5. How far back did his " prophetic soul " reach?
   6. Note the ghost's reference to his former queen.   Comment.
   7. What three definite commands were given Hamlet by the ghost?
   8. Watch how these are carried out.   They furnish the basis for the plot.
   9. Why does he swear his friends to secrecy?   Why doesn't he at once
      publicly denounce the king?
  10. What scheme for revenge is already in his mind?
  11. How do the last three lines fit in with line 31?

II. i.

   1. First Polonius distrusts Ophelia; now he sets a spy on his son.
      Comment.
   2. What signs of old age does Polonius show in this scene?
   3. What indications of considerable passage of time since Act I?
   4. What progress has Hamlet made toward his revenge?
   5. Why should Hamlet have acted in the way described by Ophelia?
   6. Does that connect up with a previous passage in the play?
   7. Why should Polonius at once want to go to the king?

II. ii.

   1. The opening of this scene suggests an earlier passage.   Comment.
   2. Why were Rosencrantz and Guildenstern sent for?
   3. Did the king suspect the truth about Hamlet? the queen?
   4. Did the queen either directly or indirectly share the king's guilt?
   5. Throughout the play watch for light on the problems of questions 3
      and 4.
   6. Does Polonius show up more favorably in this scene?   Comment.
   7. From the adjustment with Norway, what do you think of Claudius
      as a ruler?
   8. It is important that you get a vivid sense of the king's character.   He
      is by no means a minor character.
   9. Does the king show much faith in the news about Hamlet?
  10. What comedy elements do you find in this scene?
  11. What do you learn of Hamlet's condition when he says, " These
      tedious old fools " ?
  12. Why could Hamlet so readily detect the truth about Rosencrantz and
      Guildenstern?
  13. Does Hamlet suspect the motives of Polonius?   Comment.
  14. What part of the long episode of the players is important for the
      plot?
  15. For two months Hamlet has been hesitating.   What now spurs him
      to fresh resolutions?
  16. In the soliloquy, does he analyze himself correctly?
  17. The stage is now set for a crisis in the struggle between Hamlet and
      the king.   Watch for it.

III. i.

1. Does the queen really mean what she tells Ophelia?
2. What can you say about the king's remorse?
3. The "To be, or not to be" soliloquy is one of the famous passages of all literature. Study it carefully.
4. Had Hamlet thought of suicide before?
5. Does Hamlet arrive at any definite conclusion in this soliloquy?
6. What do you think of Ophelia's lie?
7. Does Hamlet still love Ophelia?
8. How do you account for his strong speech to her?
9. What effect did Hamlet's "all but one" have on the king?
10. Was the king convinced of Hamlet's madness? Explain.
11. Contrast the king's readiness for action with Hamlet's hesitation.
12. How is the action of the play kept in suspense at this point?

III. ii.

1. Sum up Hamlet's suggestions to the players, and comment on them.
2. What especially does Hamlet admire in Horatio?
3. Might the dumb show be omitted? Comment.
4. Picture the grouping of the characters during the play within the play.
5. What difference of style do you note in the play within the play?
6. Suggest a reason for this difference.
7. "The king rises." Show how this is an important crisis for both the king and Hamlet.
8. Point out passages bearing on Hamlet's "ecstasy."
9. In a few words, Hamlet's state of mind at the end of this scene.

III. iii.

1. From their remarks in this scene, do Rosencrantz and Guildenstern deserve sympathy?
2. What was lacking in the king's prayer?
3. Does this closet scene modify your estimate of Claudius?
4. Analyze carefully Hamlet's expressed reasons for not killing Claudius.
5. At this point, think of possible reasons why he has not killed the king before.

III. iv.

1. What so far has been your opinion of the queen?
2. Why was Hamlet all at once so ready to kill?
3. Would he have stabbed so quickly, had he known it was Polonius?
4. "As kill a king!" says the queen. Once more, was she a party to the killing of Hamlet's father?
5. Did Hamlet love his mother? Base your answer on this scene.
6. Why does the ghost make its appearance here?
7. Does the queen definitely promise to forsake the king?
8. Does Hamlet have hopes that she will? Explain.
9. Why does he seem so complacent about being sent away?
10. How had he learned about it?

IV. i.

1. Does the queen give a full report to the king? Explain.
2. What is the king's chief feeling over the death of Polonius?
3. Is he wise in sharing the fact with his "wisest friends"?

IV. ii.

   1. Is there any point in calling Rosencrantz a sponge?
   2. Does Hamlet maintain his attitude of madness here?

IV. iii.

   1. What qualities in Hamlet make him loved by the multitude?
   2. Did he suspect the king's purpose of having him killed? Explain.
   3. Do you feel that the action is speeding up? Explain.

IV. iv.

   1. At this point, recall all previous references to Fortinbras.
   2. Note how Hamlet conducts himself before Fortinbras' agent.
   3. In your own words, recapitulate Hamlet's problem as he states it here.
   4. Does he make any definite plans for future action?
   5. Has he previously made resolutions similar to that in the last line?

IV. v.

   1. Why should the queen at first refuse to speak with Ophelia?
   2. Was Horatio's advice sensible? Explain.
   3. Why was her soul " sick," and what " guilt " is she thinking of?
   4. Give reasons for Ophelia's madness.
   5. Elizabethan audiences were fond of " mad girl " scenes, and such were often thought funny. Could this scene have been so intended?
   6. At the " noise within," what was the king's first thought?
   7. How had Laertes worked on the feelings of the rabble?
   8. How does the queen show that she is loyal to Claudius?
   9. After the king collects his faculties, is he the same old diplomat?
  10. Show how Laertes differs from Hamlet.

IV. vi.

   1. How did the king's scheme against Hamlet fall through?
   2. Do you feel that Fate is going definitely against the king, or not?

IV. vii.

   1. From this and previous scenes, do you think that Claudius really loved the queen?
   2. State fully the plot hatched against Hamlet.
   3. Why was the king slow in proposing certain parts of it?
   4. How does Laertes finally lose your sympathy?
   5. Note once more how events pile up more rapidly.

V. i.

   1. This scene relieves the tension of the one just before. Do you find it in good taste dramatically?
   2. Compare the two clowns with similar characters in the other plays in this volume.
   3. Note how carefully Shakespeare gives Hamlet's age. Did you think he was younger? Explain.
   4. In the conversation with Horatio, does Hamlet show any signs of madness?
   5. How do you explain the fight with Laertes?

6. In your opinion, had Hamlet always loved Ophelia?
7. Had Hamlet and Laertes ever been good friends? Explain.

V. ii.

1. In your own words, tell Hamlet's story about Rosencrantz and Guildenstern.
2. Why did Hamlet feel no remorse for their fate?
3. Has Hamlet now formed definite plans for killing the king?
4. Explain why he was so willing to engage in the duel.
5. What do you think of Hamlet's apology to Laertes? of Laertes' reply?
6. Was it dramatically necessary that the queen should die?
7. Once more, do you think she knew the facts about the death of Hamlet's father?
8. Where does Hamlet learn the facts about the final plot against him?
9. At the last, do you have any sympathy for Laertes?
10. How was the ghost's command finally accomplished?
11. Why was it necessary that Fortinbras should arrive when he did?
12. Why did Horatio wish to die, too?
13. Why the order " Take up the bodies " ?
14. Why could the play not have ended with Hamlet's " The rest is silence " ?
15. Give a final summary of Hamlet's character.

DEFINITIONS

1. *Drama* is a general term; it may include every play ever written; it may mean a certain era, as the *Shakespearean drama;* or it may mean a single play.

2. A *Play* is a form of literature which tells a story through the dialogue and action of characters impersonated on a stage by actors.

3. A *Comedy* is that type of play in which none of the important characters meets death on the stage; it ends happily. A comedy does not necessarily imply anything *comic,* although humor is usually present.

4. A *Tragi-comedy* is a play in which tragedy impends, but is averted. Today we call such a play *melodrama.*

5. *Tragedy* implies that persons of high degree become involved in exceptional calamities that lead to disaster and death.

6. A *Motive* is any driving force in a play. It may be *revenge* or *ambition;* or, more concretely, something like the "pound of flesh" motive in *The Merchant of Venice.*

7. The *Theme* is that which the author intends to bring out through his story. It is the end toward which the motive or motives lead the action. The theme of *Hamlet* is not *revenge,* but how a person through circumstances over which he has no control is impelled to seek revenge, and through inner and outer conflicts meets exceptional calamity and death.

8. The *Plot* is the concrete working out of the theme through characters and action involving conflict and entanglement which lead to some sort of definite outcome.

9. A *Crisis* is an event that marks a definite turning-point in the life of a character or characters. Rosalind falls in love with Orlando; the weird sisters hail Macbeth as Thane of Cawdor; Bassanio chooses the right casket; Brutus decides to join the conspirators; Hamlet is informed that his father was murdered; these are crises.

10. The *Climax* is that particular crisis which marks the supreme turning-point of the story. When King Claudius, during the play within the play, shouts for light and abruptly leaves the scene, he finally convinces Hamlet of his guilt. That is the climax.

EARLY TEXTS

Shakespeare left no manuscripts of his plays, and it is doubtful whether he ever arranged any of his plays in assembled form. As there were no copyright laws it was customary for play manuscripts to be separated into the parts that fell to each actor. In that way no one person had the copy of a complete play, and no rival company or printer could get hold of it.

With the continued popularity of the drama, there developed a demand for printed plays. To get the " copy " for some of Shakespeare's it seems that shorthand notes were taken, very imperfectly, by printers' agents. Perhaps these may have been pieced out by the actors' parts, secretly sold when ready cash was needed. In this way sixteen of Shakespeare's plays were published during his lifetime, without his personal supervision or consent, and one more in 1622. These were printed one play to a volume, really small cheap pamphlets, and are today known as Quartos because of their format (abbreviated to Q_1, Q_2, and so on). They have proved of great value in determining the text of Shakespeare. In 1623 appeared the First Folio — F_1 — in which were included twenty plays not hitherto printed, but excluding one, *Pericles*, that had been published separately. *Pericles* was added to a later folio. The First Folio was the work of John Heming and Henry Condell, friends of Shakespeare and members of his company. Had it not been for the work of these two men the world today would in all probability have no more than seventeen of Shakespeare's plays. Of the First Folio one hundred and fifty-six copies are extant, each one of which is worth a fortune.

CHRONOLOGICAL ORDER [1]

1. Henry VI, Part I 1589–90
2. Henry VI, Part II 1591–92
3. Henry VI, Part III 1592
4. Titus Andronicus 1589–90
5. Love's Labor's Lost 1590
6. Two Gentlemen of Verona 1591
7. Comedy of Errors 1591–92
8. Romeo and Juliet 1592
9. Richard III 1593
10. Richard II 1593
11. King John 1594
12. Midsummer Night's Dream 1594
13. Merchant of Venice 1594–96
14. All's Well That Ends Well 1596–1601
15. Taming of the Shrew 1595–96
16. Henry IV, Part I 1596–97
17. Henry IV, Part II 1597–98
18. Merry Wives of Windsor 1598
19. Henry V 1598
20. Much Ado About Nothing 1599
21. As You Like It 1599
22. Twelfth Night 1600
23. Julius Caesar 1600–1601
24. Hamlet 1602
25. Troilus and Cressida 1603
26. Othello 1604
27. Measure for Measure 1604
28. Macbeth 1605–1606
29. King Lear 1606
30. Timon of Athens 1607
31. Pericles 1607–1608
32. Antony and Cleopatra 1608
33. Coriolanus 1609
34. Cymbeline 1610
35. The Winter's Tale 1610–11
36. The Tempest 1611
37. Henry VIII 1611–12

Venus and Adonis 1593
The Rape of Lucrece 1594
Sonnets 1594–1604

[1] Most of the dates are approximate only.

481

SELECTED BIBLIOGRAPHY

Adams, Joseph Quincy, *A Life of William Shakespeare*
Alden, Raymond M., *Shakespeare*
Baker, George P., *The Development of Shakespeare as a Dramatist*
Lee, Sidney, *A Life of William Shakespeare*
Neilson, W. A., and Thorndike, A. H., *The Facts About Shakespeare*

Boas, F. S., *Shakspere and His Predecessors*
Bradley, A. C., *Shakespearean Tragedy*
Brooke, Stopford A., *On Ten Plays of Shakespeare*
Brooke, Stopford A., *Ten More Plays of Shakespeare*
Dowden, Edward, *Shakspere: A Critical Study of His Mind and Art*
Schelling, Felix E., *The Elizabethan Drama*, 2 vols.
Thorndike, A. H., *Tragedy*
Ward, A. W., *A History of English Dramatic Literature*, 3 vols.

Adams, Joseph Quincy, *Shakespearean Playhouses*
Hatcher, O. L., *Shakespeare Plays and Pageants*
Mantzius, Karl, *A History of Theatrical Art, Vol. 3*
Stephenson, H. T., *Shakespeare's London*
Thorndike, A. H., *Shakespeare's Theater*